THE POETRY

AND

POETICS

OF

CONSTANTINE P. CAVAFY

Greek Poetry Archive

A series of books edited by John P. Anton, University of South Florida, Tampa, USA

Volume 1
The Poetry and Poetics of Constantine P. Cavafy
Aesthetic Visions of Sensual Reality
John P. Anton

This book is part of a series. The publisher will accept continuation orders which may be cancelled at any time and which provide for automatic billing and shipping of each title in the series upon publication. Please write for details.

THE POETRY AND POETICS OF CONSTANTINE P. CAVAFY

AESTHETIC VISIONS OF SENSUAL REALITY

by
John P. Anton

*Department of Philosophy, University of South Florida
Tampa, USA*

harwood academic publishers
Switzerland • Australia • Belgium • France • Germany • Great Britain
India • Japan • Malaysia • Netherlands • Russia • Singapore • USA

Copyright © 1995 by Harwood Academic Publishers GmbH.

All rights Reserved.

Every effort has been made to trace the ownership of the illustration on the front cover. In the event of any questions about the use of this illustration, the publisher, while expressing regret for any inadvertent error, will be happy to make the necessary correction in future printings.

No part of this book may be reproduced or utilized in any form or by any means, electronic or mechanical, including photocopying and recording, or by any information storage or retrieval system, without permission in writing from the publisher. Printed in Singapore.

Harwood Academic Publishers

Poststrasse 22
7000 Chur
Switzerland

British Library Cataloguing in Publication Data
Anton, John P.
  Poetry and Poetics of Constantine P.
Cavafy: Aesthetic Visions of Sensual
Reality. — (Greek Poetry Archive, ISSN
1074-3146; Vol. 1)
  I. Title II. Series
889.12

ISBN 3-7186-5551-9 (hardback)
ISBN 3 7186-5552-7 (softback)

*To Helen and our Sons
for their affectionate patience*

Contents

Introduction to the Series	xi
Abbreviations	xiii
Chronology	xv
Introduction	xvii

Chapter One: **THE ALEXANDRIAN ENVIRONMENT**   1
    1. The Founding of Alexandria
    2. Alexandria: The Pride of the Ptolemies
    3. The Roman Intervention
    4. Obscurity and the Rebirth
    5. The Greeks of Modern Alexandria
    6. The Poet's Environment

Chapter Two: **CAVAFY'S LIFE AND TIMES: THE EARLY YEARS**   23
    1. Growing Up in Alexandria
    2. Ancestors and Immediate Family
    3. Returning to a City of Confusions
    4. Despair and the Promise of Poetry
    5. Plumbing the Depths of Depression

Chapter Three: **CAVAFY'S LATER YEARS**   50
    1. Beyond the "Hidden Things"
    2. Vindication of an "Unorthodox Work in Progress"
    3. "Rare Poets, Like Cavafy . . ."
    4. Farewell to Alexandria

Chapter Four: **THE LONG SHADOW OF SYMBOLISM**   78
    1. The Beginnings
    2. The Encounter with Symbolism
    3. The Two "Correspondences": Baudelaire and Cavafy
    4. Prisoner of the Familiar Garden
    5. Two Poetic Worlds: Parallel or Asymptotic?
    6. Severing the Weak Ties

Chapter Five: **THE LOSS OF THE POLIS** 117
    1. The Surfacing of the Crisis
    2. In the Same City
    3. The Perimeter of the Polis
    4. Inverting the Classical Mode
    5. The Penumbra of "The City"

Chapter Six: **THE CRISIS PERIOD** 152
    1. Plotting the Province of Art
    2. The Fear of the Lonely Self
    3. The Inner Side of the Walls
    4. Erecting the Walls
    5. Fumbles and Compromises
    6. Postscript to the Inverted Walls

Chapter Seven: **THE DEVELOPMENT OF CAVAFY'S POETICS** 190
    1. In the Year 1903: *Ars Poetica*
    2. The Persisting Problems
    3. Cavafy's Self-consciousness of His Poetic Inadequacy
    4. Disillusionment and the Possibility of Progress
    5. Progress and Poetry in the *Ars Poetica*
    6. The Editing of the Collections

Chapter Eight: **THE BARBARIANS AND OTHER THINGS THAT ARE NOT** 222
    1. Insight into Decadence
    2. Cavafy Responds to Gibbon: Background for a Fictional Drama
    3. "Waiting for the Barbarians": Thematic Elements
    4. The Gods Have Not Died
    5. Defenders of Thermopylae

Chapter Nine: **EROS AND SENSUALITY** 260
    1. The Transition
    2. Eros in Life and in Art
    3. The Fear of Eros

          4. The Path of Eros: *Ars Poetica* and the Release of "The City"
          5. Reconciliation and Adjustment
          6. Eros after the Return to the City
          7. Eros and the Limits of Irony

Chapter Ten: **THE NEW VOYAGE: ITHAKA**   300
          1. "Ithaka" and the Return to the City
          2. "Second Odyssey": Background and Contrasts
          3. The Ambiguity of the Voyage
          4. The Reconstructive Assimilation of Symbolism
          5. "The God Abandons Antony": Postscript to "Ithaka"
          6. The Poetic Side of Hedonism

Appendix: **CONSTANTINE P. CAVAFY: *ARS POETICA***   339

Bibliography   347

Index A: Titles   375

Index B: General   380

Introduction to the Series

The *Greek Poetry Archive* features monographs on key modern Greek poets, from the nineteenth century to the present, and a bilingual collection of their poetry translated into English.

The monographs are by well-known specialists who present lively assessments of the poetry, supported by carefully chosen biographical facts, with reference to broader intellectual and cultural contexts, interwoven with reliable and masterly translations. Each volume is designed to provide detailed and in-depth information, to introduce the reader to the best of modern Greek poetry in the living tradition of the Hellenic spirit.

John P. Anton

Abbreviations

Inside the parentheses, after the titles of poems in English, follow the dates of composition and publication, the latter in italics, separated with a slash. When necessary, the date of the revision [rev.] of a poem is also cited before or after the slash, to indicate whether the revision was made before or after the publication date. Also printed within the parentheses are the page references to the 1963 edition of the text of the poems. I have used the Greek texts of the standard editions:

C. P. Cafavy 1963, *Poems*, ed. G. Savidis, in two volumes, abbr. A and B followed by the page number.

C. P. Cavafy 1968, *The Unpublished Poems*, ed. G. Savidis, abbr. UP or U followed by the page number.

C. P. Cavafy 1983, *The Condemned Poems and Translations*, ed. G. Savidis, abbr. CP or C, followed by the page number.

C. P. Cavafy 1942, *Cavafian Self-Comments*, ed. G. Lechonitis, abbr. *Self-comments*, followed by the page number.

C. P. Cavafy 1963, *Prose*, ed. G. Papoutsakis, abbr. *Prose*.

C. P. Cavafy 1963, *Unpublished Prose Texts*, ed. M. Peridis, abbr. UPT.

C. P. Cavafy 1983, *Unpublished Notes on Poetry and Ethics*, ed. G. Savidis, abbr. UN.

C. P. Cavafy 1963, *Comments on Ruskin*, ed. S. Tsirkas, abbr. CR.

C. P. Cavafy 1982, *Reading Notes on Gibbon*, ed. D. Haas, abbr. GB.

Key to Citations

Listed below in English translation are the titles of the Greek journals and special issues most frequently cited or mentioned in the text and the notes.

Chart = ΧΑΡΤΗΣ (Hártis)
Cavafy Cycle = ΚΥΚΛΟΣ ΚΑΒΑΦΗ (Kýklos Kaváfi)
I Read = ΔΙΑΒΑΖΩ (Diavázo)
Letters = ΓΡΑΜΜΑΤΑ (Grámmata)
Literary New Year = ΦΙΛΟΛΟΓΙΚΗ ΠΡΩΤΟΧΡΟΝΙΑ (Filologhikí Protohroniá)
Nea Estia = ΝΕΑ ΕΣΤΙΑ (Néa Estía)

New Times = ΚΑΙΝΟΥΡΙΑ ΕΠΟΧΗ (Kenoúrghia Epohí)
New Life = ΝΕΑ ΖΩΗ (Néa Zoí)
Proceedings of the Third Symposium on Poetry = ΠΡΑΚΤΙΚΑ ΤΡΙΤΟΥ ΣΥΜΠΟΣΙΟΥ ΠΟΙΗΣΗΣ (Praktiká Trítou Symposíou Píisis)
Responsibility = ΕΥΘΥΝΗ (Efthýni)
Review of Art = ΕΠΙΘΕΩΡΗΣΗ ΤΕΧΝΗΣ (Epitheórisi Téchnis)
The Cycle = ΚΥΚΛΟΣ (O Kýklos)
The Word = Η ΛΕΞΗ (I Léxi)

Chronology

1863 Cavafy is born in Alexandria, Egypt, on April 29.
1870 The poet's father dies on August 10.
1872 Cavafy's mother closes her home on Serif Street and takes her family to Liverpool.
1876 Economic crisis in Egypt. The company Cavafy Inc., dissolves.
1879 The Cavafy family returns to Alexandria.
1881 Private studies and attempts to write an "historical lexikon". Enters the private school of A. Papazis.
1882 Political crisis in Egypt. Unrest and riots. The Cavafy family moves to Constantinople. The British navy bombards Alexandria; the Cavafy residence is destroyed. The British remain in Egypt.
1884 Works on his rendition of a ballad by Lady Barnard and writes the poem, "Dünya Güzeli".
1885 More poems. The family returns to Alexandria. Cavafy takes Greek citizenship and refuses the "British protection" inherited from his father.
1886 Publishing of poems in *Hesperos* of Leipzig, also in Alexandrian newspapers.
1887 Cavafy temporarily ill from excesses of night life.
1891 His brother Petros-Ioannes dies in Alexandria. Cavafy publishes "The Elgin Marbles" and other articles.
1892 Appointed temporary clerk in the Irrigation Service (Third Circle) of the Ministry of Public Works.
1894 First version of "The City" [*I Polis*] published.
1896 Death of his maternal grandfather G. Photiades. Cavafy publishes more poems. First version of "Ionikon" under the title "Mneme".
1897 Publishes the "Walls" privately, Greek text with English translation by brother John. Cavafy suffers from deep depression. Brief visit to Paris and London.
1898 Writing of "Waiting for the Barbarians".
1899 Harikleia Cavafy, the poet's mother, dies in Alexandria.
1901 "Che fece . . . il gran rifiuto". First visit to Athens. Meets the critic Xenopoulos.
1903 Second visit to Athens. *Ars Poetica*. Favorable reviews of his poems.
1904 Private printing of first *Booklet* of 14 poems.

1905 Visit to Athens. Death of his brother, Alexander. Records his mood of depression.
1908 Writing of poem "Hidden Things"; it remains unknown until 1963.
1910 Prints privately his second *Booklet*, *Poems*, augmenting the 1904 booklet for a total of 21 poems.
1911 Writing of "Ithaka". Cavafy finishes his "Genealogy".
1915 The poet meets E. M. Forster.
1917 G. Vrissimitzakis publishes the first book-length study on Cavafy.
1919 E. M. Forster's essay on Cavafy appears in the April issue of *Athenaeum* of London. Several poems appear in English, French and Italian translations.
1922 Cavafy resigns his position and retires. Forster publishes his *Alexandria A Guide to the City*.
1923 Forster publishes *Pharos and Pharillon*, with an essay on Cavafy. Louis Roussel reviews Cavafy's "Collection" in *Libre*. More translations in *Nation* and *Athenaeum*, London.
1924 Cavafy's poetry becomes the center of discussion in Alexandria and Athens. T. S. Eliot prints the "Ithaka" in his *Criterion*.
1926 Editor of journal, *Alexandrian Art*. Greece honors Cavafy with the medal of the Phoenix.
1928 Karl Dieterich publishes translations of the poems in Germany. Gnawing controversy on Cavafy's poetry in Greece.
1931 John Mavrogordato writes about Cavafy in his *Modern Greece* (London, 1931), and in *Exchanges* (Paris).
1932 Cavafy ill with cancer of the larynx, undergoes tracheotomy, and loses his voice. Circulates his last poem, "Days of 1908". Meets André Maurois and William Plomer. D. Mitropoulos puts to music ten of Cavafy's "hedonic" poems.
1933 "I still have twenty-five more poems to finish." His situation worsens and he dies on the day of his seventieth birthday at the Hellenic Hospital in Alexandria.

Introduction

I

This book was written with the hope that it may serve to introduce the reader to the poetry and poetics of Constantine P. Cavafy from a perspective somewhat different from that of the many excellent Cavafian studies that have already appeared in print. I hasten to add that I owe more than I can indicate here to the wealth of insights I derived from the perusal of the publications of experts on Cavafy. The references to their works in the text and footnotes reflect my indebtedness to their authors.

To write an exhaustive treatise on Cavafy was not a task I had in mind when I started this work some twenty years ago. The informed reader will no doubt notice that I have not even tried to cover every aspect of Cavafy's poetry. The initial plan, one to which I have faithfully tried to adhere, was to illumine the problems that seemed to have attended his development as a poet. When I first started reading Cavafy's poetry with this purpose in mind, I was particularly impressed with the seriousness of his determination during the early phase of his creative career, working as he was against all odds and difficulties, many of them of his own making, to succeed as a poet. Artless though most of his early verses were, one can not help but admire his persistence to plant a firm foot on the first rung of the ladder of art—to use one of his own images—hopeful that he may soon begin climbing and reach the heights of poetry he had envisaged. I therefore thought it worthwhile to trace his development during the early decades, when he was gradually discovering his poetic self until he finally found his own authentic voice.

The book I have written is not offered as biography. The historical biography is one thing; the reconstruction of the poet's axiological world, the substance he transformed into poetic themes, quite another. The principle I have used in composing this work assumes that it is fair to treat each "approved" poem as an aesthetic attainment and testimony to a creative moment, which expresses the embodiment of a genuine experience into the creative result, "the work in progress", as it has been called.

Autobiographical elements in Cavafy's poems are introduced in this study mainly as guides to explore one aspect of his world: how he gradually learned to control the transformation of experience into "work in progress". The resultant interpretation was guided by Cavafy's own rule, as stated in his *Ars Poetica*, concerning the demand for thematic coherence and philosophical consistency. He refers to the rule as "the removal of flagrant contradictions". He upheld it not only when he revised the poems he found lacking in some respect, but also to govern the compositions he did for the rest of his life. It remains to be seen whether Cavafy's world hangs together as a unity, how his beliefs, values, aspirations, fears, hopes, projections, outlook on history, views on love and death, all those traits of human existence and experience a poet normally exhibits in his creations, including his reflections on selfhood and creativity, flow together and meet in a stream of light meant to illumine the path to human fulfillment.

Most scholars and interpreters of his poetry agree that by 1912 Cavafy had reached the turning point. Viewed in retrospect, the next twenty odd years of his life find him casting a wide net over select themes and ideas to firm his stance and integrate his vision. The consummate results of his mature phase are some of the finest verse in modern European poetry. The theme I sought to explore in writing this book led me to consider a complex question that, much to my surprise, George Seferis had already attempted to formulate in 1974 in his personal journal for the years 1945 through 1951. Without the benefit of knowing what Cavafy had intimated in his "unpublished poems",[1] Seferis wrote in the entry "Poros, Athens. 1946–47":

> Up to a fairly advanced age (maturity), Cavafy seems to remain at a very low level; he seems to be unable to rise above a certain very mediocre ceiling (as it is called in aviation, ceiling, plafond). What happens at and beyond a certain point? How does he cross that threshold? Here's a question that interests me—not only about Cavafy but in general. . . . For one who crosses the threshold, how many have remained below the ceiling? How many pitchers are broken for each that survives?
>
> The example of Cavafy is one of the most striking. Up to a certain point he appears hanging by a cotton thread; you think the slightest touch could cast him into forgotten ruins. What miracle allowed him to cross the threshold? I say it is faith

---

[1] They were unavailable until G. Savidis edited and published them in 1968.

in himself, the difficult acceptance of his own sincerity: imprecise, meaningless phrases, perhaps. I would like to know more.[2]

Seferis' own answer, if he had one, is another story. The interpretation I have essayed to offer in this book addresses the problem of retracing the steps to maturity rather than the search for definitive signposts. When I first began writing this study, I came across G. Savidis' *The Cavafian Editions* (1966), a landmark in Cavafian studies. He had issued sufficient warning to alert his readers to suspect blurred boundaries and arbitrary transitional phases. Yet I felt challenged to look for themes and ideas indicative of critical periods of change. As I sought to find them, I became increasingly drawn into the poetic world that Cavafy was carving out of the aesthetic materials of his visions and experiences. That is how and why the book was started. A few years ago, just as I thought that my work was nearing its completion, I came across the brilliant dissertation of a young Cavafian scholar, Michalis Pieris, who had reached conclusions by following an independent line of research that were dovetailing with my own. At first I felt uncomfortable about trying to continue with my writing; it was only after certain unavoidable postponements that I finally decided to return to my manuscript, convinced that it had a story of its own to tell. And I found myself repeating the words Cavafy wrote on September 1, 1906: "By postponing, and postponing to publish, what a gain I have had!" Whether I have indeed gained much by so doing I cannot be the judge. Instead, I prefer to take this opportunity to acknowledge my indebtedness and gratitude to all those scholars whose publications have since appeared in print and saved me from many an error.

Today we think of Cavafy as one of the twentieth century poets whose work has already received international recognition for capturing the mood and expressing the spirit of our times. His verse is often quoted, albeit sometimes out of context, as apt epigram, even as epitaph for a circumstance, summarizing as it were the high moment of a crisis or the dreaded anticipation of future disasters. Fortunately, other writers have already noted and praised Cavafy for the quality of his thought, the originality and freshness of his imagery, the boldness of his themes, the penetrating commentary on the human condition, his concrete and poignant insights, the laconic style

---

[2] G. Seferis, *A Poet's Journal: Days of 1945–1951*, trans. Athan Anagnostopoulos; intro. Walter Kaiser, (Cambridge: The Belknap Press of Harvard University Press, 1974), pp. 139–140.

disclosing sudden nuances, and not least his determination to capture in his poetry the hovering decadence in our cultural ways, reminiscent as they are of other comparable periods in Western civilization that found their way into his poems.

II

Cavafy, the modern Greek-Alexandrian poet, stretched his poetic vision over vast horizons of universal themes and perennial concerns. The light of the locale is pre-eminently Alexandrian. In its ambiance rejoice, move, suffer, and die *personae* from the pages of history real or imagined, exposing subtle shades of thought and emotion, from fear and agony to passion and affection, and even stunning apathy. Here Cavafy comes close to his great ancestors, the tragic poets of classical Greece, but with an accent of his own and a tone conspicuously modern. Adept in many periods in history, Hellenistic, late Byzantine or contemporary, he knows how to select his *personae* and, after situating them adroitly to embody a theme fashioned with confidence and dexterity, he gives a special twist to make it stare at all ages and cry quietly with its pains. He creates tunes for all seasons.

    I have repeatedly tried to delve into the intriguing facets of his so-called "decadent" themes, with the hope of showing how the poet actually gained in wisdom while touching the flames of his passions, which some of his critics identify with erotic proclivities. It was no easy task. As I tried to meet it, I could not help but notice how the elusive Cavafy slipped through the probing curiosity of many an acute observer, including the astute Nikos Kazantzakis, who once called him "the last flower of a decaying civilization", and the austere I. M. Panayotopoulos so eager to condemn him as a "man of decadence . . . possessed by the demon of debauchery". More apt proved the temperate statement of E. M. Forster who saw in Cavafy "a Greek gentleman in a straw hat, standing absolutely motionless at a slight angle to the universe".[3] He stood precisely at the "slight angle" that many of his critics proved unable to measure with requisite exactness before pronouncing judgment on the poet and his poetry.

---

[3]*Pharos and Pharillon* (1923), p. 91.

Sixty years have passed since the poet's death, and with the advantages that distance and scholarship provide, it is safe to say that we have gained the comfort of perspective to admit that Cavafy deliberately chose the "angle" to position himself in the universe just as that he cultivated its advantages with the same elusiveness Homer's mythical Proteus used on his visitors. George Seferis first drew attention to Cavafy's protean swiftness to change visible countenance.[4] It is not certain that Seferis meant to suggest that Cavafy was therefore beyond the critic's reach; rather, it would seem that he sought to alert us to the complex problems of interpretation. There is no special reason to belabor this point except to underscore the issue of complexity rather than the feature of elusiveness. There will be ample occasion to return to the protean aspect for a closer look at the difficulties that attend the tracing of the delicate undulations of the voice that speaks behind the countless masks the Alexandrian poet made and wore with consummate skill.

III

One of the main conclusions I have sought to defend in this study is that Cavafy wrestled defiantly with the seductive forces of decadence and sought to state his perceptions in acceptable didactic modalities. He attained perfect balance between the lyrical vision of the poet and the ethical refinement of the intellectual. It was no easy accomplishment. The lessons from his early mistakes surfaced slowly as he struggled to steer away from the stagnant waters of late Romanticism, the strong currents of Parnassianism and Symbolism, and the diverse lures of the dominant schools of European poetry with which he had become acquainted and even imitated during the early phases of his poetic development. But more than that, the lessons saved him

---

[4]In his essay "Cavafy and Eliot—A Comparison", *On the Greek Style* (London, 1966), p. 124: "In my view, if there is any Alexandrian element in Cavafy it is this one: he resembles that old man of the Alexandrian sea who was constantly eluding the grasp, always changing his shape—the Proteus of Homer." For Homer's reference to Proteus, see *Odyssey* IV: "Οὐδ' ὁ γέρων δολίης ἐπελήθετο τέχνης . . ." ("The old man's skill and cunning had not deserted him. He began by turning into a bearded lion and then into a snake, and after that a panther and a giant boar. He changed into running water too and a great tree in leaf." Trans. E. V. Rieu, The Penguin Classics, p. 76).

from adopting the style of pseudo-classicism that had become fashionable, especially among the Greek literati toward the end of the nineteenth century and into the twentieth. The temptation to follow a similar path came early in his life. He was able to move out of the mainstream, but not before he understood the disappointing fruits of imitation. The mediocre compositions of his early poetry continued while he wandered for over a decade into the arid lands of unsuitable trends until he was ready to make a decisive break with the past. It was the study of history during this period that helped strengthen his grasp of the precarious elements in the human condition. He engraved this knowledge on the special human situations he was to dramatize in his poems. They were the elements that formed the initial and germinal ideas destined to become part of the defining features of his style. By a happy coincidence he found the materials for the historical settings of his themes mainly in the literary heritage of his own Alexandria, the Hellenistic Alexandria of the Ptolemies and the Antioch of the Seleucids and other such centers, teeming with cultural abandon, cosmopolitanism, pretentiousness, decadence, and painfully watching the gradual loss of a cherished world.

The affinities of ancient Alexandria to our contemporary ways and modes were too suggestive and tempting for Cavafy's sharp sense of poetic relevance to miss. His affinity with the Greek mind and a natural sensitivity encouraged compassion for the ways of Alexandria in the long history of that city. The cosmopolis, ancient and modern, needed its poetic spokesman, its affectionate skeptic, and Cavafy answered the call. The response was direct, subtle, protean, as the circumstances required, but always forceful in its simplicity and convincingly personal. The poet developed his own style and remained its master to the end, as befits a consummate dramatist and director of one's own lyric stage. The person behind the complete set of its *personae* is more than what has surfaced in the 154 poems he approved from the total of his compositions. There is Cavafy's hidden wisdom, a grace as difficult to divine as it is inviting to explore. For all these and more, his is one of the finest voices of our times.

IV

The paths are open to the reader who may wish to move closer to Cavafy's poetic wisdom, but they lack the immediacy of the poet's enticing and intriguing themes. Nevertheless they are there and are worth following. One may prefer the uncharted path of his personal development; another may opt for the total vision that the study of the canon of his approved poems, in conjunction with his "unpublished" ones, affords. Fortunately there are some guideposts, certain openings and clearings Cavafy himself provided in the folds of his "work in progress", beyond what little information about his private life he allowed to slip into the public domain. Yet another path is suggested by his own insistence that all his poems form but a single theme, that they constitute the successive layers of a continuous art work. If his poetry is, as he believed, the unfolding of a work in progress, then the reader will do well to explore this path and hope to view the poet's constancy of outlook with the seriousness that a final disclosure deserves.

Throughout his life he remained a poet devoted to his art. The same verses he put into the mouth of a fictional young poet, in 400 A.D. in the poem "Young Men of Sidon (A.D. 400)" (1920/*1920*: B 16), may tempt the reader to view as being Cavafy's own stance:

> You should give, I say, all your strength to your work,
> make it your consuming concern.
> And you should still remember your work
> in times of stress or when you begin to decline.
> That is what I expect, what I demand of you—
> and not that you completely dismiss
> your magnificent tragedies—
> your *Agamemnon*, your marvelous *Prometheus* . . .

The poem was written in 1920 and published in the same year. The attitude of the young poet and critic expresses a late Hellenistic view, one that stands for the intensity of emotion in the devotion to the creative life together with the concern for the quality of the work itself—this is a principle even Aeschylus should have heeded, but unfortunately could not. Be that as it may, the dominant element in the young poet's aesthetic stance is the advocacy in favor of making poetry one's consummate concern.

Before dying, Cavafy told a close friend that he hoped he could live a bit longer as he had more poems he so much wanted to finish. The poetic edifice he left behind was already solid and remarkably complete.

V

The writing of this book could not have been completed without incurring substantial debts. Some twenty years ago the late Mary Gianos, then Professor of English Literature at the Detroit Institute of Technology, urged me to write a full length monograph on Cavafy after hearing a paper I presented at a conference to which she had invited me as Program Chairman. Later, two other friends, the late Michael Lekakis, a noted sculptor, and Mr Thanassis Maskaleris of San Francisco State University, persuaded me to accept the assignment. After many blunders and wrong starts I was about to admit defeat when I realized that the ideas I had set on paper since 1968 depended for support on the accessibility of reliable information on the date of composition of the extant poems whether condemned, published or unpublished. The impasse I had reached was finally overcome when I acquired a copy of C. P. Cavafy, *The Unpublished Poems: 1882–1923* (1968), edited by G. Savidis. I found there the needed chronology of the dates of composition of Cavafy's poems, including those listed as lost.[5]

The main body of the interpretive ideas that helped shape this book were set on paper sometime during the summer of 1968, after a visit with Professor Savidis in Greece, and have been subjected to a series of revisions before taking their present form. I owe much to the fruitful conversations I have had with specialists and friends.

This preface will be incomplete if I neglect to mention a special event related to the writing of this book. The first lecture I ever presented before an audience in Greece was on Cavafy. It took place in the island of Skiathos in August 1973, at the invitation of a group of young students who at that time were officers of their local cultural society "The Two Alexanders". It was the first time I felt that I had something of significance to say before a Greek audience without being pursued by the terrifying suspicion that my

---

[5] It is gratifying to inform the reader that at this time we can say with confidence that thanks to the efforts of Professor Savidis and his collaborators almost all the papers of C. P. Cavafy have become accessible in the original. Aside from his prose writings, the poetry output consists of three groups of poems: (a) the recognized group of 154 approved poems that have been conveniently classified as *the canon*; (b) a group of 75 "unpublished" poems; and (c) the "condemned" group of 24 poems, for a total of 253. To this we may now add a small number of "drafts" of poems that have recently come to light.

views on the subject might never advance beyond commonplaces and trivial clichés. In Skiathos I gained confidence, courage and new friends. As I listened to the comments of those young literati, I feverishly made mental notes and spent several hours later in the night revising the outline of what was to be a book. A few weeks later, on the island of Cephalonia, I finalized the table of contents that was to make the bulk of the present chapters. The rest is a story of labor, procrastinations and intermediate periods of despair when I felt haunted by the fear that this book would never be finished.

Encouragement from friends played a decisive role in my effort to continue with a work that took me almost twenty years to bring to its present stage. Professor Edmund Keeley of Princeton University was kind and generous with his expert knowledge of the subject, his fine translations and his willingness to offer helpful comments especially at the early stages of this undertaking. I wish to acknowledge indebtedness to the work of E. P. Papanoutsos, George Katsimbalis, G. Themelis, M. Vayanos, and Nikos Karydis, who are no longer with us. Part of their spirit and knowledge has already entered the substance of this book. But I am equally in the debt of the late Kimon Friar, who for years insisted that I should not abandon this task.

Professor M. Byron Raizis of the University of Athens and Professor Maskaleris read early drafts of several chapters and offered advice when it was urgently needed. I owe a special note of gratitude to Dr Katherine Zapantis Keller of the University of Central Florida for valuable editorial suggestions and a careful reading of most of the later chapters. The late Professor George Thaniel of the University of Toronto, a poet in his own right, saw enough merit in a lecture I gave at his institution to want to see the book finished. I also must thank Professor Vassilis Lambropoulos of Ohio State University for valuable criticisms. Mr George Zacharopoulos and Mr A. Apostolopoulos, both of Athens, Greece, have revealed to me a rare understanding of Cavafian themes in relation to the political side of human existence. Professors Diana Haas and Michalis Pieris of New York University and the University of Cyprus, respectively, have generously shared copies of their publications; Mr D. Daskalopoulos of Athens, Greece, made available expert bibliographical information. Ms Nancy Stanlick has offered valuable assistance in editing the MS and preparing the index. I also wish to thank Ms Eileen Kahl for reading carefully the entire MS.

The specialists will find much to which they may want to object, and I wish to state that I alone am responsible for the errors of fact or interpretation I have inadvertently failed to remove. Whatever the judgment, I accept it with trust in their good will, for my purpose in publishing this work is not so much to persuade others or even to add yet another work to the existing literature on Cavafy's poetry. My purpose is confined to sharing the results of years of scholarly labor. If there is anything left standing after the critic's judicious assessment, I should be thankful that all the labor that went into the making of this book was not in vain. A little gain for a great cause in art is no small matter. One could wish for no more.

A note of gratitude is expressed here to the American Philosophical Society for two travel grants, to the State University of New York at Buffalo and Emory University, and to the University of South Florida for providing me over the years with free time to write.

Thanks are due to the editors of *Philosophy and Literature* and *Nea Estia*, Mr D. Dutton and Mr Petros Haris respectively, for permission to include in my book the parts these journals printed in the form of articles; the former hosted what has now become Chapter 6, while the latter published an early version of Chapter 4; in both cases additions and changes were made to become separate chapters; same are due to Mr Costis Moskoff of the Greek Embassy in Cairo, for permission to include in Chapter 9 parts of the address I presented and later published in the *Proceedings* of the First Kavafis International Symposium 1991, sponsored by the Greek Embassy and Egypt's Ministry of Cultural Affairs. Earlier versions of some of the chapters were used as lectures at various universities and colleges or as papers at the meetings of professional societies. I wish to thank Professor John Koumoulides for inviting me in 1977 to give the first Brademas Lecture at Ball State University; the text of the lecture, now part of Chapter 1, was first published in *Conspectus in History*, an annual publication of the Department of History, Ball State University.

I am grateful to Princeton University Press for permission to quote translations of several poems from the Keeley and Sherrard revised edition of Cavafy's poems (1992): "In the Same Space", "He Asked about the Quality", "When the Watchman Saw the Light", "Waiting for the Barbarians", "In a Large Greek Colony, 200 B.C." and "The God Abandons Antony". All the other translations of Cavafy's poems and prose pieces as well as the excerpts from the works of other writers, unless indicated otherwise, are my own. I would be the first to admit the awkwardness of my translations. My sole aim was to render Cavafy's verse into English as faithfully as I could, being mainly concerned with conveying Cavafy's themes and thoughts in a manner that would hopefully leave the original imagery intact. Under different circumstances I would have been more than pleased to cite only from such excellent translations by superior craftsmen as J. Mavrogordato, Kimon Friar, Edmund Keeley, Philip Sherrard, Rae Dalven, and others who have spared no pain to present Cavafy's poetry in graceful English. Special thanks are due to Professor Liliane Welch for permission to quote her translation of Baudelaire's "Morning Twilight", and to Mrs Barbara Dederick, for permission to quote the translation by Kate Flores of Baudelaire's "Correspondances".

VI

The bibliography on Cavafy's life and poetry in Greek and other languages has grown impressively in quality and quantity in recent years. The tireless efforts of so many scholars, of D. Haas and M. Pieris, in particular, have resulted in the first major compilation of references.[7] The able writer and bibliographer, Mr D. Daskalopoulos, has discussed in several publications the major contributions to Cavafian studies; his work has proven to be a veritable treasure of information.[7] All the books, articles and translations in a great many languages, other than in Greek, of Cavafy's poetry have helped in no small measure to increase the number of his admirers all over the world. His recognition as a major poet of the twentieth century owes much to W. H. Auden, Peter Bien, C. M. Bowra, E. M. Forster, Kimon Friar, Edmund Keeley, Renata Lavagnini, Robert Liddell, Timos Malanos, Filippo Maria Pontani, George Seferis, Philip Sherrard, Stratis Tsirkas,

---

[6] Haas and Pieris 1984, is the most exhaustive bibliographical guide to the 154 approved "published" poems.

[7] See Daskalopoulos 1983, and the more recent work, Κ. Π. Καβάφης: Σχέδια στὸ Περιθώριο [*C. P. Cavafy: Drawings in the Margins*], Athens, 1988, for an invaluable account of the early printings of Cavafy's poems and the state of the Cavafian studies throughout the world. In a special essay he treats in depth the problems and issues related to bibliographical investigations.

Marguerite Yourcenar, and many others whose names are readily found in the bibliography. I publish this study with the modest expectation that it only be regarded as another appreciation of the fine poetry Cavafy gave to the world.

J.P.A.
Temple Terrace, Florida

Chapter One

The Alexandrian Environment.

1. The Founding of Alexandria. 2. Alexandria: The Pride of the Ptolemies. 3. The Roman Intervention. 4. Obscurity and the Rebirth. 5. The Greeks of Modern Alexandria. 6. The Poet's Environment.

1. The Founding of Alexandria[1]

Alexandria was intended to be a Hellenic city but was born Hellenistic. From the day of its founding it became susceptible to the cultural and political pressures that altered substantially whatever plans Alexander had for it. By the time he died in Persia he was already markedly orientalized. What the first Ptolemies set out to do, even if we assume their devotion to Alexander's initial vision to share the Hellenic achievement with the rest of the world he conquered, and what modifications and compromises the heirs of Alexander were led to make, are two different things. The actual events show clearly that the Hellenic was from the very beginning replaced by what the term "Hellenistic" came to mean. In fact, the roots of the Hellenistic are not an Alexandrian invention. The beginnings go back to the changes in the classical institutions and modes of life which mark the second half of the fourth century.

The cosmopolis that Alexandria was destined to become had its spiritual ancestry in Athens. The centrifugal forces that eventually shattered the cohesive substance of the classical polis were already at work when Plato wrote his *Republic*. Aristotle had just finished the writing of his *Politics*, when in 322 Alexander of Macedonia gave orders to his chief city-architect, Dinocrates of Rhodes, to build a city on the northern coast of Egypt and name it Alexandria. The philosopher's views on city-planning were left out,

---

[1]Portions of this chapter appeared under the title "Alexandria: The History and Legend of a Cosmopolis," in *Conspectus in History,* Vol. I, No. 4 (1977): 13-23.

and Alexandria was launched as a non-Aristotelian city, and less classical at that. Its founding and completion coincided with the beginning of the age of Hellenistic Empires.

2. Alexandria, the Pride of the Ptolemies

The place where Alexandria was built was known to the Greeks of the Mycenean age. Homer gave us a description of it in the *Odyssey*:

> There is an island in the surging sea in front of Egypt, and men call it Pharos, distant as far as a hollow ship runs in a whole day when the shrill wind blows fair behind it. Therein is a harbour with good anchorage, whence men launch the shapely ships into the sea, when they have drawn supplies of black water.[2]

There is the place where Menelaus, returning from Troy, had his encounter with Proteus, the elusive king of the island. Many centuries later, a young Macedonian king set out to establish a vast empire and led his armies through Asia Minor and Syria and easily conquered the land of Egypt. Alexander was scarcely twenty-five years of age when he arrived at the mouth of the Nile in 332 and selected the site for a new city from which he planned to rule the province of Egypt. It so transpired that Alexander did not live to see the city to which he gave his name and where his body was finally brought for burial. His city followed the pattern of the political centers of large states, like Rome, Constantinople, Cordova, Paris and Vienna. Alexandria, however, was never a city-state. It took on a different destiny to become the throbbing cosmopolitan center of the Mediterranean world where the molding of the Hellenistic spirit was to occur. It reflected the pride of the Ptolemies, as it grew as a great center for the blending of all cultural, religious, literary, artistic and phyletic traditions. Yet the Ptolemies saw to it that chief among them would be the glory of their ancestry, the pride and glory of their Hellenic background, or whatever they remembered of it.

It took about one hundred years and three generations of Ptolemies to make Alexandria a legend of splendor and luxury. But the city became more

---

[2] Homer, *Odyssey*, Book IV, 354-9, tr. A. J. Murray, (London 1946).

than that. Ptolemy I, the Soter (323-285), was a prudent and practical Macedonian. He ruled Egypt first in the name of Alexander's son and later in his own, but not before the political and economic conditions were made secure. He made the expansion of his kingdom and the adornment of his capital city a lifetime ambition. It is the genius of this early period that Cavafy sought to convey in one of his early poems, "The Glory of the Ptolemies" (1896/*1911*: A 28). The *persona* is a Lagides, most likely Ptolemy I Soter, son of the Macedonian Lagus, or Ptolemy II Philadelphus. The dramatic date could be sometime after 323 and much before 221 B.C. The *persona* boastfully praises both himself and Alexandria as beyond comparison to all else, be it Macedonian or barbarian, and ends on the following:

> My city is the teacher, pinnacle of the Hellenic world,
> and most wise, in every science, in every art.

Before the second century B.C. was over, Alexandria surpassed Athens as the leading intellectual and scientific center of the civilized world. The great places of learning, the Museum and the Library, established in 290 B.C. were manned in a matter of decades with hosts of industrious scholars and equipped with hundred of thousands of volumes. The city was ripe for new adventures in literature, science, art, and architecture. With the main harbor facing the Mediterranean, the inner lake Mariout directly connected with the Nile, and a water connection between the two seas, Alexandria attracted people and commerce from every land. By 200 B.C. it had a population that rose to about four to five hundred thousand, mostly Greeks, Egyptians, Jews, Persians, Syrian, Arabs, and Africans.

Every idea, value, practice, style, and attitude that was brought from Athens to Alexandria took on a different face, so to speak. In the aftermath of Alexander's conquests, the Greeks who left their land to seek new fortunes and opportunities in the budding cities of newly sprung empires experienced a transformation of character and a reorientation of outlook. Like many other fortune-seekers with different backgrounds, they contributed to the rise of the open cosmopolis and were molded by it. They helped to consolidate the new spirit of the Hellenistic world-view. So strong and far-reaching were the new ways that they proved to be of great consequence to the subsequent transformation of the city-states of Greece, including Athens. But there was still a major difference between Athens and Alexandria. Athens reached its peak as the prime example of a classical city, while Alexandria depended from the day of its founding on the co-presence of highly diverse groups of people. If the destiny of Athens was to become the heartbeat of the culture of Greek city-states, that of Alexandria was to stand out as the type of the new cosmopolis designed to serve as administrative centers of unwieldy empires. Eventually, even Rome found it impossible not to fall into the same pattern of urban growth.

There was a special flavor to the sense of loyalty the citizens of Athens, Sparta, Thebes and the other Greek cities felt for their *polis*. It was mainly a consequence of the tightly homogeneous character of their culture: their common language, their shared religious practices, their community of ideals, their public bonds of education, their legends, myths and values. The cities of the Hellenistic age, like Alexandria, attracted diverse peoples who spoke different languages, worshipped strange gods, and worked for different goals. Athens could cultivate excellence in depth for the common good, but not Alexandria. Athens developed like a cell, organically, so to speak, whereas Alexandria resembled more the accretion of molecules, to become a place where opportunities increased proportionately to the influx of talent, wealth, and power. Yet, Antioch, Syracuse and other major cities, including Rome and Athens, each in its own way followed the same path as Alexandria did. The new attitudes needed for survival and success in the cosmopolis slowly replaced the old virtues that defined the loyal Roman and the enlightened Athenian. Once all this was done, the classical age became a thing of the past. It was this powerful drama in the history of Western culture, and its repetition in modern times, that Cavafy understood so well and included in the substance of his poetry.

Early in its history Alexandria became notorious as a city of celebrations. The setting of the celebrations Cavafy revives in his "Alexandrian Kings" requires a city and a tradition that reach back to the period of Ptolemy II Philadelphus (287-246). The coronation of this king, hardly a modest affair, could never have taken place in Athens, Sparta or Pella, in Macedonia. No Greek city could provide the space or the actors for an event which required 57,000 infantry men, 23,000 cavalry, and about 1,500 chariots, which bore vessels of silver filled with perfumes and were drawn by a variety of animals from horses to antelopes and ostriches. Chief among these chariots was a gigantic one, drawn by 300 men, and carrying the image of Silenus. One can well imagine the spaciousness of the streets and open places of the city to accommodate the participants in the spectacle, from honored magistrates to the masses of on-lookers. Such was the growing cosmopolis of the Hellenistic age, with its new mores and promises, which gradually succeeded in replacing the classical polis. While Alexandria grew in size and novelty it also created the conditions for inner decadence. By the time of Cleopatra's reign, the celebrations lost all of their early significance and the proclamations of royal titles were all but void of content. As Cavafy, the modern Alexandrian poet, says in "Alexandrian Kings" (1912/*1912*: A 35):

> The Alexandrians were well aware, of course,
> that these were only words and theatrics.

The Hellenic values which the Ptolemies and their Greek companions brought with them to the newly erected capital of Egypt faded away slowly but inevitably. They were gradually replaced with a habitual repetition of ritual routines. Their initial meaning started to fade after they were transplanted to the new environment and mixed with incongruous elements. The Hellenic myths and rituals lost their original flavor. Artistic imagination responded to the changing winds of cultural taste and missed no opportunity to explore the affected, the unusual, even the trivial, until enamored of excitement for its own sake it indulged even in fears, superstitions and auguries. Yet, on the practical side, exploration in the centers of learning cultivated the practice of applied science that the demands of a complex cosmopolis required. Despite this momentum and upswing of learning, erudition and the use of practical information, the new needs which the conditions of the cosmopolis introduced in the lives of its inhabitants made it difficult if not impossible to emulate the ideal of the life of reason that the philosophies of the classical era advocated with such passion. The rational ideal became an alternative for the disillusioned, the lonely, or the very bright. When Polybius visited Alexandria in the first half of the second century B.C., he said of the Alexandrian Greeks: "they are mongrel Greeks, though they did have an exclusively Greek education." Whatever became of this education, it certainly failed to find its way into the everyday life of the cosmopolitans. Education and ethos had pulled in different directions.

This is the cosmopolis where Bacchus and the mystery religions, no longer worshipped in the wooded hillsides and mountains, were confined in the closed spaces of urban congregations. The mystery cults of Greece changed character after they were transported to Alexandria. The deities became part of an underworld cult that offered relief from boredom and hope of some eternal life removed from nature and the polis. The new religious amalgams promised flights that were not of this earth and dispensed to the needy spiritual consolations which the celebrations, the spectacles, the emporium, the harbor, and the library could not provide. Those who could resist the sensual surface of the cosmopolis sought salvation in the darker cults of the eternal. But those who wished to remain masters of men sought power and wealth, while increasing their capacity for injustice, callousness and ambition. The royal families and the administrative classes could maintain their status but not without adopting a requisite amount of selfishness, conspiracy, and calculated abuse of human talent. But the cosmopolis continued to grow, and with it emerged new styles of life. In due course everything became monumental, including loneliness.

What Cavafy tells us in his "Hellenistic" poems, as we shall see in the chapters that follow, is how a certain kind of experience, a certain attitude and mode of living, came to dim the old ways of the classical world. He tells his stories in such a way that the human beings in them, some drawn from history and some invented, re-enact dramatically the essential features of life in the cosmopolis. His personages act out each episode under the mask of "believable" history in order to help the reader grasp this gradual loss of the ways of the polis and sensitize the imagination to feel the hopelessness of the effort to escape from the clutches of the cosmopolis.

There can be no going back, no return to the by-gone realities of tradition. The cosmopolis is no place for an Odysseus to be born nor the environment to generate the passion of *nostos*. The cravings of the incurably nostalgic can only have the reality of imaginative flights, at best dreams of the excitements of different options, rarely if ever available. But actually, what is left is the thirst or need for power, the trying out of selfish ambition, and when these do not bring about the expected results, there is always the road to false pretenses, excuses for the glory that never comes. And as the pretenses wax strongly, especially when the external conditions of life in the cosmopolis get worse through mismanagement and political blundering, the actors become even more pathetic. Once in the realm of grand illusion, the chances for a *nostos* vanish for good, and the reaching out to find one in the dark is a move as doomed as it is desperate. Perhaps Julian the Emperor, about whom Cavafy wrote several poems, is the most pathetic case of doomed *nostos*. In vain did Julian try to resurrect the rituals of pagan Greece. The polis was beyond recapture, though that was not Julian's real objective. The Ithaka of Odysseus was gone; it was replaced by a non-Ithaka, the cosmopolis. Cavafy came to the conclusion that once we find ourselves dwellers in the cosmopolis, any Alexandria, if there can be an Ithaka at all, it would have to be personal, as a self-centered vision, but hardly more than that. It cannot be the polis of Plato, not even the garden of Epicurus. It is the lone path marked with a series of stops at chartered and unknown harbors of pleasures. It is an Ithaka but stripped of the object of *nostos*. And the vaster the cosmopolis the more enticing the search for the new Ithaka becomes. Actually, a no-land Ithaka is all that is left for one to create. After all, it is "a kind of solution," as the poet says in his "Waiting for the Barbarians."

3. The Roman Intervention

The Romans noticed the gradual decline of the Ptolemaic dynasty and how its weakness became stronger through inefficiency, intrigue and ruthless ambition. They moved in and asserted their own interests. The first Roman embassy arrived at the royal court of Alexandria in 273 B.C., but the first overt intervention came in 200 B.C. in the disguise of friendly protection.

The Romans found it easier to condemn the corrupt morals of the Alexandrians and the other Hellenistic centers of the Empires, than share their own righteous standards. They preferred to exploit the weaknesses of others and expand the power of Rome. Her long-range designs on Egypt proved effective, and the day came when Hellenistic kings drew up their last will bequeathing their kingdoms to Rome! The long story of Rome-Alexandria relationships during the first century B.C., when each took advantage of the other's home rivalries, rose to a dramatic pitch during the reign of the last and most fascinating of all Cleopatras, the wife and sister of Ptolemy XIV, who ascended to the throne when her brother was only ten and she seventeen. The powerful leaders of Rome became directly involved in the Alexandrian intrigues first by engineering Pompey's demise, after he sought refuge in the court of the Ptolemies, then with the victorious Caesar's direct and successful involvement in the power struggles of Egypt. The Caesar-Cleopatra affair is too well known to be retold, but she bore him a son, who was later crowned Ptolemy XVI, an event which Cavafy reconstructed with striking imagery and irony in his "Alexandrian Kings" (1912/*1912*). As it turned out Cleopatra went on to new adventures after the great Caesar was murdered in 44 B.C. Marc Antony rose to power, his legions protecting Alexandria and her queen. When the rivalry between Octavian and Antony reached its climax the Egyptianizing Roman went down in defeat taking Cleopatra with him. Her seductive powers were tried for the last time on Octavian and failed. To the alternative of being carried to Rome to adorn Octavian's triumph, she chose suicide. Sometimes the sensual are not without good sense.

With the last of the Ptolemies dead, Alexandria ended its career as a royal cosmopolis becoming the crowded capital of a Roman province. Nevertheless, its characteristic culture had taken on a distinctive flavor, and three centuries of cosmopolitanism proved sufficient to give it enough momentum not only to work out a mode of political survival, but also to invent new patterns of mixing the most divergent species of Mediterranean tastes. The Roman conquest of the Hellenistic Empires and their capitals only accelerated the transformation of what was left of the life of the polis. The ideals of wisdom and beauty of the old classical days became erudition and decorative charm, and when the past was evoked it was mainly to enhance the seductive appeal of the present. That the sciences of medicine, mathematics, astronomy and other applied fields could grow and flourish to serve the pragmatic demands of the cosmopolis is no more curious a phenomenon than is the appearance of new styles and genres in the arts and literatures to satisfy novel interests and tastes. As scientific knowledge furnished more accurate details about the world and Roman expansion made the boundaries of states fluid, the bonds which could give the individuals a sense of belonging to stable communities fell apart. The philosophers, seeing that they had no polis to call their own, preoccupied themselves with commentaries on the great books or they withdrew to a garden community. But the multitudes that had neither power nor the knowledge to save themselves prayed for different miracles to happen. Their frustrations prepared them for the wave of religious movements that swept the Mediterranean world after the Roman conquest of the Hellenistic empires.

When Alexandria ceased being a center of intrigue and power, it served as the melting pot of religious cults and as the spiritual home of theological controversy over the many sublime faces of the divine. And Alexandria changed. Though Rome divested it of its last Hellenic external remnants, it took the arrival of the gospels from Jerusalem and the theurgists of the East to appropriate the spirit. The experienced bishops of Alexandria seized the initiative and did their homework early. Thus the Egyptian Church made its mark before Constantine the Great declared Christianity the favored religion of his empire.

Not all of the long line of Ptolemies and Cleopatras, from Ptolemy I to Ptolemy XVI or Caesarion, figure in Cavafy's poems. Cavafy is writing poetry, not history. He recreates the mood of the cosmopolis, feeling the pulse of its many walks of life and grasping the dominant details of the emerging attitudes as they set the tone for a gradual involvement in the struggle for power, the search for pleasure and the effort to salvage an illusion of dignity in the face of an unpredictable future. As the cosmopolis grew, be it Alexandria, Antioch or Rome, so did the ambiguities of life multiply, and their effects were felt by persons in high places, rulers, royalty and the wealthy, as well as by those in ordinary and lowly stations, including the opportunists and the corrupt. The sense of euphoria which came with periods of expansion was no more secure and permanent than was the sense of power due to victorious wars and political maneuvering. Yet, while the fortunes and misfortunes of the individuals kept the human drama in disarray and gave it colorful variety, the cosmopolis itself could still grow in splendor, what with its palaces and public buildings, its miles of colonnaded streets, its libraries and temples, theaters, race courses, monuments, pillars, fortresses, lighthouses, and harbors.

The aspects of decadence which Cavafy utilizes in many of his poems, aside from those which interpreters read into his poems, all have to do with the fate of his city, the cosmopolis of Alexandria, and in close analogy with it, the other great centers of ancient and modern times that partake of its character. But we are dealing here with a very complex theme, and in order to keep it in proper perspective we need to remember Cavafy's concern for the fate of his own cosmopolis as well as his cultural and historical identification with it. Aside from Cavafy's broader and philosophical, so to speak, views on human life, there is this deliberate choice of concrete places where the human drama itself unfolds in depth and detail. Alexandria is both typical and intimate.

But what happened in Alexandria was typical of the fate of the Hellenistic empire-cities. The first phase displays a gradual loss of power and independence leading to the romanization of political power. The Roman victories had a profound effect on the external and material aspects of the Hellenistic cosmopolis, which in turn proved to be decisive on the fate of

Rome herself. In the closing decades of the Western Empire, Rome itself became the most parasitical cosmopolis. The other cosmopoleis and the provinces which sustained them saw the Romans carry their riches as well as moods of disillusionment to Rome. But Rome eventually became the arena of arenas, slowly readying herself for the coming of the barbarians. It was only six years before Alaric sacked Rome in 410 that the Emperor Honorius finally put an end to the gladiatorial combats. The spectacles declined and the public baths had already gone dry for lack of wood for heating. The chariot races were transferred to Byzantium, renamed at least temporarily New Rome, and then permanently to Constantinople, the new seat of the Empire. But before Rome deromanized herself, she had succeeded in defacing the external side of the Hellenistic cosmopolis. The internal side was left for religion to undo. The spiritual leaders of Alexandria, Antioch, and Constantinople were only too glad to finish the work. Within a few centuries the pagan gods were virtually forgotten and their elements carefully sifted to enrich the Christian ritual, or used negatively to stir fanaticism as needed. The pagans lost the battle of the creeds. Centuries later, an Alexandrian poet would breathe life into their shadows and when he could find none, his imagination would create them from the fabric of historical plausibility.

The spiritual end of the Hellenistic world, the human drama it involved, took place in Alexandria and Antioch, not in Byzantium, not even in Athens. Cavafy is reported to have made the following remark: "It is far more difficult for me to place my *personae* in the Byzantium period than it is in the Hellenistic. The Byzantium period, though closer to me (isn't this curious?), is restrictive, whereas the Hellenistic is more immoral, more free, and it allows me to move my *personae* as I wish."[3] This only partly explains Cavafy's

---

[3] Quoted in Malanos 1957: 77, 148. Seferis 1962: 318 quotes this comment and interprets Cavafy as not meaning to say that "the Hellenistic period suits me better because it allows me to speak more easily on heavenly concerns. That would be rather naive. My thinking is that the diverse forms of pleasure existed in all periods of history. What changes, as the times change, is man's relation to himself, to his fellow man, to God—things interconnected." Seferis has probably Malanos' Freudian interpretation in mind. He suggests that we should rather think of Cavafy as "the historical poet, that is the poet for whom the use of history—the emotional use of history—allows him to express himself better. We saw how slowly he comes to acquire historical consciousness, which means consciousness of what he can accomplish. The periods that provide him with his heroes are not mere retrogressions

preference for Alexandria and Antioch as the settings for most of his historical poems. The cycle of the "Julian" poems, set mainly in Antioch, are part of the same panorama as the Alexandrian poems—the whole civilized and Hellenistic world being replaced by the city of God on Earth.[4] Each displaced city remained a cosmopolis, albeit theocratic. And even when some of them were lost to the barbarians, the faithful would spare no effort to regain them totally through conversion. But this later phase is of minor interest to Cavafy except for those episodes in the long history of "our glorious Byzantinism,"[5] as he referred to it once, which promised sufficient ambiguity to serve the needs of poetry. The relatively minor place which the history of Byzantium occupies in his poetry will be discussed in a later chapter, but this can be explained briefly at this point by drawing attention to the fact that the cosmopolis that Byzantium was to become was from the beginning meant to be Christian in character since, at the time of its founding, the religious factor was as dominant as the administrative plan. Its destiny as a cosmopolis was sealed, and the efforts of Julian in the early phase of the Eastern Empire to revive the anemic remains of paganism were short-lived. As it turned out—and Cavafy knew this only too well—Julian had no more Hellenism in his cultural outlook than a high priest of Serapis. Just the same, Cavafy saw there the last spurts of a pathetic drama, and he salvaged them. He turned to Byzantium to view it when its monolithic spirit had lost its momentum.

4. Obscurity and the Rebirth

The last "historical" reference to Alexandria occurs in Cavafy's poem

---

or excuses; they are living entities, 'now's' that allow him to move his *personae* as his idiosyncrasy demands. The world of Homer was something else, and there is nothing strange about the fact that Cavafy realized early enough that he had to leave Homer alone" (318-319); repr. Seferis 1974b, v. 1: 398-9, also 1984: 176; comp. Politis 1930, v. 2: 451.

[4]For a detailed treatment of these poems, see G. W. Bowersock 1981: 89-104; also Renata Lavagnini 1981: 55-88.

[5]"In Church," written in August 1892 and revised twice, in 1901 and 1906, before it was published in December 1912.

"Aimilianos Monai, Alexandrian, A.D. 628-655," (1918/*1918*). This is an imaginary personage and the last of his Alexandrian *dramatis personae*. The poem tells us that Aimilianos Monai died in Sicily. By this time, Alexandria was still a livable city. The Eastern Emperor was unable to provide for adequate defense of Egypt. As a province it was divided into five parts governed by an equal number of rulers who had a greater aptitude for personal rivalries than ability for military tactics. Numerically adequate but deprived of leadership, the army was rendered even less efficient by poor civic administration and, as a result, failed to check the conquest of Egypt by the Arabs. Nor did it fare better later to prevent the capture of Alexandria by the Persians in 618 or 619. In 629, however, the Emperor Heraclius defeated the armies of King Chosroes, and Egypt, Syria and Palestine were returned to the Byzantine Empire. In both episodes the city of Alexandria suffered no major calamities. In 641, the Arabian chief Amr occupied Alexandria and sent this message of Caliph Omar in Medina:

> I have captured a city from the description of which I shall refrain. Suffice it to say that I have seized therein 4000 villas with 4000 baths, 40,000 poll-tax-paying Jews and four hundred places of entertainment for the royalty.[6]

Within a matter of a few years, the Byzantines withdrew from Egypt, never to return. The rest of the Byzantine provinces in North Africa also fell to the Arabs. Heraclius died in 641 or 642. His successor tried to recapture Alexandria, taking advantage of certain signs of unrest after the Caliph recalled Amr. The Imperial fleet arrived, the city revolted, but Amr returned and took Alexandria by force. The Arabs spared the city but time did not. For centuries it remained a minor port; but cut off from the centers of Mediterranean Christianity, the once bright cosmopolis gradually declined. The Arabs concentrated their efforts on their own city, Cairo. In 1517, Alexandria was taken by the Turks and had no spark of life to speak of until Napoleon's troops stormed the city on July 2, 1798, whose population by then had dwindled to about 4000. What was once a great cosmopolis had shrunk to the size of a small town.

Turkey, with the support of the British fleet, made an attempt in 1799 to recapture Egypt, but it ended in defeat. Two years later, the British landed

---

[6]Hitti 1937: 164-165.

an expeditionary force, partly to protect their interests by keeping open the roads to the far East, partly to support Turkey to maintain its position in the eastern Mediterranean. The French were forced to leave Egypt, and the British returned the country to the Turks. The modern chapter in the history of Alexandria begins with these events.

A Turkish subject who was stationed in Egypt prior to these military developments had managed to rise from his position of tax collector to that of Viceroy of Egypt, in 1805, and to remain in power until 1848 as virtual monarch. This man was Muhammad Ali, of Albanian origin, born in the small town of Cavala in Macedonia. This ambitious ruler almost succeeded in building an empire as large as the Ptolemaic but the combined interests of the British and the Turks forced him to a more moderate role with sole jurisdiction over the land of Egypt but still nominal subject to the sultan. For all his affection for Western civilization, Ali saw only the surface of its qualities, power and industry. While he attracted many Europeans to seek opportunities in Egypt and contributed to its modernization, he handed out privileges with a generosity that matched his donation of Cleopatra's Needles to the British and Americans and his indifference towards the plundering of Egypt's archeological treasures. While the ruling Egyptian aristocracy enjoyed the fruits of power, and the emerging cities of Alexandria and Cairo developed into commercial centers, the natives continued to live in unrequited perpetual poverty. The consequences were not felt until the last quarter of the nineteenth century when the movement of "Egypt for the Egyptians" ended disastrously with the British bombardment of Alexandria in 1882. The British rule of Egypt was to continue well into the middle of the twentieth century.

Alexandria entered the modern world of intrigue, commerce and trade as an international harbor with waterways and rail connections, but emerged as a city of random growth soon to become another modern cosmopolis, with the foreign communities in the lead. In this regard, Alexandria came to take its place as a leading city within the larger circle of near Eastern cities where Europe, Asia and Africa were once again exchanging their goods, testing their strength, and indulging their cultural tastes in a variety of mixtures. Within a century the population of Alexandria grew from 4,000 to 400,000 with almost one tenth of it consisting of foreigners—English, French, Greeks, Italians, Armenians, Syrians, Jews and smaller groups from every corner of Europe and Asia. The opening of the Suez Canal in 1869 and the building of the first dam at Aswan in 1902, proved decisive for the further development of Alexandria. Cultural pursuits and scholarly interests grew stronger through the activities of the "Service des Antiquités de l' Égypt," the "Egyptian Exploration Society," the "Société Royale Égyptienne de Papyrologie," which paralleled the appearance of a great variety of journals, newspapers in many languages, schools, bookstores, and lecture centers, museums and libraries.

Next to the Egypt of the Pharaohs, the Ptolemaic Alexandria kindled the imagination of many writers and artists who found there material for their historical accounts and plots for their novels, from Bouche-Leclercq, J. P. Mahaffy and E. D. Bevan, to P. Louÿs and Anatole France. The discovery and publication of the papyri served many purposes, not least among them the sense of excitement of living in Alexandria. The glory of the past and the sensual possibilities of the present had found an enviable mode of mutual sustenance. Both awaited their poet. Constantine P. Cavafy, from the Greek sector of Alexandria, answered the call.

5. The Greeks of Modern Alexandria[7]

Next to Arabic, French, English and Italian, Greek was one of the most widely spoken languages in Alexandria. The Greek community threw its first roots in the Egyptian soil during the opening decades of Muhammad Ali's reign. It grew in complexity and size to about 80,000 in the twentieth century giving the appearance of a small nation within a large state. Strong in its attachment to ethnic identity, the Greek community felt comfortable enough to have its share in defining the cosmopolitan character of the city. The Greeks of Modern Alexandria brought with them attitudes and values which helped them accommodate their special affection for the Hellenistic culture of the Ptolemaic era and the softer religious tone of the Orthodox Church of

---

[7]See Kitroeff 1983: 11-21, for an outline of the cultural and ideological currents of the community; Kitroeff's Table II gives the population of Alexandria according to nationality for the years 1907, 1927, and 1937 (14). Compare also Z. Lorentzatos' "Introduction" to Sareyannis 1984: 13-28. Extensive treatments of the Greek community in Alexandria in the writings of Hadginis, Halvatzakis, Keeley, Liddell, Malanos, Tsirkas, and Yalourakis, listed in the bibliography.

Alexandria; they also sustained the passion and the desire to endure as a group and to survive in economic competition. Their central concern was how to stay close to the political and cultural developments of the mainland while working out ways to prove their own worth and independence of mind.

After the long war of Independence from 1821 to 1829 against Ottoman rule, the people of the newly born state of Greece found their freedom burdened with a multitude of unsolved problems and limited only to a fraction of the land of the Greek-speaking people. The wounds from the war lay open. The worst of the disasters was inflicted by the armies of Muhammad Ali who invaded Greece to promote his own designs under the guise of assisting the Sultan to put down the revolution. Muhammad Ali became part of this drama in whose aftermath a free Greece was established on a desolate land. The failure of the Ottoman sultan to strike a quick victory over the Greek insurgents led to the decision to grant Muhammad Ali in 1822 the pashalic of Crete, although this important Aegean island was never within the Egyptian sphere of control. In exchange, Muhammad Ali was expected to bring order to this highly volatile area of the empire. He quickly seized the opportunity, and in 1824 also succeeded in obtaining the pashalic of Morea without even having tried to enforce order in Crete. In 1825, under the command of his son, Ibrahim, a strong and well-trained army landed in Morea, determined to extinguish the revolution and secure a permanent foothold on the Greek mainland. The Egyptian troops advanced from victory to victory reducing the Greek resistance to scattered instances of defensive skirmishes, bringing the war almost to an end.

Ibrahim imposed a military solution only by laying waste to the countryside, burning and killing everything that stood in his path. Eventually his forces arrived before the already weakened walls of the besieged city of Mesolonghi, where Lord Byron died in April, 1824. After months of fierce fighting, the combined army of Turks and Egyptians entered Mesolonghi, or whatever was left of that city. Starvation had forced the defenders to attempt a heroic exodus while the disabled and the sick were left with no choice other than to stay and fight to the end. In both cases the survivors were few. However, Ibrahim's success prepared his defeat. The European powers—Russia, France, and Great Britain—reacting to his excesses, destroyed the Egyptian and Ottoman fleets in the Bay of Navarino on October 20, 1827. The ruins Ibrahim left behind in the wake of the evacuation of Morea were only matched by the horrors of the victims he had put to the sword and the thousands of women and children he dragged into slavery.

With independence now made secure under the protection of the European powers, the Greeks had to attend to more than the healing of the wounds from a war that lasted almost ten years. Of no lesser urgency was the responsibility of keeping the desire for freedom strong and alive in the breasts of the unredeemed brethren living beyond the boundaries of the small state on both sides of the Aegean Sea: the Greek-speaking majorities in Epirus, Macedonia, Thrace, Pontos, the western coast of Asia Minor, Crete, the islands of the Dodecanese and Cyprus. The vital problems of Greece since its formation as an independent state and the agonizing issue of achieving the integration of all Greeks within the geographical boundaries of a single state, became a consuming cause. The Greek claims proved of small concern to the European powers except when they interfered with their own interests of diplomacy and control. National duty and hope for survival led the Greeks of the mainland to adopt a policy of patriotic vigilance. This nationalism of "the Great Idea," as it was called, cast its long cultural shadow over the lives of Greeks of diaspora. The community of Alexandria was no exception. The generation of Cavafy also lived its tensions to the hilt. The whole history of Hellenic consciousness and the profound issues of cosmopolitan humanism converged, urgently at times, and became one of the mainstreams that nourished his poetic themes. Part of his uniqueness lies in his original blending of cultural memory and personal immediacies. As it turned out, his answer to the demands of the fatherland came in the form of a different tribute. He revitalized its rich literary tradition with a new ecumenical vision.

To return to the origins of the Greek population of modern Egypt, it should be noted that there were Greek orthodox monasteries in the vicinity of Alexandria all along, but they were of no consequence to the eventual concentration of Greek immigrants in Egypt. There is reason to believe that a small number of Greeks, probably not more that 200, were living there before Napoleon's invasion. It grew into a sizable community before the Greek War of Independence broke out in 1821. Apparently it suffered repressions and punishment in no small measure. Ali's expeditionary force in the 1820's (1825-1829) enslaved a large number of women and children and transported them to Egypt, but their fate was soon forgotten. Some of the children were adopted by prominent Egyptians and lived eventually to occupy positions of high power, preserving but a dim remembrance of their origins. Somewhere around the 1840's a Greek community was formed by immigrants who were encouraged by the liberal policies of Muhammad Ali's administration. Its population grew rapidly in numbers as did its needs, and by 1860 the entire cotton industry was controlled by the Greeks who had in the meantime created their own banks, post-office, churches, hospitals, parochial schools, newspapers and journals. This was the golden age of Ismael's reign. The cultural dependence on the fatherland continued as the Greek community, lacking any interest in being attracted to Egypt's local traditions, harkened back to the literary and intellectual models of liberated Greece. It was a period when the literati of Athens, while trying to keep pace with the last romantic outbursts of Europe, were still defending the ideals of freedom and fatherland as well as entreating for political reforms.

While groping for ways to satisfy their broader spiritual and creative needs, the Greeks of Alexandria spent most of their energy in establishing themselves as firmly as they could in the economy of the land. Their efforts were successful beyond their expectations, and their leadership in finance and commerce remained uncontested until the fateful events of 1882, when the bombardment of Alexandria by the British, the defeat of the nationalist movement and the capitulation of the Egyptian leadership, led to the encroaching control of English expansionist power. These events had far-reaching effects, especially for the future of Egypt. For the thriving Greek communities they forecast more than a change in style of life. They marked the opening of an era which was to signal the new status of the communities destined to become colonies within a colony. Fortunes changed hands, adjustment on all sides became inevitable. Yet life in Alexandria had acquired enough momentum of its own to maintain its busy and cosmopolitan rhythm, with the transactions of the day and pursuits of the night.

As a whole, the Greek community responded to the crisis with considerable success and ingenuity. The fortunes of men like Averoff and Benakis were not only beneficial to the Alexandrian Greek institutions but also the source of generous assistance to the needs of the fatherland. Between 1886 and 1891, at least 34 important books were published, and they are among the best the Greek intelligentsia of Egypt produced. Generally speaking, in the decades that followed, the Greeks consolidated their interests and assessed more clearly their opportunities for cultural survival. As time went on, their feeling of attachment to their heritage and the ethnic ideals of modern Greece became even stronger. They improved instruction in the schools, built more churches, formed literary clubs, discussed with passion the political events of Greece, and when patriotic duty demanded, they rushed to fight in the wars in which the fatherland became involved, to help free the unredeemed brethren still under the Turkish yoke. Living in a city they could call their own, these Greeks felt the heavy demands of their heritage, but their style of life had a flavor the Greeks of the mainland considered lacking in purity. The Athenians were more than reluctant to recognize the intellectual output and literary attainments of their Alexandrian brothers. The poetry of Cavafy was no exception. Yet throughout their careers, the Greek communities in Egypt faced the two-fold duty of preserving their Hellenism while sharing with the fatherland the fruits of their labor and genius. They did so with devotion and eagerness without anticipating a return to the homeland. Yet, the lures of Alexandria were stronger than the call of *nostos*. There was enough Hellenism in their cosmopolis to prevent them from becoming lotus-eaters. But the day came in the wake of World War II when the realities of the awakened nationalism of the Egyptian people demanded new solutions. The sweep of events forced the *nostos,* and the exodus followed. Fortunately, Cavafy did not live to witness the forced return. He died in 1933 in Alexandria.

6. The Poet's Environment

Egypt appears for the first time in Cavafy's poetry with the writing of "Sham-el-Nessim" [Breath of the Breeze] (1892/*1892*: CP 23). Egypt, in this poem, is the native land of Alexandria, the surroundings and the people, in a day of festivities:

> The sun scorches and beats
> on our pallid Missiri (Egypt)
> with arrows full of bitterness and spite
> and wearies it with thirst and sickness.
> Our sweet Missiri
> in a smiling festival
> drinks, forgets, bedecks itself, feels happy
> and defies the tyrant sun.
>
> The pleasant Breath of the Breeze heralds the spring,
> innocent festival of the country-side.

> Empty is Alexandria and her compact streets.
> The happy Breath of the Breeze, the simple Egyptian
> wants to celebrate, and takes to the tents. . . .

It is the beloved land of the native Egyptian, with its sun beating down, its dusty streets, the thirst, the epidemic diseases, the lusty desires, the motionless thoughts.

As his poetry expanded, one by one the compelling features of the contemporary and the grand dimensions of the past found their niche in the spiraling movements of Cavafy's imagination and took their place in his poetic panorama. The haunting history of the city, its physical setting, and human drama, follow the reader like faithful shadows forcing upon him the realization that Cavafy's voice, immediate, authentic and intelligently selective, could only belong to a person whose every sentiment and thought was Alexandrian. His city remains the center of gravity even when the imaginative flights lead us to Nero's Rome, a court in Cappadocia, a night in Antioch or a theatre in Sidon. By the time he wrote his last poem, Alexandria had been granted in his poetic universe the dazzling scope of a dramatic universe, where past and present, and the many transformations in between, were turned into boundaries and contents of the cosmopolitan consciousness in a personal vision of life.

After the German armies occupied Greece in 1941, the poet George Seferis, like many other Greeks, fled to Egypt. Reminiscing on the events of his visit, he wrote:

> I found there in Alexandria a capital where Greek was still spoken, a capital at the outer limits of Greece, like ancient Seleuceia on the river Tigris, and also a Greek-speaking population which had found its poet. His shadow had not yet vanished from the streets and the gathering places of the city: but perhaps it was a somewhat different Greek world. . . .

Seferis goes on to relate that twelve years later—the year must have been 1953—when he visited Alexandria for the second time, he went to visit the house where Cavafy lived at 10 Rue Lepsius, only to find that the entrance to the house was half-blocked by a pile of rubbish. A sudden feeling of sadness overcame him and he realized at that moment the "the city of Cavafy had already gone; it was no longer there."[8]

It is interesting that Seferis thought of Alexandria as a Greek city at the outer edge of Hellenism, because in a serious sense that is precisely the character it had for Cavafy—though the modern city itself was a mixture of a dominantly Egyptian population and numerous minority communities. The Alexandrian poet could not help but apprehend the special similarity between the modern Alexandria and the changing character of the cities of Hellenistic empires. Yet his experienced eye could leisurely size up the contours of the swelling waves of the inevitable. He knew that modern Alexandria was marked to surrender its short-lived Greek flavor. Modern Alexandria held much promise for poetry though less for glory. Thus in his poem "In the Year 200 B.C." (1916/*1931*: B 88), Cavafy could place a *persona* in the climate of opinion that was still clinging to the memory of Alexander's victories, and while showing no signs of awareness that the Romans were already intervening overtly in Alexandria, to speak in the tone of a paean and praise the new Hellenic world:

> . . . And from this admirable pan-Hellenic expedition
> the victorious, the resplendent,
> the glorified, the renowned,
> glorified as no other had ever been,
> the incomparable, we sprang forth,
> a new Hellenic world, great.
>
> We, the Alexandrians, the Antiochians
> the Selefkians, and the innumerable
> other Hellenes of Egypt and of Syria,
> the ones in Media, and in Persia, and so many others.
> We, with the greatly extended sovereignties
> and the varied action of thoughtful adaptations.
> And we carried our Common Greek Language
> as far as Bactria, as far as the Indians . . .

This is the style of speech Cavafy finds appropriate to an Alexandrian Greek of the year 200 B.C., a boastful spokesman of the conquest and Hellenization of Asia, proud of the remarkable feats of cultural expansion and

---

[8] Seferis 1974b, v. I: 290.

skillful adaptations. For more than one hundred years after the death of Alexander, the confidence in the lasting power of the "incomparable expedition" in the minds of those who had inherited "a new and great Greek world," was still strong, though it proved foolhardy. Ominous clouds were gathering on the other side of the Adriatic sea. In 197 B.C., the Romans won the famous battle of Cynoscephalae by defeating the army of Philip V of Macedonia, thus turning the tide that caused the gradual displacement of the Hellenistic order of influence. Seven years later, the Romans won another decisive victory at the battle of Magnesia, in Lydia, against the army of Antiochus III the Great.[9] This military event confirmed the Roman supremacy in the East. But in the year 200 B.C. the situation seemed different to most, if not all, Greeks who could still identify with the glory of the Alexandrian conquest. Cavafy recaptured imaginatively that mood in the poem quoted. The style suits the feeling, and the hubris it intimates seems innocent enough, if not justified. The "thoughtful adaptations" went on until they ran out of ingenuity.

Cavafy's Alexandria, whether the setting is historical, contemporary or imaginative, and the themes it afforded, deserve a close and detailed analysis. As such the themes draw attention to the historical interplay between two persistent trends in the development of western man's culture: the Hellenization of the Orient and the Orientalization of the Hellenic tradition. Some may prefer to call it the on-going confrontation between mind and spirit. In the poetry of Cavafy, this interplay unfolds its drama with Alexandria at the center. The background, however, is constant: Cavafy's panoramic vision of Hellenism and humanism: how a *Hellene* becomes *Hellenikos* and how he gradually fails, once the march of events combine with a faltering sense of history—bad judgment—to render the defeat inescapable. But such falls are

---

[9]In November 1913, Cavafy wrote the poem "The Battle of Magnesia" (1913/*1918*). The famous battle figures again in the poem, "Demetrios Soter (162-150 B.C.)," (1915/*1919*). Demetrios was the grandson of Antiochos III the Great, whom the Romans defeated at Magnesia in 190 B.C. The dramatic date of the poem maybe imagined as being sometime before 150 B.C., when King Demetrios' own army suffered defeat by the Romans and he himself was killed, unable to wash away the shame of Magnesia. This poem, together with two other poems referring to the decade 200-190 B.C., provide a strong clue to Cavafy's masterful way of interweaving early Hellenistic themes: "In the Year 200 B.C." (1916/*1931*) and "In a Large Greek Colony 200 B.C." (1928/*1928*).

never total. Some day, a poet appears and undoes the work of a hundred conquerors. The poets and their Alexandrias are more lasting than the powers of kings and rulers, and more vocal than the shouts at the forum.

Chapter Two

Cavafy's Life and Times: The Early Years

1. Growing Up in Alexandria. 2. Ancestors and Immediate Family. 3. Returning to a City of Confusions. 4. Despair and the Promise of Poetry. 5. Plumbing the Depths of Depression.

1. Growing Up in Alexandria

Cavafy's personal life reflects neither the contours of the major events and adventures that transformed the conditions of life in the modern European nations and Egypt, nor the dramatic developments in cultural and artistic affairs that rocked the styles and traditions of the Western world since the middle of the nineteenth century. He was mainly a loner, a special observer, equipped with the detachment of the historian, the aloofness of a stoic and the vigilant remoteness of the spectator. He lived most of his life in Alexandria in a rather uninvolved manner, guarding his privacy with meticulous care, selecting his friends for their quickness of mind and appreciation of literary subtlety, and patiently perfecting his poetic creations. He remained a studio poet.[1] His emotional life was frequently upset with strong outbursts of

---

[1] Cavafy's own biographical and genealogical sketch, "Genealogy," was printed (with omissions) *Nea Estia*, No. 501 (May 15, 1948): 622-29. A full-length "critical biography" was published by R. Liddell, 1974. A complete and definitive biography is still lacking. The sources, from newspapers to his own personal archives, are scattered in private and public collections. Aside from the daily newspapers and periodicals of Alexandria, the future biographer will have to consult the following basic sources of information: (i) The file of Eutychia N. Zelita, compiled under the supervision of Cavafy himself; it contains clippings from newspapers and periodicals. (ii) The file of P. Anastassiadis, now part of the collection of the Benakis Museum in Athens, since October 29, 1963. (iii) Cavafy, *Self-comments*, 1942. (iv) The articles by Rika Sengopoulos in the periodical *La Semaine Égyptienne*, (Cairo, April 25, 1929), and an interview in the newspaper *Vradyni*, (Dec. 11, 1935). (v) The notes and comments by and about Cavafy in *Alexandrini Techni*. (vi) Other sources and books mentioned in Tsirkas 1963, also the bibliography in Liddell 1974: 213-16. Karayannis 1983,

passions which he was nevertheless able to contain and overcome. The crises he suffered and the pitfalls he often felt as threats to his health and identity, brought him several times to the edge of unbearable pain. Yet he is in no way comparable to the romantic poet or the rebellious artist. There is nothing extraordinary in his life to attract the attention of the biographer is in search of the colorful and the exotic. Cavafy cherished his emotions and reflections too much to dissipate them in the traffic of the cosmopolis and the excesses of ephemeral indulgence.

His relatively uneventful life is mainly of interest as the record of the development of a personality that started out with more determination than promise, and hardly any conspicuous signs of genius, to climb through patience and hard work the heights of originality. Cavafy had arrived at the mid-point of his life before he began to discover his own voice, his authentic poetic way. And while so much was happening around him and much more within him, events and persons held his attention only so long as they affected his need to understand their significance and bring forth the powers of poetry. But arriving at the level of clarity and critical assessment of his own personality was a struggle of no mean effort. It proved as difficult and prolonged a problem as were his slow and cumbersome movements to overcome the difficulties of a mediocre talent. If anything, Cavafy was born a poet. This is what makes the landmarks of his life particularly interesting to the reader who is patient enough to follow the peculiar combination of circumstances and personal determination which found a unique and felicitous expression in Cavafy's achievement.

He was born in 1863. In the same year, Ismail, the son of Ibrahim Pasha, who almost succeeded in bringing the Greek War of Independence to an inglorious end, became the head of the Egyptian government. His grandfather, Muhammad Ali, had died in 1849, at the ripe age of 80, but his father hardly enjoyed the powers of the successor, for he died within a few months. Abbas I took over the reins of state, only to be murdered in 1854. The next ruler was Said Pasha, a favored son of Muhammad Ali, a weakling who came under French influence. Prior to his death in 1863, largely due to his fiscal mismanagement, Egypt was forced to incur a national debt. His policies set the country on a course of mixed blessings by granting concessions

---

has collected the available genealogical notes and published them with commentary.

to the French and British. Ferdinand de Lesseps undertook the construction of the Suez canal while the British started the Eastern Telegraph Company and established the Bank of Egypt. These concessions strengthened the chances for the events that were to follow, leading as they did to the demise of modern Egypt's expectations for eventual independence.

Cavafy grew up during Ismail's reign, the "golden age" of nineteenth century Egypt, from 1863 to 1879. Ismail admittedly supported policies and projects that introduced a new era into modern Egypt, but his personal tastes leaned heavily toward extravagant displays. Unable to exercise prudence in public spending and private entertainment, he steered the national economy on a course which led to bankruptcy and European intervention. The fulfillment of Muhammad Ali's ambitious dreams became one of Ismail's main objectives. He used government revenues in 1866 to buy from the Sultan the special privilege of the title of primogeniture for his family. In the next year he was recognized the Khedive of Egypt. The next step was to secure the recognition of the independent sovereignty of Egypt. His efforts were crowned with success in 1873. His methods of administering public affairs were a notable improvement over the sluggish ways of his predecessors. Moved by the need for modernization, he introduced the post office service, improved the system of education and invited European contractors to undertake the construction of major public works, such as railways, harbors, lighthouses, roads and canals.

The beneficiaries of Ismail's enterprising reign were the landowners, the commercial classes, the powerful contractors, the banks and industries, the merchants in the European minorities of Alexandria and Cairo, and foremost the powerful ruling groups of administrators. The modernized ways of production and transportation made Egypt richer as the situation of the fellah worsened. The native population became increasingly poverty stricken as the administrative costs continued to exceed the income from national resources. Ismail had inherited a substantial national debt from the reign of Said Pasha, and because he had repeatedly broken faith with his creditors, he was unable to raise new foreign loans. Collecting taxes in advance proved too inadequate even as a temporary remedy and only added to the woes of the small land workers. To prevent the approaching disaster, Ismail made the equally bad decision to sell 176,602 Suez Canal shares to the British government for £3,976,582. Steps to protect the foreign investment were taken and Ismail was forced to accept European control, especially British and French, in 1876. As internal conditions worsened with the further impoverishment of the natives, political confusion and public dissatisfaction, the voices of protest sought to organize a nationalist movement. The military revolt and city riots which ensued culminated in 1882 in the bombardment of the forts of Alexandria by the British navy and the subsequent British control of Egypt.

2. Ancestors and Immediate Family

Cavafy ancestry reaches back to the beginning of the eighteenth century. The Cavafy family had lived in the Greek section of Constantinople, known as Fanari. Cavafy worked out his own genealogical tree as a project which he started in 1909 and returned to it for the last time in 1911. His father, Petros, was born in 1814. He and his older brother, George, took over the father's business and expanded it by opening branches in England and Egypt. In 1850, at George's insistence, Petros, who was already married to Charicleia Photiades (1834-1899), the daughter of a prominent leader in Constantinople, moved permanently to Alexandria to take charge of the branch there. He rented a large house on Via Franka and brought his family. The brothers decided to close the office in Constantinople in 1855 and to concentrate on the more flourishing ones at Liverpool, London, Manchester, Marseilles and Alexandria. While in Alexandria, Petros and his growing family lived rather luxuriously and enjoyed the respect of the growing Greek communities as well as the trust of the Egyptian authorities. Petros and Charicleia had nine children (two of whom died during infancy): George (b. 1850), Peter-John (b. 1851), Aristeides (b. 1853), Helene (b. 1855, d. Jan. 2, 1856), Alexander (b. 1856), Paul (b. 1858, d. 1859), Paul (b. 1860), John (b. 1861) and Constantine (b. April 17/29, 1863). The household was firmly under the direction of Charicleia, and aside from Greek servants and other personnel, it included an English nurse and a French governess. The Cavafy family was regarded as part of the higher social circles even after the family wealth was exhausted, but with the passing of time its prestige became part of the old days, much to Constantine's disappointment when he entered manhood. His sense of vanity and family pride derived from his father's role in the community perhaps more than the facts justified. However, Petros appears to have played more than a minor role in the community and to have enjoyed British protection. The parents had access to influential circles. In 1869, Petros was decorated by the government of Egypt. He died in 1870.

Charicleia, a dignified and attractive woman, was devoted to her children and kept a vigilant eye on their education. Her affectionate ways were not without a touch of vanity, nor always practical and realistic. Her emotional grip on her children went beyond the limits of thoughtful guidance, particularly in the case of the youngest child. As she had only one daughter, Helene, who died an infant, her desire to give birth to another grew stronger after the sad loss. She actually gave the yet to be born child the deceased girl's name. Again, she gave birth to a boy, but treated him in every respect like a girl. Thus, Constantine became the object of unusually tender affection. Throughout his early childhood he was dressed as a little girl, treated as such, with his hair grown at proper length and adorned in meticulous curls. Throughout his life Constantine's love for his mother remained as strong and decisive as it was during the years of his early development. When she died, he was the son who felt the loss most deeply.

Two years after her husband's death, Charicleia found it necessary to adjust to her lower income, and moved to Liverpool. It was a prudent and practical decision, especially in view of the economic crisis that came in 1876, at which time Cavafy Inc. at Alexandria was dissolved. It appears that Charicleia and the children stayed in England from 1872 till 1878, and lived in Liverpool and London. Having learned English as a child, Cavafy was well prepared for the kind of education he received during his years in England, and not only did he attain impressive mastery of the language, he also developed a strong taste for English fiction and poetry. Details about these formative years are scanty, but it appears that he became proficient in English before he perfected his knowledge of Greek. In his later years, he retained the habit of keeping notes on personal matters and studies in English, and in practical ways it helped him to earn his livelihood. Before returning to Alexandria, Charicleia consented to let her oldest son, George, remain in London with his uncle. After a brief stop in Marseilles, she returned to Alexandria with a British passport and soon established residence in respectable quarters on 32 Ramlion Avenue. In 1879, the Sultan, not without pressure from the British, ousted Ismael and appointed Tewfik as Viceroy or Khedive of Egypt. Between the year of his return and 1882, Cavafy completed all of the formal education he would ever have. It proved to be quite effective in providing him with his first serious exposure to classical ideas and values, which were not only helpful in awakening his love for historical subjects; more significantly they made evident the demand for the reorientation of his personal outlook.

Cavafy enrolled in the newly established private Greek High School in Alexandria, under the direction of an able educator, Constantine A. Papazis, a learned man with a strong sense for poetry and patriotism, well trained in the classics and holding a doctorate from a German university.[2] It was probably under his influence that Cavafy undertook to write a "*historikon lexikon,*" but the project did not advance beyond the entry "Alexander." These years of late adolescence were no doubt crucial to his development, for not only did he begin to become conscious of his own historical and cultural background, but in all likelihood he started forming then his first ideas about poetry. The environment the school provided certainly stimulated his interests and so did the tradition of the family to which he was slowly awakening. His uncle George was a man of considerable learning; Pandelis Cavafy, the son of another uncle, had published translations of Shakespeare's *The Tempest* and *Two Gentlemen of Verona* in Constantinople in 1874. The family often entertained men of letters from Athens who had occasion to visit Alexandria, just as it did in Constantinople. The poet Elias Tantalides composed the epitaph verses for Cavafy's grandfather and aunt in 1844 and 1845.[3]

A then-leading poet, Alexander Soutsos, wrote the epitaphs for the two Cavafy children who died in their infancy, which were inscribed on their tombs in 1862. But aside from such direct acquaintances with literary men, there were other circumstances which contributed to Cavafy's growing interest in art and literature. The last quarter of the nineteenth century was a period of unusual intellectual activity among the Alexandrian Greeks. Aside from newspapers and journals, they published a large number of books ranging from special monographs in the sciences and historical treatises to translations from the classics and European fiction and poetry. However, it should be noted that throughout this period Alexandrian letters hardly showed any signs of originality; dependence on Athens remained the rule.[4]

---

[2]Papazis wrote his doctoral dissertation on Demetrius of Phaleron and Athens, in 1877 at the University of Erlangen. Tsirkas 1958: 133-38; Liddell 1974: 27-8.

[3]E. Tantalidis, 1960: 248-9, (*Idiotika Stihourghimata* [Private Verses], Triesta).

[4]Tsirkas 1958: 180-181.

Within the immediate family, Cavafy's brother, John, two years his senior, took an interest in literary issues and tried his hand at poetry. He printed in 1891 or 1892 at least four poems written in English.[5] He also published his *Early Verses* in the mid-nineties and translated into English several of his brother's poems.[6] There was also the somewhat wider circle of childhood friends and classmates from well-to-do families, who were brought up with the same mixture of cosmopolitanism and insistence on tradition. It was at the school of Papazis where Cavafy and his classmates Mikes Rallis, Stephanos Skylitsis, John Rodokanakis and Kimon Periclis were drawn closer and shared interests. Except for Constantine, none of the others found their destiny in poetry. They exchanged letters later on, in English mostly, on current events, politics, personal matters, books, differences of opinion, and much local gossip.

The sweep of events broke up the intimate circle. On September 9, 1881, Orambi led a military coup which toppled the government, and the national party won the election. The unrests and riots of 1882, which followed the political crisis in Egypt, presented no small threat to the foreigners. Charicleia, with her children, moved to her parents' home in Constantinople before the British navy bombarded Alexandria. Among the casualties of the bombardment was the Cavafy residence. Cavafy was nineteen at the time, and it was in Constantinople that he became seriously interested in writing poetry. He became attached to his maternal grandfather and found in his new environment a thriving Greek community, with a deep awareness of its long historical record, its Byzantine tradition and monuments of the past. It was here that he rediscovered his ancestral ties and the full force of his native language. The parts were falling into place and a sense of cultural continuity began to take root. But more than that took place. The sensitive, somewhat withdrawn and rather reticent youth, who gave most of the time to private studies, found himself transplanted to another cosmopolis, one with decidedly oriental flavor and intrigue. Cavafy's stay in Constantinople at this critical age seems to have eased the surfacing of his emotional ambiguities. His attachment to his cousin marked the beginning of his attraction to persons of

---

[5]Savidis 1966: 119, n46.

[6]Savidis 1966: 126, n59.

his own sex, but it took years before the problems related to the expression of his intense eroticism became a theme in his poetry, with all the attendant shades of guilt and gradual acceptance. The poems he wrote during this period show little, if anything, of his emotional tensions and gropings. His shyness prevented him from publishing his verse, with few exceptions, until 1891. Most of these poems he destroyed; only the titles were preserved in a personal note.[7] Many were on themes of the Byzantine period which, as he admitted in later years, was neither suitable to his poetic plan nor a proper framework for his dramatic personages. Eventually, when he returned to this period, Cavafy had so deepened his understanding of history that his perspective was no longer affected by ancestral attachments. By the time he composed his "Manuel Komnenos" in 1905 (published in 1915) both his mother and grandfather were dead. In 1906, reflecting on the quality of certain early poems, Cavafy recalled approvingly his reluctance to print them. He left the following note among his papers, written (in English) in 1906:

> By my postponing, and repostponing to publish, what a gain I have had! Think of "Asma" . . . of trash (at the age of 25, 26, 27, and 28) of Byzantine poems [titles follow . . .] etc. speaking of rot), Cleopatra, of Porphyrios, of Threnos (with the stupid voices of wife, parents, child etc.), and many others which would disgrace me now. What a gain! And all those poems written between 19 and 22. What wretched trash![8]

Since the situation in Egypt continued fluid and unsafe, Charicleia and Constantine stayed in Constantinople until 1885. In the meantime the young Cavafy who found in his grandfather's library the answer to his quest for learning, continued his private studies, wrote a number of poems, and worked on his rendition of a ballad by Lady Barnard. After the return to Alexandria, in October 1885, Cavafy took Greek citizenship and refused the British "protection" he had inherited from his father.[9] At the same time he continued

---

[7]Savidis 1966: 106, n6.

[8]In Savidis, 1966: 107. These remarks of denunciation reveal their full flavor after one has read his *Ars Poetica* written in 1903. For the text of the *Ars Poetica* see Appendix.

[9]According to Liddell 1974: 49-50, Cavafy did not "abandon the English Protection his father had obtained in 1850."

a life of private studies for as long as his mother's situation permitted him to accept unsalaried employment. He published a number of poems, most of which he denounced in later years, but wrote almost nothing of substance between 1886 and 1891, except for two articles of some encyclopedic interest.[10] He showed a rather mild interest in the life of the community but the broader political events did not seem to have affected his views. His ethnic consciousness was further strengthened when the British authorities steadied their repressive stand toward the flowering Greek sense of community. The newly rich conveniently fell in line with the course of British interests. Cavafy remained rather aloof and sought, though not without considerable effort and difficulty, to find a workable compromise between his intensified Hellenic identity and the new forms of Alexandrian cosmopolitanism—especially the ones cultivated by some of his childhood acquaintances. It proved to be a rather difficult period for him. Intellectual withdrawal was precariously combined with night life which led to excesses, the effects of which were felt for years and led to a serious crisis and intense feelings of despair. Although it appears that for a while he was interested in both sexes, he eventually moved away from heterosexuality. The death of his close friend, Mikes Rallis at the age of 23, upon his return to Alexandria from Paris, marked the beginning of intimate losses. Two years later, in 1891, his brother Petros died in Alexandria, and so did his uncle George in London.

The year 1891 marks the beginning of a turn in Cavafy's intellectual and sexual orientation. It opened with the publication of six prose pieces, among them "Give Back the Elgin Marbles," "Shakespeare on Life," and "Professor Blakie in Modern Greek Language."[11] In the fall of the same year he re-appears as a poet with the publication of his "Builders," which drew the critical attention of I. Polemis, a leading poet.[12] The numerous poems

---

[10] Cavafy, *Prose*, 1963: 3-8.

[11] All six pieces are in Cavafy, *Prose*, 1963: 9-42. The article "Give Back the Elgin Marbles," written in English, appeared in the Alexandrian newspaper *Revista Quindicinale* (April 10, 1891); two more articles on the same subject were printed in the Athenian newspaper *Ethniki* (April 11 and 29, 1891).

[12] A poet and essayist in Athens. Polemis wrote the first critical notice of Cavafy in the *Attikon Mouseion* (Sept. 30, 1891).

and prose pieces he wrote between 1891 and 1903 reflect his widened horizon of interests in European poetry and fiction, French symbolism, problems of style and metrics, Byzantine history and classical themes. Not least among these was a slowly emerging concern to come to grips with the pressing issue of the place of his religious beliefs in the spectrum of his values, especially his as poetic themes. It was the year that marked the beginning of a practice "unparalleled in the history of our literature."[13] He decided to print, bind and circulate his poems mainly among those persons he felt were seriously interested. He followed this editing practice until the end of his life, and pursued it with meticulous patience and perseverance. This was the year that Cavafy recognized as the beginning of his creative period, even if what he wrote during the next decade proved to be of superior quality. The need to revise and rework his poems, as well as his determination to clarify his responsibility as a poet, surfaced with unmistakable force. It started with the simple device of keeping for his own use a record of his writings, an unpublished list.[14]

His relatives found it increasingly difficult to support Cavafy's style of life as poet-scholar. It was with much reluctance that he accepted an appointment in the Irrigation Service of the Ministry of Public Works, at the lowly monthly salary of seven pounds. Yet he continued to publish several poems each year. On the scholarly side, after making a careful study of Ruskin, he crystallized his ideas in a series of brief comments which reflect not only his views on the place of progress in culture but also some of the thinking that prepared him for the writing of his *Ars Poetica* in 1903. But having to work, although his duties were considerably light, proved a serious blow to his ego and self-image. "I am a poet by profession," he would state to friends who dropped in to visit him during working hours. To a person of Cavafy's social background and expectations to enjoy the life of a gentleman, the status of a low-paid civil servant was more than demeaning. He honestly expected his family would continue supporting him while he devoted himself to the noble and lofty goals he set for himself. The conviction about the high importance

---

[13]Savidis, 1966: 105, esp. 110, where he lists the representative works that reflect Cavafy's preoccupation with poetic problems. See also Seferis' remarks in 1974b, v. I: 383-8, and Cavafy, *Prose* 1963: 23-29, 66-80.

[14]Savidis 1966: 108-109.

of his mission in life ran so deep that he saw nothing unreasonable about his demands. Evidently, he felt that his success as a poet and spokesman for the deepest meaning of humanity, deserved the requisite conditions of leisure, and moreover that such support would serve to bring to the Cavafy family more lasting recognition than his father's status had done. It took him years to come to terms with the realities of his situation. In the years after the return from Constantinople, he made every effort he could to save appearances, wasting both his salary and his mother's donations to him on expensive clothes, nightclubs, theaters and society gatherings.

3. Returning to a City of Confusions

For years Cavafy found himself torn between the boredom of the daily bureaucratic routine with its monotony and tediousness and the depleting pressure to maintain social respectability by moving in the right circles. The routine led to dissipation. It is rather curious how he responded to both for the sake of his devotion to his poetic mission and need for recognition. He found himself involved in an intricate pattern of conflicts which precipitated a crisis of personality, feelings of increasing loneliness, of inferiority and insecurity, and not least, an intense sense of isolation and despair. All the personal poems of this period, especially the ones he salvaged and reworked with meticulous care, are among the ones that brought him his popularity and reflect the high moments of his personal drama. It was during this period that he gained full consciousness of the subtle threats of life in the cosmopolis. It came with his determination to find a way out, but it was more than a battle for individual survival or an attempt at finding an accommodating solution to restore the lost social status. Had it been just that, Cavafy would have achieved nothing more than most of us do in coping with problems of adjusting to the conditions of life in the whirlpool of impersonal relations in larger cities. Furthermore, his literary output would probably never have become more than second-rate "period" poetry, or at best significant only as a commentary on the issues of an age. Not born a poet, not initially equipped with a talent for flowing eloquence and easily reeling imagery, he had to fight his way to find a style he could call his own. Not having the facility to screen critically ready-made themes in the fashionable trends of poetic schools, he had to pay the price of the follower before he could identify and work with authentic experiences in the inner folds of his suffering. And when the pressures to meet the problem of livelihood closed in on him and were joined to the sudden realization of his loss of status—interpreted as directed against his idealized destiny to be a poet—the universe of his innocent outlook collapsed. It was years after the return to Alexandria that he came to realize how little he had progressed on the road to poetry. He simply was not ready for the cosmopolis.

Cavafy was not a melancholy person. His poems reveal a very sensitive human being, and much of his upbringing gave him a cultivated sense of dignity which often reached the point of vanity and affectation in his public manners. He guarded his privacy with the same zeal that he cherished his sensuality. But essentially, he was as reticent as he was articulate when he chose to discuss topics he loved. As long as he felt protected, he was free to let his introspective powers roam the range of personal interests and to press on with the quest for artistic expression. He could even feel superior in his willed isolation, as we see it in his early poem "The Walls of My Room." When the conditions of life changed and his inability to cope with them became manifest, what was previously a protective environment he saw as a restrictive prison. Slowly, he fell prey to waves of depression, to spells of pessimism, and would often have thoughts of foreboding about his future. With the passage of time, fears corroded his will to resist. He began to find consolation by trying various forms of escape only to discover he was moving from one trap to another. His sensuality was allowed to dissipate into abused hedonism, and when the force of his passions reached a frightening intensity, he took to drinking. All along, however, he remained fully conscious of the need to fight for his sanity. He would write poems with the lightness of abandon, like the "Bacchic Song," published in 1886, and talk about choosing to become intoxicated "with the heart of the god while drinking like a demi-god," but the voice was not genuine.[15] Later on, he condemned the poem, just as he did many others of this vintage when he assessed his work in 1903.

Cavafy's strength to survive his many crises was not rooted in that high quality he believed he shared with "the brave men of pleasure," and which

---

[15]The (condemned) "Bacchic Song" was probably written after the family's return to Alexandria in 1885, i.e. late 1885 or early in 1886, and published in *Hesperos* in March 1886; reprinted with certain changes in November 1892. Text in Cavafy 1983: 17, and 91-2 for variations and comments by Savidis.

some of his critics associated with his alleged preference for decadent themes. Had this been the case, he would have been defeated by his problems, which he often magnified far beyond their real dimensions. His circumstances presented nothing extraordinary that anyone with the usual sense to meet the challenge of survival could not face with some measure of success. It was his special angle of vision, his personal perspective, so to speak, that made his situation difficult to bear. His chief obsession was poetry. His strongest fear stemmed from the uncertainty he might never be a poet, either because of an inner weakness or because of external conditions. He was as apprehensive about his limitations as he was confused about his social values. As a result, he suffered and was almost destroyed in the struggle to reach an understanding of self and reality. He suffered for years while seeking escape in erotic excitement and inner withdrawal; yet he never lost sight of his highest passion and goal. What made his situation unbearably painful was his constant awareness of the distance between what quality his poetry had during his thirties and what high levels of accomplishment he had aspired to reach. The passage of time terrified him because he knew he needed years of hard work to learn the secrets of the art before he could write original poetry. In the same way, anything that interfered with this mission was viewed as a threat and a disgrace to the pursuit of the highest practice of life: the art of poetry.

The efforts in adjusting to the need to earn a living proved distasteful and humiliating but fell into an acceptable pattern as the problem of his erotic reorientation was slowly resolved. Both took a heavy toll on his pride and emotions. In a poem written in 1894 (unpublished, U 61), titled "Whoever Has Failed," he lets his feelings surface with moving sincerity:

> For one has failed and lost his standing
> how difficult it is to learn to speak
> the new language of begging, its new ways. (ll. 1-3)
>
> ... How can he listen to the words when each expression
> rends the ears—and despite it all
> you must pretend you never feel them
> as though a simpleton, to understand. (ll. 15-18)

The admirable outcome of these years of crisis is his emergence as a poet of remarkable originality. It came as a result of a radical rearrangement of his cultural values and a clarification of his attitude towards history. Both were tied up with his self-consciousness as an artist. It is true of Cavafy, as it is of many an artist, that the specific meaning one assigns to the mission of art involves the character of his cultural and historical circumstances. The passion for poetry is one thing, the particular way in which one conceives its role and selects its themes, quite another. And Cavafy's own zest for poetry, while it remained constant throughout his life as the highest form of articulating the affective side of humanity, required him to come to terms with the conditions of his own life and the traditions he accepted as his own but whose powerful messages had escaped him until the years of his crisis got well under way. The agonizing introspection into his personal dislocations eventually forced to the foreground the crucial decision of coming to grips with the problem of his subject matter and of drawing the line separating the intruding and borrowed ways of art from the spectrum of values that were truly his own. What emerged slowly during the years of his crisis was a crystallization of the quality and scope of thematic range, the immediacies of the present and the continuities of the past, away from the tenets of Baudelaire and French symbolism.

Cavafy was part of the cosmopolis and yet reached the point where he could view it with detachment. His abandonment to the risks and pleasures made him aware of the intensities of the present, but could lead nowhere unless the power of poetry could master their elusiveness and preserve their sensual ministrations. But, to carry out this poetic program, another difficult riddle had to be solved: the sphinx of the cosmopolis. Alexandria had to be captured in a network of ideas, framed, so to speak, within the lucid confines only the understanding of the passions and their reasoned acceptance provides. In an "unpublished" poem, "In the House of the Soul" (1894),[16] Cavafy pictures the passions in the form of beautiful, seductive women, occupying a mansion's rooms. In the largest one, where they gather at nights dressed in silk, they dance and revel. Awaiting outside the house of the soul are the virtues, pale and sad, peeking in through the windows and realizing that they can have no chance to replace the passions. As a poem it is a failure; its moralizing tone remains tedious. Yet it draws attention to an

---

[16]See Cavafy, *Prose* 1963: 249, for John Cavafy's translation into English and Cavafy's letter commenting on the quality of John's work. The translation was done in October, 1899. The tone of the letter suggests that at that time Cavafy was still holding the poem in some esteem.

important theme, the controlling image of the soul, full of passions, and with the excellences outside and unable to enter. It is not the timid preaching that deserves comment, but the problem. Here we have the passions locked up in the soul—all passions—left to themselves with no hope of illumination. The division between passions and the excellences is sharply drawn. The predicament is not only Cavafy's own. It pervades the mores of the cosmopolis. Nor is it one that developed overnight. It was contrived and nourished through centuries of gradual corrosion of human judgement and loss of wisdom. The search for light put Cavafy on the course of history and made it imperative that he redefine his attitude on classicism, recast his views on Byzantine Christianity, alter his perspective toward European consciousness, and most difficult of all, start the quest of identity. Regarding the latter, the problem manifested itself in full force for the first time in the confluence of Hellenistic culture and the Alexandrian cosmopolis, with their perversion of Dionysus and the mutilation of Apollo.

Monotony, dreariness, fear and disillusionment closed in on his daily life to be temporarily displaced with even more debilitating escapades. The sense of loneliness and insecurity had shattered the high expectations of his early manhood, and when the mood of despair entered the poetic domain, it surfaced in so dominant a personal note that it rendered the artistic effect of his verses unappealing and artificial. Few of the poems of this period proved salvageable.[17] And he was right in condemning them once he became aware of their self-centered and self-pitying tone. For similar reasons he rejected several religious poems, for instance "Terror" (September, 1894), where he appeals to Christ the Lord to save him from the visitation of nightmarish creatures. Nor did he fare any better with his plan to complete a collection of poems dealing with classical themes under the general title *Ancient Days*. The poems have a strained and contrived quality, full of escapes rather than insights. Even his admiration for the classical world fails to come through with an authentic ring. Although the early poems yield on occasion faint echoes of what his mature poems exhibit in the form of a profound grasp of the tragic spirit, they suffer under a thinly disguised borrowing of symbols to serve subjective needs. Burdened with the literary

---

[17]The poet did not consider most of them good enough to be included in his 1904 (1905?) approved collection. See Savidis 1966: 297.

piety of a half-hearted Parnassian, not quite able to cope with the guilt of his compulsive indulgence, he was anything but ready to probe the depths of classical hedonism.

4. Despair and the Promise of Poetry

The years of maladjustment and suffering went on. Acceptance of his condition was not in sight. The more he retreated into his private self, the bleaker his picture of the cosmopolis became. Because he was a Greek citizen, he was denied tenure at his employment, but it is not known whether he took it seriously. The first breakthrough in his poetry came in 1894, with the writing of the early version of "The City," originally titled "In the Same City," a poem he reworked carefully and published for the first time in 1910. It was in this poem that the sharp awareness of the lonely and alienated individual in the dreariness of the modern city waxed strongly as a universal theme in original imagery. Paradoxically enough, his keen perception of the imprisoning traps of the cosmopolis gave him the key to his freedom as a poet. Yet the prison had to be even more accurately defined, more truthfully understood. Its outer limits had to be set where they actually existed: the self-condemning mode of personal despair. In 1896, he wrote "Walls," and in 1897 "The Windows," as further refinement and on the same fundamental theme. But his poems were not going unnoticed. Ph. Printezis, a journalist from Athens, reporting on intellectual events in Alexandria, wrote about a certain Mr. Cavafy: "a perfect gentleman, with all the marks of the delicate and serious English up-bringing, as befits one who grew up in England."

It was about that time that Cavafy met Pericles Anastassiadis. The two became close friends. Like Cavafy, Anastassiadis had grown up in England, as the scion of a wealthy family; he became an ardent anglophile, deeply influenced by Victorian aestheticism. He was about twenty-five, with a developed taste for literature and the arts, when he returned to Alexandria and met Cavafy. Their friendship lasted till the poet's death, except for a cooling period between 1902 and 1912. Not much is known about the details of their literary exchanges but it appears that both shared a deep interest in the British novel, especially the writings of Thomas Hardy, James Thomson and Samuel Butler. It is rather doubtful that Anastassiadis, who had started a successful career in his father's brokerage firm, had found to his liking

Cavafy's sympathetic reading of Thompson's nightmarish world and Hardy's pessimistic realism. Just the same, Anastassiadis became a devoted friend, preserved with meticulous care every letter and poem Cavafy gave him, and in later years helped him gain recognition by introducing the poet to the novelist E. M. Forster as well as others. It was Forster who in turn spoke about Cavafy to T. S. Eliot, Arnold Toynbee, Lawrence of Arabia and others in England. In a letter to Anastassiadis, written April 4, 1949, Forster spoke again of his good fortune to have met "one of the great poets of our times."[18]

The next four years, 1896 to 1900, were aggravated by his personal crisis; yet they brought him closer to the only solution that held real promise. The first step towards his dislodgement from ancestral dependence came with the death of his maternal grandfather, G. Photiades, in 1896. He suddenly dropped the middle initial "F", which he was using in place of the letter "P", his father's initial, according to custom. The critics now began to identify the major features of his mood: "Cavafy is a skeptic, symbolist, philosophical, melancholy poet, with ironic bitterness."[19] In this same year he wrote a short but very important poem titled "Memory"—the first version of the "Ionic" (?1896/*1915*)—on a theme that haunted his historical consciousness throughout his life, discussed in detail in ch. 8: what the religious aftermath of the Hellenistic age did to the gods of Greece. For the first time, Cavafy dropped the historical sentimentality of his synchretic Alexandrian and Byzantine traditions to catch a quick but honest view of their ruinous displacement of the classical landscape of the human spirit. The plural "we" in the first line of the "Ionic" is not without foreboding significance:

> Because we broke their statues
> because we threw them out of their temples
> the gods did not die on account of that.
> O land of Ionia, it is you they still love,
> It is you their souls remember . . .

---

[18]Quoted in *The Complete Poems of Cavafy*, tr. Ray Dalven 1961: 216. On Forster and Cavafy, see Pinchin 1977: 82-158.

[19]T. Tsokopoulos, "Egyptian Recollections," in *Hellenic Alexandria,* 1896; quoted in Tsirkas 1963: 687.

To alleviate the unbearable suffering from deep depression he started to keep shorthand notes recording his efforts to control his "weakness." The limits of the City became the prison of the encapsulated self. In 1897 he published privately "Walls," with an English translation by his brother John. Together, they took a short vacation to Paris, while their friends Rallis and Rodokanakis went to Greece as volunteers to fight in the disastrous war between Greece and Turkey. Cavafy remained in Alexandria, facing a different and more subtle enemy, the ennui of the *fin de siècle,* and worked on his first version of "Waiting for the Barbarians" (1898/*1904*). It gained him entrance to the secrets of the fate and fall of a politically impotent cosmopolis. Having no heart for heroism, he conquered the secrets of psychic decline and cultural surrender. Still afraid to stare reality in the face, he willfully remained in his self-imprisonment, as in the agonizing poem of this period, "The Windows." Two events fractured his crystalline withdrawal: the death of his mother Charicleia in 1899 and that of his brother George in the following year. For the first time, Cavafy signed his poems: C. P. Cavafy.[20]

The last decade of the century covered the unfolding of a critical period in Cavafy's development. In 1901, with the financial support of his friend Pericles Anastassiadis, he visited Athens for the first time and made a lasting impression on the influential editor Gregory Xenopoulos as well as other intellectuals and poets. The visit coincided with the publication of the poem "Che fece . . . il gran rifiuto." Another death in the family came in 1902, with the loss of his brother Aristeides. In the next year, his brother Alexander accompanied him in his second visit to Athens, during which a number of significant events took place. The first signs of recognition came with the publication of Xenopoulos' laudatory article on Cavafy, the first of its kind.[21] A leading newspaper carried a brief but praising comment on his poems calling them "perfect, remarkably original, and it would seem, the

---

[20]Savidis 1966: 132 and notes, suggests that the successive changes of the initials may well signify the poet's gradual "return" from the maternal Constantinople to the paternal Alexandria.

[21]G. Xenopoulos, "A Poet," in *Panathenaia* (Nov. 30, 1903), repr. 1963. Actually his was the first lengthy article on Cavafy's poetry. In the same issue of *Panathenaia,* first publication of "Thermopylae" and "The Windows," together with the reprinting of other poems.

strangest poems in Greece today; few poems but good."[22] He kept a diary of this visit, with entries from 13th of June to the 5th of August. It is written in English and notes mainly persons, places and impressions, but contains no reference to his poetic activities and publications.

It is quite likely that Cavafy started his *Ars Poetica* while still in Athens. This rather brief but very important essay was composed between August and November 25, 1903. At the age of forty, the poet paused to take a close critical scrutiny of his life and work and also to project reflectively the further development of his outlook on poetry. This document was also written in English. His tone and intent are evident from the opening sentences:

> After the already settled Emendatory Work, a philosophical scrutiny of my poems should be made.
>
> Flagrant inconsistencies, illogical possibilities, ridiculous exaggeration should certainly be corrected in the poems, and where the corrections cannot be made the poems should be sacrificed, retaining only any verses of such sacrificed poems as might prove useful later in the making of new work.

The discussion of Cavafy's poetics is reserved for chapter 7, but suffice it to note here the poet's crucial decision to go beyond the technical revision of his poems, and his determination to proceed in a methodical way to remove discrepancies and flaws with the aid of "a philosophical scrutiny." The rewarding effects of this undertaking proved both immediate and of long range, leading to the completion of this critical period in 1911. But by way of immediate results we have not only the poet's decision to denounce a great number of poems written prior to 1899 but, on the positive side, the rewriting and first private printing of "Waiting for the Barbarians" in 1904. Towards the end of this year, he printed, also privately, his first *Booklet* comprising 14 poems, all of which had passed the test of "philosophical scrutiny" as stated in the *Ars Poetica*. The resolution to clear up the cobwebs which had in the past hindered the development of his own creative voice became an abiding principle, but offered no help in the equally sensitive area of his private and emotional life. A new crisis broke out which almost brought him to the edge of despair. His suffering took the form of a deep agony over the persisting

---

[22] In the newspaper *Neon Asti*, Sept. 11, 1903.

problem of his heavy drinking and the timid acceptance of his homosexuality.[23] In January 1904 he revised a poem, "September, 1903" (U 135), written a few months earlier:

> At least I should not fool myself now with illusions
> so as not to feel my empty life.
> And yet I came so close so many times;
> and yet how paralyzed I was, how timid I became.
> Why did my lips stay sealed
> when my empty life was weeping inside me
> and my desires were dressed in mourning.
>
> To have been so close so many times
> to the eyes and the erotic lips,
> to the body dreamed of, the beloved body;
> so close so many times.

5. Plumbing the Depths of Depression

After his brother John moved to Cairo, the poet and his other brother, Paul, rented an apartment on 17 Rosseta Street. In the meantime, his brother Alexander fell ill in Athens. Cavafy visited him there before death came in August 1905. No doubt the loss grieved him deeply and aggravated his psychological crisis. Fears and attacks of depression kept him in a state of emotional exhaustion, and drinking became uncontrolled. To lighten the burden somewhat he started the practice of shorthand notes in which he ciphered his state of mind. The note of November 19, written at 2:00 a.m., reads:

> I am in torment. I raised myself . . . Now I am writing. What shall I do?
> What is going to happen to me? What shall I do? I am lost.

These personal notes, written between 1905 and 1907, together with the poems of this period and other writings, furnish valuable information for

---

[23]The first "daring" poem, as it may be called, appeared in 1911, in *Nea Estia* (Nov. 1911), p. 28, under the title "Dangerous Things" (*Ta Epikindyna*).

understanding his inner turmoil and determination to bring it under control in order to write. Throughout this period he continued to resist the fact of his employment, partly because it compromised his previous social standing, but more importantly because he believed he was a poetic genius, and therefore should be free to devote all of his time to his art. Sometime in June, 1905, he wrote:

> . . . Many a time during working hours a beautiful idea, a rare image, like ready-made sudden verses, come to me but I am forced to neglect them because the assignment cannot be postponed. Later, when I am back home, having somewhat recovered, I try to recall them but they are gone. And justly so. It seems as if Art is saying to me, "I am not a servant so you may dismiss me when I approach you, come as you wish. I am the greatest Lady in the world. Since you have rejected me—traitor and lowly man—for your pitiful nice home, your pitiful nice clothes, your pitiful nice social standing, content yourself with those things (which you cannot) and with the few instances when my visits coincide with the times you are ready to receive me, standing there by the door waiting for me, which is what you should be doing every hour of the day."[24]

In another note, written six months later, on December 15, 1905, he shifted the angle of blame to indulge in self-pity and lay the burden on the doorstep of the external conditions:

> The miserable laws of society—results neither of health nor judgment—diminished my art. They fettered my expression, restrained me from offering light and emotion to all those who are made like me. The difficult circumstances of life forced me to struggle to master the English language. What a pity . . . . Had I instead mastered French—on account of the conveniences of its pronouns, what they conceal and suggest—I would have been able to express myself more freely. But now what is there to do? Aesthetically, I am unjustly wasted. I am destined to become the object of guess. They will understand me more fully from all those things I had to exclude.[25]

---

[24]Translation mine; the Greek text in Savidis 1966: 170-171.

[25]Translation mine; the Greek text in Savidis 1966: 171. Three years later, in 1908, he wrote on this very theme a poem titled "Hidden Things"; text in *Unpublished Poems*, p. 151. This poem remained unknown until Savidis' edition of Cavafy's unpublished poems in 1963.

By this time, his passion for poetry, his confidence in his mission and his determination to create a work of lasting value had taken deep root and given sustenance to his inflated self-esteem. Still in a period of groping for crystallization of style and clarification of thematic content, his poetry was more promise than finished achievement. The signs of originality were undoubtedly there. One could hardly rely upon Cavafy's known poems to predict the brilliant, creative output which was slowly building up to justify the image the poet had of himself in 1907, as it is projected in the following note of March 1, 1907:

> At times when I reflect and conceive difficult notions and relations, including consequences things have, and an idea comes to possess me which others are not in a position to think and to feel the way I do, I feel "uncomfortable." For immediately this is what goes through my mind: How unjust it is, for me to have such genius and not to be talked about everywhere, not to be rewarded. But then, the idea that perhaps I am deceiving myself and that there are many others who also think greatly and correctly, brings me comfort. What a thing it is, this Interest or Desire for Reward! The idea of being equal among the many gives me more comfort than to be superior and deprived of my reward.[26]

In the end of that year, Cavafy and his brother Paul moved to an apartment at 10 Lepsius Street, where he lived until his death in 1933. About this time, Cavafy joined a circle of bright young intellectuals in Alexandria which was formed in 1904 to promote their literary and artistic interests. They launched a journal *Nea Zoe* (New Life), which eventually gained wider influence and rivaled in quality the best of its kind in Greece, especially when in due course it succeeded in securing the cooperation of the leading writers and university professors of the mainland. The *Nea Zoe* and another Alexandrian journal *Grammata* (Letters), kept the movement going and became so prominent that it reflected more adequately the new developments in modern Greek literature than the best of Athenian journals; it stayed in the lead past the end of World War I. However, it is certain that the leaders of *Nea Zoe* either ignored or failed to notice the presence of Cavafy. Evidently, the attention he received in Athens did not impress the Alexandrians, nor did his 1904 Booklet stir any excitement or discussion. This absence of

---

[26]Translation mine; the Greek text in Savidis 1966: 172; comp. Peridis 1948: 91-92.

recognition in his own environment was the main cause of his chagrin and disappointment. Yet the "desire of reward" remained unrequited, and in the years to come it became the driving force behind his cultivated facade and calculated efforts to ensure the fame he wanted.

He made his first appearance in the pages of *Nea Zoe* with two short critical notes, in 1908.[27] In the following year, Cavafy devoted much of his time to the subject of his genealogy, going back to a Petros KAVAFIS of Constantinople, who died in 1730.[28] The meticulous care with which he went about it for almost two years, gathering details, making additions, changes, annotations, shows clearly how seriously he was preoccupied with the issue of his personal importance, his historical roots and the fate of his poetic work. In a way, it can be said of the "Genealogy" that it came to complete the critical task which began with the *Ars Poetica,* to take full measure of his own personality, his antecedents and his creative orientation. Both undertakings were crucial to his need for self-understanding and his inner cry to overcome the recurring states of depression, alcoholism, erotic hunger and feeling of social dreariness, so powerfully projected in the poems of this period. Yet his sharp sensitivity to pain, his preoccupation with his emotional conditions, his almost frantic concern for his future, were hardly features manifest in his public conduct. The frequent references in his poems to a "mask" or a "personal panoply" are part of the dignified front he maintained as are his mild eccentricities and affectations. In October 1905 he crystallized his canon of conduct in the poem "As Much as You Can" (1905/*1913*: A 25):

> And if you can't make your life as you want it,
> try this at least
> as much as you can: do not degrade it
> in the crowded world,
> with constant gesturing and talking.
>
> Do not degrade it by dragging it along

---

[27]The first note (February 1908) was on the Greek poet M. Avgeris, and the second (April 1908) on the short-story writer A. Papadiamandis; both reprinted in Cavafy, *Prose*, 1963: 103-104, 105-106.

[28]The manuscript in the Benaki Museum in Athens; published in *Nea Estia* (May 15, 1948): 622-629.

> moving often around and exposing it
> to the mindless ways of gatherings and parties
> until it comes to be like an alien burdened life.[29]

By a curious coincidence the keeping of ciphered shorthand notes on private matters ceases to be a pressing need. According to M. Peridis, the shorthand confessional notes start in 1897 and end about 1909; he also states that "after 1912 his erotic problem subsided." However, G. Savidis, who seems better informed since he has had access to the Cavafy papers, notes: "His confessional notes with reference to his lone erotic passion end in November 1911."[30] His gaining better control over his psychological turmoil, combined with his intense attending to his historical identity, had a beneficial and stabilizing effect on him. But there is another factor that seems to have played a role, and it may well have to do with his craving for approval which remained starved since the loss of his mother and the degradation he felt after he became a low-paid civil servant. There is no doubt about his strong dependence on maternal affection and the sense of importance he derived from his family's social standing. When both were gone, he found himself totally unable to cope with these needs and became a victim of withdrawal. In the process he was almost destroyed, and the disintegration would have been total and fatal if it were not for his passion for poetry, which fortunately, in his case, had grown strong during the formative years of his adolescence. The fact that he turned to literature earlier in his life literally saved him when the waves of loneliness and insecurity threatened to swallow him whole. But there was more in his favor, particularly his insatiable thirst for learning which brought him into direct contact with his historical and cultural roots. The assimilation of his heritage slowly transformed and enriched his sense of personal identity.

On April 23, 1909, a young medical doctor with a strong taste for poetry, Paul Petridis, gave the first public lecture on Cavafy, titled "An Alexandrian Poet, Konstantinos P. Kavafis," in the conference hall of the literary club of *Nea Zoe*. He had heard about Cavafy and paid him a visit in 1907. Petridis' lecture was attended by several dozen persons and was

---

[29]The original title was "*Bios*" (Life); the poem was revised and published in 1913.

[30]Peridis 1948: 49; also, Savidis, 1965: 195, and 1985: 29-55.

received without much enthusiasm. The text of the lecture, prepared substantially in cooperation with the poet himself, was published in *Nea Zoe* (vol. 5, No. 55. April, 1909, pp. 201-206). Though the response was mild, it signaled the beginning of talking about Cavafy not merely as a name in the social register but as a person of considerable promise among the intelligentsia of Alexandria. He had finally begun to emerge from his obscurity. For the first time he tasted in his own environment the sweetness of fame he so much wanted. It was precisely what he needed to overcome the weaknesses of his persisting dependencies. For the rest of his life, Cavafy carefully cultivated every person he believed could be added to his circle of admirers and widen his public that would ensure lasting admiration for his poems. If he was unusually sensitive to adverse criticism, it was not simply because his emotions needed the reassurance which comes with approval, but mainly because his confidence in his originality and creative promise was unshaken. He was reserved, shy, insecure, vain and affected but he never doubted his worth as a poet. He must have felt elated when P. Yannopoulos came to Alexandria from Athens for a visit and urged the members of the *Nea Zoe* circle to pay attention to the poet of their city, or when *Nea Zoe* reprinted in the same issue that published his "The Satrapy" a favorable article by Galateia Kazantzakis.[31] A year later, Z. Papantoniou, a much respected poet and critic, made a profound observation: "Cavafy is the only one who reacted against the affectations of lyricism." At last Cavafy's poetry was not just receiving praise: its special qualities were being noticed. With it came the end of his agony. The worst was over. Athens was not beyond his reach.

The prolonged period of his personal crisis determined much of the thematic content of the poems he wrote for that duration, but the repeated bouts of suffering had little if any effect on his pace of work. He devoted himself to his task with unusual industriousness, clarity of direction and a conception of system reflected in the revisions of the older poems he regarded salvageable as well as in his fresh compositions. A direct outcome of this labor was the private printing of the augmented *Booklet* of his *Poems* (Alexandria, 1910, pp. 32) which more so than its predecessor, testifies to the

---

[31] Galateia was the first wife of the poet-novelist Nikos Kazantzakis. Her article appeared originally in the influential Athenian journal *Noumas* (Feb. 14, 1910), 2-5; reprinted in *Nea Zoe* (May-June, 1910).

fact that Cavafy had definitively concluded his search for a principle of serial arrangement of his poems on which he could found the claim that his life-work must be understood as one continuous poem. He planned the selection for *Booklet* 2 as far back as 1907, to replace that of 1904, but for a number of reasons he kept postponing it.[32] Characteristically enough, it does not contain his remarkable poem "The City," (1894) which had been rewritten in the meantime but published eventually in the April 1910 issue of *Nea Zoe*.

Between May 1910 and May 1911, Cavafy made the most impressive creative leap of his career. It was destined to help him span the gulf between the despairing self of the desolate world of "The City" and the aspiring self of the long voyage to inviting harbors intimated in the symbolic and hortatory "Ithaka." The writing of "Ithaka" was done in October, and that of "The God Abandons Antony" in November 1910; the latter was published in May 1911, and the former in November 1911. With the completion of his search came the full vista of the poetic panorama which only the rigorous application of the "philosophical scrutiny" of his poems could offer. The attunement of his creative energy to his outlook on life brought with it the serene acceptance of his erotic drive, lucid and balanced between reality experienced in recollection and precious projections of fantasy. The fragments of the self began to fall into place. In June 1911, Cavafy wrote the unpublished poem "On Hearing of Love" (U 153):

> On hearing of powerful love, tremble and be moved
> like an aesthete. Yet, being fortunate,
> remember how many such things your imagination made for you;
> these first, and then the others—the lesser ones—in your life
> you had and enjoyed, truer and tangible.—
> You were not deprived of such loves.

It is a far cry from the view expressed in the poem "Walls":

> Without consideration, without pity, without shame
> they built around me great and high walls.
>
> And now I sit here and grow hopeless.

---

[32]Due to financial, medical and artistic problems Cavafy was facing at that time, according to Savidis 1966: 181-3.

or the depressive mood of "Monotony" (1898/*1908*: A 22):

> The one monotonous day another
> monotonous follows. The same things
> will take place, will happen again.
> Similar moments find us and leave us.
>
> A month passes and brings another month.
> One easily guesses the things that are coming:
> they are those of yesterday, the weary ones;
> and each tomorrow comes to look no longer like a morrow.

The prospects which the writing of "Ithaka" heralded were carefully prepared throughout the long period of agony and testing. The gropings in the twilight were all authentic yet inescapable; and with the light of day, the gateway came into full view (A 23):

> As you set out on the journey to Ithaka,
> wish that the road will be long,
> full of adventures, full of learning.
> The Laistrygonians and the Cyclopes,
> 5 angered Poseidon, do not fear,
> you will never meet with such things on your way,
> if your thought can stay high, if an exquisite
> emotion touches your spirit and your body.
> The Laistrygonians and the Cyclopes,
> 10 the fierce Poseidon, you will not encounter,
> unless you carry them inside your soul,
> if your soul doesn't raise them up before you . . .

Chapter Three

Cavafy's Later Years

1. Beyond the "Hidden Things". 2. Vindication of an "Unorthodox Work in Progress". 3. "Rare Poets, Like Cavafy . . .". 4. Farewell to Alexandria.

1. Beyond the "Hidden Things"

Between 1911 and 1912, Cavafy made a fervent and renewed effort to free his own work from imprecisions and flaws for the preparation of a new collection which could genuinely reflect his liberation and break from the confusions of the period of emotional turmoil. The new selection and arrangement of his fresh, revised and salvaged poems was finished by April 1912, but 1911 was the year he recognized as the turning point that signaled the completion of the opening phase of his poetic maturity. Suddenly, what was all along a special concern for dress and social appearance lost its appeal. At a more basic level, something else emerged with impressive boldness. The hidden eroticism, whether as nocturnal escapades or haunting fantasies, recorded in cryptic confessional notes—which stopped around November 1911—had been in many instances transmuted into poetic conceptions. Like all passionate lovers, Cavafy reached the point where he could no longer contain the experience in the private chambers of the unexpressed. The cry to speak, to declare, to preserve in shared artistic form the intensity of his passion could no longer be suppressed as cautiously masked concessions to social custom and moralistic convention. Once he freed himself from his emotional ambivalence and accepted his erotic proclivities for what they were, the problem of the place that eros as feeling and art occupied in his life became of paramount importance. That is why the solutions in such poems as "Hidden Things," had to be ruled inadequate. This may well be the reason why the poem was never published. Yet it contains a key to the transition toward the mature years. It was written in 1908 (U 151):

> From what I did and what I said
> they should not try to find out what I was.
> An obstacle stood there transforming
> the actions and the mode of my life.
> An obstacle stood there and stopped me
> many times as I was about to tell.
> The most unnoticed of my actions
> and my writings, the more veiled ones,
> from these alone they'll understand me.
> But maybe it isn't worth spending
> so much care, so much effort to know me.
> Later—in a society more perfect—
> someone else made like me
> will certainly appear and create freely.

Recent critics have remarked about "Hidden Things" that it "must be among the most overtly personal poems Cavafy ever wrote, and it is probably the most revealing about the torment as an artist—about his long incapacity to tell things as they were . . ..The language of the poem (in the original) is as direct and unpretentious as any the poet used."[1] When seen in the light of Cavafy's mature years and in connection with older unpublished yet explicitly erotic poems, the revelatory value assigned to "Hidden Things" seems excessive. The obstacle intimated as "his long incapacity" was not just psychological. Aside from the intensified need he felt during the period prior to 1911 to express his passionate side, there was the equally demanding problem of arriving at the appropriate technical solution for composing erotic poetry. The above covert erotic poem of 1903, and other more explicit ones, written prior to the renewed and more severe application of his "philosophical scrutiny," simply were not found adequate, and the same holds for the unpublished ones written after 1911, when the first "daring" poem was printed. They compare unfavorably to the explicitly erotic poems "I've Looked So

---

[1] See "Introduction" by Keeley and Savidis in C. P. Cavafy, 1971 *Passions and Ancient Days,* where it is claimed that the poem "would seem to explain why a number of his most honest and realistic love poems ("The Bandaged Shoulder," "Half an Hour," "At the Theater," "On the Stairs") remained among his papers; and it also suggests why these 'hidden things' now seem to speak with particular truthfulness" (xix). It should be noted that of the four poems mentioned above the first two were written in 1919 and 1917, and the other two in 1904; text in *Unpublished Poems*: 179, 169, 143, 141.

Much" (1911/*1917*) and "When They Come Alive" (1913/*1916*). Faithful to his principle, Cavafy refrained from publishing any poem, erotic or otherwise, he considered imperfect. He was determined to defy conventional morality, at least as far back as June 1903, when he wrote the "Growing in Spirit" (U 103):

> Whoever desires to strengthen his spirit
> must go beyond respect and submission.
> He will retain some of the laws
> but for the most part he will break
> both laws and customs and will move away
> from the accepted and inadequate uprightness.
> He will learn many things from life's pleasures.
> He will not fear the destructive act;
> half the house needs to be pulled down.
> It is thus he will grow virtuously in knowledge.

In 1908, when he wrote "Hidden Things," he was still within the walls. To a great extent they were of his own making. He was still unable to solve the problem of form for this thematic region. The fact remains that after 1912 his erotic passions and preferences were not among the "hidden things." This fact not only dated that poem; it rendered it almost unsalvageable except for the autobiographical relevance it could have, which may well have been the reason he kept it among his papers. As a poem it has too many flaws. A close reading of its message shows Cavafy's conceit dressed in sentimentality while rationalizing his timidity. The accent is on self-pity and a feigned surrender of hope of being recognized during his life-time. The reference to "a more perfect society'" weighs heavily as an appeal to the reader for compassion. The loss of aesthetic merit becomes more noticeable once the *persona* projects its wishing for a more tolerant society, one purged of hypocritical moral institutions. It simply was not true that the city of Alexandria at that time, or even earlier, was as prudish and moralistic as the poem suggests, although the same cannot be said of the moral climate of opinion in Athens. The fear of scandal was no less real, but it must be remembered that Cavafy was still courting select social groups in order to maintain his birthright to social standing and respectability. His brother Paul appears to have been more defiant, and so were other scions of well established families. The main defect in the poem is rooted in Cavafy's reluctance to face his predicament with courage and honesty. The problem he foisted onto society was mainly due to his own inhibitions. His fears magnified the issues, for he was still carrying "inside his soul" the Cyclopes and fierce Poseidon. Within a few years, and especially after the composition of "Ithaka," he finally learned how to cope with the burning desire to transmute eros into poetry. With this knowledge, Cavafy was able to pass through the gateway to maturity. He could write as one of the "brave men of pleasure."

2. Vindication of an Unorthodox "Work in Progress"

Beginning with 1911, a number of events began to unfold. They were destined to keep Cavafy's work at the forefront of literary movements in Alexandria and Athens, and later on to international attention: his close association with literary journals, his final shaping of the principles for the editing of his "collections," and his meeting with English literary persons in Alexandria during the first World War.

Early in 1911, several of the editors of *Nea Zoe*, the progressive faction, insisted on presenting radical and original literature, and decided to start a journal of their own. The occasion for parting was a disagreement over the printing of a poem entitled "Sacrifice" (*Thysia*) by the Athenian leftist poet C. Varnalis. Thus, the *Grammata* (Letters) was launched under the editorship of D. Zachariadis, C. Zervos, and S. Pargas. It featured in its very first issue poems by Cavafy. From the start it was vocal, critical, unorthodox, and daring enough to print an unfavorable article on the celebrated and leading poet of the mainland, Costis Palamas. Cavafy remained friendly toward *Nea Zoe*, and when, in 1912 a vitriolic attack on his poetry was made in a pamphlet by someone writing under the pseudonym Robertos Campos, the less progressive *Nea Zoe* rushed to condemn Campos' views, not only upholding the originality of Cavafy's poetry, but also predicting boldly "it will start a new school in modern Greek poetry."[2] Cavafy continued to publish in *Nea Zoe* until 1916, when the journal stopped its circulation for six years. But his relation to *Grammata* was not without occasional strains. His contributions ceased to

---

[2]It is certain that "R. Campos" was the pseudonym of Petros Magnis, author of *The Poetic Work of C. P. Cavafy* (Cairo, 1912), reprinted in *Epitheorisi Technis* 18 (Dec. 1963): 640-44. The rebuttal was written by C. N. Pappas, *Nea Zoe,* No. 5 (March, 1912): 266-68.

appear after 1913. They were resumed in 1917, then stopped completely after 1919 when *Grammata* took a decisive socio-political direction. The first break with *Grammata* occurred either because Cavafy expected special attention or because he hoped for a place on its editorial committee. For instance, one of its contributors, Michael Peridis, who met the poet in 1914 and later became Cavafy's biographer, had plans to write a "critical" essay which was announced rather irreverently in the July 1915 issue. However, the article was printed first as an independent pamphlet and did not appear in *Grammata* until May 1917. As a conciliatory gesture, the issue also carried several of Cavafy's poems, "Tomb of Iases," and "In the Month of Athyr," including some of his most "daring" ones, "Grey" and "I've Looked so Much." The decision no doubt must have pleased the poet. By this time, however, his name was well established in Alexandria, as well as in Athens.

After the writing of "Ithaka" and the intensive period of revising his poems in 1911 and 1912, Cavafy arrived at the final clarification of the canon upon which to base the collecting and editing of his work. The series of collections he made available constitutes one continuous growing body of poems. Each is marked with minor variations in the number of poems. As each successive "edition" came to replace, so to speak, the preceding one, he moved in a cautious and deliberate manner to incorporate into his post-1911 work only those pre-1911 poems which he regarded as complete and finished. This third and final phase of editing lasted till the end of his life, and the cumulative results of this labor brought the total of his approved poems up to 154, including his one apparently finished poem, written in the last year of his life and published posthumously, "On the Outskirts of Antioch."[3] The underlying principles of the system of editions that render his poems an organic unity, despite the topical diversity and *genre* variety, will be discussed in more detail in conjunction with his "poetics" in chapter 8. What is of direct relevance here is the fact that the beginning of the mature period reveals a parallel and coordinate cresting of his persistent labors to break through the psychological barrier and the technical obstacles and in order to ensure the longed-for consistency between experience and expression. When all of these

---

[3]The basis for arriving at a total of 154 poems includes both the post-1911 *Collections* and "autographed" sets he sent to persons who had requested his poems. The evidence and relevant data have been carefully discussed by Savidis 1966, esp. ch. 6.

aspects are considered together, they provide a reliable way of understanding Cavafy's maturity and they also vindicate the thesis advanced by two of Cavafy's most serious critics, first by G. Seferis and later G. Savidis, advocating the view that Cavafy's work be read in a special way:

> My own view is that from a certain point onward—and I should place this point at about 1910—the work of Cavafy should be read and judged not as a series of separate poems, but as one and the same poem, a "work in progress" as James Joyce would have said, which is only terminated by death. Cavafy is, I think, the most "difficult" poet of contemporary Greece, and we shall understand him more easily if we read him with the feeling of the continuous presence of his work as a whole. This unity is his grace.[4]

Cavafy turned fifty years old in 1913. The maturing process took its toll, and though it came late in life, the fruits were far from disappointing. The remainder of his years were given to composing more poems and securing their place in the world of literature. By this time, his circle of admirers had expanded beyond the limits of Alexandria. The course of events during the early part of World War I had brought to Egypt a number of Englishmen, some with pronounced interests in the arts and letters and others who had already acquired considerable distinction as poets and writers. Cavafy's close friend, Pericles Anastassiadis, who had all along maintained social and business relations with the English sector of Alexandria, introduced the poet to many visiting intellectuals and others who had government assignments in Egypt, among them R. A. Furness, a professor of classics and literature, Sir John Forsdyke, who later became the director of the British Museum, Sir Bartoll Frere, John Marshall, and the novelist E. M. Forster. It was mainly through the efforts of Forster that Cavafy's poetry became known in England. Although he studied the poetry in translations, which G. Valassopoulo, a graduate of Cambridge University, prepared for him at that time, it wasn't until after the war that he was able to publish them in English journals. As the biographer Peridis notes,

> Forster's devotion to the poetry of his Alexandrian friend ran very deep. He arranged for the publication of several poems in England.... This interest continued after the poet's death and finally he was able to persuade John

---

[4]Seferis 1966: 125; also 174-77.

Mavrogordato, a professor at the University of London, to translate all of Cavafy's poems.[5]

In 1917, Cavafy renewed his relations with the journal *Grammata* and published in it four "daring" poems, among them the "In the Month of Athyr," which he handed in person to the editor S. Pargas and said: "Please, take this masterpiece, take it for it burns my hands."[6] Never before or since did Cavafy use such extravagant expressions about any of his poems.

> I read with difficulty on the ancient stone
> "Lo[rd] Jesus Christ." I can see a "Psy[ch]e."
> "In the mo[nth] Athyr" "Lefkio[s] went to sleep."
>
> Where age is mentioned "He li[ve]d years"
> the Kappa Zeta indicates he went to sleep quite young,
>
> Worn lines, but I see there "hi[m] . . . Alexandrian."
> Then come three lines quite mutilated;
> But I make out words like "our t[e]ars," "grief,"
> then again "tears" and "mourning to u[s] [f]riends."
>
> It seems to me that Lefkios was greatly loved.
> In the month of Athyr Lefkios fell asleep.[7]

Cavafy's strikingly unconventional poetry had by this time become the object of discussion, ranging from open praise to direct condemnation. It was this very poem, probably because it was published together with other "daring"

---

[5] Peridis 1948: 104. The complete correspondence between Forster and Cavafy has not been published yet. Savidis has announced an edition of Cavafy's letters, but the project still awaits its completion. See G. P. Savidis, "Cavafy and Forster," in *The Times Literary Supplement* (14 Nov. 1975), reprinted with additions in Savidis 1985: 169-78.

[6] Mentioned in Pieridis 1965: 73.

[7] Compare also G. Valassopoulo's translation, which does not observe the brackets; printed in Forster 1923 [1962]: 29. The Greek letters *Kappa Zeta* stand for the numerals "27". The month of Athyr in the Egyptian calendar covers the period between October 10 and November 8. Athyr is a female divinity. She lends her name to the month in which her brother Seth drowns their brother Osiris in the Nile.

poems, that provoked the ire and irony of Timos Malanos who attacked Cavafy's style and themes in a series of caustic articles. Many of Cavafy's close friends rushed to his defense, chief among them G. Vrissimitzakis, who then published his book—the first extensive favorable analysis of Cavafy's work—appending a selection of twenty-one poems.[8] This critic had mixed motives in taking a position in the front line of the pro-Cavafy forces. He had hopes of enlisting the poet's support in a movement of cultural radicalism organized by himself and other restless young intellectuals who called themselves "The Apuans."[9] The eccentric orientation of this group had no appeal for Cavafy, especially at a time when his sole interest centered around the furthering of his creative work. However, Vrissimitzakis' analyses were not without merit and some of his insights, especially his observations on the "political" dimension in Cavafy, must be recognized as landmarks in the literature about this poet. As his radical concerns grew stronger, his loyalty to the poet did more than diminish. Eventually, he took a polemical stance and accused Cavafy of indulging in "tomb worshipping and mysticism."

While more serious and high level critical essays began to appear in Athens, Cavafy moved more decisively, this time engaging his devoted and life-long friend Alekos Sengopoulos, whom he later appointed executor of his will, to give a public lecture on his poetry. The event took place on February 29, 1918, the text having been prepared under the poet's direct supervision, and probably whole sections written by his own hand. It consisted mainly of an analysis of several poems and was intended as a guide to educate the public on how to understand the poet. The text, with prefatory remarks by P. Modinos, was printed soon after the event.[10]

The appearance of adverse criticism did not seem to have surprised Cavafy. He bore the bitter remarks with polite irony and gentle detachment. The attention, even when he was an object of controversy, could not be denied. He was more fully compensated when E. M. Forster published in the

---

[8]Vrissimitzakis 1975 (revised ed.), with introduction by G. Savidis.

[9]For a brief but biased account, see Malanos 1971: 75-80; also Tsirkas 1958: 441; Yalourakis 1974: 120-21.

[10]Reprinted in *Epitheorisi Technis*, special "Cavafy Issue" No. 108 (November 1963): 614-21.

April 1919 issue of the *Athenaeum,* in London, a brief essay "The Poetry of C. P. Cavafy," with Valassopoulo's translations of several poems, including "Alexandrian Kings," "In the Month of Athyr," and "The God Abandons Antony." This essay was reprinted with certain alterations in the May 17 issue of the *Egyptian Gazette.* In bringing Cavafy to international prominence, Forster praised the poetry while maintaining a certain distance. In the concluding paragraph he stated that Cavafy "has the strength (and of course the limitations) of the recluse, who, though not afraid of the world, always stands at a slight angle to it. Which is better—the world or seclusion? Cavafy who has tried both, can't say. But so much is certain—either life entails courage, or it ceases to be life."[11] Following suit, the Italian-Alexandrian, A. Catraro, who became one of the intimate devotees of Cavafy's work and also introduced him to F. T. Marinetti, the futurist, published his first translations in Italian, thus marking the beginning in Italy of a literary and scholarly interest in Cavafy.[12] Before the year was over, there were translations of several poems into French and also a substantial article by Philéas Lebésque, "Lettres neo-grècques: La Poésie de Constantine Kavafis," in the December 16, 1919 issue of the *Mercure de France.*

Cavafy's brother, Paul, his senior by three years, died in France, early in 1920. To what extent the loss affected the poet is not known. What is certain, however, is that Paul had lived in a libertine manner. The scandalous conduct of his youth had almost led to the cancellation of the 1909 lecture of P. Petridis. Paul's character contrasted rather sharply with the reserved, cautious and deliberate manners of his younger brother. S. Tsirkas, in his detailed study of Cavafy's times, makes the interesting observation that it seems quite unlikely that Cavafy did not in fact indulge in conduct that fed the rumors about his sexuality during and after that period. Whatever his experiences of homosexual affairs, they were rather limited, particularly during

---

[11]Reprinted in Forster 1962 [1923]: 97.

[12]See Renata Lavagnini, "Cavafy and Italian Literature," in *Proceedings of the Third Symposium in Poetry: C. P. Cavafy* (July 1-3, 1983): 363-72; references to G. Ungaretti, A. Catraro, F. M. Pontani, E. Pea, E. Montale, and F. T. Marinetti. A number of distinguished scholars in Italy, among them, F. M. Pontani, R. Lavagnini, M. Peri, M. Vitti, V. Mascaro and R. M. Minucci, have published in recent years important monographs and articles. See also Lavagnini 1982.

his early manhood. Tsirkas adds that "from the moment Cavafy realizes that the notoriety of having had a scandalous youth can serve his hedonic poems, he decides to appropriate the rumors about Paul's conduct."[13] Whatever the case may be, the five poems he circulated in 1920 give no indication of grief or mourning, and the only somewhat explicit poem, "For the Shadows to Come," is but a distant echo of past experience recollected in reverie. By this time he had severed his relations with *Grammata*, as this journal, waving a "socialist" banner, started a new period under the leadership of S. Pargas and M. Peridis. In the ensuing years, it neither mentioned Cavafy nor published any of his poems. His style, unique and original though it was, no longer appealed to its editor's changing taste, and the themes he treated lost the initial fascination they once held. The post-war quest for social ideas and progressive reforms provided his former admirers with goals of their own, and as in the case of Vrissimitzakis, a platform to write an ironical article about Cavafy. The Poet was now being seen as "an old man" of Alexandria.[14]

The interest in the poetry of this strange poet did anything but subside. His was a voice to cope with and a challenge to literary critics. Athens was beginning to pass the point of patronage and mild acknowledgement. Unlike the defecting former supporters in Alexandria, several respected Athenians began to study Cavafy's poetry. In March 1921, the critic Tellos Agras gave the first serious public lecture, which he later published under the title "The Poet C. P. Cavafy." He declared that Cavafy had already left his mark on modern Greek poetry.[15] With the appearance of new poems, more European critics began to show interest. Karl Dieterich in Germany took notice of Cavafy, and more so, Hubert Pernot in France, in his book *La Grèce actuelle dans ses poètes*.[16] But the event that helped more than any other to break the ice occurred when the celebrated poet Costis Palamas, who for decades dominated the literary circles of Athens and Greece in general, wrote

---

[13] Tsirkas 1958: 179.

[14] Cf. Vrissimitzakis [1921], rev. ed. 1975.

[15] The text was first printed in the *Bulletin of the Society on Education* (Deltio tou Ekpaideftikou Omilou, 1922): 3-46; reprinted in Agras 1980, v. I: 31-81.

[16] Paris, 1921. The book included translations of six poems by Cavafy.

a note on the Greeks in Egypt and mentioned in passing the following: "There is a poet of admitted originality, Cavafy, who is exceptionally honored by the youth there."[17] This was about as far as he ever went in recognizing the significance of Cavafy, but before the twenties were over a strange and bitter controversy over the two poets broke out in which both tried to stay in the background while their more vocal partisans kept the flames alive. We may open a parenthesis at this point to trace some highlights of the controversy because of the importance it had in the later period of Cavafy's life. The biographer M. Peridis evaluated the conflict as follows:

> For quite some time Palamas, who was highly respected as a person and great poet, had noted with displeasure the increasing neglect younger people were beginning to show for him as they turned to Cavafy. As a critic, Palamas had promoted understanding in order to appreciate the thoughts and feelings expressed in viewpoints contrary to his own. He would have recognized the value of his Alexandrian rival had fate not turned them into opponents. Had he elected to write on Cavafy's poetry he might have said some very interesting things. However, once Cavafy's fame started spreading and the younger people began to praise him as the leading poet, Palamas found it impossible to tolerate this ranking, especially after being for over half a century the subject of the devotion and admiration of his contemporaries for his prolific productivity. The blow to his pride was far too heavy. A man of his stature could hardly watch himself being suddenly brushed aside by someone only four years his junior, unknown until yesterday, rising abruptly at the age of sixty to the heights of artistic distinction.[18]

In the eyes of the people, Palamas was the new national poet of Greece, the successor of Dionysios Solomos and the indomitable defender of the demotic movement in language, literature, and culture. His epic and lyric poetry, as well as his prose, had set the tone for the articulation of the national ideals and aspirations of Greece since the closing decades of the nineteenth century. Cavafy was only a Greek of the diaspora, a withdrawn and peculiar Alexandrian with a talent only for minor chords, the limited pitch

---

[17] The note was published in *Embros* (December 4, 1921) and signed "W."

[18] In Peridis 1948: 113 (translation mine). Further details on this controversy in Yalourakis 1963: 1584-1589; Petridis 1961; also Souloyannis 1983: 50-55.

of whose voice could never span the awesome range of the perennial values embedded in the three millennia of the Hellenic tradition. Such, apparently, was Palamas' way of viewing Cavafy, the outsider. At another level, their differences ran somewhat deeper but hardly surfaced during the years of the controversy that raged over the laurels. Palamas' dionysian outbursts and his torrential lyricism, so strongly sustained by the last waves of the Romantic movement, stood in sharp contrast to the direct yet subdued erotic hedonism of Cavafy's explicit poems. Palamas' almost mystical idealization of female beauty could not conceivably make concession to alternatives. Whatever the case may be, Palamas made several slight remarks about that side of Cavafy: "a case of base sensual versifying"; ". . . and here profligacy is transformed from a Witch to a Muse."[19] The disapproval was not so much over the issue of prestige, for Palamas managed to maintain his privileged position to the end.

The two poets never met each other in person. On the whole, the dispute was carried out by their circles of admirers and only occasionally encouraged by pointed and direct, at times inadvertent, statements by the poets themselves. If Palamas wanted to grant Cavafy a place in Greek letters, he could have done so any time between 1922 and 1926, the year when the dispute entered its critical stage. While he kept his silence, his friends in Alexandria organized a literary festival in his honor. Cavafy sat in the audience and heard the speakers extol Palamas as the greatest poet of Greece. Later, when he was asked for his opinion he said, guardedly, that he could think of better poets.[20] After this opinion appeared in print, it took no time at all for the *literati* to split into pro-Cavafy and pro-Palamas camps. The attacks and counterattacks thickened in the columns of the newspapers in Alexandria and Cairo. Palamas finally broke his silence in an interview which was forced upon him by Lukas Christophidis, a reporter and mediocre poet from Cairo. Nevertheless, Palamas expressed serious reservations:

— I believe he is not deficient in wisdom . . . but is he a poet? I don't know, I may be mistaken. Rather, his is a case of reportage. His writings

---

[19]Translation mine; text in Peridis 1948: 268.

[20]Rika Agallianou, who later married Alekos Sengopoulos, solicited the interview and printed it in the newspaper *Tachydromos* (February 18, 1926).

> seem as if his concern is to bring us a report from the centuries . . . . Let us try to be just . . . . Some of his poems look like they are on their way to become sketches of ideas, about to become songs, but whose master prefers to keep them in the shape of plans . . .[21]

The Cavafians were outraged and sought help from Athens. Replying to their request, Kleon Paraschos and especially Alkis Thrylos went out of their way to maintain peace, careful not to injure the pride of either party. Yet the latter wrote:

> Today, more so than ever before, I believe that Cavafy is one of the very few modern Greek poets with a contemporary European consciousness and style, and at the same time, a most sensitive and unusual personality. I am convinced that his work is one of the few in our own literature that can claim one of the first places in world literature.[22]

While the mood in Athens seemed conciliatory, Palamas' evaluation of Cavafy had an unfavorable effect on the Alexandrians, but the moderate critics at least were quick to lay the blame on journalistic irresponsibility. After all, Cavafy was a poet of their city. A month after A. Thrylos' note appeared, Palamas defended his judgment, this time by appealing to the aesthetics of technique, and referred to Cavafy as "legislating the amorphous in versification." The differences of opinions ran deeper than the level of vanity and personality. For the first time, a Greek poet of the diaspora was rising on the horizon of literature bringing forth a message and style which did more than present a challenge to the established conceptions of art and values. He heralded a point of departure in task and technique of unprecedented consequence. Palamas saw but one aspect of the issues the controversy had engendered. And when *La Semaine Égyptienne* brought out a special issue on Cavafy, Palamas felt sufficiently irritated to write a long letter to his close friend G. Katsimbalis, in which he said:

> . . . I have no appetite for counter attacks . . . nor do I intend to disturb the

---

[21]The interview appeared in *Othóni* (October 16, 1926); reprinted in Yalourakis 1963: 1585. Translation mine.

[22]In *Isis*, (November 13, 1926, Alexandria); reprinted in Yalourakis 1963: 1586.

peace of those persons in Alexandria, Cairo, the Panegyptians in general, who believe they have the one and only poet of the centuries.[23]

As the artistic issues and convictions separating the two poets were brought into the open with increasing sharpness, the initial camps for and against Cavafy rekindled their differences by turning the comparison of Cavafy with Palamas into a battle cry. There were mixed motives involved, too. Many of the anti-Cavafy writers were themselves poets in Alexandria and Cairo who came to feel that his presence among them stood in their way to glory, failing to realize that some were already slavishly imitating Cavafy's language and technique. But in the case of Palamas, no such interest ever emerged. He had made the irrevocable decision to dismiss the Alexandrian as an impressive yet still mediocre poet who had become fashionable, but was definitely undeserving of wider attention. When the French-Greek writer C. Photiades declared at an interview that he had selected Cavafy for translation into French, Palamas, who had read and praised Photiades' book on G. Meredith, felt indignant upon reading Photiades' statement that "Cavafy is a poet, a true poet, which is also the opinion of my friends Henri Renier and the Countess de Noailles." To which Palamas retorted, in a letter to the newspaper *Ethnos* (Nation): "He is all theirs to enjoy!"[24] The bitterness remained deep-seated. Palamas, in his August 15, 1929 letter to Katsimbalis, complained that the articles in *La Semaine Égyptienne* on Cavafy went beyond the point of hurting his personal pride. Then, noting how it declared the Alexandrian poet "the great one, the one and only with whom Renaissance commences, the Greek Renaissance," his protest took on a stronger accent: "Now it is he who brought poetry, language, thought, verse, art to us. As for the demotic movement—nonsense!"

The February 17, 1930 issue of the same journal was dedicated to Palamas, whose note of gratitude for the honor was prominently displayed. The attention he received had a softening effect, yet in another interview he

---

[23]The special issue of *La Semaine Égyptienne* appeared on April 25, 1929. The letter to G. Katsimbalis is dated August 15, 1929; reprinted in Yalourakis 1963, 1588; the complete text of this letter in *Nea Estia*, special issue on Palamas, (December 25, 1943): 293-294, reprinted with notes in Palamas 1981: 24-27, 287-8.

[24]The full text of the letter in Palamas, *Apanta* (Collected Works), v. 16: 584-86.

granted to Pieridis for the *Tachydromos*, he repeated his old views but in a milder tone.

Palamas' cultural commitments, more than anything else, prevented him from finding anything of value in Cavafy. The possibility of envy must be readily dismissed, not only because his nobility of mind and gentle manners prevented such a feeling, but because his fame had already been firmly secure as a major European poet with many of his works translated as well as discussed in a score of languages. Romain Rolland, in 1930, had stated that Palamas "is the greatest of the living European poets," no mean recognition, to be sure, when added to the fact that Palamas about that time came close to winning the Nobel prize for poetry. When Cavafy heard of this prospect, Peridis reports him to have said: "I do wish Palamas to get the Nobel. Not for his sake; I am indifferent to the man, but it will be an honor for Greece."[25] Another comment he made in 1930 summarized his views best: "Costis Palamas is a great lyric poet, but lyric poetry does not appeal to me. That's just about it."[26]

Seen in perspective, the controversy was in no small measure due to unfortunate misunderstandings instigated by journalistic sensationalism and shallow partisanship. If anything, it was not Palamas who gained from the prolonged dispute. Rather, it was Cavafy's name, less prominent by comparison, that was kept in the foreground and made publicly visible. In this regard it stands to reason to say that he welcomed the entire affair and probably encouraged it. Be that as it may, the dispute continued by partisans in Egypt and Greece for years after Cavafy's death in 1933. As for Palamas himself, he never changed his opinion. In a letter to Glafkos Alithersis, whose book on Cavafy he had received and read, Palamas wrote on January 1, 1935:

> . . . Of course Cavafy has certain merits, but they cannot stand up to dispassionate observation . . . . Perhaps you are familiar with the opinion I expressed in *Figaro* (France) which was printed in September 18, 1928. What I said then about Cavafy, I shall say again: Cavafy is innovative, peculiar, and has to his credit that he reminds us often of the ancient command: "Poet, make myths, not speeches." Up to this point, this praising

---

[25]Peridis 1948: 119.

[26]See also Cavafy's comment on Palamas in *Prose* (1963): 248 notes.

remark raises Cavafy almost to classical rank. But let me proceed. I also said there that precepts are of no help. What counts above all is the man himself, the person behind them. To be brief about it, putting aside the details about his poetic art, or lack of art, call it what you wish, and his philosophy, I come to the following conclusion. The works of Cavafy, verse, language, expression, form and substance, seem to me like notes which either cannot or deign not become poems . . .

(Signed) Costis Palamas[27]

The dispute ended on a note of mutual exclusion. Although neither poet was denied popular acclaim and public recognition, they never met in person, nor tried to understand each other's way of perceiving the world. Yet both probed attentively and with consummate compassion into the fate and fortune of mankind. They stood at the extreme points of different tangents on the same circle, their trembling hands eager to touch the same center, as all the beloved of the Muse are expected to do.

3. "Rare Poets, Like Cavafy . . ."

In 1922 Cavafy, approaching sixty, decided to retire after 30 years as an employee in the Irrigation Service of the Ministry of Public Works. His resignation became effective on April 1. His pension and savings were sufficient to provide for his needs. During that year he printed privately three new poems while older ones continued to appear in journals. His friend A. Catraro wrote an article for the daily *Il Popolo Romano,* and E. M. Forster published in England his *Alexandria: A History and A Guide,* the second edition of which he dedicated to C. P. Cavafy. When the book was reissued in 1961, he wrote in his Introduction:

> One of the joys of those years was my friendship with the great Greek poet who so poignantly conveys the civilization of his chosen city. C. P. Cavafy was not then widely known and the translation of "The God Abandons Antony" by our friend George Valassopoulo represents his first appearance

---

[27]The entire letter in *Nea Estia*, 34 (December 25, 1943), 309-310; reprinted in Palamas 1981: 202-4. In translating this comment I have altered the punctuation slightly to preserve the tenor of the letter.

in English. He has been fully translated since, and widely eulogized—for instance by a late lover of Alexandria, Mr. Lawrence Durrell."[28]

A string of unhappy events followed the defeat of the Greek army in Asia Minor. The conflict with Turkey that ensued on the wake of World War I, ended in the burning of Smyrna in 1922, the holocaust of its predominantly Greek population and the savage uprooting of over one million Greeks from their traditional homeland along the western coast of Asia Minor, Pontos and Thrace. The defeat was a national disaster and a fatal blow to the long-nourished hopes of recovering the ancestral lands and extending the boundaries of the small state of Greece to include all the unredeemed brethren in one political unit. The aspirations of centuries, which began to materialize with the Greek War of Independence of 1821-1829, came to an abrupt and disastrous end. Polys Modinos, one of Cavafy's close friends, preserved in striking detail an account of the painful and disturbing effects the events leading to the conflagration of Smyrna had on the poet:

> People who never met Cavafy personally have wondered what impact the debacle and slaughter perpetrated against our nation had on the poet and what was his reaction. I can answer this question without hesitation. Cavafy experienced intensely all the phases of our history, its glories as well as its misfortunes. However, the then current events did not move him poetically, did not stir his poetic disposition . . . . By mid-September 1922 the catastrophe of our Hellenism in Asia Minor was complete, ending in uprooting and annihilation. I remember Cavafy sitting in his usual place in his living room, gloomy, silent and sad. We were alone. Suddenly he broke out in cracking voice and said: "What is happening to us is terrible. Smyrna is lost, Ionia is lost, the Gods are gone." He was unable to continue. Under the light of the lamp I saw tears streaking down on his wrinkled face. I learned then and there what it means to evince and express a deep pain.[29]

Only months before the debacle of Asia Minor in 1922 Cavafy had

---

[28]Forster 1961: xvii.

[29]Translation mine. Greek text in Modinos 1980: 9-10.

printed his poem "Those Who Fought for the Achaean League,"[30] an epigram in honor of the fighters who fell in the last battle against the onrushing Roman legions, in 146 B.C. ending thus the independence of the Greek city-states.[31]

Cavafy's brother, John, died early in 1923. More than any other member of his family, he had stood by Constantine and expressed an active interest in his poetry. He had tried his hand at poetry, written several poems in English and a few in French, and published at his own expense a small collection titled *Early Verses* (probably in 1896). He was close to Constantine and felt a strong affinity for his work. The few translations he made into English were conspicuously inferior to the originals, and Cavafy who was well aware of their quality, discouraged the undertaking. John had moved to Cairo in 1904, where he became quite successful and ended as a partner in the R. J. Moss Company which cooperated with the London and Lancashire Insurance Company. After his retirement, he moved to Alexandria in 1917, but for the remainder of his years contacts with his brother became less frequent. John was the last member of the family, and when he died Cavafy was deeply grieved and also felt disappointed that John left him only £1000. Five months later, Cavafy wrote his own will:

> This is my last will and testament. I appoint Alexander D. Sengopoulos Executor of my will. I bequeath to my niece Charicleia Valieri the amount of 200 pounds. I bequeath to my niece Helene Cavafy 700 pounds. I bequeath to Alex D. Sengopoulos all of my remaining property; all other such items which belong to me.
>
> Written in Alexandria on July 8, 1923
> Sign. Constantine P. Cavafy[32]

---

[30]I have discussed the coincidence of these catastrophic events in relation to this poem in my 1975: 13-25.

[31]Cavafy's concern for the fate, misfortunes and historical significance of Hellenism, is a vast topic. Seferis 1974b, v. 1, was perhaps the first to intimate the relevance of this poem to the ominous developments and the political blunders which lurk in the background of the catastrophe of Asia Minor (126-127, 136).

[32]Translation mine; Greek text in Peridis 1948: 15, n2. Peridis estimates the value of Cavafy's property at the time of his death in 1933 to have been about £10,000-12,000.

For the next ten years Cavafy was finally free to devote himself entirely to his poetry, to the completion of his work. Never for a moment wavering in self-confidence, never lacking in perseverance or feelings devoid of ideas, he moved on with new compositions. On the practical side, he was determined to gain the place he knew he deserved in the world of letters. It was about this time that he started attracting devotees from different quarters and walks of life. New poems circulated, others were reprinted and also anthologized. K. Skokos included in his *Neohellenic Anthology* (1923) eleven poems, together with an appreciative note, and Forster reprinted his 1919 essay on Cavafy in *Pharos and Pharillon*. But there were also the bitter attacks and rejections. In 1923, Ph. Politis published a satirical article in *Politeia* (Athens), making "Cavafy" the pen-name of a "real" poetaster named G. Exarhopoulos Kavafis Matthaiou, merchant in Alexandria; in France, Louis Roussel wrote in 1923 in *Libre* a negative review of the "Collection."

The decisive turn of events which established firmly Cavafy's fame as a poet came in 1924. Critical opinion, first in Alexandria and then in Athens, became increasingly divided around a slowly growing body of poems whose message and quality had engaged the attention and interest of friend and foe alike. Timos Malanos, who was later to write an ambitious psychoanalytical study of Cavafy, opened the year with a public lecture in Alexandria in which he attempted to show that the "historical" poems should be considered "vulnerable." A physician, S. Lagoudakis, published in a newspaper opinions of his own which contained innuendoes damaging to the private life and personality of the poet. A torrent of protests and condemnations followed, and a demonstration was staged to prevent Lagoudakis from giving his lecture. To his credit, Malanos was among the protestors. Athens became similarly excited as Cavafy's admirers grew in numbers and stature.

A young student of pharmacology at the University of Athens, Marios Vayanos, made Cavafy's recognition a literary cause, and protested in writing when the poet was not given the coveted "Award of Excellence."[33] The old guard defended itself with rigor and more often with caustic replies. The undaunted Vayanos arranged interviews and succeeded in securing the cooperation of thirty-one personalities to bring out a special "Cavafy" issue of

---

[33] See Cavafy 1979, *Letters to Marios Vayanos*, ed. E. N. Moschos (Athens); also Tsirkas 1963: 698.

the journal *Nea Techni* (New Art),[34] an event which cost him his career as a scientist. Vayanos' perseverance in his cause drew out into the open most of the leading writers and intellectuals. It was about this time that Palamas joined the anti-Cavafy movement with an official statement of his own. Far away from the tense atmosphere of Greek letters, Cavafy's poetry received more positive acclaim. Again, with Forster's initiative, new translations by Valassopoulo appeared in *The Nation* and the *Athenaeum* (October 6, 1923, April 5, 1924, June 21, 1924), among them that of the poem "Theodotos." Of special significance was the fact that T. S. Eliot not only noticed the poems but published the "Ithaka" in the *Criterion* (September, 1924).[35] Again, with Forster's help, the circle of sympathetic readers in England came to include Lawrence of Arabia and Arnold Toynbee.

The literature on Cavafy continued to gather momentum though most of it proved of uneven quality. It consisted mainly of articles, brief essays, notes and comments, none of which matched the penetrating insight and power of his poetry. If anything, it became clear that Cavafy was a poet of magnitude and one who continually eluded the interpretive efforts of his contemporaries. He was clearly a poet of the future. It was under these circumstances that "the Cavafy problem" emerged and was debated for many years as the most unsettled issue in modern Greek letters. The anti-Cavafy circles, even when conceding a certain value to his work, did so only reluctantly. The enthusiastic support of his admiring friends was carried out without the benefit of adequate conceptual tools required for methodical study. However, several competent articles by I. M. Panayotopoulos, Tellos Agras and G. Vrissimitzakis began to show the way towards more fruitful explorations. Sensing how crucial the controversy about his person and work had grown, Cavafy seized the initiative to secure a forum, even a platform, to keep interest alive and also project his work in a more judicious light. Thus, toward the end of 1926, a new monthly journal devoted to art and literature, *Alexandrini Techni* (Alexandrian Art), was launched under his titular directorship and financial support. The journal became known as Cavafy's

---

[34] This was the July-October 1924 issue but circulated in December.

[35] Cavafy refers to T. S. Eliot in two unpublished letters to Forster, dated August 1, 1924 and October 15, 1929.

mouthpiece, but what really counts in this connection is that it carried a large number of important comments, written anonymously by Cavafy himself, which throw valuable light on problems of interpretation, technique and style.

His opponents took advantage of every opportunity to malign him, as they did, for instance, when the then head of a dictatorship in Greece, Theodoros Pangalos, honored Cavafy with the Medal of the Phoenix, which the poet finally accepted despite pressures to refuse it. The meaning of this gesture was blown out of proportion. It must have surprised his socialist and radical critics when they learned that Cavafy's name appeared on the letter which was printed in the newspaper *Democratia* (April 21, 1925) to protest the dismissal of the socialist poet Costas Varnalis by the Greek government. But what counted more heavily during the last period of his life was the annoying misunderstanding of the philosophy of life his poems expressed. Most of his interpreters had seized on the motifs of the pre-1911 poems, reading in distorted ways both the "hedonic" and "historical" themes of the post-1911 poems, and thus came to project Cavafy as a pessimist, disillusioned, egocentric poet, indulging his personal passions and wallowing in the cultural sickness of decadence. This trend was partly due to the fact that most of the "approved" pre-1911 poems, like "Walls," "The Windows," "Trojans," "Monotony," "The City," and "Waiting for the Barbarians,"[36] had become immensely popular, but much of it can be attributed to the surging reconstructive ideology after the shock of the 1922 national disgrace had subsided. Cavafy's perspective on history and interest in the Hellenic political adventures of the post-Alexandrian era could not be properly fitted into the progressive mood and the revitalized patriotism of the late twenties in Greece. His stance was at a slight angle to the Greek world.

When N. Kazantzakis visited Alexandria in January 1927, filled as he was at the time with his Nietzschean-Marxist vision of a modern Odysseus, designed to replace the Homeric model for the centuries to come, he went to see Cavafy at his residence. Later he wrote only what his personal anticipations allowed him to note:

---

[36]This last poem does not appear to have been included in the definitive *Collections*. Savidis correctly defends its inclusion in the canon of approved poems on the basis that it was part of the folder of the poet's trusted friend, P. Anastassiadis.

> A brave soul, saying farewell to Alexandria . . . with an expression in his beautiful dark eyes, full of decadence and exhaustion . . . Cavafy is one of the last flowers of a decaying civilization . . . . He has all the typical features of the extraordinary man of decadence—wise, ironical, hedonistic, fascinating, full of memory. One who lives as if he is indifferent, as if courageous.[37]

So firm was the image of a "decadent" Cavafy in the minds of the progressive ideologues that the significant but brief essay of Vrissimitzakis, "The Hellenic Dimension of Cavafy's Poetry" (1928), went unnoticed.[38] Kazantzakis made no attempt to correct a view that was simply repeating what others before him had already projected. Palamas had set the tone for the moral and patriotic evaluation, but it took the forceful mind of a representative among the younger aspiring reconstructionists, G. Theotokas, looking for dynamic new policies to direct the nation, to pronounce the castigation in the wider context of the search for progress. Theotokas wrote in 1929:

> Cavafy is the culmination of a direction in Greek poetry toward death . . . He is a defeated who never in his life dared to fight; he is defeated not by the idea of life itself, which he never really felt, but by his own self . . . Frankly speaking, an ordinary bandit of the Greek mountains interests me more than the poet from Alexandria.[39]

By 1939, Theotokas had discovered a new and different Cavafy: an original poet, profoundly moral, a genuine teacher of freedom and a paradigm of human dignity.[40]

As time went by, new compositions added significantly to the "work in progress." In 1928, one of the most productive years, he circulated nine poems, a feat never to be equalled again. Cavafy proceeded slowly and

---

[37] Kazantzakis, *Travels: Spain, Italy, Egypt, Sina* (1927); I have based my translation on the second edition of 1965: 78-83; also Anton 1974: 3-15.

[38] Reprinted in Vrissimitzakis 1975: 61-72.

[39] In *Eléfthero Pnévma* (Free Spirit), Athens 1929: 67.

[40] Theotokas, *Pnevmatikí Poreía*, (Spiritual Journey), Athens 1961, revised edition; the essay on Cavafy, 235-47, originally written in 1939, reflects his mature views in which he rejects the negative opinions he had expressed in his 1929 article.

confidently with his work. Critical discussions, as such, had no direct bearing on the methodical exploration of his themes and no effect on his stylistic principles. His responses to his interpreters were either on issues of correctness or protestations against improper references to aspects of his personality. What irritated him mostly was the printing of opinions which calculatedly questioned the quality of his work. He knew how remarkably different his poetry was, and for this reason he resented comparisons. It was precisely this awareness of his originality, which once it came to its full fruition, led him to disown all the early poems he knew were not only imperfect, but obviously derivative. He considered himself a poet who came to his own "in older years." It is reported that in an interview held in 1929, Cavafy complained about an article Peridis had written in which he expressed the opinion that the poet's work was just about "exhausted":

> This is precisely Michael Peridis' mistake in writing that critical article in *Grammata*. Just because he regarded me somewhat older, he imagined that my work had been done. As a result, what he wrote looks like it refers to something finished. Many wrote after their forties. The great Anatole France wrote his monumental work after he was forty-five. The list is long. In my case, what sets me to work is not the immediate impression. The impression has to age, to vitiate itself with the passage of time, without my having to do it. I had two features of my own. To make poems or write history. History I did not write, and now it is too late. I know what you will retort: And how do I know I could write history? I understand. I make the experiment and ask myself: Cavafy, can you write fictional works (*mysthistorima*)? Ten voices in me reply: *no*. I put the question for a second time: Cavafy, can you write for the theatre? Twenty-five voices reply again: *no*. I put the question for a third time: Cavafy, can you write history? One hundred-twenty-five voices exclaim: You can, yes, you can.[41]

4. Farewell to Alexandria

Toward the end of his life Cavafy became the celebrated poet of his city. His influence had become apparent in every literary expression and cultural discussion, even when his opponents tried to ignore it. For the European

---

[41] I have used for the translation the text in Peridis 1948: 121.

intellectuals who visited Alexandria, he was "the one" to see and visit. The special "Cavafy" issues of journals became more frequent and many of his better known poems were finding expert translators in Italy, France, and Germany. *The Great Hellenic Encyclopedia* (1929) included a lemma on Cavafy, written by Tellos Agras; A. Politis devoted ten pages to Cavafy in his two-volume work, *Hellenism and Modern Egypt* (1930). On the other hand, the Greek critic A. Hourmouzios who gave a lecture on Greek literature in London without ever mentioning Cavafy, was met with open resentment. In the next year J. Mavrogordato made reference to Cavafy in his *Modern Greece,* published in London, while G. Valassopoulo wrote an essay in English for the Parisian journal *Échanges* titled "An Alexandrian Poet." A substantial number of articles, many of them showing careful treatment and close analysis, appeared between 1930 and 1932 notably by E. P. Papanoutsos, I. A. Sareyannis, C. Th. Dimaras, and T. K. Papatsonis, marking thus a decisive turn in the study of Cavafy. Sensitive to the problem of interpretation, he finally acceded to a proposal by G. Lechonitis (1930?) to dictate personal "comments" on his poems, which the latter published under the title *Cavafian Self-comments,* in 1942.

For a number of years Cavafy was suffering from pains in his larynx. He was advised to cut down on his smoking, which he did, but the fear of illness depressed him and he would often fall into periods of silence and melancholy. He was literally filled with terror when the medical diagnosis showed he had developed cancer of the larynx. His health deteriorated and he was urged to seek treatment in Athens. In July 1932, he was hospitalized and a tracheotomy was performed. As he could not speak at all, he communicated with his visitors by writing brief statements on sheets of paper. During his stay at the Red Cross Hospital, the literary journal *Kyklos* sought and secured the contributions of leading writers for a special "Cavafy" issue. The issue appeared in November, after the poet's return to Alexandria, and proved to be a landmark in the critical study of Cavafy. Among other items, it contained the first thorough and reliable analytical bibliography by G. Katsimbalis. About the same time Cavafy circulated the last poem before his death, "Days of 1908." The last year of his life brought with it a few deep satisfactions, as when André Maurois, who visited Cavafy in Alexandria, praised him in an interview for the *Panegyptia*; and later, in December, *Nea Estia* in Athens announced the news that Dimitri Mitropoulos had composed the music for ten of Cavafy's hedonic poems. In the meantime, a young poet,

William Plomer, published a collection of poems in London which included one on Cavafy.

Even during the last months, when he knew his illness was terminal, Cavafy could still summon courage to attend to the literary disputes and misrepresentations of his views, despite the fact that the operation he underwent had caused total loss of his voice. But the most urgent task of his last days was the completion of his work. Before returning to Alexandria he "told" some of his friends, "I have twenty-five more poems to write! Twenty-five poems!" Still he was able to work and finish one more, "On the Outskirts of Antioch," which was published posthumously in 1935; it was found among his papers, carefully copied and signed.

His situation became grave in April, 1933 and he had to be hospitalized. He could still receive close friends and write brief notes. He was not a religious man, although in some of his early poems he expressed the need to seek in religion protection from fear and evil. It was his art that consumed whatever devotional feeling he had. When on the deathbed his friends suggested that he should receive the Patriarch of Alexandria, he changed the subject quickly and asked Rika Sengopoulos to look up some historical information in the municipal library. She reported later what happened when the Patriarch arrived and his visit was announced to him; she stated the following:

> Cavafy, who never asked for this, declined, became angry, persisted, but in the end yielded to his friends or rather to the thought that it would be improper and a display of bad manners not to receive a Patriarch of the Great City of Alexandria. When the prelate entered the patient's room he found Cavafy propped up, pious, with an expression on his face at once serious and eager to follow all the formalities of the Orthodox Church.[42]

On April 28, he suffered a massive stroke and died at 2:00 a.m., Saturday, April 29. The funeral took place in the afternoon of the same day and his remains were buried next to his parents, brothers and sister, in the Greek cemetery. The voyage of his Ithaka was over.

He left all his papers in good order, but there were no written directions about the use of his personal documents. The archives and books

---

[42]Translation mine; the Greek text in Sareyannis, *Nea Grammata* (March 1944): 140.

in his library were later moved to Athens. The system he had followed for the arrangement of his poems and notes suggests that he had kept in mind the posthumous study of his work. In the "Genealogy" he included all the information he considered essential and of public interest. Most of his life he lived alone yet admired by devoted friends. He selected his company, avoided crowded places, walked the same streets, stopping occasionally to whisper something to himself, or lean sideways to study an object on display in a store. He was curious but reserved, a brilliant conversationalist, witty, a master of the playful phrase, a kind host, cultivating his well-disposed acquaintances and guests, sizing up intentions when they concerned his poems, but always polite, composed, and reticent in the presence of strangers. He rarely ventured to speak on subjects beyond his interest—and they were anything but narrow—nor did he discuss current politics unless the issues were definitely vital.[43] He spoke clearly, always articulating his thoughts with utter precision, and when the company was stimulating and eager to listen, he would elaborate a point at length, exhibiting logical vigor and vast erudition. Much of the effect on his listeners he owed to the marvelous control of his hands and facial expressions and, more especially, the fascinating intonation of his speech, due to his unusual accent, a mixture of Constantinopolitan idioms and English vocalisms. His entire mode of life had something of a minor ritual to it, calculated, intended, meant to entice, to engage attention and lead to admiration. Uncontrolled expression of feeling and spontaneity disturbed him as would any instance of bad taste. In his style of life, just as in his poetry, he imitated nothing. He remained peculiar, unique, elusive, self-centered, a master of his many masks. In a word, he was inimitable.

    He studied many of his contemporaries, English and French writers and poets, remained impressively abreast of literary movements and fashionable currents, and was influenced by none. His appreciation of the work of others, especially after the writing of his *Ars Poetica,* remained balanced, distant, and one of thoughtfully distilled judgment. His personal library reflected his range

---

    [43]One notable exception is his reaction to the newspaper reports on the events leading to the massacre of the Greek population of Asia Minor and the burning of Smyrna by the Turks in 1922. K. N. Constantinidis, who was with the poet at that time, writes: "I can never forget with what agony he followed the heartbreaking news about the Asia Minor debacle." I have used for the translation the text in the *C. P. Cavafy: Commemorative Issue,* ed. M. Vayanos (Athens, 1973): 13.

of readings. Most major authors were there, the classical Greeks and Romans as well as the modern classics in poetry, history, politics, philosophy, fiction, folklore, biography, theatre. The collection of books was rather selective. He bought books rather conservatively. A large number of them came from his friend P. Anastassiadis, others were gifts from admirers or autographed copies from authors. His biographer Peridis mentions that the collection included more than twenty volumes of erotica. Cavafy was a careful and critical reader, often making marginal notes on passages of direct interest to his work.

Cavafy left a body of 154 approved poems. In addition to these are the 24 he published between 1886 and 1896, which were later rejected. The total of published poems came to 177. A large number of unpublished poems, about seventy-five, have come to light since his death; copies of some he had given to friends, but most of them were found in his archives. They were brought together, edited and arranged in chronological order of composition by G. Savidis, and published in 1968. Not included in this edition were thirty "plans" or "sketches" for poems which the poet never managed to cast in verse form. Notably, 22 of these "plans" were written between 1921 and 1932; it may well be that Cavafy had these in mind when he said in the year before he died that he had twenty-five more poems to write. The record shows that his oldest poem was written in 1882 and the last in 1933, a span of fifty-nine years of poetic activity. Valuable though these unfinished compositions may be for understanding his poetic development, they confirm what we already know. For the specialist or devotee they offer supplementary touches to the well-wrought edifice the poet bequeathed us.

Cavafy was never uncertain about his artistic mission, nor modest about his poetry. He was his own critic in more ways than one. He passed technical judgment on his poems every time he reworked them to meet the standards of mastery he had so painstakingly articulated. He provided the appropriate clues for correct interpretation of thematic content. And finally, he showed no hesitation whatsoever when the moment came to state his own evaluative judgment. Cavafy was determined to leave nothing so important to accident, to his contemporaries or any future public. The opportunity came one day when in the bookstore of S. Pargas, someone representing a French periodical approached the poet to give his own opinion on his work. Cavafy, it appeared, had gone to the interview well prepared. He took a note from his pocket and dictated in French what he wanted to say. The alert Mrs. Pargas reacted quickly and took down the entire statement *verbatim et literatim*. No one seems to know whether it was ever printed. The Pargas copy was given to M. Peridis years after the poet died, and was published for the first time in 1963:

> I do not share the opinion of those who contend that the work of Cavafy, being one of its kind and not pertaining to any of the known schools, will forever remain a specialty, so to say, in poetry, and will never have imitators.
>
> Imitators, truly superficial for the most part, I already discover, and not only among the Greek poets. Rare but striking examples of Cavafy's influence have more or less been noted everywhere. It is a natural consequence of every work of value and progress.
>
> Cavafy, in my opinion, is an ultra-modern poet, a poet of the future generations. Aside from his historical, psychological and philosophical value, the sobriety of his impeccable style which at times verges on the laconic, his balanced enthusiasm arousing intellectual emotion, his accurate phrase resulting from an aristocratic naturalness, his light irony, are elements which the future generations will appreciate even more, once impelled by the progress of discoveries and the subtlety of their own mental mechanism.
>
> When that time comes, rare poets like Cavafy will occupy a prominent place in a world more mindful than that of today. Because of these facts, I maintain that his work will not be forgotten locked up in the libraries as a historical document, as part of the development of Greek Literature.[44]

Had this statement been printed at the time it was dictated none but his most ardent admirers could have hailed it as prophetic. If nothing else, it would have sufficed to silence the other side which never tired of calling Cavafy the poet of death, decadence and doom.

---

[44] I have used the text in Cavafy, *Unpublished Prose Texts*, (1963): 82-85. Alexiou 1983, gives a slightly different translation of paragraph 3: "Cavafy in my opinion is an ultra modern poet, a poet of the future generations. In addition to his historical, psychological and philosophical worth, the fastidiousness of his style, which at times verges on the laconic, his measured enthusiasm, which arouses mental excitement, his correct syntax, the consequence of an aristocratic disposition, are elements which generations of the future will enjoy even more, impelled by the progress of discoveries and by the subtlety of their mental process" (9).

Chapter Four

The Long Shadow of Symbolism

1. The Beginnings. 2. The Encounter with Symbolism. 3. The Two "Correspondences": Baudelaire and Cavafy. 4. Prisoner of the Familiar Garden. 5. Two Poetic Worlds: Parallel or Asymptotic? 6. Severing the Weak Ties.

1. The Beginnings

Cavafy wrote his first exercise in verse before he reached twenty. There is little, if anything, of poetic quality present in the first three poems he wrote in 1882 in English. His years of study as an adolescent in a private school in England added significantly to his mastery of that language. His proficiency in it, more so than in Greek, held promise as a medium for literary work but he decided to turn to the latter for the creative work of his life. The beginnings were considerably modest and without much promise. When in Constantinople, he wrote to his friend Mikes Rallis a letter on December 12, 1883, asking him to copy a poem by Alfred Tennyson; most likely it was the "Ulysses," part of which Cavafy translated into Greek in 1894 (C 87). Between 1882 and 1884, he wrote several poems and also translated in a somewhat free style poems by an unknown French poet and some lines (62-74) from Shakespeare's *Much Ado About Nothing*, (Booklet 13). To the youthful first poems he wrote in Greek while in Constantinople [among them "Like a Generation of Flowers," (Οἵαπερ Φύλλων Γενεή), revised later and published in 1895 under the title, "The Elegy of Flowers" ('Η ἐλεγεία τῶν λουλουδιῶν: CP 37), and "Niochori" (Νιοχῶρι: U 15)], we must add the "Bacchic" (Βακχικόν, 1885?/*1886*: CP 17) and "The Poet and the Muse" ('Ο Ποιητὴς καὶ ἡ Μοῦσα, 1885?/*1886*: CP 18), all of which he later rejected.

In the fall of 1885, the family returned to Alexandria and settled in a new residence. Without doubt, it was a time-consuming chore with little leisure for poetry and studies. The records he kept for the year 1886 list the publication of three poems but no new compositions.[1] It is quite likely, however, that he composed one poem, although not mentioned in the list: "Memory" (Μνήμη), which was published ten years later, in 1896, in the *Asty*. He rejected the early version of this poem but decided to revise it in 1905 and changed the title to "Thessaly". Still not satisfied with that new version, he revised it once more in 1911. It was published in its final form and with a new title: "Ionic" ('Ιωνικόν).

Sometime before June 1886, Cavafy translated Lady Anne Lindsay-Barnard's (1750-1825) popular ballad "Auld Robin Gray" (1771), gave it the Greek title "Μάταιος, Μάταιος Ἔρως" (="Futile, Futile Love"), and published it in June 1886.[2] He also worked on two brief essays, "The Coral from a Mythological Point of View," and "The Inhuman Friends of Animals," both in Greek, and published them in 1886.[3]

We know very little about Cavafy's activities between August 1886 and October 1891. Although information is lacking that would allow us to reconstruct his literary record, if there was one, the main events in his life of this rather barren period have been successfully related by R. Liddell.[4] Suddenly in June 1891 Cavafy writes a (lost) poem, ("Images" or "Icons"), and spends the next month correcting various poems. In August he writes the poem "Correspondence According to Baudelaire" (Ἀλληλουχία). It remained unknown until Savidis printed the text in his *The Cavafian Editions* (1966).

The year 1891 was special for Cavafy.[5] While he sought to reach a broader range of poetic themes, his prose writings, mainly brief essays and reviews, showed a widening of interests to cover vital concerns about tradition,

---

[1] See the list in Cavafy, *Unpublished Poems*, 1966: 18.

[2] Text in Cavafy, *Condemned Poems* (1983): 122-6.

[3] Reprinted in Cavafy, *Prose* (1963): 9-22.

[4] Liddell 1974: 49-61; esp. ch. III, "Return to Alexandria."

[5] Ilinskaya 1983, agrees that the year 1891 was a "special landmark marking the beginning of a new career no longer marred with blind acceptance of importations and imitation of alien styles" (44). The thesis is well argued and it indicates how fruitful it would be to use it to explore Cavafy's relation to the tenets of Symbolism.

language and culture. In April 1891 he published two essays in which he advocated the return of the Elgin Marbles to Greece.[6] The strongly worded message defending the demand for Greece to recover her national treasures, the review of P. Gritsanis' treatise on poetic metrics, and the article on the views of the English classicist J. Blackie (1809-1895) on the continuity of the Greek language, together form a solid list of inquiries in an area that anticipates the development of a lasting devotion to the study of history and the idea of national identity as encompassing all phases of Hellenism, from early antiquity to the present. The genuineness of his patriotic feelings expressed in those pieces cannot be questioned any more than his sincere admiration for the greatness of the classical achievement. His writings display a heightened sensitivity that lasted undiminished over the years in the face of Greece's national misfortunes, adverse events and his own personal disappointments. Nor was this sense of loyalty ever displaced in favor of other current affections as it happened in the case of some of his former schoolmates and friends who either grew indifferent to the tradition or proved quick to embrace the fashionable cosmopolitan values.[7]

The ink on the manuscript of his own version of Baudelaire's "Correspondances" and "Builders" had hardly dried when he wrote in a brief essay "Byzantine Poets," occasioned by D. Vikelas' review of K. Krumbacher's *Geschichte der byzantinischen Literatur von Justinian bis zum Ende des oströmischen Reiches* (527-1453), the following paragraph:

> We Greeks have an obligation to study our poetry with the attention it deserves—the poetry of every period of our national life. We will find in our poetry the genius of our people, all the tenderness and the most invaluable

---

[6] The text in Cavafy, *Prose* (1963): 9-22.

[7] Peridis 1948: 28-29, raised the question whether the adolescent Cavafy actually shared the "anti-Hellenic" attitude, however shallow, of his friend Pericles Rallis. Peridis thinks that Cavafy never harbored similar feelings. Papoutsakis, the editor of Cavafy's early prose writings, notes that Cavafy's opinion regarding "the genius of our people" never changed, although later on it was toned down somewhat. His greatest pride, writes Papoutsakis, "was phyletic, and it was nourished by his constant readings of historical works, to which his own poetic imagination added something aesthetic." See Cavafy, *Prose* (1963): 49-50, marginalium.

heartbeats of Hellenism.[8]

He borrows a few phrases from Vikelas's review and goes on to state his reflections on the quality and value of Byzantine poetry, pointing out that "we Greeks do not know who our Byzantine poets are and why they are worth studying." He refers to them as "the connecting link between the glory of our ancient poets and the grace and golden hopes and aspirations of our contemporaries."[9] Filled with so ardent a love for his own artistic and cultural traditions, he ventured out to meet the leading spokesmen, mainly poets and historians, of the modern European experience on a one-to-one basis.

Cavafy's spiritual wanderings in the European space of literary ideas and currents proved rather temporary, despite the beneficial effect they had on his career. Whatever grounds he covered during his wanderings, he still yearned for the return. This multifaceted feeling of *nostos* may also be related to an awareness of "loss," the deep sense of which has been masterfully discussed by Keeley 1976, arguing that the longing to return to a state of existence that could do justice to the human condition, was vividly portrayed in Cavafy's latest poems. Evidently, Cavafy was consistent on this point. In fact, during the first phase of his literary career we see him returning to the Grecian tradition of *Logos*-reason and at the same time pressing for the return of the Elgin Marbles. Person and art went hand in hand longing to return to the spiritual land to which the poet felt both belong. In his thoughts, he would address, even defy, obstacles that appeared formidable or simply impossible to overcome. His advocacy for the return of the Elgin Marbles, quite understandably, went unheeded. At a more personal level, his misperception of the city during the crisis period added to his feeling of self-imprisonment the certainty that all exits were forever blocked. It was a period of depression casting a long shadow on the mood of the themes in the poems "The City," "The Windows," "The Satrapy" and others. On the practical side of diurnal affairs, and without the fanfare of wailing statements, Cavafy decided to drop his English citizenship as part of his preparation to "return" to Alexandria. He became officially a Hellene and poetically a *Hellenikos*.

---

[8] Cavafy, *Prose* (1963): 50.

[9] Ibid., 43-44.

Yet he never took up permanent residence in Greece.

2. The Encounter with Symbolism

Cavafy's encounter with Symbolism, the tenets of the movement and the poetry of Charles Baudelaire, was one of the most significant events in the early career of our poet. Like Baudelaire, but for different reasons, he did not retreat to an Ivory Tower. On the negative side, the encounter complicated his determination to clarify the goals of his poetic mission. At that time, Cavafy was innocent of the complex nature and of the difficulties attending the search for an aesthetic guide to launch a literary career. In 1891, he was projecting his goals with the mentality of an unsuspecting citizen curiously unaware of the covert pitfalls of public life in the cosmopolis. Not yet stung by the restlessness and the emptiness that could set in with the first signs of alienation, he clung to a lofty idealism. He was carrying deep in his heart the lessons he had learned from his teacher, Papazis, trusting that somewhere in the present the prospects of the dream to live in the well-founded city of ideas were still lurking regardless of their fate for the future generations. He was Greek in his outlook and European enough to believe that the modern mood could engender novel ways to recapture the lofty style of the classical past and with a new spurt of creativity.

The details of his initial encounter with the Symbolist movement and at what point in his life he first felt the impact of Charles Baudelaire's aesthetics and poetry, along with the significance of Edgar Allan Poe's theory of composition, have not been preserved. We have little to go by to reconstruct the story.[10] Since Cavafy does not refer to Baudelaire in his prose writings of this period, his encounter with Symbolism can only be related through the "translation" that was found among his unpublished poems of Baudelaire's famous sonnet "Correspondances":

> La Nature est un temple où de vivants piliers
> Laissent parfois sortir de confuses paroles;
> L'homme y passe à travers des forêts de symboles
> Qui l'observent avec des regards familiers.

---

[10] Comp. Savidis 1966: 139-41 on the influence of Symbolism and Parnassianism.

> Comme de longs échos qui de loin se confondent
> Dans une ténébreuse et profonde unité,
> Vaste comme la nuit et comme la clarté,
> Les parfums, les couleurs et les sons se répondent.
>
> Il est des parfums frais comme des chairs d'enfants,
> Doux comme des hautbois, vert comme les prairies,
> —Et d'autres, corrompus, riches et triomphants,
>
> Ayant l'expansion des choses infinies,
> Comme l'ambre, le musc, le benjoin et l'encens,
> Qui chantent les transports de l'esprit et des sens.[11]

The relation of Cavafy's early poetry to the Symbolist movement and Baudelaire in particular deserves special consideration, if only for the reason that tenets of the movement reached Alexandria as well as Athens. We now have evidence that Baudelaire, in particular, exerted a certain influence on Cavafy's development more so than the Parnassian poets. Cavafy's flirtation with Romanticism and Parnassianism lasted only a brief period and virtually ended around 1903, when he took the decisive step to review his technique and revise as many of the salvageable poems as possible. The "philosophical"

---

[11]
> Nature is a temple from whose living columns
> Commingling voices emerge at times;
> Here man wanders through forests of symbols
> Which seem to observe with familiar eyes.
>
> Like long-drawn echoes afar converging
> In harmonies darksome and profound,
> Vast as the night and vast as light,
> Colors, scents and sounds correspond.
>
> There are fragrances fresh as the flesh of children,
> Sweet as the oboe, green as the prairie,
> —And others overpowering, rich and corrupt,
>
> Possessing the pervasiveness of everlasting things
> Like benjamin, frankincense, amber, myrrh,
> Which the raptures of the senses and the spirit sing.
>   (Translation by Kate Flores)

basis for the revisions is treated in detail in chapter 7, but suffice it to say at this point that certain romantic traits that survived and may be discerned in some of the post-1903 poems cannot be regarded as having any significance as determinants of style or content. Of the three aforementioned "schools" of poetry, Symbolism came closest to occupying a special place in his mode of expression and understanding of the poetic tasks.

A piece of solid evidence concerning the place of Baudelaire in Cavafy's early work came to light when Savidis published his *The Cavafian Editions* in 1966, and again when in 1968 he brought to light and printed a collection of poems Cavafy had kept hidden from the public eye. Probably Cavafy saved some of those poems with the intention of salvaging some for "future" use or even "publication," and others for personal reasons though they were hardly salvageable at all. Some of these "unpublished" poems were written as early as 1884. One can understand why their publication, particularly the early ones, would have embarrassed the poet had they been released during his lifetime. The printing of these compositions proved to be an invaluable source of information and an indispensable guide to understand Cavafy's development. Savidis included in the edition of the *Unpublished Poems* chronological data, variants of verses and other pertinent information.

Cavafy's acquaintance with Baudelaire's poetry and the Symbolist movement was known to his critics. What had not been made public, except perhaps to his intimate friends, was that Cavafy had translated as early as August 1891 one of Baudelaire's most influential poems, the sonnet "Correspondances." Savidis printed the text of the translation for the first time in an article in which he discussed the early phases of Cavafy's development and the poet's search for guideposts to identify the periods of his creative work. He showed that criticism now could make use of an available and reliable key to analyze the earlier transitional phases of Cavafy's poetry. The key was the until then unknown and unpublished poem titled "Correspondance According to Baudelaire" (1891: U 19).[12]

---

[12]"Ἀλληλουχία κατὰ τὸν Βωδελαίρον." See the December 1967 issue of *Nea Estia* dedicated to Charles Baudelaire, commemorating the centenary since his death, especially the three studies of the place of Baudelaire in Greek poetry by P. Karavias, H. Klaras and M. Demakis. The latter identified a common strand between Baudelaire and Cavafy but gave no indication that he had read Cavafy's "translation." He notes: "Baudelaire and Cavafy, as each moves from poem to poem, working with different data, offer whole worlds that continue to

The fact that Cavafy had become familiar with the work of Baudelaire before most of his contemporaries in Greece does not answer the question of influences. Savidis 1966, carefully avoided the issue of influence but went as far as to say that the available evidence shows that Cavafy was basically adjusting to his own needs both the Baudelairian view of action, as suggested in *Les Fleurs du mal*, and the theory behind the "Correspondances." Savidis' main conclusion was that Cavafy built on that theory his own poetics in 1891, which proved to be the first formulation of the idea of "the work in progress" (177). The point is well taken, but it does not remove the lingering problem of the extent and quality of influence. The question is whether the translation of a singular poem, no matter how central it became to the entire Symbolist movement, was so fundamental to Cavafy's groping for a theory of poetics as to account for the first formulation. In this connection Savidis is right in saying that for the correct answer one would have to include the full body of ideas that run through the entire *Les Fleurs du mal*, not just the "Correspondances." The reference to "action" indicates arrangement of the outcomes of poetic productivity in a continuity that reflects awareness of the creative process as the work moves toward qualitative completion and thematic cohesion. Whereas in Baudelaire the contours and the content of action are clear, Cavafy, at the time he was translating and paraphrasing Baudelaire, felt tempted to adopt the idea of action, as Savidis meant it. His verse reflected the beginning rather than the conscious crystallization of a point of view. At any rate there can be no doubt that in 1891 Cavafy attempted the selective assimilation of features from Baudelaire.

The text shows that Cavafy builds on Baudelaire's poem by incorporating a foreign poem into his own composition. On a broader scale, and here Savidis is right again, Cavafy receives and adopts as he moves forward from poem to poem, following the very principle of "work in progress" on which his work will depend for its organic unity. But there is a difference in intentions between the two poets, especially as it relates to the place the translation occupies in Cavafy's own poem.

Baudelaire once asked himself the question: "Why does one poet

---

grow and become more complete. As we approach the end of their unique work, we have the feeling that these poets satiate us with their worlds. We grow richer in sensitivity and fuller in understanding of human events that no other poet even with voluminous works can help us do" (971). Translation mine.

translate another?" and gave the following answer: "Because he resembles me." He had in mind Edgar Allan Poe.[13] We have nothing to go by when it comes to explaining Cavafy's motivation to undertake the translation of "Correspondances." A suggestion is hinted in one of the verses where the phrase "accidental magnetic nearness" occurs. It may be taken to mean "resemblance" or "closeness," but this is only a guess and it should be used with caution. We would be on firmer grounds if we read it as intended to refer to a certain receptivity of appealing features of Symbolism. But again, one cannot be too sure. There may be reservations and objections to this way of stating the motive. But on the whole one fares better by appealing to poetic experiences and convictions. One could, for instance, introduce at this juncture a difference between the idea of "voyage" as Baudelaire expressed it and as Cavafy understood it, not as this motif was recast in his "Ithaka," in 1910, but as he expressed it three years later in January 1894, when he wrote "The Second Odyssey," and in conjunction with the prose piece, written three months later, "The End of Odysseus."[14]

It is difficult to trace with accuracy the connections between the views he expressed in 1910 and his poetic stance in 1891, but the surrounding lines he composed to envelop the Baudelairian poem allow for useful comparisons, as we shall see. Whatever the similarities and the differences, the fact is that there is enough evidence to show that Cavafy, unlike his contemporaries on the mainland, did not come under the spell of Baudelaire's *Les Fleurs du mal*. In this regard, Pieris 1982, has convincingly argued that "Cavafy's path crosses theirs [viz. the Parnassian and Symbolist themes and poetics], particularly the second, actively." In essence he agrees with Savidis.

We now return to the question of influences. A comment Cavafy made about Baudelaire allows us to delimit the points of contact and place them between two dates: 1891 and 1907. In view of the paucity of information, everything counts here, including the title of the Cavafian 1891 poem, namely that it is not a literal rendering of the French "Correspondances." While it may be merely accidental, it may also be viewed as a sign alerting the reader

---

[13] Quoted in Beebe 1964: 129, n29.

[14] Cavafy 1974: reprinted in Savidis 1987, with introduction and notes. The Cavafian "voyage" motif is fully discussed in ch. 10, "The New Voyage: Ithaka."

to an important device: Cavafy's intention to proceed conceptually in a direction of his own, one that while acknowledging 'correspondences' and admitting a relation to the original, also seeks to preclude the impression that an identity of pursuit is at work. Years later, in September 1907, he wrote:

> Tonight I was reading about Baudelaire. The author of the book was somewhat epaté [shocked] about *Les Fleurs du mal*. It has been some time since I last read *Les Fleurs du mal*. From what I remember, I did not find the poems so shocking [epatants]. It seems to me that Baudelaire was locked in a very narrow circle of pleasure. Last night unexpectedly, or last Wednesday, and so many other times / I lived / and did / and fantasized, and silently arranged far stranger satisfactions (*apolauseis*). 22. 9. '07.[15]

All we know about the author of the book is that he was French. More important is Cavafy's view on the topic of emotions as he relates his reading of the book to his own experiences. Baudelaire had ceased to surprise him in 1907. But what is more important is that the intensity and quality of pleasure conveyed through the poetry of Baudelaire no longer compared favorably to his own personal experiences, which are mentioned in the note but not named. The gist of the remark—alluding to sexuality—is that Baudelaire was tied to "a narrow circle of pleasure." By 1907 the two features of pleasure, intensity and quality, were lifted to the heights of valuational criteria. In the meantime, Cavafy had begun to write hedonic poems, particularly since the early years of the first decade of 1900. Therefore, even before 1907, Cavafy was more than ready to underscore the limitations of Baudelaire's erotic thematics and view the poet "from above."[16]

Despite the distancing Cavafy felt from Baudelaire's thematics, the influence that was exerted during his early poetic phase and perhaps even later is not easy to ignore. In 1891, Cavafy approached the "Correspandances" in a manner that indicates a certain affinity, but it is one that holds a surprise for the reader who undertakes a close inspection of what Cavafy does with this poem. The first thing to be noticed is that Cavafy encloses his translation of

---

[15] Cavafy 1983: 42; bibliographical references in Pieris 1982: 62, n1.

[16] The expression 'from above' with reference to Cavafy's superior feelings, in Savidis 1983: 175, n23, "Comment."

the sonnet within verses of his own. The reader begins to suspect that this conscious move on Cavafy's part is intended to incorporate that poem within a composition of his own. It is a case of appropriation within the limits of propriety. Cavafy selects this foreign sonnet to project comparable sentiments and personal feelings as well as personal attainment. The poem is projected as a literary act conspicuously deviating from the model of strict translational work. Secondly, Cavafy breaks up the sonnet form and interferes with the motif. Thirdly, we know from Cavafy's readings of that period that he was well informed on the art of versification and had attached much seriousness to observing its rules. Thus one is tempted to conclude that the interference was neither accidental nor the result of artistic ineptitude.[17]

This departure from the original strengthens the suspicion that translational fidelity was not his real purpose. As will be shown later, Cavafy was hardly moved by the Baudelairian metaphysical agony. Rather, he remained aloof towards Baudelaire's psychological and religious convictions, although it is clear that he shared many features of Baudelaire's aesthetic orientation. Finally, as can be discerned from the poems Cavafy wrote prior to the 1891 rendition of "Correspondances," especially from the poem "Logos and Silence," written shortly before his own "Correspondence," Cavafy had gained confidence in the expressive power of logos-reason bringing him closer to "truth, life and immortality," ideas that have received their formulations through the exercise of Greek rationality rather than Gothic mysticism. Absent from Cavafy's ideational world is not only the mysticism of Baudelaire but also the inexpressible world of the beyond. The poem "Logos and Silence," to the extent that it is representative and free of self-deception, shows that Cavafy had shed some of the inferiority and trepidation he had felt when he was writing the poem "The Poet and the Muse." It also suggests that five years later he was both ready and confident to create the work which the Muse ordered him to make in 1885. "Logos and Silence" carried him beyond the strictures of "The Poet and the Muse." He felt compelled to declare his readiness to undertake the grand mission.

---

[17]Cavafy seems to have been familiar with the work and technique of Victor Hugo who had experimented with the caesura and introduced "enjambement," i.e. the extending of a sentence over to the next line. Needless to say that this was a departure from the rigor of the traditional verse restricting the sentence to the length of the Alexandrian verse of a single line, twelve syllables with a caesura after the sixth.

3. The Two "Correspondances"

A close look at the vocabulary Cavafy used to render in Greek Baudelaire's idea of "correspondances" makes the reader suspect that faithful translation was not his primary purpose. The differences are significant for the understanding of what Cavafy apparently had in mind to accomplish. The nuance of "interconnections" the French term communicates to the reader, even when it is not silenced in the translation, is less prominent in the Greek text. The noun ἀλληλουχία (sequence), in the singular, is offered for the French plural 'correspondances.' The interference is also noticed in the handling of the title. The reader is led to suspect that Cavafy intended to maintain a certain degree of independence from the original in order to create something of his own, though not totally discontinuous with the original. The alterations were probably planned but without the introduction of arbitrary features. Actually, the spectrum of meanings in Baudelaire's poem has not been distorted, and hence the requirement for translation has not been compromised. However that may be, the plan for a poem to encompass another poem is evident from the opening verses of Cavafy's prologue.

Upon close inspection it seems that "correspondence," rather than being denied, is actually reinforced and introduced at another level: a sequence between two poems suggesting a shared sensibility between the two poets and an affinity of sensuous thought. The central question now becomes: What precisely did Cavafy hope to accomplish by translating Baudelaire? If we exclude faithfulness of translation, subscription to the tenets of Symbolism, or the need to express agreement with the Baudelairian system of values, then the answer must be sought elsewhere. For one thing, Cavafy gives no signs in 1891 of having studied Baudelaire to gain mastery of his values and ideas. For another, there are no indications that he was consciously seeking to follow fashionable trends or literary movements. Whatever the answer, the fact remains that Cavafy opens the poem with verses of his own:

> The perfumes inspire me like music,
> like rhythm does, and like beautiful words,
> and I rejoice when Baudelaire
> interprets with harmonious verses
> all those things which the soul dimly
> feels in sterile emotions.

The sentiments are those of Cavafy and only incidentally, one surmises, Baudelaire's. Certain differences with reference to perfumes, music, rhythm, beautiful expressions/words are silenced. Baudelaire speaks only of colors, sounds and perfumes. The inclusive "sounds" (les sons) are broken into music, rhythm and words. One cannot help but think of comparing here the elusive and metaphysical status of aromas and their dominant place in Baudelaire's "Correspondances," on the one hand, and what Cavafy does with aromas in this translation and in many of his own poems, on the other. One notes, for instance, how concrete and evocatively erotic the aromas have become in the poem "Ithaka" and other compositions. Cavafy creates the strong impression that a memory, at once sensual and sensuous, is as much visual as it is musical, and that it is profoundly tied to the sense of smelling through the effects of select perfumes.

There is no room in the prologue for a separate *persona*, as is the case in the "The Poet and the Muse." Baudelaire is basically a source of enjoyment.[18] The presence of certain ideas and sentiments, not directly derived from Baudelaire's poem, may be taken as intended indications that Cavafy's composition must be taken seriously in the sense that the sonnet is incidental to the passion to express the poet's comparative superiority vis-a-vis the sensibility of the ordinary person. There is nothing new about this belief except for the appeal to a different framework to justify the conviction. It refers to the artist's expressive powers and unusual perception of things no one else can see or even suspect such things exist.

In contrast to Cavafy's opening verses, where the lyrical "ego" introduces the thought, in Baudelaire's sonnet the ego is submerged. It speaks from afar as if intoning an apocalyptic truth: Nature is seen as a temple, and it is as though its pillars, utter with the power of symbols in the manner of a primordial speaker, though not as the voice of "God," and there human beings

---

[18]Ilinskaya 1983, believes that Cavafy expressed excessive admiration for the great skills of Baudelaire. Actually all that Cavafy says in lines 3-4 is "I rejoice . . ." It does not necessarily follow from the admission of agreeable feelings that "Cavafy also accepts the symbolist correspondence between the graceless objective world, where human beings grope for a wearisome path, and the world of dreams and memories, that could offer them for a while rays of light from its source" (45). This way of understanding Cavafy's position, Ilinskaya contends, is valid once we admit that Cavafy's development in fact proceeds from a pure anti-realism and advances toward a realist position.

walk through a forest of symbols; the latter stare at them with familiar glances; and at the end, where finally all converge and seem to fuse into a unity—"tenebreuse et profonde"—all the opposites disappear. Baudelaire means to project deep personal convictions.[19]

Nature contains within itself both innocence and corruption, and only by transcending both can one touch the spirit of God. Corruption builds its nest in the heart of purity, and purity gives birth to corruption. Nature-Temple is always God's creation, but so are human beings. The latter, being transient, sensual pedestrians, pass through the correspondences of things and symbols trying to perceive the secrets of the parallel sets in their ultimate unity. Baudelaire's sonnet closes without the surfacing of the lyrical *persona*; pythian in tone, it speaks as the alter ego and partner to the vision.

Cavafy takes over again after the sonnet has done its work. The lyrical "ego" resumes the theme of the prologue, and proceeds to complement it with a concluding declarative note on the nature of the poet's mission. The gist of the epilogue is a message to the world. It informs the reader of the profound difference between poets and the "other human beings," those of a lower type of sensitivity, the "many," who lack the piercing glance of the poet. An abyss separates "the others" and the poet. The former move in a "dark paradise"—the bliss of ignorance?—but a paradise nevertheless. To the poets, nature is the "familiar garden,"—a notion brought in to replace Baudelaire's "La Nature est un temple." In essence, the thirteen verses of the epilogue, mainly the unity of the last ten, comprise an explanation for the contrast as much as they are a compassionate representation of the limited mode of

---

[19]Beebe 1964, notes that Baudelaire assumed three roles: "The dandy becomes an esthete; the demon is no longer an experimenter in vice, but a Gilles de Rais or Marquis de Sade; and the visionary in Baudelaire, so easily reconciled with Christianity and the Hermetic tradition, is carried beyond the search for a hidden spiritual reality which is outside him to the point where he achieves a descent into the neant which is both within and beyond the 'I'. The major difference is that whereas Baudelaire wore all three of the masks, few of his followers were able to combine more than two" (139-40). The point is of interest as it provides us with a way to consider the parallel to Cavafy, who made masks for his own use and for his *personae*, as we see in poems that speak of concealment of the *persona*'s deeper desires and forbidden pursuits. It contrasts rather sharply with the role of masks in Baudelaire. Cavafy's motive for propounding masks to hide one's real face behind them, is on the whole erotic and hedonic. It is a protective shield against the aggressive and hostile attitudes of the puritan and the frantic anti-hedonist.

grasping of the sensual possibilities wasted in the dark paradise of "the others."

> Believe not only what you see.
>
> The poets' glance is sharper.
>
> Nature is to them a familiar garden.
>
> In dark paradise human beings,
> the others, feel out a tortuous path.
> And only the flash, which sometimes like a spark
> short-lived brightens their way
> in the night, yields a certain quick sensation
> of an accidental magnetic nearness—
> a brief nostalgia, thrill of a moment,
> dream in the hour of dawn, a joy
> uncaused suddenly flowing
> in the heart and suddenly fleeing.

In Cavafy's epilogue all the metaphysical elements of Baudelaire's "Correspondances" have been carefully brushed aside; presumably they were not needed. It gives the impression that the poet has fully tasted the suggestive flavor of the original "Correspondances," saw agreement with the idea of "the sharper glance of the poet," and used the opportunity to build on it. It is not clear from the epilogue that the motive was to admit a deeper affinity and continuity with French Symbolism and Baudelaire's world. The fact that he paraphrases rather than translates, and also the flanking of the rendition he did of the original with the adding of two units of his own, the prologue and the epilogue, support the inference that Cavafy had in mind a plan for a poem that would help him create a mood and ambience of his own. In any event, there is no logical transition from the "translation" to the epilogue, like the one connecting the prologue to the sonnet. The epilogue pictures Cavafy enlisting Baudelaire's assistance to see with a clearer eye the perceptual and sensual limits of the "common man," in contrast to the poet who, by transcending them, is free of errors and compromises. If so, Cavafy's overarching goal was to find a powerful ally in his effort to posit the privileged existence and sensibility of the poet. And even beyond that, to project the value of the poet's superb contribution as builder and co-worker in the construction of culture, independently of the historical participation in the securing of Progress, as conceived in the "Builders." And here again, we find another point of contrast between the two poets. Baudelaire was against industry and progress; he called them "despotic enemies of all poetry" in his 1859 critical essay on Théophile Gautier.[20]

Baudelaire's sonnet gave Cavafy the opportunity he needed to further the thinking that alerted him to the problem of the self-consciousness of the poet. From that point on he had to strengthen the means to refine the conviction about his unique stature as an artist, as a human being, select and different, apart from the multitudes who live as prisoners of their limited sensibility within the confines of a dark paradise.

Repeated in the epilogue are all those things the Muse told the poet in the 1885 poem and again in "Logos and Silence." There is nothing here that catapults the idea to a doctrine of unusual value. Cavafy is simply repeating self-assuring beliefs. And he continues to speak about convictions he had embraced from the time he wrote his first poems, added here with only slight variations of the phrastic cliches to which artists invariably resort when the urge to underscore the special place they deserve in the world becomes insufferable. Although there is nothing novel about the conviction that the poet is a privileged entity, Cavafy found the perfect opportunity to confirm it along with his connection with "the spirit of the Symbolist tradition."[21]

---

[20]*Oeuvres Complète*, édition de la Pleiade, Paris, 1961: 700. For the diverse meanings in Baudelaire about progress, see Cyril and Lilian Welch 1973: 30-31. Baudelaire raised serious doubts about the continuation of progress. "Infinite progress might be humanity's most ingenious and cruel torture" (*Oeuvres*, 958-59). He also said: "I understand by progress the progressive diminution of soul and the progressive domination of matter" (1032-33). Beebe 1964: 132, quotes Baudelaire: "There cannot be any Progress . . . except within the individual and by the individual himself" [*Intimate Journals* 27].

[21]The expression in Ilinskaya 1983: 44. The strong impression of this connection which Ilinskaya's characterization conveys is softened further down, where she writes: "However, the proximity with the Parnassians and the Symbolists will never take the form of membership in the school, or full acceptance of its aesthetic program" (59). Haas 1984, has discussed this connection in an original way. Haas and Ilinskaya have given two different views on the central thesis which Savidis 1966 first stated regarding Cavafy's going from Romanticism to Symbolism: ". . . in the first revision, we saw a fallen "aesthete" founding his poetics on the essentially anti-social theory of Baudelaire concerning the mystical or secret correspondence of Nature (a correspondence which, as Cavafy declares, only the poet can grasp) about the

It remains to be seen whether Cavafy's relation to the Symbolist tradition was one of direct influence, whether Cavafy felt an affinity with Symbolism, due to shared interests, and whether he discovered in its tenets new truths about the nature of poetry and the mission of the poet.

4. Prisoner of the Familiar Garden

In 1891 Cavafy, still working with Romantic vestiges, was not ready to see that nature was not something to be innocently branded a "familiar garden" for the poet's evening walks and morning browsings. It did not take long for "nature" to be removed from his thematic cycle. Comparably, he had taken for granted the unfathomable depths of his sensibility. By relying so heavily on his subjective states and indulging contrived feelings about "familiar gardens" and other unreal entities that he let crowd his imagination, he was actually courting the imprisonment of his more genuine desires. Evidently, there was no external support to help him clear the air to avoid winding up, as he did, captive of his own contraptions described in the semi-dirge songs of "Windows" and other poems of the crisis period. As though punished for the innocence of 1891, he found himself within a few years in a situation worse than that of the non-poets who inhabit the "dark paradise." Cavafy was convinced that he had the glance of the poet and that he could exercise it at will to bring only rewards and no punishments.

Baudelaire was far better prepared than Cavafy for the encounter with "nature" and the challenge of sin. But Cavafy did not suspect that he was heading in a direction that would require of him a descent of the rungs on the ladder of guilt, one by one, a slow voyage into the psyche's internal Inferno. Later, when he put some order in his actions and retrieved the memories of his eroticism, he actually learned how to avoid the entrapments which the psychology of Symbolism had provided for the covering of guilt under the illusion of poetic privileges. Only then could he move forward to recover his right to be an Alexandrian and claim openly the world of feelings and emotions that was his from the start. During the descent Cavafy was using his imagination to compete with the diverse schools of poetry, the established

---

futility of Progress" (196). Also Seferis 1974, v. 1: 325.

names, and the preaching of their tenets, eager to set up a parallel cosmos of his own. What he created was an artifact unsuitable for the cultivation of the rare flowers he wanted to grow. Until that time, Cavafy was anything but the "brave man of pleasure" he praised in one of his later poems. This type of courage contrasts sharply with the lukewarm sensuality in the verses of the Cavafian "Correspondence," hardly a corrective to that of Baudelaire. However, in 1905 he could write "I Went" (1905/*1913*: A 59).

> I didn't bind myself. I let myself go completely and went.
> To the sensual pleasures that were half-real,
> half-turning in my mind,
> I went into the luminous night.
> And drank from the strong wines just as
> the brave men of pleasure drink.

"Brave men of pleasure" (ἀνδρεῖοι τῆς ἡδονῆς) captures the intended inversion of the classical virtue of courage, now assigned to a different urge and determination: the bravery becoming to the pursuit of *hedonê* and the unreserved acceptance of *eros*. But the attitude Cavafy entertained in 1891 was anything but that of the courageous hedonist of 1905, and more concretely in 1913, when this poem was published and its contents were made public. At twenty-eight he was clinging to an alien mode of perception, one of reaction, and it led him on a path towards self-imprisonment, so that by 1894, he would feel compelled to confess in "The City" that

> My heart, like the dead, lies buried.

The encounter with Symbolism proved to be counterproductive at the level of experience and thematic development, but not in the area of technique and artful devices useful for the communication of the near-ineffable and the metaphysical. But that was not Cavafy's own world, and years later, after much wandering, he moved on to his own real world, the realism of his Hellenic soul.

Cavafy's early poems on Romantic and Parnassian themes did not advance beyond the level of exercises in versification. That phase of artistic exchange was no more than a chance meeting at the marketplace of current trends and with no theoretical training on his part to embrace the world of art as a commitment to a way of life. One might even be tempted to say that he stumbled upon poetry and accepted its seriousness only after he came to realize its significance as an expressive medium. But by the time he made his first acquaintance with the poets of the Symbolist movement, he was better equipped to understand the function of artistic tenets. Thus he responded to this post-Romantic development with spontaneity rather than the experience of a skillful artist in search of novel ideas. And when he detected a suitable mode as he did in the case of Baudelaire and other poets of the period, he simply admitted his attraction to it and proceeded to use whatever he thought he could. The surviving poems of that period indicate that Cavafy adopted whatever elements of technique he could extract through his readings to his need for poetic expression and particularly in response to his inflated conception of the poetic mission.

We have no way of knowing whether Cavafy could decide for himself whether Symbolism had the intellectual scope or the ideological vision of Romanticism. By the same token we cannot say for certain that he went to the Symbolist poets with the expectation to find in their works a set of principles on which to rely for enlarging his idea of poetry while strengthening his confidence in the social role of the artist. Probably, he was disappointed to find the Symbolists unable to contribute to his expectations, and this may be one of the reasons for his gradual withdrawal from their camp. Since Symbolism concentrated exclusively on "poetry," it would be expected from a person with Cavafy's sense of civic role to want to move away from Symbolism for fear that subscription to its demand for artistic purity would compromise his sense of social and cultural mission, as he understood it in 1891. Thus, the lack of the commitment to the "polis" in Symbolism is something Cavafy did not find satisfying, and that despite the fact that Baudelaire's poetry reflected a strong metaphysical and ideological concern. But the question is still whether Cavafy had deeper sympathies with the outlook of Baudelaire and what we may loosely call his metaphysical stance.

After the writing of his own "Correspondence" Cavafy composed in the latter part of 1891 a number of poems, all of which exhibited in varying degrees traces of Symbolist influence and all of which were mediocre. Some he published but eventually condemned. Others, marked "lost," were either destroyed or thoroughly rewritten. Even the ones that were saved, the "unpublished" ones, show that Cavafy had not really assimilated nor had faithfully followed the basic principles of Symbolist aesthetics: that poetry is a laboratory art; that the social and ideological programs of Romanticism had no special place in the artistic pursuit; that the discarding of the routine use of words must precede the use of language for the cultivation of musical effects in poetry; that even precise emotional content functions obstructively in the poetic communication of the infinite; that in the poetic act indeterminate internal situations can only be projected by the imagination when combined with analogous visible symbols; that effecting an organic correspondence between symbol and its referent so as to reach the utmost limit of identity demands the suppression of logical relations between symbol and referent; that the poem to attain the best form possible in the conflation between symbol and what is symbolized must make full use of the power of suggestiveness; that whereas the poet projects the experience of the limitless world of the dream, the poem must be understood as a wholly created reality independent of criteria of scientific truth, and the feeling it communicates must be free of moral and didactic messages.

Baudelaire, in his "Correspondances," alleges familiarity with a relationship between two worlds, the material and the spiritual, but also expresses confidence in the great suggestive power the poet has when he exploits the special translatability that obtains among the senses, especially the power of smell. Given the emphasis Baudelaire placed on unorthodox ways of penetrating into worlds inaccessible to the ordinary ways of experience, and also the strong interest in the artificial paradises of opium and the exploitation of decadent situations, Cavafy was at a definite disadvantage. He would soon discover his limitations when trying to attempt vicariously comparable adventures to approximate the extravagant reaches into esoteric worlds as did Baudelaire or Arthur Rimbaud, who had died exactly in the year Cavafy wrote his own "Correspondence." The calculated derangement of all the senses required of the poet to become a seer, as the latter demanded, was far too threatening to Cavafy's mentality. There was little hope for him to rise to the heights of poetry through such practices.

The claim for the superior status of the poet agreed with Cavafy but the simultaneous acceptance of the dream world in which the poet can reign supreme, even apart form the common world, proved rather difficult to hold without considerable pretending. Certain aspects of the creative role of the poet he found appealing but not the conditions the Symbolist poets had attached to it. For Cavafy, it was sufficient that the poet should partake of *sophia* but not as magus and seer. There is a difference between what the poet reveals and what can be reasonably said about correspondent realities.

He saw danger in claiming as real all the things that the poet's excited imagination posits as real existents in the firmament of the imagination. For a while, however, he espoused the Baudelairian definition of the beautiful and sought to write poetry by employing the device of suggestiveness. The beautiful, writes Baudelaire, "C'est quelque chose d'ardent et de triste, quelque chose d'un peu vague, laissant carrier a la conjecture . . . . Le mystère, le regret sont aussi des caractères du Beau.[22]

What can be encompassed in this definition becomes virtually unpredictable, and it can range from the pleasant to the abhorrent and from the noble to the grotesque, allowing all shades and variations to enter into the making of the idealization of the universe of the dream—a universe more real to the poet than the reality of nature. But Cavafy could stay with this tension only so long as his mind could endure the demands placed upon it without erupting in despair. Yet endure he did, and after the composition of his own "Correspondance" he wrote a number of poems in the Symbolist vein. Of the poems written between October and the end of December 1891, four are listed as lost, and two were published and finally condemned.

The year 1892 turned out to be an important one in Cavafy's life. It brought deep satisfaction and also marked the emergence of guilt, due to failure to carry out the message of his "Builders." In the poem "Timolaos the Musician"—the title was changed later, to "Timolaos the Syracusan," published in 1901—there is talk about the superior quality of the "unheard music" the musician tries in vain to express through his art. It is basically a Plotinian aesthetic concept. The motif, as Savidis remarks, points to "the emotional deposit that remains inexpressible or hidden." Inexpressibility becomes a haunting concern and while it provides a platform for claiming superiority it also conceals deep frustrations. Whether it refers to the natural limitations of means, to the artistic failure to meet the demands of the emotions, or to the timidity to disclose a private satisfaction or craving, the result is the same: a gaping rift within the self. The presence of the motif of hiddenness persisted in several later poems. In the 1918 poem "Comes to Rest" (Νὰ

---

[22]"The Beautiful is something passionate and sad, something a little vague, leaving room for conjecture . . . . Mystery and regret are also characteristics of the Beautiful." Quoted in *The Penguin Book of French Verse,* ed. and introd. by B. Woledge, G. Bereton and A. Hartley (1980), p. 341.

Μείνει 1918/*1919*: B 8), the poet recalls what took place long ago—an erotic encounter:

> Enjoyment of the flesh . . .
> the vision of it, passed by twenty-six years ago;
> and now it came
> to stay in this poetry.

The year that experience took place must have been 1892. It was "recalled" in 1918, indeed twenty-six years later, but in 1892 Cavafy had neither the courage nor the forthrightness to compose daring poems on homosexual experiences. In fact none of the poems written after 1892 and before 1903 offers any clues about the theme of "Comes to Rest."

The "Timolaos" poem is sad, even depressing. The people admire his music but only he knows that his superb art has failed to articulate the "mystical sounds" that harmonize deeply in his soul. Timolaos, the *persona*, masks Cavafy's fears and also his conviction about the elevated status of the artist. This covertly autobiographical poem is projective. Cavafy has created his own poet-musician who is "most wise with the lyre and the guitar." But, we are told again, "his most perfect harmonies" remain unexpressed. The poem is thematically related to the unpublished February 1897 composition, "Things Impossible" (U 97), in which he repeats the suspicion that "the best music is that which remains unexpressed," and also that "the most select life is the one that cannot be lived" (ll. 5-8). Art parallels life in the sense that the best is "untold and unlived," varying here the familiar voice of John Keats in the "Ode on a Grecian Urn":

> Heard melodies are sweet, but those unheard
> Are sweeter; therefore, ye soft pipes, play on:
> Not to the sensual ear, but more endeared,
> Pipe to the spirit ditties of no tone.[23]

Seen in another way, since Cavafy had not succeeded in becoming an

---

[23] Cavafy translated in 1892 (?) Keat's "Lamia" and also five lines from "Sonnet to the Nile." The motif of inexpressibility of hidden harmonies is repeated in a condemned poem, "The Inkwell" (1894: C). The failure to express the richness of his inner world the poet attributes to the ink or the inkwell, not to his own limitations. See Savidis 1966: 121-22.

accomplished poet by 1892, the poem serves him in two ways: it provides a vicarious outlet for a vision of fame and recognition while placing him above the ordinary people who cannot rise to the higher level of his experience. It allows Cavafy to cover his failure by rationalizing his inability to articulate his "closeted" homosexuality or to admit he is a mediocre poet. One cannot exclude a deliberate avoidance of responsibility for his inadequacy. The discrepancy between what "returned" at the hour of reverie and remained in "that" poetry in 1918, and what he claimed to be beyond expression in the 1892 poem, is rather puzzling. This obscure relationship makes sense once we see how Cavafy hides behind the sentimentality about inexpressible musical sounds. The culprit, in this case, is the poverty of means and preparation. The blame is placed squarely on the medium. Even the best poetic means fail to do justice to the "music felt." Guilt and fear, the accompaniments of his homosexual gratifications, are suppressed here, but then surprisingly enough they emerge symbolically wearing the innocent mask of unspeakable harmonies. Eventually, the motif became outmoded and abandoned, but not before he realized that it was *then*, during those years and through those experiences that his verses had their *beginning*, as he confesses in the poem of his mature period "Their Beginning," a poem in which there is not the least trace of Symbolism to intimate Baudelairian ghosts.[24]

In 1892, still in the shadow of Baudelaire's Symbolism, Cavafy would use "sad" shades of beauty to compose, but hardly anything that could approximate even remotely Baudelaire's power of expression. The poem "Hours of Melancholy," February 1892, is a compilation of sadness, sighs, sorrows and sobbing, an abortive experiment to embody Baudelaire's definition of beauty, marking the nadir point of his apprenticeship in Symbolism. In May 1892, Cavafy made a timid, yet significant move in a direction that signaled the beginning of emancipation. He wrote the first version of a poem that remained unpublished, originally titled "The Secrets of Flowers," which he revised in 1903 and changed its title to "Artificial Flowers."[25] He meant to include this, along with other poems, in a group

---

[24]This poem may be the "lost" one Cavafy wrote in December 1908 titled "Degenerate Eros," to which he probably gave a different title after making extensive revisions.

[25]Savidis 1966: 123-4, esp. 123, n52; also Peridis 1948: 159, 169.

to be titled "Our Art." Nothing came of that plan, but in the poem itself he expressed an idea that proved to be of great value to his development: acknowledging that the domain of art is his exclusive concern. The idea is cast in extravagant similes and ornate expressions, but the main theme stands out rather clearly: nature's flowers are ephemeral while the works of art—the "artificial" flowers—have an everlastingness of their own, like theories and rhythms and truths do. The inflated and "metaphysical" nature of Symbolism began to recede from the foreground of his themes until finally it became irrelevant to his poetry.

5. Two Poetic Worlds: Parallel or Asymptotic?

The encounter with Baudelaire's poetry was brief, though not short-lived, and left undecided the question of identity of concerns and affinity of views. The few poems of that period that have survived the revisions and the rejections do not give us enough to draw conclusions about strong influences. One thing for certain is that Cavafy's contact with the school of Symbolism helped him cut loose from the grip of Romanticism but only to fall in the net of a different type of difficulties attending the search for an answer to the quest for the poet's mission.

Where the Romantics sought to articulate the experience and the sense of deep loss over the vanishing of Beauty, the symbolist Baudelaire believed that we rarely find a consummate experience that makes life palatable, because ultimately it is but a sordid affair. He saw nature replete with evil, and the passing of experience only repeats what is basically a sequence of low points on the scale of possible values. Only in art, and rarely in ordinary experience, does life offer occasions for celebrations. They occur in the exquisite expressions of art, and they in turn are the high marks in the history of civilization. Humanity is split between the ideal and the sensual, between the divine and the satanical, between purity and darkness. Suspended as we are between the two, with freedom to move in either direction, we can choose to dissipate our energies in futile acts or elevate our existence to the level of the sublime. This is what makes possible the bringing forth of flowers of evil. The poet sees both possibilities and can move to explore the promises either direction holds, and through his poetry reconcile good and evil in a superior embodiment of truth and insight: the poem.

As Cavafy drew closer to the Muse his sense of orientation became stronger. He knew that he had to solve the enigma of the poetic mission. His thinking about the role of the poet had been conditioned early enough by his awareness of two opposing currents of thought: the classical view that wanted the poet to be a citizen, and the modern way, which had also nourished the growth of the symbolist movement, demanding that the poet be a hero of mystical truth. The modern role allowed for the expression and use of eroticism in ways quite unlike what the ancient tradition of philosophical eros prescribed. The modern asked that a price be paid for its performance: the intensification of the awareness of sin, of guilt and a feeling of alienation so that "eros crucified," to use a phrase from Angelos Sikelianos, would make it possible to enhance the chances to ensure salvation through the union with the transcendent Whole. For a while Cavafy had embraced the latter but he knew that it did not represent him.

Cavafy came across Baudelaire at a time when he was barely beginning to understand the need to make a distinction and contrast between the ritualistic elements of Christianity and the classical way of conjoining values to actions, especially aesthetic values. His deepest desire was to become recognized as a citizen in "the City of Ideas," a desire awakened rather early in his life and prior to his encounter with the modern currents. When he came under their spell and after the first fascination wore out, the signs of resistance began to appear. Whatever the degree of involvement, the encounter did not alter his initial orientation nor did it affect his creative energy.

Above and beyond the encounters that took place about the same time that he was learning from Baudelaire, there was the problem of finding a way to clarify the dark relation between salvation and *politeia*. Lacking preparation for so demanding a task he soon found himself wandering in a state of temporary confusion. Response and fulfillment of desires became a major problem. Three years after the writing of his own "Correspondence" Cavafy wrote "The City." Three years later came the writing of "Walls," and following that he slid downhill in the condition of insularity so vividly pictured in "The Windows."[26]

---

[26]Sareyannis: 1964, 121 makes the interesting remark that "Walls," "The Windows" and other poems of this vintage were influenced by Mallarmé.

Baudelaire, even on the limited contact Cavafy had with his poetry, was not the right ally in the battle whose target was hidden behind the thick mist of mystery. The struggle to find a solution to the question of mission lasted for years. Eventually, the effort turned to another direction, that of history. It is obvious now, even to the non-specialist, why the theoretical doctrines and the manifestoes of the European literati did not interest him then or later. True, he studied Gibbon, Macaulay and the great ancient historians of Greece and Rome. But it was poetry that was foremost on his mind. Given this dominant interest during the period of concentrated studies between 1891 and the first decade of the twentieth century, his response to the tenets of Symbolism was, understandably enough, one of utility.

Most of the poems, though not all, written during this period, whether published or otherwise, are often less than mediocre. Savidis has argued convincingly that looking back at Cavafy's work from the time he wrote the *Ars Poetica* in 1903, it is possible to arrive at a reliable guide that enables us to assess his development through a careful analysis of the revisions and improvements Cavafy made on the poems he had produced. Thus, according to Savidis, the first phase comes around 1891, after a period of silence that had lasted from three to four years, leaving behind him the Romantic outlook when Cavafy wrote the "Builders" and the "Correspondence According to Baudelaire." The second came about twelve years later, in 1903, with the formulation of the philosophical elenchus as the guiding principle for another round of revisions and arrangement of selections, a process that also led to the rejection of a large number of poems. By this time, Cavafy had put considerable distance between his technique and the teachings of Symbolism, although it was years before he was able to divest himself of the last vestiges of Symbolism. The rejection was gradual, to be sure, and it required certain adjustments in outlook, foremost one of coming to terms in part with the ideal of progress, the acceptance of the demotic language and the problem of subjective truth. The third phase, Realism, is marked by definite signs of self-assurance as expressed in the "Ithaka," and though Cavafy was still in the shadow of Symbolism the compositions after 1910 have all the features of the new free style of expression. At the beginning of the third phase, as Savidis notes, "We now see an ascetic poet who recognizes his true self, accepts his portion of responsibility for having excluded himself from nature and society, and who is devoted to the perfection and recognition of his art."[27]

The most important of the three phases is the one that marks the transition from the period of Symbolism to Realism. Maronitis has made a special study of this aspect of the second transitional phase:

> I would propose that the Symbolist phase be distinguished from Cavafy's Realist period on the basis of three additional distinct features: (a) Cavafian Symbolism is identifiable as being primarily mythological as to its literary sources; (b) metaphorical as regards its poetic expression; and (c) suggestive in its reference to the poet's erotic preference. By contrast, Cavafy's Realism can be seen as historical in relation to its grammatical references, literal by way of structures and constructions, and confessional, even provocative, with regard to the poet's erotic experiences and preferences.[28]

Correct as the observation may be, it requires a supplementary note to provide for the mode of Cavafy's handling of the "inversion of the classical" device. It is a device that helped replace a number of elements in the Symbolist technique as the poet developed his diverse modes of expression. While advancing to the realist period he widened his themes and tightened the dramatic dialogue.

Seferis was among the first to defend Cavafy's uniqueness, especially in the context of the relationship of his poetry to the tenets of the Symbolist movement during the early phase of his poetic career. While it cannot be denied that he "breathed" the atmosphere of the movement, the more serious question is whether he was overshadowed by its doctrines, and if not, what was his precise relation to its tenets and technique. Seferis writes:

> I know of no other poetry so isolated as his. From many aspects—and this is one of them—he appears as a boundary mark or limit. He remains outside the great thoroughfare that was opened to us by Solomos, and at the same time he appears to have no connection whatsoever with any European figure of his own generation or before his time. There is, I mean, no close affinity which affects his work organically. The only thing I observe here is that Cavafy has certainly breathed the atmosphere of contemporary European poetry as it was when he was between twenty and thirty-five years of age.

---

[27] Savidis 1966: 197.

[28] Maronitis 1983: 74; translation mine.

> That is the atmosphere of the school of Symbolism from which have sprung the most important and the most dissimilar figures in prewar poetry. But he does not show the influence of any one specific writer; the marks of this school which he retains are merely the general characteristics of his generation and they soon fade away or, as his work progresses and his first attempts are left behind, take on a completely personal and individual tone.[29]

Seferis arrived at his conclusion without the benefit of knowing the existence of the Cavafian translation of the sonnet "Correspondances." And though his judgment is amazingly accurate, we still have to answer the question of possible influences that might be present in Cavafy's earlier work, even they are absent from his later work. The issue that must be decided is whether the apparent affinity is due to acceptance of doctrines. This is open to interpretation.

The two main sources from which Cavafy drew ideas were the literary Alexandrian tradition of the Hellenistic period and the modern post-Romantic developments. What we do not know is whether he was sufficiently and expertly cognizant of both traditions at the time he translated Baudelaire. It is not enough to say with Liddell (1948), that "Cavafy is the heir of Callimachus, Apollonius Rhodius, and the Alexandrian poets of the Greek Anthology— though born out of time, he belongs with them; and he holds a high place among them." He continues:

> Cavafy does not merely write as if he had been born in A.D. 400, instead of 1863. He has come into an older world, and later into the history of Hellenism. He does not only draw on Alexandria for inspiration, but on all the Greek world—ancient, medieval and modern. But he looks at it from an amused sceptical Alexandrine point-of-view. Moreover, he has read the Symbolists, and has assimilated such modern themes as *Taedium Vitae*. This has inspired several of his early poems, notably 'The City.'

While Liddell objects to Baud-Bovy's view that the poem states the poet's "desire to escape from the consequences of his anomaly," he offers an insight which he builds on T. S. Eliot's reading of Baudelaire and views Cavafy as one who had "felt the torturing impact of the great modern city upon the

---

[29] Seferis 1966: 123-4.

lonely individual," and concludes that from the Symbolists "Cavafy also learned how to tell a story, and Browning may have been another influence here—though, happily, Cavafy never wants to point a moral."[30] Liddell leaves the question unanswered or rather gives the impression that he suspects rather strong influences as in the case of the important poem "The City." The inadvertent error, if an error it is, is understandable especially in view of the fact that the existence of the translation was not known in 1948.

In his 1986 article, Papanghelis brought together the results of extensive comparative analysis of two sets of literary thematic parallels: (a) between Propertius and Baudelaire and (b) both Propertius and Baudelaire and Cavafy. In the concluding section of his article he identifies and discusses the passages which "allow the reader to appreciate the extent to which the 'Hellenic' poet is close to the other two from a point of view indicated in the title of the article": "*Spiritus in toto corpore surgit:* A Function of the Erotic Body in Propertius, Baudelaire and Cavafy" (280). He identifies parallels and differences between Propertius and Baudelaire by referring to antecedents in the Alexandrian poets, especially Callimachus, and Baudelaire's conception of the sensuality of the body of the *femme fatale*. He then draws attention to the multifaceted second half of the nineteenth century: Aestheticism, Decadence, Symbolism, *L'art pour l'art*, Pre-Raphaelitism, *fin-de-siècle*. The syndrome common to all, he states, is "the sensual, transporting disposition of mysticism; the sensitiveness of the heroes of the period toward aromatic substances is but one of the symptoms" (294), which though present in Cavafy had a long history that was known to him. Hence proposing parallels rather than influences seems to be a stronger case, for it rests on firmer grounds. He has one serious reservation about Seferis' thesis: "What is absent in Seferis' perceptive remark with regard to influences is the 'emphasis.' Cavafy's entire poetic work presents highly sensitive twists that are particularly visible in the school of Symbolism." Having said that, he proceeds to close his discussion by examining Cavafy's mode of writing about the sensual exuding of bodily aromas, and uses it as a basis to propose streamlining the modalities in Cavafy with those in the other two poets.

The important thing is that Cavafy, regardless of what he assimilates from the practices of the Symbolists, especially Baudelaire, has also another

---

[30]Liddell 1948; reprinted in *The Mind and Art of C. P. Cavafy* (1983): 22-23.

tradition with which he is familiar, as Seferis, Liddell and others have said, one that serves as a source of sensual imagery, the same source, with Callimachus at the head, that provided the Roman elegiac poets with theirs: the Alexandrian poets. Papanghelis is fully aware of the literature on Cavafy's affinities to the European poets from the middle of the nineteenth century to the beginning of the twentieth, and concludes that the drawing of comparisons and strong parallels between Baudelaire and Cavafy has yet to be fully explored (302, n50). This is a commendable position to take, given the *status questionis*. The fact is that we possess the text of the Cavafian poem that contains Baudelaire's sonnet. Even if the closest analysis may not succeed in giving us definitive answers with regard to the degree of Cavafy's affinity to the Symbolist movement and Baudelaire's influence, in particular, at least we are provided with an opening that invites fresh investigations. The text seems, at this point, to favor the conclusion about an initial parallel between Cavafy and Baudelaire that eventually transforms itself into a conscious and gradual withdrawal from the shadow of Symbolism. Seferis was right when he insisted that Cavafy was on his way to uniqueness even in his early poems when he was timidly perhaps foraying into directions where he thought he could find the materials and the modes he needed to forge the first bridge to the art of poetry.

Whatever the case may be, Symbolism in Cavafy's early poetry did not take the depth and scope of a doctrine indispensable for the exercise of direct influence. Rather, it seems that Cavafy was from the very start an outsider to the movement and a unique poet. And he remained one.

6. Severing the Weak Ties

Cavafy's ambivalent attitude toward Symbolism, viewed in retrospect and in conjunction with the personal problems he faced while trying to cope with the strong currents of his sexuality, led eventually to a withdrawal into a private Mausoleum, dark and ominous, drab and menacing. Far from being able to find an opening from which to survey the *correspondences* and the blending sequences of realities and symbols, all he could sense was the surface of the inner walls of his self-made prison, which issued no invitation to unity and allowed no merging of qualities to form a single vision of life. Such is the unfolding of poetic thematics that form the sequence of "The City," "Walls" and "The Windows." They were written in the shadow of the Symbolist movement, though not with any special trust in the veracity of its doctrines, whether aesthetic or philosophical.

The young Cavafy went to Symbolism with the hope of the eager yet inexperienced searcher expecting to find there a universe similar to his own. Instead, what he inadvertently brought back was the materials with which to begin the construction of a prison. Such were the workings of fate for the Hellenic dreamer of Alexandria who wanted to read the messages of the intellectual-poets of Europe as promises to themselves and to those willing to adopt the doctrine of a new freedom of the creative spirit. But what they delivered to the on-lookers like Cavafy, was a threnody for his thwarted hedonic expectations. The symbols of handsome youths dying in the hour of their prime had their origin in the pallid blooming of Europe's exquisite flowers of evil. Cavafy's biographer, M. Peridis, reports that Cavafy, the avid reader of European and English literature in his younger days, stopped perusing all those importations sometime around 1903. This final loss of interest coincides with the writing of his *Ars Poetica*. He slew no Minotaur in 1903, but he did find the other end of the thread of Ariadne that gradually guided him out of the dark mansion of his own making, the labyrinth of the confused soul.

Cavafy moved away from the tenets of Symbolism but not away from the usefulness of the symbols. The world of Symbolism, a world glued together with the suggestive power of metaphoric imagery, remained foreign to his needs. He could not attune to it. If Cavafy felt close to Symbolism for a while, when he was groping for means to express his own dimly lit cravings, it was because he was responding to a world he could not understand fully.

As a poet, Cavafy was not temperamentally suited for commitment to the Symbolist movement, except as an imitator of a fashionable and powerful technique. In fact, Cavafy's early poems written in the shadow of Symbolism went beyond the normal utilization of symbols as he tried to convince himself that he could adjust his heritage to the world of Symbolism, or work in the manner of its heroes, particularly Baudelaire. His temporary attachment to the movement proved to be a costly pretension, and was purchased at a high price. For while he could translate Baudelaire and add something of his own to the "Correspondances," it was a contrived effort to place himself in a world of the imagination which had few if any real points of contact with the experiences he was trying to render poetically significant. The imaginative cosmology of the Romantics and of the Symbolists had few fruitful parallel correspondences-correlatives to Cavafy's ideas about the world. It was a view rather foreign to the cultural needs he could call his own. As for the correspondences that obtain among the senses—the doctrine of their continuity —he could readily find them in the philosophies of the ancient Greeks, the Presocratics and Aristotle. Unlike Baudelaire, Cavafy neither sought to explore the feelings of sin and guilt, nor derived any special meaning from their presence in conduct to theorize about the ways and functions of poetry.[31] Cavafy had his difficult moments when he felt most uneasy about guilt, and he tried to cope with it, not as something *primordial* but as induced and due to disapprovals, fears, and confusions. Symbolism aided and abetted this induced sense of guilt, but it also gave him the incentive to make his first panoply. His interest in masks goes back to a prose piece he wrote during the stay in Constantinople in 1884-1885, titled "Masks," which was never published.[32] Symbols for Cavafy have protective function and thus resemble the shielding that a panoply provides. They help their user to hide behind ambiguities while charming the reader with their suggestive power.

Symbolism, though a creative mode of art designed to enhance poetic expression, proved to be in Cavafy's case a mixed blessing. It provided him with a technique that remained useful so long as he relied on crutches of guilt to maintain emotional intensity. However, as a doctrine it proved detrimental in two ways: (a) It made him an imitator and follower of a style essentially foreign to his temperament and affected him in ways that delayed his search for original expressions. (b) It provided him with the means to conceal his

---

[31]Cavafy was not touched by the modern theologizing of poetry. Even the interest in the "ceremonial" and "telestic" practices of his own religious tradition as found in several of his early poems, do not reflect any special effort to come to grips with the notion of original sin. On Baudelaire's sharp sense of sin, Chiari 1960 writes: "He had, to a degree shared by no other, even the Catholic Claudel, a sense of sin and an awareness of the decay of flesh which is puritanical, or one might say Augustinian" (121). Baudelaire left us a testimony of his self-projection of an artist: "The artist depends on nobody but himself. To the centuries to come he offers nothing but his own works; he only commits his own responsibility. He dies childless, after having been his own king, his own priest, his own God." Quoted in Chiari, *op. cit.*, 125.

[32]Cavafy, *Prose* (1963): 167-68.

eroticism and hence gave him the covering his guilt needed to hide behind the veil of pretentiousness and artificiality. In sum, the closer he came to its tenets, the longer it took him to arrive at the authentic presentation of his poetic genius and existential demands.

In 1903 Cavafy dissolved his weak ties with Symbolism and moved away, theoretically at least. Still, it took him years to shake off the last vestiges of his dependence on its technique and redesign it to function productively. The definite signs of his emergence from its shadow came when he formulated the revisionary principle of "philosophical scrutiny," when he felt obliged to remove "flagrant" contradictions and inconsistencies in the thematics of his poems and the power of imagination was brought in line with the principle of rational correctness. The return to the *logos* tradition had started.

In the meantime, Symbolism as an artistic movement, represented by Jean Moréas, Maurice Maeterlinck, Émile Verhaeren, and others, intensified the search in a direction that diverged significantly from the road familiar to Cavafy. Mainly in France, the poets concentrated their effort on dissolving the logic of poetic discourse. They arrived at the conclusion that this could be effectively done by introducing into poetry the aesthetic purity of music. The later practitioners of Symbolism cultivated poetry without the communicative function of language. They conceived of poetry as a veil to be used to stave off logical discourse. The poet's duty to his art became one of transcending the sensible world by way of absorbing and dissolving its inherent contradictions, in good faith that the symbols and their illogical connections manifest higher reality. With Stephan Mallarmé, the ideal of art is best approximated by means of those rigid symbols that succeed in excluding the reality of nature and effacing the basic emotion that gave the artist the initial push. The road from nature to the realm of ideality and its mysteries was now believed to have been made secure. Cavafy reacted instinctively against this trend as leading the poet to a barren and non-hedonic idealism. The end of his apprenticeship in the shadow of Symbolism marked the beginning of his new poetic phase: realism.

But for a period of about ten years Cavafy, like the French Symbolists, attended to the Poe principle, so clearly stated in Poe's *On Poetic Composition,* whereby beauty is declared the province of poetry. It was a principle that excluded the writing of long poems. Cavafy's poems are brief. It is tempting to conclude that this practice originated from his acquaintance with the aesthetics of Poe. However, as a modal form it goes back to Herondas and Theocritus, indeed, to classical lyric poetry. The practice is ancient, the rationale for its particular defense in Poe is modern. As a consequence of its acceptance, the epic length became inappropriate to the Symbolist mode of disclosure. Cavafy, who never tried his hand in the epic form but admired the art of tragedy, refrained from writing tragic drama; the most he ever did was to praise the spirit of ancient tragedy in one of his early poems (1897: CP 52).

The decision to restrict his compositions to short forms, in which he frequently intimated the rudiments of tragic situations, was made independently of the Poe principle, though it may be argued that the decision found support in both Poe and the Symbolists. But unlike the latter, Cavafy could not and did not escape the impact of his own Hellenic tradition. He selected from it what he thought could best serve the modern sensibility. It was a decision based on conscious exclusion. Life could not be treated *tragically*, at least not in the classical sense of tragic dramaturgy. That way of viewing life seemed at odds with the rising cult of poetic individuality and the preoccupation with the discovery of the inner landscape of the psyche and its quest for unity with the absolute rather than the clarification of the place of the individual within the controlled freedoms of the *politeia*. To state the same thing in a more tangible way, it did not appear that the texture of contemporary life was in harmony with the principle of the common good and the securing of suitable social conditions indispensable for the pursuit of personal fulfillment. The aesthetics of pathos had in modern times become so prevalent as to blur the last traces of the Greek concept of *hubris*. The moderns had ushered toward the center of art their own conception of poetic style. Poetic sensibility settled for the short poem and the lyrical cry of the individual for mystical unity, not for the return to the city. Symbolism had succeeded in pushing over the precipice whatever was left of the Romantic advocacy of the social mission of art.

Cavafy eventually returned to the city; he recaptured Alexandria as theme and sentiment. On the surface of it, this return seems to be quite in line with the way in which Baudelaire saw the poetic use and transformation of urban materials into poetic experience. However, the similarities end rather abruptly. For Cavafy, after he moved out of the shadow of Symbolism, saw the problem of his own alienation from the city in personal terms and not as one that was due to the advent of technology, industrial progress and its ambivalent benefits to humanity. The reaction he felt went back to his early twenties and the emotional tensions of that period. He saw a city where opportunities became increasingly limited, blocking the satisfactory expression of desires. Much like Baudelaire, Cavafy emerges as a poet of the city, although each has his own "political poetics," that is, what poetry does with and to the city as experience.[33] While Baudelaire responded basically to the problems of the *modern* city, how to assimilate it into the texture of his poetry, Cavafy viewed it the way that an Aristotelian, more so than a Platonist, would: as the environment to nurture excellence and fulfillment, as the material framework for citizenship and statesmanship, as the natural milieu for poetry, friendship, community bonds and sensual enrichment.

Like Baudelaire, Cavafy had to face the problem of revitalizing the city, especially after deciding to publish "The City." In this poem Cavafy had emptied the imaginative space of his nameless city and drained it of every vital element until both he and the city stood in opposition as well as tied to each other with an indissoluble bond: "the city will follow you." Baudelaire faced a similar challenge and tried to give an answer in his "Le Crepuscule du matin." He expressed his determination to work with two kinds of enduring forces, two types of interrelated materials, the sensuous and the historical, as they were filling the city to the brim with things emerging from the stupor of the night and the misery of chilled existence, things only the forceful will of a poetic vision could unite:

---

[33]Vayenas 1980, has formulated the related Baudelairian thesis with clarity: "For Baudelaire, the artist tries to express the inner sense of his theme. And this because nature is but a heap of elements and images, unable to provide a moral meaning. It simply forces us to satisfy certain basic needs keeping us in a condition of inhumanity. Baudelaire writes characteristically that 'nature offers us advice only for crime'" (130). Ref. to *Oeuvres*, ed. Y-G LeDante, Paris, 1954, 783. Again, Baudelaire states: "True civilization is not to be found in gas or vapor, nor in the little wooden tables where the spirits of the dead are invoked. Civilization is found in the effort to wipe off the traces of the original sin" (1224). As Vayenas notes, for Baudelaire dualism is metaphysical and its cause lies in the primordial sin. Since salvation in this world is not possible, all attempts to attain it are condemned. What cannot be done with religious means is achieved through aesthetics, "which explains why Baudelaire's religious outlook has many common features with the kind of heightened experience poets have in their most creative moments" (160).

> ... It was that hour when swarms of maleficent dreams
> Twist brown adolescents upon their pillows ...
>
> It was that hour when, amidst the cold and misery,
> Women's labor pains increase ...
>
> A sea of mist was bathing the buildings,
> And from the interior of hospitals, the dying
> Were emitting their last breath in convulsive rattles.
> Debauched revelers were coming in, broken by their labors.
>
> Dawn shuddering in her rose and green dress,
> Was slowly advancing on the deserted river Seine,
> And somber Paris, rubbing its eyes,
> Was taking up its tools, an aged toiler.[34]

Seen from the perspective of the revitalization of the city, it may not be far from the truth to say that from 1903 on, and especially after the publication of "The City" in 1910, whatever Cavafy wrote was but part of his work in progress, one work-poem aiming at the rebirth and the rehabilitation of the self in the condition of the modern cosmopolis haunted by the dream of the *polis*. After 1910 Cavafy, no longer the nostalgic reformer and dreamer

---

[34]
> ... C'étais l'heure où l'essaim des rêves malfaisants
> Tord sur leurs oreillers les bruns adolescents; ...
>
> C'étais l'heure ou parmi le froid et la lésine
> S'aggravent les douleurs des femmes en gésine ...
>
> Une mer de brouillards baignait les édifices,
> Et les agonisants dans le fond des hospices
> Poussaient leur dernier râle en hoquets inégaux.
> Les débauchés rentraient, brisés par leurs travaux.
>
> L'aurore grelottante en robe rose et verte
> S'avançait lentement sur le Seine déserte,
> Et le sombre Paris, en se frottant les yeux,
> Empoignait ses cutils, vieillard laborieux.

In *Les Fleurs du mal*, texte présenté par René-Louis Doyon, Paris: R. Rasmussen (CXII, 161-2); tr. C. and L. Welch (1973).

of the resurrected classical polis, knows that he must work mainly with the poetic materials the modern city provides and the experiences it makes possible. Baudelaire had to struggle with the inescapable barbarism of the industrialized modern city together with his profound preoccupation with sin and guilt, whereas Cavafy had a different and at least equally difficult task to meet. Being an Alexandrian and deeply steeped in history, in the culture of his city, its philosophy and its legends, he had to come to terms with the ineradicable memories that were clamoring for aesthetic justice. Acting on behalf of his city, as its poet and consciousness, the task became more than an artistic responsibility. It was equally tied to his survival as a person.

In Cavafy we encounter a conflict between two frameworks for defining the role of the poet: (a) the classical-Platonic of the poet-*polites*, and (b) the romantic-modern role of the poet as aesthetic hero of selfhood. In the early Cavafy the dominant note is on the Romantic. It took precedence over the classical, mainly because of the displacement of the erotic element in his life and the loss of opportunity to serve as one of the builders of progress. His training as a student under Papazis alerted him to the classical, but in the absence of reinforcements, no clear set of concepts emerged to help him cast his lot as a poet within his own Hellenic tradition. His schooling in England, and his fascination with the modern, allowed the then current views of the role of the artist to provide the foundations for understanding himself as poet and person, so much so that he even persuaded himself to think and believe in his own alienation and social estrangement. As a result, he cast his role in a mold that proved to be unsuitable to his temperament and cultural identity. He gradually lost sight of his erotic inclinations as well as confidence in his poetic mission. Cavafy started as a Romantic in a Greek "chiton" only to become increasingly confused about both.

Between 1890 to 1903-1904, for almost fourteen years, he struggled to find a firm ground on which to build his poetic edifice, only to see it rise and fall, leaving him with few useful materials but hardly enough for the completion of the architectural masterpiece he had so much aspired to be its builder. Cavafy as a modern was caught in the transition between the last waves of Romanticism and the spiral ascent of the Symbolist movement. For a brief time, he was tempted to answer the riddle of the Baudelairian sphinx: the enigma of the artist's alienation.

The attitude of suffering for the sake of art we find projected in one of Cavafy's early poems, "The Pawn" (1894), where the "pawn" or the artist, depicted symbolically, is sacrificed for the Queen-Art. Soon, Cavafy altered slightly the stance to one of living for the sake of art. The "Pawn" remained among the "unpublished" (UP 63, 221).[35] The "pawn" stands for a journey, presumably the poet's own, symbolized here as the defiant process to meet death for art's sake. The poet dies and is transformed as poetry or as art: the Queen. Death and resurrection, or what amounts to the same thing, giving one's life as an individual to gain the life of art and to be one with poetry or art. The message is clear. Art is born from the death of the artist-martyr. In principle, then, Cavafy's "Pawn" is a variation on a theme common to Poe and Baudelaire in that the artist must suffer and die for the sake of his art, but with a difference in the imagery in which the respective versions are cast. Cavafy's view of the imagery of the journey is unlike that of Baudelaire's journey of the poet, which is one of descent into vileness that lands the poet at the "Vanishing point of spiritual ambition"—"away from illumination" and into Saint John of the Cross' "Dark Night of the Soul."[36]

Cavafy did not seem to possess either the stamina or the inclination to adopt Baudelaire's attitude of defiance. Eventually, he redesigned the journey in a mode completely different from the Baudelairian conception when he wrote his "Ithaka." This should not come as a surprise. In the tradition of the "art for art's sake" movement, there is no united front in response to the undertaking of the journey. Often the views seem unreconciled. Even Baudelaire, as M. C. Beardsley has pointed out, did not maintain a consistent view of the end of art as the end of the journey.[37]

Thematically, Cavafy was no stranger to Baudelaire's rebellion of the imagination. Bertocci 1964 has noted that "the final cry in *Les Fleurs du mal* is for a ship to weigh anchor and to bear him into the unknown to find the new" (112). It is rather doubtful that the image of the ship in Cavafy's "The City" in 1894 is taken from Baudelaire. However, by the time he wrote his "Ithaka" the idea of the endless voyage had become a dominant motif, and for

---

[35] The Folio #11, as Savidis reports in Cavafy 1968, contains a note dated 23.3.'11: "Not for publication. But may remain here" (UP 221). Also, Cavafy, *Unpublished Prose Texts* (1963): 58f.

[36] Zweig 1968: 229.

[37] Beardsley 1966: 286.

reasons other than those related to the unleashing of the imagination. Admittedly, Baudelaire had assigned to this faculty an unusually powerful role. Bertocci (1964) has aptly summarized this point:

> [Imagination] decomposes all creation, and, with its materials amassed and disposed according to rules whose source can be found only in the profoundest depths of the soul, it creates a new world, it produces a sensation of the new. Since it created the world (one may say that, I think, even in a religious sense), it is just that it should govern it (57).

It is the same imagination that instructs us in the "moral meaning of color, sound and perfume" (56).

The open voyage to discover the unknown came back later to haunt Cavafy, and he probably remembered what he thought was worth retaining from the symbolist model when he embarked on his new poetic quests. The fact is that "Ithaka" contains certain elements of Baudelaire's Symbolism, but what is more significant is that in this poem Cavafy is able to assign a counter-Baudelairian meaning to the concept of "voyage" by mapping a totally different and open-ended course, one that is genuinely suited to the "courageous men of pleasure," the ἀνδρεῖοι τῆς ἡδονῆς.

Before the fledgling poet could claim his place among the select men of pleasure he had to suffer the full agony of self-alienation, and pain had to run its course in the labyrinth of the lost polis. The tortuous path of a convoluted meandering in the dark corridors of a windowless existence refused to yield the secret of the exit to the world of light, not before the wisdom of desire was finally ready to prevail over fear. The insight of the "second odyssey" did not become the joyous vision of Ithaka until the loss of the polis had run its full cycle of despair and Eros could return unscathed to guide the soul of the poet in its search for understanding.

Chapter Five

The Loss of The Polis

1. The Surfacing of the Crisis. 2. In the Same City. 3. The Perimeter of the Polis. 4. Inverting the Classical Mode. 5. The Penumbra of "The City."

1. The Surfacing of the Crisis

In the "Prefatory Note" to the edition of Cavafy's poems, Savidis remarks that the poet's "entire conscious life remained a study of death."[1] Taken quite epigrammatically and without further explanation, the expression sounds rather ponderous and fraught with implications. However, one could not be blamed for assuming that the poet devoted himself to the mastery of his art in anticipation of death. The contrary is also true, namely, that confident in the quality of his life-work, even if unfinished, Cavafy saw his poetry taking its permanent place in the "Banquet of the Future."[2] He was not sordidly and consistently preoccupied with the vanity of life and the glorification of death, although there were moments during the period of the "crisis" years when death was welcomed as "a kind of solution." At times the need to put an end to the unrequited agony may have pushed the poet closer to the death wish, but that is a different problem. The poems of this period abound in symbols and feelings conveying such a state of mind.

The themes of the poems written throughout the crisis period, viewed collectively, range over a broad horizon marked by sharp rises and declines, from despair and total hopelessness to renewed efforts and humiliating compromises. When the poet is not walking along the paths of an inner cemetery, his fearful vision is scanning the landscape of past history, often coming to rest on the deeds of the dead as though he is forming a series of

---

[1] "Prefatory Note" in Cavafy, *Poems*, A (1963): 9.

[2] The expression is from the title of the 1897 unpublished poem (U 95); the poem consists of two three-verse stanzas. Translation in Dalven, 1961: 200.

monuments to failure and futility. Yet the inner eye, vigilant and eager, a glowing amber in the dark rooms of the mansion, patiently waited for the moment when it would light the torch of hope that would show the path to the gateway. A modern Orpheus, he has to descend into the dark regions of the inner Hades in the cosmopolitan self before he could return to the fullness of life, pursuing on the way down and the way up his real and faithful Eurydice: *poetry*.

The "crisis" period in Cavafy's creative life had already begun when he wrote, in 1894, the key poem "The City," originally titled "Again in the Same City." It waxed strongly as the years went by and reached its turning point in 1903-1904, before entering its waning phase to end around 1910. What defines his state of mind and also finds lyrical expression in most of the poems of this period is a deepening sense of self-alienation and estrangement from his environment. Eventually, it gathered such emotional force that it almost succeeded in defeating both the person and the poet. In 1894, Cavafy was able to find enough determination to face the strong waves of despair and come to grips with the fear of a growing and constrictive loneliness. In 1894, his poetic self lashed out in order to throw in sharp relief the outer circumference of fear. The writing of "The City" brought into fullness the anomalies of his predicament though not what caused them. But the experience persisted and led to more serious forms of withdrawal until he was eventually confined to a windowless existence. The self-image Cavafy exhibits through the *persona* in the poems during the first phase of the crisis, reflects faithfully the lyrical self though not the *mundane* Cavafy with the remarkable external self-control, hiding behind the masks, an expertly made panoply perfectly suitable for the affairs of Alexandrian life.

"The City" draws the widest of three perimeters within whose areas the poet will display the drama of his impending self-imprisonment. The middle perimeter, inside the first, appeared two years later with the writing of "Walls" in September 1896. The constrictive process reached its final stage in an image of inexorable finality in August 1897, when Cavafy wrote "The Windows," a poem showing the *persona* locked inside a symbolic mansion with no doors and allowing no exit. But the most threatening feature of the symbol is the mansion's lack of windows, or what amounts to the same thing, the *persona*'s inability to locate the windows, and even if perchance encountered in the darkness still unwilling to open them. At this point the poet has reached the narrowest limits of self-alienation. It all happens in three successive moves, three lyrical implosions of the swelling crisis:

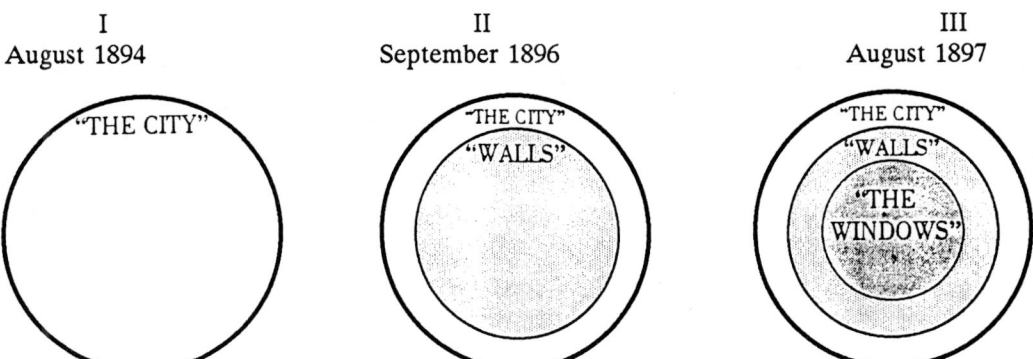

In those years Cavafy had made plans to prepare thematic collections of his poems. One of them, titled *Prisons,* was meant to include the poems on the theme of confinement. This particular plan was abandoned, as we shall see. What is more pertinent to our discussion is the relationship between the dates of composition and publication of these three crucial poems.

Date of Composition	Time lapsed to	Date of Publication
"The City": August 1894	16 years	April 1910
"Walls": September 1896	4 months	January 1897
"The Windows": August 1897	6 years	November 1903

A comparison of the dates of publication leads directly to the question: Why did Cavafy postpone for sixteen years the release of "The City," a poem he considered to be thematically significant and "from one point of view, perfect"? The question becomes more enigmatic in view of the fact that the experience which the theme of "The City" projected so powerfully in 1894 no longer represented the poet's state of mind in 1910. Although Cavafy released the poem for publication sixteen years later, after making a few important changes, the substance remained intact and truly expressive of the early phase of the crisis period. Since "The City" antedates chronologically and thematically the other successful poems of the crisis period, the search for an answer to our question must take precedence, despite the fact that the poem was published as late as 1910 in *Nea Zoe*. It was not made part of the 1910 booklet but was given the first place in the *Collection of 1912*, which consisted of 14 poems. He gave a copy to Pericles Anastassiadis. On February 27, 1914, Cavafy gave to D. Anastassiadis (Pericles' brother) a *Collection* of 19 poems, *Alexandria 1910-1914*, and again "The City" was the lead poem. Its importance for understanding Cavafy's development cannot be overestimated. One could dramatize this point by assigning the poem "internal recognition," as Cavafy himself would want it.

In February 1895, Cavafy wrote a poem titled "The Last Step," revised later as "The First Step" (1899: A 101). When placed in the context of his poetry as "a work in progress," this poem cannot be denied some autobiographical significance. The theme here is poetry and poets. The Syracusan poet Theocritus (third century) gives advice and encouragement to the young poet Eumenes (a fictional *persona*), who complains:

> . . . I have been writing for two years now
> but composed , one idyll.
> It is my   te work . . .

And Theocritus replies with the authority of a master:

> . . . To have come this far is no small thing.
> . . . Even this one step, the first,
> is quite above the common world.
> To set your foot on this one rung
> you must in your own right be
> a citizen in the polis of ideas.
> . . . It is no small thing to have come this far;
> to do this much is a great glory.

If this is covert autobiography, then Cavafy is giving internal recognition to one of his own compositions. One would have to guess in this case that Cavafy's own "first step" corresponds to Eumenes' one idyll. Going back to Cavafy's compositions since 1893 to assess the quality of his poetic output, and by extending the search back to 1884, the only outstanding poem that strikes the reader as worthy of recognition, though not an idyll, is "The City," whose existence was known only to his close friends when "The First Step" appeared. For reasons of his own, Cavafy decided to postpone publication, and when time came to select one special poem as the signpost that would mark the end of the crisis and also serve as the preface to the mature years, he made an excellent choice. The prize went to "The City."

If "The City" pictures in bold brushstrokes the *persona*'s abrupt admission of self-alienation, the poem "The Satrapy," written in July 1905, the first to be published after the release of "The City," recounts in brilliant light a set of circumstances that could lead a *persona* like the one in "The City" to denounce one's *polis* and "take the road to Susa." Ten years after the writing of "The City" the loss of the *polis* continues to haunt the poet, asking to be cast in concrete setting. The parallel predicament in the two poems may well make the latter the "twin portal" to the former,[3] but discussion on this affinity must be reserved for the next chapter.[4] Be that as it may, it would be helpful to suggest in anticipation that "The Satrapy" offers another counter-productive solution to the *impasse* of self-estrangement. Cavafy's resorting to either of the two "forced" and negative solutions as ways to handle the depleting situation that culminated in the loss of the *polis* succeeded only in prolonging the period of the crisis and in deepening the sense of agony. Not before the landscape of life's ruins had come into full view could the crisis end in creative understanding. When Cavafy published "The City," in 1910, he also revealed the shocking scale of the lasting predicament. One could say with confidence that he intentionally used this poem to serve as a major statement against which to measure the disclosures of new thoughtful solutions, as with "Ithaka" and its exquisite companion, "The God Abandons Antony," both written in 1910 and published in 1911.[5]

---

[3] See Savidis 1966: 197.

[4] Chapter 6, section 5.

[5] Keeley 1976 has taken the position that Cavafy selected "The City" to head the *Booklet* 1909-1911 and the thematic *Collection* of 1917 because the poet came to see "this particular work as a kind of turning point, more precisely, a culmination that might signal a new beginning" (18). He develops the argument for this view in chapter 2 (15-23). He writes: "The implication of the revised text is that the poet exonerates the city of blame for the predicament of his protagonist; the city is no longer seen as a cause of the predicament but as a metaphor for it" (20). The view assumes that the revisions allow the conclusion that the *persona* (=Cavafy) has accepted full responsibility for the predicament. This is also the position of Liddell 1974 and Ilinskaya 1983; it carries Savidis' observation beyond its original limit when he stated that "by 1911 we see an ascetic poet understanding his real self, accepting his *portion* of the responsibility for his exclusion from nature and society, and

2. In the Same City

According to Cavafy's notes found among his personal documents, the first version of "The City" was written in August 1894, almost six months after his first attempt to formulate the idea of the voyage in "The Second Odyssey." It seems that "The City," originally titled "In the Same City," shortened in the same way as the poem "Like the Trojans," underwent certain minor revisions before it appeared in final form in 1910. In a letter to his friend Pericles Anastassiadis, written sometime after August 1894, but not later than July 1896, Cavafy wrote (in English):

> Dear Pericles,
> These lines are a general introductory notice to 3 articles and 3 poems herewith enclosed.
>
> My article on "The End of Ulysses" is simply a "curiosity of literature" and I only hope it isn't tedious and that the translations are not too bad.
>
> "A Night on the Calinder" is an old article which I have retouched. I am rather satisfied with its diction, over which I have taken many pains. I have tried to blend the spoken with the written language and have called to my help in the process of mixture all my experience and as much artistic insight, as I possess in the matter—trembling, so to speak, over every word. The same remarks apply to "The Mountain."

---

devoting himself to the cultivation and recognition of his art"(197, italics provided). Savidis' cautioned approach has the better argument, for it avoids the pitfalls of Keeley's claim about Cavafy's exoneration of the city from blame that turns Cavafy's *rapprochement* with his environment into a moral issue and an aesthetic device. Had Cavafy intended his revisions to imply acceptance of the responsibility for the *persona's* predicament, he would have made them more explicit and definite. In that case the revisions would have demanded the removal of the symbolist use of ambiguity, which lies at the heart of the poem and accounts for its special appeal. Keeley's proposal that the city is viewed in 1911 not as the cause of the *persona*'s predicament but "as a metaphor for it," tends to make his original position somewhat enigmatic. It is not clear that the antecedent of "it" is the cause for the predicament. The assumption is that the movement is from "the literal city" to "the metaphoric city" and thus it secures the requisite advantage of aesthetic distance, rather than from a symbolic city to a real city, as Savidis, Ilinskaya, Pieris and Dallas have suggested. Keeley's work, however, is important for bringing to the open a crucial issue for debate: to clarify the relationship between Cavafy's aesthetics and his personal development.

"Candles" is one of the best things I ever wrote."

"In the Same City" is from one point of view perfect. The versification and chiefly the rhymes are faultless. Out of the 7 rhymes on which this poem is built, 3 are identical in sound and 1 has the accent on the antepenultimate. But I have *parakamei* (overdone) it and somehow got cramped on the exigencies of the meter; and I am afraid I haven't put in the second stanza as much as should have gone into it. I am not sure that I have drawn the 2nd, 3rd and 4th lines of the second stanza an adequately powerful image of ennui—as my purpose was. It may be however that by trying to do more, I should have overdone the effect and strained the sentiment, both fatal accidents in art. There is a class of poems whose role is "suggestif." My poem comes under that head. To a sympathetic reader—sympathetic by culture—who will think over the poem for a minute or two, my lines, I am convinced, will suggest an image of the deep, the endless "désespérance" [sic] which contain "yet cannot all reveal."

Yours
Constantine F. C.[6]

Careful consideration of the contents of this letter, written when Cavafy was still in his early thirties, reveals two important sides of his personality as a poet. First there is the developed sense of distance he is able to put between himself and the thematic content which permits him not only to suggest to the reader the appropriate mode for appreciation, but also allows him to raise critical questions about technical aspects. Secondly, he wishes to make sure that the poem will not be treated as a strictly autobiographical piece, so to speak, nor as depicting a permanent or even universal aspect of the human condition. In the *Self-comments* which decades later (1930) he dictated to G. Lechonitis, he stated the following thoughts:

---

[6] Quoted in Peridis 1948: 311-12. The title "In the Same City" differs slightly from the one given in the handwritten copy, presumably the one Cavafy had enclosed, where the title in Greek reads *Páli stin ídia póli* (=Again in the same city). The handwritten copy, now in the Benaki Museum in Athens, is dated August, 1894 (photo in Tsirkas 1958, plate 5). Peridis reprints the poem (173) using the original title "Again in the Same City" but gives "August 1897" as the date on the copy to Anastassiadis. Savidis 1963 discusses this error (123). Cavafy used the title *Páli stin ídia póli*," but gave its equivalent in English "In The Same City." Both variants disappear after the revised version was printed in 1910.

"Monotony," "The City"... concern situations of definite individuals, not general situations. The life of certain people, whether they are themselves responsible, or because of the circumstances, becomes such that "one monotonous day follows another monotonous day." However, Cavafy does not mean that the life of every human being is such—only for some, and as a phenomenon in life he thinks it worthy to become the theme for a poem. In "The City" he does not mean that whoever spoiled his life cannot straighten it out somewhere else. Yet there are individuals who once they spoil their life in one small corner, "they ruin it everywhere on earth" (43-4).

The special "self-comment" on "The City" reads as follows:

> The man who spoiled his life will try in vain to recapture it again on a better and morally higher plain. The city, an imaginary city will follow him, overtake him, and wait for him with the same streets and the same neighborhoods. Certainly, the poet does not face generalities in this particular poem but a particularity, since he frequently treats isolated themes or exceptional cases (24-5).

Cavafy is also quoted to have said that "the city is what you carry with you. When you leave on a journey the homes and the streets also walk; they don't stay behind."[7] These reflections are explicit enough to alert the reader to the intended scope of the theme as well as the relationship of the situational mood to the poet's experience, whether personal or vicarious. Any approach which ignores the warning given in these comments, precluding as it does assigning finality and ultimacy to the mood, cannot but be misleading.

Evidently, Cavafy was aware of the thematic flaws and technical defects of the poem in its original version. He sent a copy to his friend, P. Anastassiadis, but decided to keep it unpublished, along with other poems, for another fifteen years. It appeared first in 1910, in *Nea Zoe*, with significant changes in the first stanza. However, the fact that he felt it necessary to write special comments on it is sufficient evidence of his uncertainty about its adequacy. Yet he regarded it as having special importance and as being, in a definite way, irreplaceable as a poetic moment in the entire cycle of the "crisis" compositions. It summarizes the predicament by way of collapsing the inner and outer sides of the walls, and casts the net of the symbol over a wide

---

[7] Quoted in Tsirkas 1958: 245.

area to collect the related intensities in their darkest hour. Thus, the experience conveyed is stretched almost to the breaking point. The resulting ambiguities, necessary to enhance the element of suggestiveness, become unavoidable flaws in the poem.

Whether through ineptitude or design, the poet made phrastic revisions affecting the sentiment, not the symbol, probably realizing that the removal of all ambiguities would simply destroy the mood or alter its substance beyond recognition. It may sound paradoxical to say that the poem's flaws are essential aspects of its merits, but that is precisely the case. The character of the poem is but an extension of the poet's own ambivalences which provided much of the body and bloodstream of his poetic growth. Concluding the "crisis" period, although written fifteen years earlier, the poem in its final form reads (A 15):

> You said: "I'll go to another land, go to another sea.
> Some other city will be found, better than this.
> Each one of my endeavors is a written verdict;
> and my heart—like the dead—lies buried.
> My mind, how long will it remain in this decay?
> Wherever my eye turns, wherever I gaze
> I see my life's black ruins here,
> where I spent, and spoiled and ruined so many years."
>
> Other places you'll not find, you'll not find other seas.
> The city will always follow you; the streets you'll walk
> will be the same. In the same neighborhood you'll grow old,
> and in the same houses, hair turning white.
> Always in this same city you'll arrive. Don't hope for other places.
> There is no ship for you, there is no road.
> Just as you spoiled your life here,
> in this small corner, you ruined it everywhere on earth.

The changes he made are not without interest.[8] Evidently, in the revised form of "The City" he left out the expression "I hate" as a case of

---

[8]Lines 6-7 originally read: "I hate the people here as they hate me, / here where half my life . . .

"strained sentiment."⁹ Had he kept it in, the poem would suffer from a "flagrant contradiction," since as he informs us in a comment, "the city is what you carry with you," and hating it would be tantamount to self-hatred. The city can only become what one makes of it. The contradiction had to be removed, especially in view of what his city, Alexandria, was to become for him and his poetry in 1910.

In a letter to his friend Rallis, written in 1883, when Cavafy was still in Constantinople, he seems to have expressed strong disapproval of the social and cultural life of Alexandria; to which Rallis replied: "When you claim that you hate Alexandria and 'all this futility', I don't believe you."¹⁰ Cavafy was only twenty years old at that time. The special circumstances that gave rise to this "hatred" need not concern us here. What matters is that the feeling of hatred, in varying degrees, persisted long after his return to Alexandria in 1885. The fact is that it was decades before he accepted the city in which he was destined to spend the rest of his life. Even at the age of forty-four he had yet to come to terms with the Alexandrian environment and its limitations. It was not until after he had sufficiently matured that he learned how to speak of life in the city in other than depressing imagery. When he decided to revise the poem, sometime after the spring of 1907, he removed the reference to "hatred." At the age of forty-four he could say:

> By now I've gotten used to Alexandria, and it's very likely that even if I were rich I'd stay here. But in spite of this, how the place disturbs me. What trouble, what a burden small cities are—what lack of freedom.

---

⁹The expression 'hatred' appears for the first time in the early (and condemned) poem "Bacchic Song" (1886), where the poet says that wine has the power to efface "every frigid effect of envy, shame, hatred or slander," which he felt, and others presumably did for him, and hence drinks to drown his sorrows. When "Bacchic Song" was published in 1892, the word 'hatred' was expunged and the entire stanza replaced. See Tsirkas 1958: 222. The same expression occurs once in the unpublished poem, "Addition" (1897: U 99): "I hate being counted in their multitude." The word 'hatred' (*mísos*) appears only once in the 154 approved poems, and is found in "Thermopylae" (1901/*1903*), where the *persona* states that those who have elected to guard Thermopylae in their lives are, among other things, "always speaking the truth but without hatred for those who lie."

¹⁰Quoted in Peridis 1948: 36.

I'd stay here (then again I'm not entirely certain that I'd stay) because it is like a native country for me, because it is related to my life's memories.

But how much a man like me—so different—needs a large city. London, let's say. Since . . . P. M. left, how much it is on my mind.[11]

There is another important aspect to the publication of the poem, directly related to the issue of internal consistency. When we stop to consider the fact that by 1910 Cavafy had gone beyond passive reconciliation with his environment and reached the point of seeing Alexandria for what it was, historically as well as culturally, the question as to why he bothered at all to publish a poem like "The City" still lingers on and calls for an answer. The plain truth is that the situational mood of the poem did not represent him in 1910, regardless of what it meant to him in 1894. Nor is it likely that he intended its publication to communicate in some didactic way the incipient dangers waiting to harass the unsuspecting dwellers of his city, destined to be caught in the snares of disillusionment and self-alienation. The crumbling of his own inner walls had already begun with the writing of the *Ars Poetica* and the post-1903 poems. Hence it is difficult to understand why so many years later he would want to revive the ghostly past.

The explanation of his decision to publish "The City" only a few months before the composition of the poems "Ithaka" (October, 1910) and "The God Abandons Antony" (November, 1910), must be sought elsewhere. Between the end of 1909 and the beginning of 1910 Cavafy had completed the major part of his revisions and brought out *Booklet* 2, augmenting his *Booklet* 1 of 1904-1905. If this period is seen for what it is, namely one of intense creativity adumbrating the approach of the exit, his concern to compose poems on themes that were soon to find expression in "Ithaka" and "The God Abandons Antony," written only a month apart, must have preoccupied him for quite some time. Although special details on his day-to-day activities are lacking, we have some evidence in support of a plausible explanation. Thematically speaking, the germinal idea for his "Ithaka" came shortly prior to the first writing of "The City," while an unpublished poem "The End of Antony,"

---

[11]The note was found among the poet's papers by Savidis and printed for the first time in Keeley's article, "Cavafy's Metaphorical City," *The Southern Review* (Winter, 1976); reprinted in Keeley 1976: 19.

composed in June 1907, anticipates in certain respects, especially as regards the stance taken by the *dramatis personae* in this poem, what will be said of Antony in 1910. Such are the prevailing circumstances at the time of the publication of "The City." Still, it is rather remarkable that Cavafy did not include this poem in his *Booklet* 2 (1910). Instead, he assigned it the place of the leading poem in the canon of the approved published poems.

Although the crisis period which ended shortly after 1910 is both relevant to and significant for our understanding of the relationship between Cavafy's psychic states and the poems he wrote, the main issue here is to determine the extent to which the last compositions of this period reflect the solution he sought to give to the technical and thematic problems emerging at this stage of the development of his art. Thus, his decision to grant "The City" a place in the approved poems, makes even more complex our task of tracing his development toward maturity, especially since the poem is not representative of the new period. Yet the fact remains that even in 1910 Cavafy was still a prisoner of his walls, still groping for solutions, although he was feeling his way toward the exit. What holds for "The City" is equally true for his "Ithaka." Both poems contain noticeable imperfections, but "Ithaka" is in many respects a superior poem. However, whereas thematically the "Ithaka" reflects quite faithfully the poet's own mood around 1910, "The City" had long before that time lost its situational pertinence. Actually, these two poems provide the sharpest contrast and, when read together, express aspects of the human condition that seem beyond reconciliation. Therefore, it strikes us as paradoxical that Cavafy would want to publish "The City" at all, particularly at a time when he was intensely working on the "Ithaka" themes and making plans for a new policy for the editing of his poems. The only reasonable explanation would be one which assumes that Cavafy was fully aware of his nearing the gateway to the exit and that he needed to put into effect a principle of editorial arrangement of his poems that would demarcate the end of the crisis period and announce the expected passage through the gateway. The poem which had best captured the dominant mood of the crisis years, beginning with 1894, is none other than "The City." As recapitulation of what preceded the sighting of the exit, it remains an outstanding statement on the darkest hour of alienation foreshadowing the phase of the windowless existence of self-imprisonment. Cavafy could not have made a better choice with which to open his *Collections* period.

There is no need to recount here what has already been said in chapter

2 about the circumstances of his life during the mid-eighteen-nineties. What is more pertinent to the problem of explaining the curious and paradoxical place of "The City" in the canon of Cavafy's approved poems is its thematic contrast not only to "Ithaka" but more so to a special group of unpublished poems he wrote after June 1903, and also its agreement with the crisis poems of *Booklet* 2. It should be noted that not a single poem in either *Booklet* 1 or *Booklet* 2 is explicitly erotic, including "Desires" with its covert overtones of unspecified suppressed passion. Between June (?) 1903, when he wrote the unpublished "Growing in Spirit" in which he declared his intention to learn from pleasure as one who "will not fear the destructive act," fully aware that "one half of the house must be pulled down"—and 1910, he wrote at least the following erotic poems: "September, 1903" (1904); "December, 1903" (1904); "January, 1904" (1904); "On the Stairs" (1904); "At the Theatre" (1904); "Memory of Pleasure" (1904, later revised as "Come Back" and included in *Collection* 3); "The Tobacco-Shop Window," published in 1917 and included in *Collection* 3); and "March, 1907" (1909, later changed to "Days of 1903," first publication in 1917, included in *Collection* 3). Of these ten erotic poems none was published before "The City," and only five eventually found a place in one of the *Collections*. They were held "prisoners" until such time as Cavafy was well beyond the gateway.

The fact that Cavafy wrote at least ten, that we know of, explicitly erotic poems prior to 1910 may be appealed to as irrefutable evidence that he had come to grips with his passionate side, and was well liberated from the inner controls and fears so powerfully symbolized in the crisis poems. However, such an appeal would leave the decision for the delayed publication of "The City" in a state of confusion, to say the least. Evidently, Cavafy exercised good judgment by not allowing the expression of his emotional and subjective experiences to take command over his creative life just because he had bestowed upon them the credentials of erotic poetry. By postponing the publication of the erotic poems he was tacitly admitting certain reservations which exercised a binding hold so long as the perimeter of the self-imprisonment was serving as constant reminder of his artistic predicament—uncertainty about his technical maturity. Admit his eroticism he did, but only as a "hidden" thing, a confessional record written in privacy, and for exclusive use. Despite the sincerity and integrity of these poems, he was not ready to present them as substantively integral parts of his *public* "work in progress." Though written a decade later than "The City," and more advanced in their technical aspects, they could not receive his final approval so long as the state of mind which had its roots in the experience articulated in "The City" continued to manifest itself in ways beyond his control. Therefore, their premature recognition and release would have been artistically inauthentic if not a gesture of defiance. All these considerations lead to the conclusion that the best way to understand the place of "The City" in the canon is not through his erotic poems prior to 1910, even if they constitute reliable signposts of his personal and artistic development, but in connection with such crisis poems as "The Windows," "Walls," "Trojans," "Waiting for the Barbarians" and "Desires."

3. The Perimeter of the Polis

The interpretation of the crisis poems, to be discussed in chapter 6, owes whatever advantage it may have to a deliberate approach that assigns priority to strict chronological order of composition. The purpose there is to identify the co-centric perimeters of self-imprisonment and define the corresponding states of Cavafy's development with reference to representative poems. Thus, "Desires," although written in 1904, unmistakably intimates its place in the long process of self-alienation which was completed with the entombment of the desires in a mausoleum. The widest perimeter within which this process was destined to unfold his personal drama, coincides with the reaches of a depersonalized city in the 1894 composition. The retreat to the two inner perimeters follows with inexorable logic until the exterior limits steadily contract to form the inner wall of utter loneliness inside a windowless structure. Between the outer circle and the narrowest point of "The Windows" lies the blurred surface of the inner sides of the "Walls," revealing dimly the planes of the intervening region. Only three years separate the first conceptualization of the outer circle in "The City" from the strict confinement presented in "The Windows." The 1898 poem "Waiting for the Barbarians," occasioned by his reading of Gibbon's *The History of the Decline and Fall of the Roman Empire,* when viewed in this context, is nonetheless a restatement of the impasse cast in objectified imagery and social symbols, and therefore could be treated in conjunction with "The City" as an inverted critique of political decadence and cultural exhaustion. Cavafy's repeated attempts to rationalize the predicament, as reflected for instance in the 1899 poem "Che fece . . . il gran rifiuto," are intimately related to the futile efforts to break through the walls of the besieged self, as in "Trojans," and to the fumbles and compromises which dominate the themes of a number of poems, among them "Thermopylae" and "The Satrapy." Parallel to all the work it took to conceptualize and explore the nature of the predicament, is the gradual emergence of his acceptance of his eroticism.

We may now turn to the substance of "The City" and its ambiguities. Thematically, it presupposes a finished individual drama: the squandering of a life and the ensuing *impasse*. The desperate groping for a hope to escape, given in the first stanza and the harsh pronouncement of a condemned future in the second, are presented as two movements set on a course of collision. The first already contains all the ingredients of the anticipated doom. The second follows like the seal of fate and with the sound of heavy hammering to secure the prisoner back in the cell of his own making. The situation Cavafy describes here is unique—it pertains only to the despondent *persona* in the poem—though if by accident it should happen to suit other *personae*, the validity of the predicament obtains with equal force. Beyond this type of probable recurrence there is no intended general extension of the truth which the poem claims.[12] The thought that what is an endemic element may spread as an epidemic, receives no mention in the poem; and since it is not a thematic ingredient, Cavafy carefully refrains from turning his concern into a cultural diagnosis, least of all a prognosis of some impending universal decadence.[13] The situation of the pathetic, which is what "The City"

---

[12]Contrary to Cavafy's carefully phrased comments, which prohibit the generalizing of a particular situation, e.g., that of "The City," there have been critics who prefer to extract from special circumstances a message about a universal element in the human condition. For instance, one critic goes so far as to rewrite certain verses in order to prove his point. Thus, "my heart" in line 4 of the first stanza is changed to read: "And our heart is buried like someone dead." By substituting the plural pronoun for the singular, the critic Elias Ganoulis forces the verse to conform to the use of the plural in "Trojans." Similarly line 3 is made to read: "Every effort of ours . . ." See Yalourakis, "Elias Ganoulis on Cavafy," *Nea Estia* 99 (Feb. 15, 1976): 234.

[13]Vrissimitzakis 1975, along with many other critics, finds "The City" overwhelmingly pessimistic, and goes to special pains to explain its dark outlook by introducing *dramatis personae* from other poems. Thus, he writes: "But if in one respect the person in this drama cannot break the chains, in another respect he is still able to free himself from other bonds.

embodies, like that of the tragic, requires the presence of special circumstances in the lives of individuals in order to emerge with the inevitability of a destiny. And, once it makes its appearance the victim can either accept the consequences with dignity or bleed to death in a hopeless struggle from which there can be no escape: "There is no ship for you, there is no road." Such is the reached *impasse*, but the reader does not know, nor has any grounds to infer, the manner in which the *persona* in the poem succumbed to the pathetic. The rest of the drama is acted out in the secrecy of withdrawal while the reader is free to guess and sympathize. To add more to the poem than Cavafy intended would destroy the logic of the pathetic, namely the dependence on the unpromising ambiguity of the future; for without it, the sense of suspension vanishes.[14]

If the more personal elements of the pathetic themes are traceable

---

There are living currents which run in all directions through the city, if one only knows how to find them" (19). The issue of pessimism, once it is introduced, poses a problem which is more of the critic's own making rather than Cavafy's. As a result its defense forces a strained interpretation. If Cavafy wanted to salvage the *persona* in "The City" he would have done so himself, but then it would not be the poem it is. For Cavafy's answer to his critics on the issue of pessimism, see the poet's "self-comment" devoted to this issue in Cavafy 1942: 43-45.

[14] At the heart of the ambiguity is the absence of a clear assignment of responsibility for the situation of the *persona*. One of the verses declares that all attempts are doomed to fail, and that means past, current, and future efforts. It would hardly be an adequate explanation to say that the cause is to be found in the last three lines of the first stanza; and to say, as some commentators have, that we have here "an image that symbolizes personal responsibility" is to claim more than the poem allows, and furthermore that the element of ambiguity has been thereby removed. Neither the early version nor the emendations Cavafy made before publishing "The City" support the position on responsibility Ilinskaya 1983: 69, defends in her otherwise insightful book. The "self-comment" already quoted, made in 1930, leaves no doubt about the ambiguity on the issue of responsibility: "The life of certain people, whether they are themselves responsible, or because of the circumstances, becomes such that one monotonous day follows another monotonous day." The controlling image Cavafy sought to suggest in this poem is precisely the one he phrased in his 1896 (?) letter to P. Anastassiadis, that of "deep . . . endless '*désespérance*'." The context makes it clear that the expression 'endless' does not imply permanence, nor does the poem as a whole call for a search to identify the causes of the squandering of a life and the assignation of guilt. For other interpretations of "The City" see: Keeley 1976, ch. 2; Malanos 1957: 72-73, 301-2; Michaletos 1952: 28-36; Seferis 1974, v. 1: 414-5; Sherrard 1956: 83-96; Tsirkas 1958, ch. XII.

back to the experiences of 1894, the situational truth loses none of its intensities. Comparable circumstances in the life of another individual may appear, foreboding the eventual surrender of all hope and the raising of walls. Still, technically, "The City" belongs to the crisis period and suffers from the characteristic weaknesses other poems of the same vintage have regardless of Cavafy's decision to grant it a leading place in the *Collections*. Judged in a more narrow way, "The City" is without doubt the strongest of the twelve poems Cavafy wrote in 1894. His own editorial judgment confirms this fact. Thus of the entire poetic output of 1894 only one poem, "The City," was finally included in the *Collections*; "Second Odyssey" falls outside these considerations since it was not published; two poems "Sweet Voices" (="Voices," published 1904) and "An Old Man" (published 1897) were incorporated in both *Booklets,* 1 and 2; one was published but condemned later; four remained unpublished and three others listed only by title.[15] According to Cavafy's own early thematic list, "The City" was given a place in a group of poems under the special thematic designation *Prisons,* which included "Walls," "The Windows," "Like Dead" (written in August 1897 but lost), "The Souls of Old Men" (written in 1898, published in 1901 and included in *Booklets* 1 and 2), and "Confusion" (U 1896).[16] Thus, this plan to group certain poems under the heading *Prisons,* and the general mood of the 1894 compositions, help to build the background needed to view "The City" in its proper perspective.

Let us now turn to the poem itself. In the first stanza, the poet is quoting himself, and more precisely, disclosing his need for hope, his fall into desperation, and his admission of failure. The psychic state is clear enough but the setting is left uncertain, if not opaque. The city has no name, no

---

[15] The titles of the three poems are "Second Odyssey," "In Vain," and "Injustice." The five unpublished poems are "Whoever Has Failed," "The Pawn," "Terror," "In the House of the Soul," and "Rain." The dates of the 1894 twelve compositions, according to Cavafy's records, are as follows: (1) "Second Odyssey," January; (2) "The Inkwell," February; (3) "Whoever Has Failed," June; (4) "The Pawn," July; (5) "Sweet Voices," July; (6) "In The Same City," August; (7) "In Vain," August; (8) "Injustice," August; (9) "Terror," September; (10) "In the House of the Soul," September; (11) "An Old Man," October; (12) "Rain," November.

[16] For the unpublished poem "Confusion," see Savidis' note in Cavafy 1968: 225; the thematic list is F 82.

identity and no character of its own. It could well be any city, provided that at least one individual living there has fallen into a comparable state of despair and alienation. In the poem, this particular city remains unnamed; the details are left to the reader's imagination except when the poet paints its contours through adroitly chosen subjective reactions. Purposely omitted from the total image are the city's bustling activities, market-places and night life; above all, there is no mention of its inhabitants. Yet the temptation to compare it with other, and better cities, also left unnamed, is under strict control; the speaker as he surveys his ruined life simply assumes their existence. But, regarding his own city, it is quite certain that its drab and dreary conditions will continue to provide a depressive environment so long as the inner state is forced upon the outer landscape. In fact, the inner intensity generates so bitter an attitude as to preclude a change of mind. And the decay stays on course moving at a steady pace.

As the poem opens, the squandering of a life appears to the *persona* to be an irrevocable fact. The focal point is not the fact, but the intensity of the feeling the perception of "the fact" has generated. There is nothing in the first stanza which gives information about the *persona*, his initial expectations and goals, his specific desires, wants and ideas, of the circumstances responsible for the squandering. No clues are given to reconstruct the past and see what caused the damage. The *persona* stops short of assuming full responsibility. His weaknesses and errors are guardedly shrouded in silence. All efforts to escape have ended in failure.

The ominous signs of doom mark a terrain far bleaker than the one we see in "Trojans" (1900/*1905*), where at least for a while a new start could be made and hope was still alive. The *personae* in "Trojans," besieged in their citadel, at least appear determined to defend it. Clinging to their love of it, they prepare to face the fall and meet their fate while the threnody of the elders recants memories of yesterday and glories of old. In "The City," there is no reference to the homeland. If anything, the city is already turned into a wasteland, a place of ruins holding neither promise nor redemption. The poet could go no further than this in the cleaving of city from inhabitants. The second stanza comes to shatter not only the possibility of reconciliation, but even the chance of making a new start somewhere else. Once one's own city has been turned into a replica or a projection of the inner landscape, the pitiful outlook will repeat itself with the same affective gloom: "Always in the same city you'll arrive." In this sense, every city is destined to become an occasion for the ruined self to reproduce its image. The city conforms to the person, and if the heart is deadened so is the world around it. When the poet asks: "My mind, how long will remain in this decay?", the only hint toward a hopeful solution lies in the full resurrection of the heart. The mind cannot alone discover the exit so long as the desires remain prisoners of the windowless self. In Cavafy's own case, it took years before the poet's power of mind could cut through the walls of emotional darkness and discern the roads to other lands and other seas, and above all find his own city, Alexandria.

4. Inverting the Classical Mode

The choice of title was indeed a rare gem of poetic ingenuity. Although the word "city" is employed in the widest symbolic way and therefore Cavafy fails to muster the needed concreteness to satisfy the rules of composition in the *Ars Poetica*, it serves to generate a subtle paradox. The title must be understood as an integral part of the poem, yet the theme of "The City" is not about a *polis*; in essence, it is a subjective state in its implosive moment revealing the horrid details of self-ruination. The city itself, whatever its locale, stays in the background, unaffected, detached, beyond the grasp of the reader except as it must be imagined as the stage on which a personal drama is being performed. It has neither history nor identity, and thus it is simply a field of opportunities to which the *persona* responds with a closed mind or, to put it more mildly, without the requisite preparation to find his niche in it. Whatever the case may be, the result is the same. There is no indication that the *persona* ever identifies with the city, and consequently no sign that it feels any loyalty towards it. The separation is total: the self on the one extreme of the polarity, the city on the other. All expectations for the convergence of the two end in frustration. Noticeably absent from "The City" is the moving force that inspired the "Builders," giving the impression that the two poems were composed by different poets.

Since nothing flows by way of obligation from such a disengaged self, the *persona* cannot even conceive of possible efforts he could have made to declare his presence as a citizen. There is no hint at being a willing participant in civic affairs prepared to contribute his share to public life. The concern is so exclusive as to emerge as a pathetic preoccupation with one's own salvation, which, as the first verse declares, compels the *persona* to want to depart for any other city, hopefully better, where the desires may blossom and the mind recover its strength. The second stanza, in which the *persona* replies to itself, shatters the fiction of self-delusion: "Other places you'll not find . . . ", "Always in this same city you'll arrive." Given this self-defeating outlook, all cities become alike, neither better nor worse, just depersonalized.

But let us turn to the paradox itself. Although the poem is not about the factual city, or any particular city, the title is still part of the meaning of the poem. The title builds on an element of expectation since the word *'polis'* carries with it a wealth of associations, reminiscent of Aristotle's celebrated definition "man is by nature a political animal," Socrates' loyalty to Athens, and generally the classical ideal of civic virtues. In those times, fatherland and culture could not be separated in the minds of the citizens without splintering the meaning or dimming the prospects of the good life. Ideally, the citizen's identification with his own *polis* was so deeply rooted in his consciousness that leaving the city against one's will was tantamount to a fate worse than death. In contrast, with Cavafy's opening line in the poem all these cultural and historical connotations of the word *'polis'* are being swept aside once the *persona* states the decision to leave for another place in search of a city "better than this." Immediately, the emphasis switches from the realities for which the classical *polis* always stood to the inner world of an estranged person set on escaping. Even if the city had once provided a livable environment for the poem's *persona*, by this time the rejection had become final and irrevocable. Thus we cannot help but suspect that for this particular individual the city had always been nothing more than a place of fleeting affections. It is precisely this outlook that subverts the *polis* into a *cosmopolis*. Hence, the readiness with which the *persona* feels free to walk out of that maze of streets and neighborhoods, which have never been his. The self has prevailed over the city at the costly price of an illusory freedom. Probably, there was no feel for the city to begin with, but Cavafy has left this part unsaid. The suppressed elements of the context allow the reader to suspect that this state of mind of the *persona* could arise only in response to the conditions of life in a cosmopolis that forces the individual to retreat behind the fences of privacy and suffer there the bitter consequences of withdrawal.

Both the title and the thematic content, the first as the inversion of a classical idea and the second as a bold projection of self-estrangement which has ended in despair and condemnation, converge to convey the same result:

the fate of the individual after the loss of the *polis*. In this poem Cavafy is more than a self-conscious observer who depicts a true-to-fact situation in a forcefully confessional tone. The implicit promise in the title announces a seemingly objective reality which claims to represent nothing less than the most complex organization of collective human life, the city of man. However, by the time the poem ends, Cavafy has drawn the wide perimeter of a prison rather than of the luminous outlay of a city. Only a poet with strong historical consciousness, who was also a student of the human condition, could have accomplished so much within the limits of two stanzas. Cavafy is able to do this, not merely by utilizing wide and suggestive symbols, but by projecting from the outset the illusion of objectivity which the device of statement-counterstatement creates. Since the "dialogue-in-the-monologue" presents the predicament as a personal situation with full awareness of its consequences, form, content, and title, are brought to bear on one another. Whether Cavafy was fully aware that he had discovered in 1894 a technical element that he could develop into a powerful device for *double entendre*—presented here as the inversion of the classical mode—is not the issue. The original title "In The Same City" was too literal and far too faithful to the content to credit it with the invention of so ingenious a device so early in his development. Sixteen years later, when he was able to remove certain imperfections and revise the title, he was well on his way to giving full reign to what was perhaps only dimly felt at the time the poem was composed.

What counts is the final result. The inversion of the classical mode through a single word in the title prepares the reader for the full message of the poem: by losing the city the individual loses his self, and when the experience is honestly seen for what it is, the self reflects the image of a city as the wasteland of the psyche. By striking out the words "In the same" in the title, Cavafy gave his key symbol unexpected ambiguity and scope. It could now cover not only the fate awaiting one who must live in the same city, but also the curse of being condemned to repeat the same error of judgment everywhere. With the cause of the real prison properly located in the self, the physical limits of the city suddenly matter less, but so does the identity of the city. As the realization of the predicament which Cavafy diagnosed as being his own deepens, the contraction of the outer perimeter gradually tightens its hold until the sense of space is reduced to the inner surface of a windowless life. The process that would end with the closing of all exits was dramatically announced in 1894. The subsequent poems of the crisis period should be read as further elaborations of the same basic theme and also as special statements on the successive phases through which the narrowing of the outer perimeter of the self had to pass. Quite masterfully Cavafy avoided the temptation to make "The City" the lyrical outcry of a personal problem. Subjective though the situation of the *persona* is, the objective character of the drama of the broken bonds between self and city in the condition of a cosmopolis is preserved intact and cast in modern mold. After its publication, with the noted emendations in 1910, Cavafy, decided, quite wisely, to use it as the opening piece in his mature *Collections*, thus prefacing the new creative period with a major statement on the darkest hour of his life: the moment when all exits had been blocked, and the process of retreat had severed one by one all traditional ties to the city.[17]

It took him almost sixteen years to learn how to walk confidently in the streets of his own city. With the writing of "Ithaka," Cavafy made a joyful exit, but it was no more than a spectacular flight from the rusty cage. The rediscovery of his city came in the wake of a voyage in reverse with his "The God Abandons Antony."

Not more than three years separate "The City" from the writing of the "Builders" in September 1891.[18] The sense of social mission was then wedded to the cultural role of the poet, and served as a source of inspiration to Cavafy who in his early manhood had developed such a strong interest in the meaning of progress. Untutored as he was in the complexities of practical affairs, he adopted a facile theory of the cycles of civilizations. He put his hazy reflections on historical progress into oracular verses in which he expressed a naive pessimism about how progress, when it reaches the point of perfection, also comes to reveal its very imperfection: "Its own perfection will bring the work to ruins."

His high-flung idealism, though far from helping him to clarify his serious objectives, convinced him that he qualified for membership in the caste of builders who bring "reason and council" to the "great edifice." If the

---

[17]Savidis notes that "according to Cavafy's thematic order "The City" and "The Satrapy" are twin portals to his mature poetry at least up to 1916." See Savidis "Notes to the Poems," in Cavafy 1992 [1975], rev., tr. by E. Keeley and Ph. Sherrard, pp. 224-25.

[18]This poem and other early poems are discussed with reference to Cavafy's poetics in chapter 7.

external circumstances and shifts in his family's affairs deprived him of opportunities to make his contribution to public life as a man of ideas, his own theoretical preparation was far from adequate for the ambitious role he envisaged in the excitement of poetic aspiration. Within three years the spark that had fired his imagination to dream of noble deeds had reduced the spectacle of progress to "the black ruins of my life." His own imperfections did not have to wait for the completion of the edifice of progress to show their depleting effects. The force of habit and the misdirected convictions on which he depended for his self-esteem did the rest. When he wrote "The City," the heart was buried "like the dead," but the reflective poet was very much alive to ask the saving question: "how long will it [his mind] remain in this decay?" A shaft of light was still lingering on to help make the black ruins of a squandered life visible enough.

Cavafy, the disappointed citizen-builder, unable to bring his heart and mind together, soon enough found himself pacing feverishly the dark chambers of a psychic labyrinth until the withdrawal is sealed in self-estrangement. The fall from the lofty heights of the "Builders" is what marks the first chain of the events which in retrospect provide the proper background to understand the man in "The City."[19] If the historical components of the dream were rooted in the cultural tradition of the classical ideal, the realities of Cavafy's modern Alexandria displayed a different texture. Had Cavafy given free rein to his emotional outburst of frustration, "The City" would probably have amounted to nothing more than a moving autobiographical cry. The form saved the theme, first by leaving the background sufficiently vague, and then by staging the drama with aid of the two masks that the same speaker uses. The constructive power of poetic thinking succeeded in transmuting the pain of

---

[19] The experiential background of the poem should be distinguished from the literary sources. Cavafy is reported to have said that the city in the poem is an imaginary one, a *phantastiki polis*. See Cavafy, *Self-comments* (1942): 24-25. Tsirkas 1958 believes that the source of the poems can be traced back to James Thomson (1834-1882), whose poem "The City of the Dreadful Night" contains parallel lines and similar expressions, and is therefore a most likely candidate (251-56). Tsirkas' proposal, based on a Marxist thesis, tends to read into the poem more social realism than the content allows. This emphasis leads him to conjecture that Cavafy's disillusionment is directly caused by loss of social standing and also to conclude that the "escape" need was already present during the period of Cavafy's stay in Constantinople.

personal suffering into a poem of wider relevance.

5. The Penumbra of "The City"[20]

None of the other poems written in 1894, ever came close to the achievement of "The City." Their real significance, even when allowances are made for the ones he published, lies in their forming the penumbra of "The City." Of the five poems which precede it, only three seem reasonably certain of falling within the first half of the penumbra by way of anticipating in some respect the eventual emergence of the dominant theme of "The City."

A few comments will help to exhibit their continuity with this theme. On the surface of it, the first poem of the year 1894, "The Inkwell," written on January 2, seems unrelated to the wider context of the closely knit themes that form the penumbra. A careful look convinces the reader otherwise. In a way, the poet is trying here to cover his tracks without losing face in the event of artistic failure. The inkwell, endowed with the power of a fountain, yields a whole world of poetic meanings, "diamonds of our imagination," as the poet draws ink from it and the words drop from the pen. But what if the poet should be overtaken by deep sleep some night never to awake? In the closing lines, Cavafy laments "the many people who will be lost" to poetry; still, he finds consolation in that the words will always be there and no other strange hand will be able to bring them to us, for the inkwell, "faithful to the poet, will refuse."

The symbolism is fatefully artificial and hardly able to conceal the sentimentality of self-pity. He cannot quite bring himself to admit his technical deficiencies, nor can he honestly face, at this period of his life, the truth that open confession may bring to the surface. His poems turn out as failures—either disguised confessions of rationalized inadequacies, or mediocre imitations of fashionable techniques through which his thought could never move beyond the range of a monochord. Lost in the mist of wishful thinking,

---

[20]The chart in section 1 of this chapter indicates the place of the penumbra poems preceding and following the composition of "The City" in August 1894; of the thirteen poems written within a year, January 1894-January 1895, four were published, seven remained unpublished, and two were lost.

he can hardly rise above the level of a mediocre versifier writing a poem about the genius of the poet, the blossoms of which may never grace the world.

It is quite evident that by trying to transmute his problems into poetic content with such poor means, he could not claim that he may have reached "the first step," as suggested in the 1895 poem of that title. If anything, and at best, his state of mind was what he voiced through Timolaos in the 1892 poem "Timolaos the Syracusan": "though his soul is filled with music . . . in vain he tries to sing his secret notes." Yet Timolaos—Cavafy's own self-projection in a fictional identification—is pictured as the first musician of the first city of Italy! Small wonder that beginning with 1894, the harsh realities were pounding hard on the door of the house of illusion. Almost two years had lapsed since Cavafy's circumstances had forced him to seek and accept employment in the Irrigation Service of the Ministry of Public Works. That he felt disgraced was but part of his state of mind. The lowering of social standing, which he associated with the loss of opportunity to fulfill the role of poet-builder that would make him a paragon of social progress, slowly corroded his confidence in himself. In the unpublished poem "Whoever Has Failed" (U 61), written in June 1894, only two months before "The City," he painted a vivid picture of the compromises and degrading pretensions that await one who has fallen below his status and now must face the bitter prospect of humiliation, pity and lowly employment:

> For one who has failed and lost his standing
> how difficult it is to learn to speak
> the new language of begging, its new ways.

Immediately, in the next two verses, come two words, "houses" and "streets" which also figure strongly in the picture of "The City":

> How can he go to the miserable, strange homes!
> With what heart walk in the street . . .

Horrified at the thought that in his former circles he will be stared at with cold eyes, regarded as a burden, and realizing what is in store, he exclaims:

> Now, how can the proud lips
> begin to speak in humble ways;
> how can he lower the disdainful head!

In the closing verses we witness a sudden shift in form. While the preceding verses are written from the viewpoint of an observer describing the state of falling of another *persona*, suddenly we hear the same observer whispering intimate advice:

> ... How can he listen to the words when each expression
> rends the ears—and despite it all
> you must pretend you never feel them
> as though a simpleton, to understand. (ll. 15-18)

This masking of the pain of humiliation which in later, mature poems was artfully exploited as a panoply of pretention,[21] provided Cavafy with a device for introspection as well as a poetic mode for the private dialogue between the two sides of a divided self. The poem is thematically inferior compared to the heightened drama of "The City." Yet both share the same lack of concreteness. Neither poem reveals the background and foreground necessary to reconstruct an adequate picture of the causes of failure. The nature of the flaw of the *persona*, that could help the reader form some judgment and go beyond a compassionate response, is carefully concealed. It may well be that in 1894 Cavafy himself did not quite know how to assess his situation in order to cut himself loose from the bonds of false expectations, nor how to control his obsession with social standing as the means to secure his recognition as a builder-poet.[22] Working against these handicaps, which

---

[21] The phrase occurs in "Aimilianos Monai, Alexandrian, 628-655 A.D.," written in 1918, if not earlier. The deeper the relationship this poem has to the defensive mood of the 1894 poem "Whoever Has Failed" is worth exploring. By 1918 Cavafy says unabashedly that the panoply covers "wounds, vulnerable parts, under the lies." It may be no accident that within the fictional chronology of the Alexandrian themes, the dates of the *persona* 628-655 A.D. mean to convey the idea that we are dealing here with the last in the line of Cavafy's fictional Alexandrians. The co-incidence is a curious one.

[22] The view taken here on this poem differs from that of Ilinskaya 1983; following Tsirkas, she states that "the antagonistic relations of the individual and the social whole

could have easily defeated a person of lesser stature and determination, Cavafy made at least one important advance by writing the penumbra poems. He learned to objectify his situation by staring at it in the mirror of the self. Along with the admission of suffering, and the acceptance of his exclusion, came the first forging of the defensive mask and the setting of the stage to perform the drama of private dialogue. These elements merged later, through conscious use, into a powerful poetic device.

The time came when Cavafy could no longer hide from himself. However, the distance he had put between himself and his social image was not enough to set him free from his miscast conception of his mission as a poet. He evidently could not see the futility of his demand to find in the cultural mosaic of the modern cosmopolis the conditions which gave birth to the poets of the classical *polis*.

His sense of high mission continued to haunt him, but when he tried to give it flesh and bone, he could not advance beyond the composition of artificial verses, contrived Parnassian themes, and mediocre symbolic devices to disguise autobiographical situations. In July 1894, he wrote "The Pawn," where the persisting idea of mission is rather pitifully burdened with the passion for dignity and chivalric self-sacrifice to resurrect the dead Queen. The symbolism is at once facile and transparent. The poet identifies with the

---

emerge as a result of the economic deterioration of the lyrical subject who falls below his class and is now condemned to deprivations and humiliations" (67; translation mine). This could have been the case had Cavafy's aspirations been tied to the acquisition of wealth of his own as the condition to maintain his social standing. But the failure of the *persona* intimated in the poem, notwithstanding the paucity of information, must be sought elsewhere. We know, for instance, in what high esteem Cavafy held the poet in the role of a builder. He expected to be recognized in this capacity, and never changed his mind on the subject. In 1894, self-alienation took also the form of failure in two respects: (a) Cavafy *the artist* is disappointed in his own work, and (b) *the citizen-poet* with his strong expectations to serve as "builder" and co-equal in some way with the other political paragons in the community, perceives that no such social recognition is forthcoming. Liddell 1974, has done much to correct the misapprehension of what this "failure" could have been by showing that the poet was hardly in a destitute state in those years (esp. chapters 3 and 4). The reference to "deprivations and humiliations" adds little to the understanding of the poem. If anything, one is tempted to infer from what Cavafy fails to say in the poem that he did not know exactly what his real situation was, who was responsible for it or how to resolve his difficulties; rather he allows the *persona* to wallow in self-pity. The *persona*'s failure parallels the failure of the composition.

lowly pawn on its high mission, all the while threatened by castles, knights and hostile pawns, hoping to reap the pleasures of the reward upon arriving at the last line. Yet, the moment of triumph brings with it the pawn's own death as well as its fulfillment. Cavafy's good sense stopped him from publishing this piece but the conviction it embodied, though significantly modified in later years, was never abandoned. Curiously enough, the sense of mission in "The Pawn" was so carefully concealed when he wrote "The City", that the reader hardly suspects it is hovering over the ruins and a squandered life.

Quite likely, Cavafy felt so despondent and discouraged that he could only offer "The Pawn" as an epitaph to the withering vision of the poet-builder, which he had earlier expressed with such high expectations. It proved to be the best poem of the period, but did not prevent the formation of the other half of the penumbra. In the same month, and after "The City," he wrote two lost poems. Only their titles have been preserved but they indicate the mood: "In Vain" and "Injustice." No doubt, he recognized their artless quality and destroyed them. The two poems he wrote in September 1894 did not fare any better, and for personal reasons he decided to let them stay among his unpublished papers. Both bear all the familiar signs of agony over the effects of nocturnal dissipation and the ensuing pangs of guiltiness, but at the same time fail to allow the confessional urge to break through the barriers of shame. In "Terror" (U 67), also written in September, the poet prays to his Lord Christ to protect his mind and soul, particularly when "Creatures" and "Things" steal in the dark night on fleshless feet, running in circles around his bed, with eyes fixed upon him and uttering "voiceless yelps." He asks for help not to return to "those abominable former times," hoping that they will not be repeated since he is "saved and baptized in the name of Christ."[23] And

---

[23]Haas, a careful student of Cavafy's work, sees in this poem "a struggle between the powers of Christian ritual, concentrated in the symbol of the cross, and the 'daemonic' forces of paganism," and moreover a motif present also in "Julian at the Mysteries" (1896) and even a later poem, "Kleitos' Illness" (1926/*1926*). See Haas 1982: 56 and 1983: 593-4, esp. note 9 (in Greek). Haas makes a number of observations on poems and prose pieces of this period that deal with the complex theme eros-temptation-guilt-damnation-deliverance. To press Haas' point a step further, there seems to be no doubt that during this phase of Cavafy's crisis his attachment to religious symbols and fascination with religious personages, saints and saviors, re-enforce his dependence on the technique and theory of symbolism. Haas' penetrating analysis of this aspect in Cavafy's early writings complements the discussion on

exclaims: "Hide me, Lord, from their sight." In the last stanza, he implores:

> And when the creatures talk or crackle, let none
> of their cursed words ever reach my ears
> lest they bring back to my soul
> a horrid reminder of secret things they know.

The poet here seems lost in a sea of suffering. He shows no more courage to plumb the depths of his soul and let the "secret things" rise to the surface, to be seen and understood for what they are, than he does in "The City," where he similarly leaves unnamed the acts responsible for the spoiling of a life. The next poem is more forthright in tone and content. "In the House of the Soul," obviously mediocre, has as its special saving feature not the pitiful outcry of guilt and trembling but an element of detachedness and signs of introspection.[24]

> In the Soul's house the Passions circulate.
> They are handsome women elegantly dressed,
> and sapphires glimmer darkly in their hair.
> They rule the whole house—from outer gate
> to the innermost and secret rooms.
> And when the night's incontinences rouse
> the riot in their blood they congregate
> tumultuously in the hall, and there,
> with hair dishevelled and with bosoms bare
>   they dance and they carouse.
>
> Out of the house the Virtues badly dressed,
> pale-visaged,—conscious of their being clad
> in things disused, disvalued past recall,—
> hear the carousal and the wild unrest
> of the depraved Hetairae and are sad.
> Up to the lighted windows they advance

Cavafy's development from symbolism to realism in two recent books (in Greek): Ilinskaya 1983, and Vayenas 1980, chs. I and III. Vayenas' book is one of the best studies of the influence of the symbolist movement on modern Greek writers.

[24] The English translation of this poem was done by the poet's brother and signed: "Alexa[andria]. Oct. 5th 1899. Tr. by John Cavafy."

> in pensive silence and, their foreheads pressed
> against the glass, they contemplate the hall,
> and stare at jewels, flowers, and lights, and all
> the wonder of the dance.

Aspects of this poem have already been discussed in chapter 2. What needs to be emphasized here is the poet's awareness of his divided self, but with one difference: instead of imploring his Lord and Savior for help, he now sees his helplessness in a more palpable way. The house of the soul is pictured as one ruled by the passions, where a state of frenzy and debauchery persists so long as the Virtues are denied entrance and the chance to replace the Passions. The symbolism is too elementary, and the moralistic framework too transparent, to give the personal problem artistic depth. The division between Passions and Virtues has all the pretentiousness of a contrived polarity. It is worth noting that Cavafy's persisting evasiveness about specific passions and virtues has all the marks of facile generality, as well as psychological subterfuge, in intended concealment. Furthermore, the image of the house, one which figures repeatedly in many of the crisis poems, is in this case a direct borrowing from a poem by G. Rodenbach. The point is not simply that it has no originality. Rather, it lacks the conceptual precision of the device he needed to bring the problem of the divided self within sight. The dependence on prayer in the "Terror" has now been replaced by the expected performance of a miracle which would open the doors of the "house" to allow the made-to-order Virtues replace the Passions. Quite likely, it didn't seem odd to Cavafy to recognize the ruling role of the passions one month after he had already cried out in "The City" that his heart "like the dead—lies buried." Perhaps the only commendable feature of the poem is that it preserves the illusion of detachment. Here, the poet has suddenly become an observer, an outsider looking at an object, a mind reporting on what takes place inside and outside one's own soul, without the help of the pronouns "I" or "mine." Once again, Cavafy scribbled on the written page in red ink: "NOT FOR PUBLICATION, BUT MAY REMAIN HERE."[25]

---

[25]See Savidis' comment on this poem in Cavafy, *Unpublished Poems* (1968): 223. The title of the poem is from a verse in one of G. Rodenbach's poems:

> Plus au fond, tout au fond dans la Maison de l'Âme,

About a month later, and still a young man of thirty-two, Cavafy wrote his "An Old Man" (1894/*1897*: A 98), by far the most distinguished poem of the penumbra group. It was included in *Booklets* 1 and 2 but not in any of the *Collections*. Two lines in "The City" anticipate the theme of old age:

> ... In the same neighborhoods you'll grow old
> and in the same houses, hair turning white.

So young and yet so old, he compressed whole decades of the future and stepped into the land of fantasy with no other prospect but to live the last phase of unfulfillment reminiscing in loneliness the things he never did.

> And in the scorn of miserable old age
> he thinks how little he enjoyed the years
> when he had strength, and eloquence, and looks.

The vivid recalling of lost opportunities and futile postponements haunt him:

> He remembers ardors he bridled, and how much
> joy he sacrificed. Every lost chance now
> His brainless knowledge mocks.

For a brief time Cavafy had convinced himself that life had passed him by. The feeling was no doubt sincere and it enabled him to project in bold brushstrokes the image of his aged self. The carefully disguised self-portrait reveals much, but withholds even more. The third stanza is painfully true to the situation:

> He knows he has aged much, feels it, sees it.
> And yet the time he was young seems like yesterday.
> How short a distance, how short a distance.

> Où vont et viennnent et s' asseoient autour d' un feu,
> Les Passions avec leurs visages de femmes.

Cavafy quotes the first three lines directly as the motto under the title of his own poem. A photographic reproduction of the text of John Cavafy's translation into English, together with Cavafy's own comments on it, are printed in Cavafy, *Prose* (1963): 247-49.

Indeed it was. In fact, it all happened within a month's time. He had completed his identification with the infirmities of old age. He seemed ready to collapse the difference between the unhappy present with its shattered dreams, disappointments and splintering of desires, and the projected misery of the imagined future. He needed the license to state what guilt and pride forbade. Thus, what memory could now recall in reverie was not the nightmares of "Terror," not even the frustrated aspirations of the poet-builder, but sorrow for joys never had, and resentment for the sacrifices that prudence had sternly demanded. The unfulfilled desires flood the old man's memory until exhaustion overtakes him and:

> He falls asleep
> slumping over the table of the coffee-shop.

Far from entertaining serious thoughts about death, though not free from depression, Cavafy sought momentary relief in the imagined resignation which only the poetic treatment of the theme of old age affords. Yet, in a sense, while this device enabled him to focus more clearly on his erotic fears, it also helped him to substitute fictional impotence for moralistic atonement. By assuming the position of the observer of his distanced self, he composed a remarkable poem but advanced no solution.

Cavafy wrote only one more poem for the remainder of 1894. Sometime in November, he expressed in melancholy verses his autumnal feelings. "Rain" (U 75) is a conspicuously inferior poem. Someone, presumably the poet, is looking out the window facing a garden, then turns his attention to the saddening visual patterns the raindrops make on the windowpanes. Slowly the thickening film of water blurs in misty wetness the outside objects, streets, houses and carriages. For a moment, the poet shifts from the external happenings to the human side, recounting the difference between the cheerful reactions of children to the rain and the pensive responses of old men, who gaze

> with gloomy patience,
> with tiredness and boredom;
> for they instinctively
> feel no love at all
> for wet ground and shadows.

Chapter 5: The Loss of the Polis

The thought of creeping old age, bringing death in its wake, and the last event of repose and burial, preoccupied Cavafy for months to the point of acquiescing in fantasies filled with symbols of doom. In a January 1895 poem, under the borrowed title "La Jeunesse Blanche" (U 77), again from G. Rodenbach's collection of poems published in 1886, he tries to capture the meaning and hour of youth at that very moment of death that he may shroud in its whiteness the lifeless body. Probably, this is the worst of the penumbra poems, but the last four verses may be quoted for their bearing on this theme. The poet believes that "white" youth, rather than vanishing forever, actually withdraws in the white horizons of our past only to return at the moment of death, when,

> With its white hands it will take us,
> and with a fine shroud made of its whiteness,
> with whitest shroud made of its whiteness
> it will cover us.

The loss of youth, pictured here as a death which precedes the second and final death, is lamented in more strongly plaintive tones than the anticipated coming of the latter. The only consolation for the occurrence of the former is the sudden return of white youth from "the frosty regions of white horizons" to sweeten us with the illusion of listless rejuvenation the moment before it falls into eternal silence. In later poems, composed in the style of epitaphs, Cavafy will have all the *personae* die young, sparing them, and his readers, the agonizing scene of the second death. What "La Jeunesse Blanche" lacks in quality, it gains through one of its few thematic components that contains the seeding idea for the glorification of death at the hour of ripe youth. However that may be, in 1894, Cavafy could still distinguish between his personal associations with death in imagined self-reference and the death of others dear to him. In the July 1894 poem, later revised under the title "Voices" (A 95) he wrote:

> Ideal and beloved voices
> of those who died, or of those who are
> lost like the dead.
> They may return for a moment, and then reach us
> like sounds from the first poetry of our life—
> like a distant music fading in the night.

The opaqueness of the penumbra poems is noticeable in many of the post 1894 poems which Cavafy wrote while he struggled with the problem of the divided self and continued to experience relapses into states of guilt. Consider, for example, the March 1896 poem "Confusion" (U 83):

> In the middle of the night, my soul is
> disturbed and paralyzed. Outside,
>   outside it, is where all its life takes place.
>
> And it waits for the improbable dawn.
> And I wait, I waste and am bored,
>   I, within my soul, or with it.

We see him waiting in vain for some miracle to happen. He implores his Savior for protection from the surging force of passions, yet he would not resist indulging them in the stealth of night. The spoiling of a life, so pathetically paraded in "The City," had entered its destructive course. Voicing its horrors and fantasies, and projecting them in symbols through poetry, did more for Cavafy than all his implorations to his Lord and Savior. By keeping intact his loyalty to poetry, he proved that he was able to secure the best available means to conceptualize his predicament and also was able to gain enough experience to refine the tools of artistic creation.

Artless though the penumbra poems are, they form the foreground and the background of "The City." They throw considerable light on the formidable problem Cavafy had to face over a long period of time as a person and a poet before he could safely reach the shores of his art. Discussion of these poems was further called for if only because the crisis poems, composed after 1894, show how limited his scope was with regard to themes, symbols, imagery, and vocabulary. Yet, during this very period, Cavafy shows deep sensitivity, acquires a wider knowledge of history, and learns how to adjust to the pressures of diurnal life. That it took him years before he could balance the inner and outer sides of the self, and thus transfer the artistic potential of his external world to fill the world within, should be of no surprise. It was only thus that he finally freed his poetic mind from the clutches of self-pity and the fear of failure. This is exactly what the exit signaled to him. But there were more stops to be made. "The City" stands out as the signpost of despair on the landscape of ruins. Fifteen years later, the poet returns to it and uses the ruins to build there a grand mansion of consummate poetry. It took the mind of a great poet to build a monument of art from the ruins of a squandered life.

Chapter Six

The Crisis Period

1. Plotting the Province of Art. 2. The Fear of the Lonely Self. 3. The Inner Side of the Walls. 4. Erecting the Walls. 5. Fumbles and Compromises. 6. Postscript to the Inverted Walls.

1. Plotting the Province of Art

Cavafy formulated the canon of "philosophical scrutiny" in 1903 and continued to refine it through practice. However, the difficulties of applying it to revise his salvageable poems persisted even beyond 1911. Being aware of the demands of the canon and writing new poems which met them with full satisfaction proved to be two different things. This struggle for artistic maturation set the tone for the agonizing period of the crisis years which lasted down to 1911 and 1912, when he finally approached the gate of the exit.

The sense of confidence which marks his *Ars Poetica* notes is somewhat misleading. Cavafy's search for a definitive canon is intimately related to his hesitation to come to a final decision about what poems should be excluded from the *Booklets* 1 and 2. This winding path of his literary development, provisional and tentative as it was, fits well within the broader picture of his psychological crisis, which as his private notes tell us became so acute as to create unbearable phobias before he was able to resolve it. In this chapter the main phases of Cavafy's crisis period are studied as a revealing series of escalating episodes that ultimately led to his discovery of the exit. The pain and intensity highlighted in the poems of this period were the accompaniments of his search for sincerity, wholeness and total self-acceptance.

Before proceeding with the analysis of certain representative poems of this period, we need to consider a general thematic issue. Numerous critics, especially those who wrote on Cavafy when he was beginning to be recognized as a new voice in modern Greek and European poetry, have misinterpreted many of the "crisis" poems of this period mainly due to lack of sufficient information about the complex issues of this phase of his development.

Almost without exception the poems of the crisis period conform to the principle of "guesswork," as made clear in the *Ars Poetica*:

> ... care should be taken not to lose from sight that a state of feeling is true or false, possible and impossible at the same time, or rather by turns. And the poet—who, even when he works the most philosophically,[1] remains an artist—gives one side: which does not mean that he denies the obverse, or even—though perhaps this is stretching the point—that he wishes to imply that the side he treats is the truest, or the one oftener true .... He merely describes a possible and an occurring state of feeling—sometimes very transient, sometimes of some duration. (40-42)

The crisis poems have a foreground and a background. Whereas the former presents a focal projection of incident and feeling in authentic circumstances, the latter serves only to insinuate the working of elemental forces of human motivation, waiting to be transformed into historical, cultural and personal incident. The poems offer very little help to the curious reader whose interest may lie in reassembling the hidden components of the background for the sake of making explicit Cavafy's philosophy of human nature. It is the foreground which matters most in his poetry: the authentic states of feeling and action, or frustrated action and thwarted emotion, as these come to prevail under certain circumstances. Given the emphasis which Cavafy placed on the authenticity of foreground, the crisis poems, and in a more integrated way, the mature poems of the later period, are not commentaries of universal and permanent truths about human nature in general or laws of historical developments, in particular. Thus, attempts to infer from the "crisis" poems that Cavafy is a poet of gloom and cultural decadence fail to carry conviction.

Given this central guidepost, no interpretation of Cavafy's poetry which seeks to extract a theory of life by linking together the incidents of situational themes can hope to piece together his achievement or the purpose of his art. If he has a basic philosophical outlook—by no means original—it is carefully and intentionally kept in the recesses of the background. In this regard, he is not a poet who indulges in parading philosophically didactic poems, or general diagnoses of human culture offering the reader lessons on history.

---

[1] By this expression Cavafy means working with profound themes and applying the criterion of consistency.

Nevertheless, the "crisis" poems exhibit a certain blurring of contours of the thematic incidents. This feature, which so tempts the reader to risk a general diagnosis about human nature, Cavafy knew was a weakness, but he could not at that time bring it under full control. As a result the "crisis" poems came to be regarded by the poet himself as belonging to a special class. He could never revise them enough to remove their elements of ambiguity without affecting seriously the quality to which they still owe their special appeal.

Unlike the Romantic poets, including those of the mainland, Cavafy refused to embark on the quest for the "deep truth" and to go back to nature or to the presumed unspoiled primitiveness of human nature.[2] To the domain of nature he counterposed his understanding of human history. He replaced postulated poetic visions of the human psyche with events which flow from human activity and visions of progress. He held up the mirror not to nature but to what human beings do and become in civilized life, what acts they perform and how these may be recalled in memory. The one basic lesson Cavafy had to learn from his reflections on human events, one that he had adequately conceptualized by the time he wrote the *Ars Poetica*, was that neither inscrutable *fortune* nor any other mysterious force controls human destiny. The wisdom the poet needed to frame his judgments had to be sought elsewhere. Only the historical concreteness of personal and political crises could provide a field of experience to glean there the pattern of human predicaments. If sensibility focuses on the deviations and distortions of human action or thought, it is because the compromising of capabilities for fulfillment "fails to give works of immediate utility and works of beauty" (*Ars Poetica* 46).

In the *Ars Poetica*, Cavafy explicitly states his view of truth as factuality and also refers to true events as recurring situations of action and emotional states. If the poet were to limit himself to this commonplace observation, he would hardly be worthy of his craft. His art begins where selective judgment registers incidents for special consideration. When Cavafy isolated from the past certain historical parallels to his own present, he was deliberately re-creating in poetic memory an atmosphere of cosmopolitan conduct. His aim was to juxtapose an environment of action similar in character to his own in order to project the miscasting and abuses of human resources. So long as we remember this poetic employment of history and deliberate selection of

---

[2] On the influence of English Romantics in the earlier period see Keeley 1976: 178 n3.

epochal incidents, Cavafy's ambivalence toward the modern cosmopolis need not be viewed as a cipher or, even worse, a riddle. Nor should it serve as the ground to call him a pessimist or a decadent poet. These and other inferences like them follow only when the interpreter tries to construct the poet's outlook by means of a forced concatenation of the thematic episode, by ignoring the organic context and sequence of insights. The moods of the crisis poems properly belong to the completed phase of the expanding vision that enabled Cavafy to discover the "exit." They contain the seedlings from which the designs of his poetry grew and blossomed. They are the experiences of which he could say in the poem "Understanding" (1915/*1917*: A 64):

> The years of my youth, my sensual life—
> how clearly I see their meaning now.
>
> What needless repentances, how futile. . .
>
> But I could not see the meaning then.
>
> In the dissolute life of my youth
> the intentions of my poetry were being formed,
> the province of my art was plotted.
>
> That's why the repentances were never firm.
> And my decisions to hold back, to change,
> would last two weeks at the most.

2. The Fear of the Lonely Self

The fourteen poems which comprise *Booklet* 1 were written between August 1893 and September 1904, representing a period of activity spanning over eleven years, and selected according to the criteria of the 1903 *Ars Poetica*. When Cavafy completed his plan for *Booklet* 2 in 1910, he added only reworked poems written before 1905 but none of the ones he composed between 1905 and 1910. Of the twenty-one poems in the augmented *Booklet* 2, only the following six, "Trojans," "Monotony," "Dionysos and His Crew," "King Demetrius," "The Footsteps" and "That's the Man" were definitively approved for inclusion in the post-1911 *Collections*.

Two interesting aspects begin to show themselves clearly when we compare the poems of *Booklets* 1 and 2 and those of the *Collections*: (a) what types of themes and moods characterize the total pre-1910 period, and (b) which poems written during the crisis years were selected, reworked and revised for incorporation in the mature period of the *Collections*. Beginning with the second aspect, we are surprised to see that, aside from approving only six poems from *Booklet* 2, and keeping all the *Booklet* 1 poems in a state of suspended judgment, he made a renewed effort to review the pre-1905 vintage for a fresh appraisal. For decades and until the last years of his life, Cavafy seems to have struggled with the problem of deciding what poems of the "crisis" period had sufficient merit to represent his thought and moods. Thus from the large number of poems written before 1905, he finally incorporated in one or another of the post-1911 *Collections* the following (dates of composition are given in parentheses):[3]

1. "In the Same City" (1894), slightly revised with new title, "The City," published in 1910.
2. "Impending Things" (1896), published in 1899; revised with the new title, "But the Wise Perceive Things About to Happen," and published in 1915.
3. "The Glory of the Ptolemies" (1896); revised and published in 1911.
4. "Walls" (1896), published in 1897; revised at a later date and reissued.
5. "Memory" (1896), after a number of revisions and changes of the title, published in its final form as "Ionic" in 1911.
6. "Absence" (1897), revised title, "If Dead Indeed."
7. "As if in the Past" (1898), revised title, "Monotony."
8. "One of Them" (1899), revised title, "One of Their Gods."
9. "In the Church" (1901).
10. "Amphora" (1903), revised title, "Artisan of Craters."
11. "Memory of Pleasure" (1904), revised title, "Come Back."
12. "Demaratos" (1904).

It is also noteworthy that even the augmented *Booklet* 2 contains none

---

[3]"Second Odyssey" (January, 1894) was virtually discarded. The poem, considered to have been "lost," became known only recently, in 1987, when a photocopy of the manuscript was found in a private collection of papers, now in the Hellenic Literary and Historical Archives in Athens. The romantic motif of the voyage was used in a conventional way close to Tennyson's *Ulysses*. See chapter 10 where reasons are given why this poem should not be regarded as containing the seed for the theme of Cavafy's "Ithaka" (1910/*1911*). Actually, aside from the use of the voyage motif, the two poems have hardly anything in common. The text of the poem was printed in Savidis 1987: 196-7.

of the poems which were composed (in their first form) between 1905 and 1910. The "finished" poems of this period became gradually incorporated in the mature *Collections*. They are:

1. "I Went" (1905); first publication, 1913.
2. "The Satrapy" (1905); first publication, 1910.
3. "Life" (1905); new title, "As Much as You Can," first publication, 1913.
4. "Lustfulness" (1905); new title, "He Swears," first publication, 1915.
5. "The Ides of March" (1906); first publication, 1911.
6. "Philhellene" (1906); first publication, 1912.
7. "The Covered Coach" (1907); new title, "The Tobacco-Shop Window," first publication, 1917.
8. "March, 1907" (1909); new title "Days of 1903," first publication, 1917.
9. "The Displeasure of Selefkidis" (1910); first publication, 1915.
10. "Things Ended" (1910); first publication, 1911.
11. "Ithaka" (1910); first publication, 1911; its thematic idea goes back to 1894.
12. "The God Abandons Antony" (1910); first publication, 1911.

The complete list of the "unpublished poems" written between the 1894 and 1910 reveals the pattern of his working habits and the growing refinement of his critical judgment. The likelihood that he was able to salvage a poem written as early as 1894 should not be dismissed lightly. Even if "Ithaka" were to be shown remotely related to the motif of the "Second Odyssey," there is still another 1894 poem that received approval for inclusion in the first collection: "The City." In point of fact, it alerts us to seek there the beginnings of his first creative response to a crisis which eventually forced him into full recognition of the encroaching predicament.

The twelve "canonized" poems he selected from the lot of 1905-1910 production should be regarded as evidence in favor of Cavafy's intensified anticipation of the coming final solution, the "exit" poems of 1911-1912. Therefore, those who have said that Cavafy's artistic maturity occurred in 1911 ignore the preparatory stages as integral phases of the process of maturation. The crisis was in fact part of the search for the exit. Without it, Cavafy could not have found his "Ithaka." As the years went by, the thematic means, that is his own personal experiences and the special circumstances of select historical personages and groups, received clear and sharp delineation. These pieces of "remembered" history, so to speak, took on the prominence of actors on the stage of his poetic imagination. More concretely, Cavafy retrieved the neglected aspects of a lost humanism to do what the tragic poets of Greece

3. The Inner Side of the Walls

Although the poem "Desires" or "Longings" (A 96) was written in 1904, Cavafy very aptly placed it second in the arrangement of the poems of *Booklets* 1 and 2. It is a prelude to the surging feeling of loneliness, however transient and recurring it proved to be as an emotional state. The poem explains and illumines in retrospect the gradual rise of self-encasement:

> Like beautiful bodies of ones who died before growing old
> and then sealed, with tears, in a splendid mausoleum,[4]
> with roses at the head and jasmine at the feet—
> desires that passed without fulfillment
> resemble them; they were granted not even
> one night or one gleaming morning of pleasure.

This dirge song to suppressed desires and unfulfilled erotic passion has all the force of a lamentation. The deep pain, well under control, becomes a plaintive lyrical murmur. The real dead, entombed in a mausoleum, not a public cemetery; and the lament is over the death of desires rather than that of their objects. These desires, so highly revered and valued, not only resemble the bodies of beautiful dead—and they must die young to be remembered in their full beauty—but change the mausoleum of the psyche into a sumptuous monument. The imagery of the public burial of beautiful young bodies, tied to the lonely funereal ceremony of the poet's desires, accents the inner landscape of a private world, tenderly preserved in the mausoleum of unexpressed love and raised to a dubious immortality in memory of a world too personal to ask for compassion or even public commemoration.

The poet walks within the walls of his own mausoleums to inspect the bodies of beloved dead, blossoms of unfulfillment, victims of timidity and intense passion, so we are led to suspect. Yet there are no accusations here, no words of bitter resentment, only a tone of dignity and self-acceptance to

---

[4]The word 'mausoleum' in the text.

register the deaths and insinuate the circumstances. Nothing heroic is claimed; just the fact of unfulfillment, of what never happened. How many dead? The poet refrains from counting, yet enough is gleaned to suspect the many long years of suppression. However, this is only one side of the poet. The mausoleum of desires is not exhaustive of the world of plaintive erotic memory. The desires which found expression and met their erotic object received equal attention, as for instance in the poem "I Went."[5] What concerns us here is mainly the situational aspects which underline the fear of loneliness and the theme of self-enclosure of the crisis period.

What is striking about this 1904 poem is not so much the unmentioned incidents of his encounters in Athens in the year before, which became the themes of particular poems as in "September, 1903," "December, 1903" and others, but that Cavafy is now familiar with the details of the inner surfaces and the contents of the mausoleum: what he has entombed and why. At least this much can be said of "Desires": we have there a turning-point in a phase of groping experiments to measure the tone of feeling and identify the landmarks of a definite though desolate emotional region. Somehow, the outer perimeter, we suspect, hazily touches the forbidding limits of social mores and erotic resistance; fuzzy boundaries, to be sure, which inner controls prevent their crossing for fear of generating unbearable pangs of guilt and threat of punishment. Yet the desires kept gushing forth with their own unceasing force only to crowd the mausoleum with more untimely dead. Yet while the search for modes of fulfillment lasted, the choking uncertainty of where the limits of erotic action lie pushed Cavafy to find at least a temporary point of rest in the subterfuge of dignified self-pity. Albeit embroidered with artificial cliches of heroic resignation, his early poems are perfect mirrors of a disposition to abandon himself to the inevitability of the encroaching loneliness, a process which originated with the first signs of his determination to become a poet, a builder in the city of ideas.

Certain remarks may be in order to capture the special flavor of the "crisis" poems and introduce certain safeguards against misinterpretation. His prose and poetry written between 1891 and 1903 show a growing awareness

---

[5]Many other poems refer to memorable erotic experience which in later years found a place in his poems: for instance, "The Afternoon Sun" (1918/*1919*) and "Comes to Rest" (1918/*1919*).

toward critical demands for poetic precision as well as a widening interest in poetic themes. While religious concerns gradually receded, his sense of creative mission became a forceful preoccupation, and this despite the adverse change in social status, the humiliation he evidently felt in seeking employment and the pretensions he used to save the appearances of belonging to a special class in his community. His unrealistic expectations of recognition as a cultural leader, mainly on the strength of his belief in the poet-leader role, served only to add to his maladjustment. That the conditions of the Alexandrian cosmopolis presented ample and tempting opportunities for sensual indulgence was both a constant invitation to a dissolute life and a factor which intensified his inhibitions.

Uncertain about the quality of his poetic output, Cavafy found it easier to attribute the causes of his predicament to external circumstances. Unable to resolve his conflicts and torn by the ambiguities of his sexuality, he took to various forms of escape, including a dependence in his artistic expression on poetic styles alien to his real needs. When dissipation, abused hedonism and other such trappings led to uncontrolled drinking, playfully glorified in the condemned poem "Bacchic Song" of 1886, the awareness of psychic convulsions posed with utmost urgency the issue of sanity. The fear of loneliness, pounding the corroding shores of his existence in successive waves, was dealt with and eventually overcome only by the perseverance of his mission as a poet-builder. The successive layers of defeat and conscious response formed the early rock on which he was able to erect the body of the mature poems but only after many years of agony in search of the exit. Whether the splendid sight of the exit, so clearly expressed in "Ithaka," is another half-disguised escape is an open question. More pertinent at this point is the theme of loneliness in the "crisis" poems and the debilitating effects of the cosmopolis.

The inner perimeter of Cavafy's loneliness defines his self-encapsulation in a sequence of moods alternating between contraction and expansion of a region divided between despair and anticipation of defeat. It is expressed as a movement of doomed emotions, voiced in the lower register, at times in the personal "I" of the poet's constrained tone of subjective protest, at others as a widening psychic state in the plural "we" or "they," as the situation demands. The poet has issued ample warning in the *Ars Poetica* that in principle and in effect the thematic situations of the "crisis" poems were not meant to claim universal truths about permanent human conditions. The statement is worth repeating as the guideline for correct interpretation:

> If even for one day, or one hour I felt like the man within "Walls" or like the man of "Windows," the poem is based on a truth, a short-lived truth, for the very reason of its having once existed, may repeat itself in another life, perhaps with as short a duration, perhaps with longer (56).

If the chronology and the date of composition of the first draft of such key poems as "In the Same City" (="The City") are taken as indicators, we are allowed to follow the process of constricting movements pushing the poet into a "windowless" enclosure. Thus, in "The Windows" (1897/*1903*: A 105):[6]

> In these dark rooms where I'm spending
> weary days, I wander up and down
> to find the windows.—When one window opens,
> it will be such a relief—.
> But the windows are not there or I cannot
> find them. Perhaps it's better if I don't find them.
> Perhaps the light will be a new tyranny.
> Who knows what new things it will expose.

The image of a mansion was strongly drawn first in the unpublished poem "In the House of the Soul," written in 1894, where the passions had taken over, parading themselves like women with heavy make-up, dressed in dazzling attire, while the virtues, unspecified whether Christian or Hellenic, denied entrance, were watching from the outside, pensively staring through the windows at the orgiastic dances of debauchery. Three years later, the mansion became a prison of the self. In "The Windows" we find no mention of passions and no reference to virtues. The situation now is clearly one of paralyzing fear and hopelessness. The mansion has enveloped the poet, but there is no word how he got there or why, or for how long. Mid-way between the writing of "In the House of the Soul" and "Desires," the contained passions became the container, and the mansion was gradually transformed into a model for the mausoleum. The *persona* of "The Windows" lacks the ability to make the finer distinctions we see the poet making in "Desires" where the entombed contents are identified as the unfulfilled longings. Yet even

---

[6]Comp. Seferis' brief remarks on this poem in 1974, v. 1: 312.

"Desires" suffers from the burden of ambiguity; the poet still hesitates to specify what these desires are and what conditions they require in order to blossom. They are left general and vague. The reader may feel tempted to supply the rest, but at least he knows that the poet has broken out of the situation of total entombment and is now carefully attending to the affairs of his unrealized passions. But such is not the case in "The Windows." We cannot see or hear the poet except through his confessing tone. But this is a paradox, although excusable in the context of poetic freedom.

Granting all that, Cavafy's predicament in "The Windows," despite its vivid description, is shrouded in mystery. We imagine the poet, or whoever can be like him, trapped inside the mansion, moving restlessly from room to room, day after day, searching for any window. No door, no exit, is mentioned. A single window would suffice, enough to bring "some relief." But the self proves powerless, either because there are in fact no windows, or because it cannot find them. Then comes the soft whisper of timidity, a withdrawal: ". . . perhaps I'd better not find them." This is a softened cry, compared to the harsh and final tone of "The City," where the voice announces the irrevocable: "You will not find another city." Memories of contacts with what is outside recall nothing but hurtful wounds, old tyrannies. Even a shaft of light, to say nothing about leaving the mansion, may well prove to be another tyranny. One never knows what new things the light of day will reveal. And the reader is left to his own imaginative resources to conjecture those new things. It could be the tyranny of another one-sided erotic attraction, another short-lived affair with its resultant disappointment, or remorse, or a renewed effort to try again one's hand in cultural statesmanship, only to be told that there is no room for poets in the making of public policy.[7] In "The Windows" the urge to retreat and the fear of exits set the dominant tone. The situation, no doubt authentic, one of a mansion containing a mausoleum, had its place in the chain of Cavafy's moods and phases. But before we consider its antecedents, it would be helpful to discuss briefly certain implications which the suppression of the quest for a window—a

---

[7]Tsirkas 1958: 424-7, placed strong emphasis on this aspect of a political role. For Tsirkas, Cavafy's indecisiveness to open a window from which to view the possibilities of political action can be explained on the basis of the social and economic consequences which the British occupation of Egypt had for the enterprising leaders of the Greek community.

solution—have for understanding the predicament of self-imprisonment.[8] This early poem throws into sharp relief the problem of pessimism and escape from responsibility, at least for the period under consideration.

It is not clear that "The Windows" is part of an artist's autobiography, that the *persona* speaking in the poem is the poet himself. What is disclosed there emerges only as the tip of the iceberg. The submerged part, his full range of concerns, in a word, his fuller personality, remains hidden. The windows are shut, and though we hear of the restless movement of the person within we can neither see nor apprehend the entire scale of the drama. The dark rooms of the mansion protect the intended ambiguities of the poem. The poet's voice announces only what he wishes to circumscribe in the compact burden of his message. This is not so because he has come to accept or, even worse, cherish the predicament, but because he needs to illumine it. The fear of "new tyrannies" need not mislead one to draw facile generalizations about a total pessimism or the reaching of a psychological breaking-point. There are other sides to Cavafy's complex personality, other *windows* of which "The Windows" gives no hint. They can be found in the poems which precede it: the January 1894 composition "Second Odyssey," the "assuring" theme of "The First Step," composed in 1895, the "Memory," 1896, later revised as "Ionic" and included in the *Collections*, the thematically significant but technically unsalvageable "Addition," written six months before "The Windows," to say nothing of his prose writings during this period. If "The Windows" is a documentation of a highly tense moment of the "crisis" period, it is neither without its antecedents nor does it stand alone, apart from the sequel of poetic statements which highlight the way to the "exit."

About seven years after the writing of "The Windows," when Cavafy was still working on the "philosophical scrutiny" of his poetry, he also wrote a number of comments on certain poems, among them "The Windows." However, an attempt to correlate strictly the analytical and reflective statements of the comment to the lyrical mood of the poem and its intended ambiguities, would probably end in being anachronistic, notwithstanding the benefit of insight it may afford. Aside from the question whether Cavafy had in fact sorted all his thoughts at the time he composed the poem, the

---

[8]The idea of being imprisoned against one's will occurs in one of the earliest poems, "Dünya Güzeli" (1884?).

comment shows that its purpose is not meant to remove the built-in ambiguities, but mainly to illumine their source and implications. We see here a reflective Cavafy revealing the workings of the imagination of his lyrical self. The comment is presented here in rough translation:

> *The Windows*: the difficulties of life. Wretched incidents and habits form a moral darkness (the dark rooms), which we try to illumine by searching for causes and beginnings ("the windows"). And we fail because the causes remain hidden due to the lapse of much time and the intervening of many circumstances. The beginnings, when applied to present things, to past events and the promises which present things create for the future, appear to be sometimes contradictory and sometimes unsuitable. On occasion, one could suppose that it is better that the search, mainly the one for beginnings, should end in failure, because if successful it would perhaps show many errors and much ugliness and indecency, inevitable although unbearable, when brought to full light.[9]

4. Erecting the Walls

From the standpoint of Cavafy's awareness of self-imprisonment, "The Windows" marks the narrowest point in the straits of loneliness. Two related poems hold the key to the growing sense of his predicament, two co-centric perimeters of defense, one within the other; both bear the same alternating tension between a reluctantly accepted restriction and the impulse to escape the fear of loneliness. As the outer perimeter narrows, the need to locate the exit waxes stronger only to find the gateway securely chained. Finally, when the tension reached the limits of endurance, the windowless mansion, or what the *persona* in "The Windows" thinks it is, enveloped him in its dark rooms raising at least temporarily the frightful possibility of a permanent impasse.

A telling testimony to this alternating tension, a dialogue, so to speak, between the sense of imprisonment and the urge to escape is the fact that in 1894, when Cavafy first expressed his uneasiness about growing old, ending in the awful situation of being lonely, decrepit, and hanging on to life through

---

[9] The Greek text was published for the first time by Haas in her 1983 important paper, "Comments by Cavafy on His Poems: A Report on Unpublished Material from the Archives of Cavafy," in *Kyklos Kavafi* (91).

reminiscences with questionable consolation of the days when one had "strength, and wit, and looks" ("An Old Man,"), he wrote the two poems on themes that expressed the tension of the crisis period, "Second Odyssey" in January and "In the Same City" in August. The important thing here is that the generative ideas for both poems occur at about the same time. Assuming that the dreary image of "The City" was also in some definite manner the dominant note in the first draft, it appears that the outer perimeter coincides with the limits of the poet's city, Alexandria, but as his psychic state and circumstances had forced him to view it. However, the picture he draws there is a far cry from the Alexandria we see in the later poems, especially of the mature period associated with the exit and its related themes.

It took Cavafy two years to complete the first phase of withdrawal, from the condemnation to live in the same city to the realization of the presence of the inner walls. The components of the symbol remain constant, only to be recast as needed to express new intensities of the encroaching self-isolation. Thus in September 1896, Cavafy wrote the poem "Walls," and published it in the next year (A 106):[10]

> Without consideration, without pity, without shame
> they built around me great and high walls.
>
> And now I sit here and grow hopeless.
> I think of nothing else: it is a fate that gnaws my mind;
>
> for I had so many things to do outside.
> Why wasn't I mindful when they were building the walls?
>
> But I never heard the noise or the sound of the builders.
> Imperceptibly they shut me up from the world outside.

The "Walls" has been the subject of much discussion.[11] The interpretations abound and the differences of opinion often seem beyond

---

[10]The poem underwent revisions and appeared in its final form in the text of the lecture of P. A. Petridis (*Nea Zoe,* May 1909); also Tsirkas 1958: 263.

[11]Comp. Seferis 1974, v. 1: 330-331; also G. Michaletos 1952: 41-46.

reconciliation.[12] As one critic says, this is one of the most symbolic poems to be found in Greek literature.[13] There is also disagreement on the literary sources of the seminal concept on which the poem is built. Papanoutsos offers an extended argument in favor of André Gide's *Palludes*;[14] Tsirkas, on the other hand, appealing to the evidence of hand-written notes which Cavafy gave to his friend, Pericles Anastassiadis, together with what the latter had scribbled on the manuscript, proposes that Cavafy took his cue from reading Thomas Hardy's *Jude the Obscure,* esp. Pt. II, ch. 1 (p. 92 in the original edition).[15] He then draws the further conclusion that the builders of Cavafy's own "walls" bear no resemblance to those who appear in the 1891 poem "The Builders," namely workers of progress and men of social action with whom he believed then to have a direct affinity. According to Tsirkas, Cavafy switched the meaning of "wall" from that of a separation between rooms, as in Hardy's novel, to that of "walls" marking the defenses of the city, in order to give this symbol a new breadth. Thus, Tsirkas concludes, "from the isolation due to the wall of a house, the 'excluded' person suddenly finds himself a prisoner within the walls of a city." The center of gravity now shifts from the individual to the group, from the personal problem to social criticism. This observation is particularly interesting because of the critic's contention that this "is Cavafy's first social poem, because in it 'the others.' emerge for the first time, behind whose masks hide the enemies of his happiness."[16]

We may leave the question of literary sources, to consider more closely the substantive issues. To begin with, it is not true that this is Cavafy's first

---

[12]See on this, Papanoutsos 1955: 151-152, who also refers to the interpretations by Xenopoulos and Sareyannis. The latter contrasts the *persona* of "Walls" and the prisoners in the Cave in Plato's *Republic*: "The Cavafian hero is born free . . . and only later, after he develops his consciousness of externality, much later, becomes imprisoned," unlike the Platonic men who are born in a prison-cave. Sareyannis 1964: 52-53.

[13]Tsirkas 1958: 260.

[14]Papanoutsos 1955: 152ff.

[15]Comp. Liddell 1970: 119, note 4, against Tsirkas' thesis that *Jude the Obscure* is the source.

[16]Tsirkas 1958: 272.

"social" poem. The evidence does not support this claim, for just about every poem, from "The Builders" to the first version of "The City," written during this phase of the "crisis" period, contains a strong social element. Taken together, the poems disclose an intense concern either for public values or their impact on the individual, whether positive or inhibitive. The issues involved are too complex to support the position that Cavafy may have come close to becoming an idealogue groping for more stringent positions of social criticism, especially as a result of disillusionment and conscious dissociation from his own socio-economic class. Be that as it may, there is no evidence whatever that Cavafy ever contemplated making a special effort to project himself or even conceived it practical to cast his role in the form of active statesmanship in the arena of politics and community affairs. The issues, therefore, run in deeper streams.

At the level of thought and intellectual criticism, Cavafy felt as free as his scope and learning allowed. But the discrepancy which he experienced so painfully and which made the "crisis" years so acutely anomalous, had its source in the difference between the two sides of his outlook: being a citizen in the "city of ideas" and at the same time unable to provide gratifying outlets for the compelling streams of his emotional urges. For Cavafy, the conditions for poetic fulfillment called for more than securing the comforts of leisure; he also needed the tactics to by-pass a system of mores and social values which either distort one's initial potential or call for a heavy armor of hypocrisy. During the "crisis" years, Cavafy came to realize how much of his problem was due to the former and how unprepared he was to acquire the latter. His early poetic fumblings match perfectly his feeble probings into the shifting grounds of his emotional demands. Partly because of his idiosyncracy, partly due to his upbringing, Cavafy had internalized the ambivalent character of his middle-class society with its double standards, together with its scheming intrigues of conduct and confusing rhetoric. The way out of this maze proved long and arduous, for the issues reached far beyond having the right strategy for the pursuit of pleasures; they touched the nerve of cultural quality and social sanity.

The Petridis lecture which contains valuable suggestions, directly supplied by the poet, refers to "The Walls" as "that beautiful poem in which the poet pours much pessimism and melancholy and so much bitterness over certain social crudities (σκληρότητες)." If these are "approved" intentions, the mode of expression required to sustain them for directness and eloquence, deserves a close look. Whether or not Cavafy took his initial image from the "separating wall" in Hardy's novel becomes a wholly secondary matter. It may be seriously doubted that he even needed to borrow a symbol conspicuously different from the dramatic situation enacted in this poem, despite its similarities to the portrayal of social bleakness in the nineteenth century novels of Gissing and Hardy. The prevalence of oppressive social conditions, class distinctions, and moral hypocrisy was hardly confined to the organization of life in the modern city. But to return to the matter at hand, there was no mention at all of anything in the poem reminiscent of a "separating wall." From the title itself and throughout the four two-verse stanzas of the poem the same word, "walls," occurs three times; the Greek is unmistakable: τείχη. The expression "great and high walls" leaves no room for doubt.[17]

There is no intended transference of image from a dwelling to a city. On the contrary, the notion of the city, already worked out before in poetic symbolism, is fully kept intact. The difference lies in the sudden announcement of a new restrictive perimeter. The Homeric world of fortified cities, the clash of armies before their walls, the persistent sieges, the resolve of the defenders, were all too familiar to the history-minded poet from his teacher's lectures and apprenticeship in Parnassian poetry. But more significantly, we have here the echo of a rising consciousness of the conditions and ideals of the classical *polis*, of men as citizens in search of honor, truth, courage and the

---

[17]Nehamas 1983: 296, has summarized insightfully the interpretations of "Walls," from G. Xenopoulos to James Merrill. His own interpretation differs from the one presented here on two points. Nehamas is confident that the poem can be fully understood in isolation from the other poems on the general theme of "prisons," which to a certain extent compromises the "work in progress" principle. The second point concerns the difference in meaning of two nouns, both translatable as "walls": *ta teiche* and *oi toichoi*; the former means city walls and the latter, the walls of a building. Cavafy writes *ta teiche*. The choice is anything but accidental, and the simile in place leaves no doubt about the meaning: the self is like a city. "Walls" bears a definite resemblance to the theme and imagery of the poem "Trojans" (1900/*1905*). The word "outside" (ἔξω), carries much of the burden in both poems and draws a strong parallel between insulated self and besieged city by referring to the open space beyond the "walls," be it where the bustling activities of the crowds take place or where Achilles dominates the battlefield. However, there is a difference between the two thematic settings: in "Trojans" the walls protect the besieged, whereas in "Walls" they draw attention to the inverted meaning of an encroaching insularity which imperils the freedom of the *persona*. The ambiguity stems from the malfunction of "walls."

other virtues. Higher than personal honor stood the defense of the city, and for the performance of this duty the walls of the city had their physical location and proper function. Within their enclosure throbbed the heartbeat of civilized life, institutions and ideals. With a single stroke of poetic genius, Cavafy inverts the location and the function of physical walls to convey the psychic condition of the modern man in the cosmopolis. The walls for the defense of the cities have now become the limits of individual expression, and what was once built to protect appears radically inverted into a trap and a prison. The contrast is complete; and only one word, 'walls,' denoting nothing that belongs to the physical apparatus of modern cities, suffices to evoke the rich associations of a world carefully kept in the background. And justly so, for in this case Cavafy's intentions call for imagery suitable to the crudities of the modern conditions, among them the paradox of freedom and the defenselessness of human individuality. The first two-verse stanza is addressed directly to the process and the result:

> Without consideration, without pity, without shame
> They built around me great and high walls.

The dictum of his *Ars Poetica* must again be kept in mind here, and hence it is premature to ask whether Cavafy purports to insist on the permanence of the experience. Rather, his attention is fixed on its presence as an effect and the possibility of its recurrence, in other words what "they," the agents of alienation, cause the poet, other poets like him, and possibly the agents themselves, to suffer. The accusing finger is pointed toward "the others," who cause the harm, and by implication to the social thoughtlessness that generates the act of aggression. Whatever the social quantity of the "they," the victims, regardless of numbers, live in isolation, in the private worlds behind the walls of their self-envelopment, unknown to each other and condemned to withdrawal. The possibility of their social salvation is not part of the poem, and does not have to be raised to round off the intended meaning. The poet's own solution came with the final phase of the search of the "exit." In any event, it never took the form of social gospel nor did it sound the call for political or social revolutions, much to the disappointment of some of his critics.[18]

---

[18] Varnalis 1958, v. 2: 191-4; also Tsirkas: 1958, ch. XIV.

In the Greek text we have only the verb form *ektizan* (they were building); the pronoun is omitted and the subject left unspecified. The reader, with little to guide him, supplies the "they" as he tries to guess the states of mind at work, all with a negative intent. The text allows for no hint of motive. The ambiguity is fascinating and invites guessing. Who are these "others," how many, how long did it take to do their insidious work, what brought about this hostile act? No ready answer is given. The reader is tempted to identify them with those men of action who are ignorant enough to dismiss the significance of the poet's role as a statesman of ideas. Given the conditions of Egypt during that period, "the others" might well be any socio-economic and political group, native or foreign, including the establishment or the newly rich in the Greek community, which directly or inadvertently affected Cavafy's status. But all this is speculation, especially since the poet says no more about his frustrated objectives than the vague, "I had so much to do outside." Then suddenly, he modifies the unqualified blame on "others" to say: "When they were building the walls . . . I never noticed."

There must have been reasons, but he does not state them. Caught in the vise of hopelessness, he can only think of one thing: the fate which gnaws his mind. Yet all along he never heard the builders, not a sound. The identity of the builders and the isolating effect, puzzle and predicament, lock the entrance with doors shut tight, prelude of a drama to be acted in the dark rooms of the mansion. But the reader can go on in search of the "others," probably to find among them all those who in one way or another had a part in his character formation, especially his mother, other members of his family, the mores of the community, the taboos, the inhibiting force of social institutions, the quest for political power, the relentless demands for economic success, the fear of punishment and sexual refusal, all the indignities of the impersonal city which dam up or lead to the abuse of the individual's emotional and intellectual resources. Whatever the associations and conjectures the reader is free to make about the compact meaning of the "others," whatever the labyrinth of psychological complexes that generate aggression and phobias, the poet leaves no doubt about his intentions, however guardedly phrased, to indicate his share of negligence. By not noticing what was happening to him, he had passively accepted some degree of responsibility for his fate. The wailing started only after he saw the finished work. The next phase of the predicament follows with inexorable logic in "The Windows." It would seem that all could have ended there but for the power of remembrance urging him to follow the one light of promise: "the many things to do out there." The mind can think of hopelessness, but the passions make demands of their own. And in due course, Cavafy wrote his "Desires," but not before he explored all the ominous surfaces of the inner sides of his walls. Among the 1898 poems one is titled "Monotony" (A 22):

> The one monotonous day another
> monotonous one follows. The same things
> will take place, will happen again.
> Similar moments find us and leave us.
>
> A month passes and brings another month.
> One easily guesses the things that are coming:
> they are those of yesterday, the weary ones;
> and each tomorrow looks no longer like a morrow.

The poetic theme is genuine and illustrative of the recurring yet intense state of persistent loneliness. The *ennui* is there making its presence felt day after day. Such is the reaction to the hustling activities and aimless commerce of the world outside the personal walls. And the poet, for a moment, extends the self to include others who like him are caught in the snares of a monotonous existence: the same things will happen to *us* again and again. This "us" is not some recognizable community or well-knit group; rather, it motions a compassionate gesture to include those unknown fellow-travellers along the lonely path of boredom, whose names he does not know but whose existence he suspects. Whoever they are, whatever their number, each with his own walls, more will follow sooner or later, when their time will come to understand the workings of their fate. Whatever the degree of alienation, no matter where the boundaries of the restricting perimeter are placed in each case, the individuals who make up this "us" remain strangers to one another, mysteriously tied together with the imaginary bonds of a common destiny of prolonged isolation, each talking to himself, walking up and down in the dark rooms of private mansions.

Nothing is to be gained by trying convert this bleak painting of the inner landscape into a literal description. The fact is that the blocking of Cavafy's desires, left unnamed in these poems, did not paralyze his creative passion. Expressing his emotional problems through a series of poems which scan the full spectrum of frustrations is itself a set of acts, which on the artistic and intellectual side, counters the foreboding claim of the relentless, bland future, whereby "each tomorrow looks no longer like a morrow."

The poems he wrote between August 1896, for instance, and the end of 1898, both published and unpublished, give the impression of a mind traveling far and wide in the realms of the self, history, legend and myth. The change of poetic scenery and the scope of his themes show both excitement and variation, gropings and discoveries, intense self-awareness and refinement of aspirations. At least five of these poems found a place in the *Collections*, and another five were included in the *Booklets*.[19] In these and the unpublished poems we see his first attempts to plumb the riches of Alexandrian life, to capture the essence of the "Julian" period, widen the geographical horizon for the location of his themes, recast the relevance of homeric myths, come face to face with the vanity of political power and the possibility of cultural decadence, project in anticipation the infirmities of old age, and last but not least gain new insights into his own motivation as a factor in his self-imprisonment. Since the latter aspect is directly related to the "crisis" period, two unpublished poems, both written in February 1897, leave no doubt about Cavafy's feelings of self-esteem. In "Impossible Things" (1897) one verse goes ". . . the most select life is the one impossible to be lived." In one move he strikes for an ideal totally out of reach. And to make his uncompromising idealism more emphatic and remote, he declares in the poem "Addition": ". . . as for the great addition . . . I am not to be found there."

Cavafy knew full well he had willingly stepped outside the ranks of the ordinary. Ambition and impossible dreams fed his deep-seated need for self-esteem and recognition. "The others," among them the "builders of progress" he had once so eagerly identified as allies, either ignored or shattered his expectations. Having no early spectacular achievements to support him, he fell back in the murky swamps of dejection. Lacking the requisite early titles to join the aristocratic company of poets, his determination grew stronger though not his understanding of the price he had to pay. Not knowing how part of his walls were of his own making, he feared his self-imprisonment as

---

[19]In the *Collections*: "The Glory of the Ptolemies," "Walls," "Ionic," "If Actually Dead," "Monotony"; in the *Booklets*: "The Windows," "The Souls of Old Men," "That's the Man," "Waiting for the Barbarians," and "The Funeral of Sarpedon."

much as the urge to find the windows.[20] Barring help from without, he could only appeal to what frightened him most: his desires. But the road to freedom was neither paved nor straight.

5. Fumbles and Compromises

As the years of the "crisis" went by and the personal agony persisted, Cavafy continued to add to the stock of ideas from which he drew his poetic themes. Yet, the walls of his imprisonment were made of solid psychological stuff and proved impregnable, at least for a long while, to the sorties of the massing forces of desires from within. Much had to be settled before the walls could crumble under their own weight, and the much needed self-illumination to take place before the search for the windows were to become superfluous. In June 1900, Cavafy wrote the first draft of "Trojans" (A 26, original title "Like the Trojans,") but published it in 1905. It is a remarkable poem both for its excellent choice of simile and its dramatic setting and originality.[21] Technically impressive and free from restrictive rhymes, the poem rises as an elegy to the fumblings and attempts of the poet—and others like him surrounded by their personal walls, all the condemned,—to break through the walls and end the siege.

---

[20]Liddell 1970 is stressing a point too far when he makes claustrophobia the theme of "Walls" and "The Windows," among other poems. This interpretation denies these poems their special ambiguity. For instance, the search for the windows is as strong as their avoidance, and the fear of light is as intense in "The Windows" as is that of imprisonment. The *personae* in these poems exhibit deep uncertainties that give the central symbols their forcefulness and appeal. Liddell stated his position as follows: "The claustrophobia of 'Walls' must repeat itself in many lives, and it is the theme of 'Windows' also. It is connected with the boredom behind 'Waiting for the Barbarians'; it is certainly the inspiration of 'The Town'" ["The City"] (64). It cannot be doubted that an element of claustrophobia is present in varying degrees in these poems, but it is an effect rather than a cause. It is not correct to elevate the effect to the position of theme or inspiration, especially in the case of so deliberate a poet as Cavafy.

[21]For contrasting interpretations of this poem, see Seferis 1974, v. 1: 397-400; also Malanos 1957: 71-72.

> Our efforts are those of people stricken by misfortune;
> our efforts are like those of the Trojans.
> We succeed a bit; and then a bit
> we recover; and begin
> to have courage and good hopes.
> But always something turns up and stops us.
> Achilles in the trench in front of us
> comes out and with loud shoutings scares us.—
> Our efforts are like those of the Trojans.
> We dare think that with determination and boldness
> we will change the downward course of fate,
> and we stand outside to do our fighting.
>
> But when the great crisis comes,
> our boldness and determination vanish;
> our soul shakes, paralyzed;
> and we run around the walls
> seeking to escape by fleeing.
>
> Our fall though is certain. Up,
> on the walls, the wailing has already started,
> mourning memories of our good days and feelings.
> Priam and Hecuba bitterly weep for us.

The poem, except for few names and elemental symbols, shares nothing essential with the heroic world of Homer's epic. Absent are the gods and the heroes, even Achilles is undistinguished, except for his terrifying shoutings; there are no dead, no duels in the battlefields, no clamor of well-wrought arms. There is no great story to be told, except the certainty of the doom. The grand epic of the ancient world has given way to a psycho-drama. The brave armies of the Achaeans and the Trojans have been replaced, and in the imaginary landscape of the besieged city one discerns only those who are prone to disaster or have been defeated. The poet is one of them. Their *efforts* are like those of the Trojans. The similarity ends there but has served its purpose; the inversion of the heroic follows with a series of felicitous strokes. The real *dramatis personae* declared in the opening verse. "Our" efforts and attempts may well include among them the gropings of the man in the mansion. Since the simile precludes identity, and the walls of the city differ in their function from those of the lonely psyche, neither the nature of the threat nor the virtue of courage is the same. The difference also holds for the purpose of the efforts. Much in the opening verses is left intentionally vague. We don't know what specific character these efforts take, how frequently they are made and what exactly they seek to accomplish. Despite some minor successes and short-lived hope, the besieged are easily frightened to withdraw. The formidable "Achilles" steps forth and terrifies them with his shouts. Precisely what this symbolic Achilles means, except that he belongs to the enemy camp, is left vague. It could be the enemy within—the voice of guilt, the weakened will and force of inhibition—or the enemy without. The answer to this ambivalence came later in "Ithaka," when the voyage started with the discovery of the "exit" and the absence of "Achilles":

> The Laistrygonians and the Cyclopes,
> the fierce Poseidon you will not encounter
> unless you carry them inside your soul,
> if your soul doesn't raise them up before you.

So long as the predicament of the "Walls" situation prevails, all efforts to escape end in hopeless frustration, and courage and determination eventually vanish. The soul is paralyzed, the besieged scurry in disarray, running round and round the walls to find the gates and escape behind the protection of the walls. To be sure, the survival is temporary and the fall is inevitable. The inglorious end is in sight, and the threnody to the memories and feeling of days past has already begun. The originative powers of the soul—Priam and Hecuba—mourn bitterly. With the writing of the "Trojans," Cavafy concluded his diagnosis of the situations of self-imprisonment and underscored the futility of all efforts to escape the predicament, so long as the soul remains confused and helpless lacking the courage to assert the legitimate claims of the world of desires. Sooner or later, each person, however one has perceived the limits of his walls, whatever the inner and outer repressive forces, is accountable to oneself for the quest for happiness and fulfillment. The hell-like existence in the mansion must come to an end and the situation of ambivalence and indecision regarding thought and emotions must be resolved. Perhaps not every person can face this predicament responsibly; quite likely evading the challenge is preferable. But those who do should be prepared to accept the consequences, whether their answer is one of self-acceptance or self denial. If one cannot honor what his nature asks of him, at least he should be honest if not correct. Such is the dilemma of the day of self-judgment, when it finally arrives, as the poet put it in "Che fece ... il gran rifiuto" (1899/*1901*: A 104):

> The day comes for certain people
> who must say the great Yes or the great No.
> Whoever has the Yes ready within him
> is seen immediately, and by saying it goes
>
> straight to honor and his conviction.
> He who disavows does not repent. If asked again,
> he would still say No. And yet that No—
> the correct No—depresses him throughout his life.

Despite the dignified, almost priestly, tone of the voice speaking in the style of a ponderous oracle, much remains hidden. The poem was written in July 1899, and its title borrowed from a line in Dante's *Inferno*.[22] By ignoring the concrete circumstances of the infernal story in Dante, Cavafy is able to retain the distant echoes of torment by making suffering an aspect of the living, but the omission and commission are handled with a logic of evasion. The dilemma is final enough but cast in generalities, and even the adjective "great," with all the intensity it introduces, is of no help. This special breed of people eventually come to their crossroads. Unlike the legendary Hercules who had to choose between virtue and vice, in this case the alternatives here are not named, only the decision is required, the great Yes or No. By saying "Yes," one goes "to honor and his conviction." That is all. The denial, presumably never repented, correct though it is, drags one down "all his life."

One cannot help but wonder why Cavafy sought such subterfuge in this logical fumbling where "attempts" laden with a decisive finality are transformed into obscure alternatives, except for their associated rewards and

---

[22]*The Portable Dante* (tr. Lawrence Binyon, Viking Press, 1947), 16, line 60: ". . . Who made the great refusal, from meanness"; for an alternative reading see Dante Alighieri, *The Divine Comedy* (anon. tr., Doubleday and Co., 1947), 12: ". . . who to base fear/yielding, abjured his high estate"; a note explains that the lines refer to the following event: "Commonly understood to Celestine V who abdicated as pope in 1294 and made way for Boniface VIII" (432). For commentary on the poem, see Seferis, v. 1, 1974: 388-92; Malanos 1957 states: "As we know, Cavafy omits the expression '*per viltate*' to give the poem its requisite universality" (295). Cavafy takes the expression to mean 'from cowardice or weakness.'

consequences. Even the negative decision has its reward: the satisfaction of not repenting for making it, the knowledge of its correctness. We can imagine someone, like the poet himself, reading this poem to the man in the mansion or one who is among the besieged as in the "Trojans." Could a poem which reads like an oracle help his state of indecision? The problem is not whether he wants to say "yes" or "no" to his predicament, but whether he knows what ends he can accomplish. This is what the poem fails to articulate. Yet it seems paradoxical that although the poem is deficient in thematic clarity, by itself it is a creative and affirmative step, a confirmation of the poet's own artistic mission and "strong conviction." A closer reading of the poem yields the suspicion that the poet meant perhaps to maintain some kind of link between the great "Yes" and "No," for there is always the price of exclusion to be paid by either answer. Having the requisite strength of soul to decide on the day of self-judgment is one thing, knowing what one must refuse, quite another. By remaining silent on the special demands involved in the issue of ends and the dialectic of the alternatives, Cavafy prolonged the "crisis" and the announcement of his own "great Yes."

The themes of defeat and exhaustion continue to recur. The negative answer, the "great No," however admirable, takes its toll for the rest of one's life. Deep inside, Cavafy knew he could never extinguish the flames of desires, the hedonic urges, and above all, the aspirations to his ideal of poetry, a life-work which subsequent generations of young men will read and recite.[23] Not knowing exactly what conditions of life and what attitude of mind they require to blossom, "the work of the gods, we, the hurried and foolish creatures of the day, interrupt" ("Interruption" (1900/*1901*: A 102). Fears and uncertainty, agents of dubious self-protection, destroy the chances of the gods' favorites elected for bestowment of "immortality." But, then, how does one defend the precious resources of nature's gift to mankind? That

---

[23]In 1911, when Cavafy was forty-eight, he wrote the poem "Very Seldom," in which he tells us that the strong sentiment of expectation of fame and recognition, although met with renown, perhaps suffices to compensate for the infirmities and loss of vigor and looks that come with old age. The title, however, is odd. The comment he dictated to Lechonitis clarifies its meaning: "The title is a comment on the poem. The duration of a work of art which appeals and moves one generation after another, is not a characteristic of ordinary art, but only of art extraordinarily good; and this is something that happens "very seldom" (*Self-comments*, 30).

Cavafy appears so preoccupied with the notion of defense and all the ambiguities which surround it, is not surprising. Nor is the problem mainly psychological. The political and cultural consciousness he had shown as early as the "Builders" had alerted him to the social conditions which his poetic mission demanded to function. But the city was not a *polis*, nor were the prevailing values of the cosmopolis setting men free to do "the work of the gods." If anything, they turn their users into victims, the leaders into slaves, until the network of confusion drags them all into the labyrinths of self-imprisonment, a common fate awaiting the tormented and tormenting alike. And who can say that at some time or another, even for a moment, he has not felt like the person in the "Walls" or that his efforts are not like those of the "Trojans?" It is no minor admission, and once equipped with this much awareness, one has no choice but continue the defense. Thus, the poet went on, and a year after the "Trojans" wrote his "Thermopylae" (1902/*1903*: A 103):

> Honor to those who in their lives
> elect and guard Thermopylae.
> Never wavering from the duty . . .
>
> And still more honor becomes them
> when they foresee (and many do foresee)
> that Ephialtes will appear in the end
> and the Medes will finally pass through.

Two years later he noted in his *Ars Poetica*: "If 'Thermopylae' fits but only one life, it is true; and it may, indeed the probabilities are that it must" (56). The tone and identity of the defensive situation has changed markedly from that of the "Trojans." The threnody gave way to an ode of praise, and the plural "we" and "our" dropped along with the cries of self-pity. Cavafy introduces here the element of distance between himself and his gnawing problem. Technically, the perspective is different but the expectation of doom and the final outcome retain their feature of inevitability. The few borrowed elements from the setting of the famous battle in antiquity that stemmed the tide of the Persian invasion have the power of symbols of faint sounds from afar to recall the by-gone times of a glorious defensive battle to protect the fatherland, enough to alert the reader to an intended contrast.[24] Leonidas is not mentioned, nor are the Spartans; only the location, the name of the traitor, and that of the faceless aggressors. The theme is modern and without heroes, except for the unnamed defenders of an insinuated cause. The enemy is expected to arrive like the force of destiny, yet the reader is left without so much as a hint to tell why the Medes will pass or why the traitor should appear on the scene. Despite the strong beat of the encomium in the opening verses of the first and second stanzas, the poem is heavily enigmatic.[25]

Much has been written about this poem, but little has been written to suggest the place it occupies in the sequence of poems related to the psycho-drama of the "crisis" years.[26] In "Thermopylae," Cavafy advanced a step further his remarkable innovation of "inverting the classic." Aside from the distance in perspective he gained through this device, Cavafy discovered a way to lay a new and unexpected pedestal on which to place the living statues of the *personae* speaking in "Walls," "The Windows" and "Trojans." Suddenly in "Thermopylae" we see for the first time *their public side*: the qualities of their conduct in social intercourse.

The frenetic man in the dark rooms of the mansion, the hopeless *persona* behind the walls, the frightened Trojans, asking only for postponement of the doom, all failed themselves in the same fundamental way. They lacked the needed self-respect and self-esteem to recognize and value the treasures put in their trust. Not that Cavafy was ever in fact such a man, but on certain occasions he did feel sincerely and intensely the situations he so powerfully captured in the "crisis" poems we have considered. They made their demands on his poetry and he met them. But what seemed as total despair, a sort of wasteland, from the view within, became a luminous outlook from the distance

---

[24] For suggestions on the "literary" sources of this poem, see Tsirkas 1958: 406.

[25] Bowra 1949 observes that the poem is good but contains a number of defects due to a certain "abstract ring to it" (35). Other critics have praised the originality of force of the idea, especially as stated in the opening verses and the second stanza, but weakened by the "filling in" of the rest. See Themelis 1970: 96-107; also Michaletos 1952: 57-58.

[26] Beaton, 1983 interprets "Thermopylae" to mean "Not the historical pass defended and lost in 480 B.C., but any crucial moral 'pass.' A Thermopylae is a historical metaphor for a contemporary and generalized dilemma, the purpose of the appeal to history is to illustrate a perennial, and especially a present moral truth" (23-44, esp. 24-25 and 43).

of the public perspective. The defensive efforts were given a new name, in fact, a heroic name: Thermopylae. The place of a fatherland, as the symbol demands, is now replaced by the inner universe of promising potentialities waiting to blossom as creative acts and thoughts in the inner "city of ideas." They may never come to full fruition, and most likely they will not, so long as the conditions of life in the cosmopolis distorts them. However, this modern fatherland, the world of individuality, needs its defenders to protect the inner *polis* whenever the Medes, the barbaric forces of the modern, would reach the site of Thermopylae. Cavafy has shown us the inner side of the fighters' psycho-drama, but for the public faces he reserved a special word and the praise it carries with it: "Honor to those who in their lives elect and guard Thermopylae."

The critics who have found the remaining verses of the first stanza "mere filling" and trite, have missed the poet's point. The ordinary character of the moral virtues of the "defenders" is one thing, and it should be admitted that there is nothing heroic or exceptional about them. At least they possess what the offenders do not. They show pity, compassion, forthrightness, love of truth and lack of hatred, unlike the aggressors who "with no consideration, no pity, no shame" build walls. However unimpressive these "soft" virtues may be, they have a legitimate place in the poem; they are the only guides to recognize the defenders of a Thermopylae, guarding the new precious territory of their own psyche. Honor belongs to them, and even more honor to those who can foresee the outcome of the clash. The Medes will finally prevail: treachery and barbarism will cut down the flower of the creative promise. To foresee the victory of aggression and still remain determined to resist to the end, is no minor feat. Enigmatic though the poem is, its suggestive richness makes it an extraordinary epigram to the curse of awaiting fate: burial in the labyrinth of the modern.[27]

The low-key praise of the soft virtues of the vanquished guardians and those destined to be defeated lost nothing of its tone in the later poems of this period. When these virtues are not directly mentioned in the thematic body, they glow with a peaceful constancy in the background. They form the last line of defense of the individuals's inner resources. When one's circumstances

---

[27]"Thermopylae" is re-introduced for discussion in chapter 8, section 5, in connection with the theme of cultural exhaustion and inertia in "Waiting for the Barbarians."

leave no room for generosity of heart and mind, when the temptations to return to the affected manners of pretentious social circles and the diurnal shallowness of pedestrian associations prove difficult to resist, at least one should try not to cheapen his ways. To preserve one's dignity, although not up to the style that suits the ideal of the creative life, is a respectable alternative. So runs the flow of his reflections in the "As Much As You Can" (1905/*1913*: A 25):

> And if you can't make your life as you want it,
> try this at least
> as much as you can: do not degrade it
> in the crowded world,
> with constant gesturing and talking.
>
> Do not degrade it by dragging it along,
> moving often around and exposing it
> to the mindless ways of gatherings and parties
> until it comes to be like an alien, burdened life.

Such is the public side of the lonely person at its best. Yet dignity, when it takes its place next to the "soft" virtues, makes demands of its own and requires sacrifices which in the long run few are prepared to pay. Maintaining a dignified style of life is more a response to the crowding trivialities and superficial pursuits of the cosmopolis than an answer to needs of the passions or the noble aspirations to lofty ideals.

6. Postscript to the Inverted Walls

The swelling pressures of the world within require a public domain to reach their full fruition as creative acts with social significance. The dreams of the poet-statesman involve strong desires for, and dependencies on, the "things out there" than he is willing to admit or sometimes able to recognize. Estranged though he is from the external world, a locked-up mansion in the maze of countless streets, the time comes when he must end his self-exile. To keep up a way of life in continuous lack of public success and social encouragement harbors the fear of death in spiritual deprivation. The delicate bond of existence cannot endure the cruel stretching of polarized urges, and the day of yielding will inevitably come, as indeed it does. The fatal crawling along the path of compromise commences. The outcome proves to be a false exit, ending in humiliation, in just another version of a life not worth living, as described in "The Satrapy" (1905/*1910*: A 16), a twin poem to "The City":

> What a disaster, whilst you are made
> For beautiful and great acts,
> This iniquitous fate of yours ever
> To refuse you encouragement and success;
> Always do littleness and base customs,
> And indifference stand in your way.
> And how terrible the day on which you yield
> (The day on which you abandon yourself, and yield),
> And you leave, a wayfarer for Susa,
> And you go to the monarch Artaxerxes
> Who admits you with favour in his court,
> And offers you satrapies, and the like.
> And you, you accept these things in despair;
> These things which you do not desire.
> Other things does your soul demand,
>   For other things is your soul weeping . . .—[28]

There is a variant of the third line that reads "this city of yours." According to G. Savidis it helps us to understand why in the thematically arranged *Collections* Cavafy always placed the poem immediately after "The City."[29] As I tried to show in chapter 5 and again in chapter 10, another element may be added to Savidis' view and hopefully lead to a fuller explanation. It seems that one could make the case somewhat stronger by suggesting that Cavafy chose "The City" to lead his *Collections* because it represents the dominant mood of the pre-1911 period of his poetic development and summarizes the deeply felt alienation. "The Satrapy" as a twin poem projects the most important compromise one can possibly make in

---

[28]The translation is Cavafy's own, done sometime after 1910, shortly after the date of the first publication of the poem. I have rearranged the lines to parallel the original verses. The text of the translation in Cavafy, *Unpublished Prose Texts* (1963), pp. 86-89.

[29]Savidis announced the existence of the variant in his article "Are There More Unknown Poems in the Cavafy Archives?" in the newspaper *Vema* (April 24, 1983), p. 5.

one's life as poet and citizen. The decisive feature of the compromise lies in its lasting effects on one's style of life and relationship to creative work. The temptation of a satrapy lies in the promise of immediate and rich compensations it offers for injury done to one's pride. But the crucial question remains: once a satrapy is accepted what consequences follow for one's art and belief in being a citizen and one of the builders of progress in the city of ideas?

The theme of compromise is worked out with masterful dexterity. The poem opens with the misfortunes of exceptional persons, who though cut out for grand and noble acts, through fate, weakness or unfair circumstances, suffer frustration and disappointment. And then the terrible day of yielding arrives and in consequence dubious pursuits replace high-minded goals. Along with the proffered rewards comes the humiliation of acceptance. It all started when the person addressed in the poem departed, wayfarer, to seek the favor of the King of the Medes. If this citizen is one who counted himself among those who had a Thermopylae to defend, his fall is twice as dreadful. He will live to taste every drop of the poison of his decay, obliged from then on to receive in prostration all those things he does not want, and to lament the irretrievable loss of the chance to win a priceless laurel and the applause of people in a worthy republic. He gains a satrapy only to lose his place in the city where ideals are cherished and honor is earned. Worst of all, he has surrendered his soul in exchange for a gilded survival.

The thematic idea of the poem is lucidly stated from the start leaving no doubt about the generative forces of the conflict. The polarization between noble aspirations and cheap habits, itself a calamity, has laid ground for the ensuing failures. The seeds of the doom are already there; the rest is only a matter of time and opportunity. The process of decay gains momentum as the poet introduces with unexpected boldness an "inverted classical setting" to stage the drama of compromise. The borrowed classical elements require no conspicuous reference to any actual past to reveal their full meanings. With one masterful stroke, Cavafy brought together the pathos of the modern and the conflict of cultures which, as politics of ideas and ideals, has been brewing over three thousand years. The Grecian *polis*, on the one hand, and the Asian kingdoms and Hellenistic empires with their cosmopolitan capitals, on the other, have always stood for two different and completely opposed political settings of human opportunities, two irreconcilable ways of life. One could tell them apart for a while in antiquity, but the distinction was lost after Alexander's conquest. In later times, neither the appeal to geography nor the cult of personal outlooks could tell the difference between the orientalization of Hellenism or the hellenization of the Orient.

The fusion and confusion of the two traditions eventually conditioned the modern and defined its character. The person in "The Satrapy," polarized *ab initio,* has hopelessly mixed the Hellenic and the Asian, thus craving for both the demos and the satrapy but also pretending to be unaware of the incompatible demands they pose. The road to Susa and the road to Athens stand at cross purposes, with different expectations, and distinct solutions to the political, social, cultural and philosophical problems of humanity. By taking the road to Susa, the man in the poem finally sealed his fate: intellectual death in the luring opportunities of the cosmopolis. Perhaps the choice was preordained since there is no *polis* to which he can go. What preoccupied his mind at that time was the imaginative exploration of the treacherous alternatives that lurk behind the compromise solutions to the problem of self-alienation.

The "satrapy" solution contains the seed of destruction and begins to blossom as soon as the temptation takes root. The prospect of satisfaction derived from the acceptance of dubious values is known to the *persona*, and so is the anticipation of death in a state of permanent exile. The road to Susa and to the court of Artaxerxes remains open to any disgruntled citizen. Considering it as a possible solution to a bad situation generates a lingering suspicion that refuses to go away: how gratifying is the answer and how authentic is the voyage that has its beginning in a decision that opts for self-exile? The only way a traveler can feel comfortable about this type of prospect would be if he could wipe off the past and pretend possession of the innocence of a naughty child. Nothing however can be that easy, especially when the stakes are so high. For willingness to accept a satrapy from an enemy whose motives are fraught with expectations for services against one's political self, even for an ex-citizen, exposes the wound of the divided psyche to irritants that cause permanent bleeding. The road to Susa, far from being a voyage, becomes an escape from bad to worse and a refuge to compromise that leads to an existential dead end.

When Cavafy wrote the "Builders" in September 1891, he was assuring himself of an assignment in the grand mission of securing Progress, despite the belief that as progress reaches a state of perfection, it announces the hour of its demise. This was hardly a disturbing thought. What mattered most at the time was the margin of activity allowed each generation of builders and the honor to contribute. The poet-builder, the role in which Cavafy had casted himself, could readily point to a visible reward: the satisfaction due to the opportunity to participate in the constructive phase or cultural work. There was a note of mild pessimism, or rather fatalism in the poem, hardly concealed from the reader. It was hiding behind another belief: the counterbalancing inevitability of regeneration warranted by the cyclical view of history. It echoed a variation of an Empedoclean theme with a cast of human actors in the place of the primordial elements in the cosmic drama of eternal revolutions. At the more earthy level, the pessimistic stand in the "Builders" gave the assurance of the joy of work though not the promise of permanence for the product. The workers as individuals were granted the privilege of personal fulfillment despite the catastrophe that awaits their collective effort. And so it is with that of each successive generation. At the core of existence, death always spins a new beginning, heralds a new cycle.

Five years later, when Cavafy wrote the "Walls" in September 1896, he was the poet-builder who had come to the realization of being walled in by builders of a different mind. A peculiar activity, unnoticed and relentless, had been under way while he was dreaming of perfection. What the unnamed builders were constructing was not the work of cultural progress but a prison for one of their own unsuspecting co-workers. At least such was the perception of the poet. By 1896 Cavafy had come to the conclusion that the art of building the edifice to Progress was convertible into the art of prison-making. Whether intended or not, the activity portended bitter consequences for some and perhaps for all participants dedicated to social construction. What concerned Cavafy in 1896 was the fate of the role of the poet when lopsided values force him to restrict his desires to choices that limit the creative performance. With the gradual realization of the effects of the disabling victimization of his desires came the need to break out into a reactive but pathetic lament, almost a dirge to the loss of creative initiative. The cause of the predicament was conveniently rationalized: the progress builders had surreptitiously transformed themselves into prison builders of others. But there is an ambiguity built into the poem, and it allows the reader to infer that the rationalized diagnosis is not the whole truth or perhaps not the way things happened.

The *persona* of the previous poems, as it moved along the path that eventually brought it to the situation descried in the "Walls," suffered a change of heart followed by a shift in perception. To use Cavafy's own imagery, a disturbance in the spectrum of values was enough to alter the use of the walls erected for the protection of the city. What he had failed to observe all along was that walls can also serve as the means to deny one's fellow workers the right to creativity to further the work of progress. Desires, the bloodstream of creativity, became suspect, and the poet passively accepted the verdict as his own decision.

Once the citizens, poets or not, misread or abuse the initial purpose of "walls" the whole city becomes endangered and in due course runs the risk of becoming a prison unto itself. From that point on, building becomes a menace to the individual and eventually graduates into a condition for insularity. When the poet awakens to the reality that acquiescence and misplaced trust in others have brought about it is already too late. And the worst is yet to come. As the crisis deepens an inexorable process of self-doubt and self-alienation leads to the concluding phase of retreat into the interior of one's psychic space until the self is transformed into a windowless existence. The initial and spasmodic reaction to such a predicament can only be a frantic looking for one of either of two types of exit: the threnody of despair, as in "The City" or the melancholy wayfaring to Susa, as in "The Satrapy." Both attitudes had to be carefully assessed and patiently clarified as lyrical states before a new alternative could be found.

"Builders" was not a successful poem, and Cavafy found it necessary to include it in his list of condemnable poems when he reviewed his poetic output in 1903. The ideas, however, and the values that fill the poem mark the initial point of departure and therefore form the relevant background for the proper appreciation of the dramatic change of scene in the crisis poems, especially the fumblings and the gropings for solutions that turn out to be but embarrassing compromises. Understandably, it was no accident that while the "Builders" was condemned, the "solution" poems, viz. "The City" and "The Satrapy" were assigned a privileged place in the canon as integral parts of the "work in progress." The two poems reveal the two extremes that flank the new alternative proposed in 1910: "Ithaka." Yet, from the bleak external world of "The City" to the dark internal world of the "Walls," Cavafy slowly moved forward to shape the new phase of his art, one that was as much a personal achievement as it was social in scope.[30]

The confinement of the "walls" was hardly restricted to the poet's existence. Many other individuals like him, members of the human heap in the alienating modern cities, live inside invisible walls, in places that hardly qualify to be recognized as community sustaining cities. Each person's insularity points to the invidious workings of social degradation and political impoverishment, a sterilization of the psyche. And as the process of negative building continued, the resulting *ennui* created situations that shockingly enough produced a mood to protest in acquiescence, in the kind of civilized resignation we see in "Waiting for the Barbarians." The poet tells us there that the coming of the barbarians held "a kind of a solution," and yet those people were not coming for they were nowhere to be found. The insinuation is unmistakable: there is a grade of decadence below which, once reached, even barbarism cannot affect the hardened *ennui*.

"Walls" and "The Satrapy" are two sides of an unwanted coin. Before one can move forward to the solution intimated in "Ithaka" there is more on the uncharted path to cover. One recommendation is made in the "As Much As You Can" (1905/*1913*: A 25): self-respect. By 1905, Cavafy appears to have fully understood the pretensions of *le monde*, and the psychic burden of the *ennui* owed to the vanity of mingling with social circles. He knows that there is an answer to the question he posed in the "Walls," but it cannot be found unless one is willing to combine the experience of pain with the insights of a wisdom gained from staring steadily and bravely at the desolateness of the "city." The direction intimated in "The Satrapy," the acceptance of Artaxerxes' offer, suits only a person in utter despair, leading to a different dead end, to a temporary postponement of the inevitable. In a note dated December 15, 1905, written about the same time as the "As Much As You Can," Cavafy confesses intimate fears about the fate of his work:

> The miserable laws of society ... have made my work less than what it could be. I have lost unjustly in the way of aesthetics. I will become the object of guess; they will have to understand me more fully from all the things I have

---

[30]For a different interpretation see Dallas 1974: 146. It is suggested that by comparing the "Walls" and relating the meaning of the poem to Dante's *Divine Comedy* we can see how Cavafy engages in apologetics to speak from the stance of isolation which he feels as an aesthete or a sophist "of the Hellenistic period."

denied.[31]

The agreement between the note and the poem is striking. Together they form a preliminary answer to the predicament of "Walls" and perhaps the only one that could be used while the cause of the crisis continues to prevail. As such, however, it is a positive alternative compared to the escapist one, delineated as well as regretted, in "The Satrapy." By extension, it is also appropriate to the situation of the *persona* in "The City," once the realization of the impasse is fully reached. The fact remains that as the crisis period approached its end, Cavafy's poetic *persona* finds a variety of means to cope with the painful confinement of "Walls." For a while, but only for a short while, the poet will venture into the world of fantasy pursuing an ideal escape, that of "Ithaka." But it would be foolish to sanctify the message and ignore the irony. Cavafy had to cope with definite personal problems associated with the situations as projected in the crisis poems. What he needed was not escapes into fantasy and exotic dreams of journeys. The urgent need called for determination to overcome the tendency to indulge in self-deception, alcohol, guilt, including the craving for public applause.

Eventually Cavafy worked out his own solution: devotion to poetry and to the creative life. Symbolically, the solution is embodied in his "Ithaka," but the voyage projected in the poem had no meaning as direct action in the real world. There was room for an Ithaka in the space of imagination, in the realm of art where each new poem proves to be another rich port, a delightful harbor, a marvel of continuous adventures, forming together a work in progress, culminating in a life of authentic pursuits. It bore no resemblance to the Homeric *Odyssey*—could not, since the times of the modern are not heroic. The inversion of the classical mode is demanded of the modern predicament, in fact the latter makes the former unavoidable. The real challenge lies in acquiring the skill and the knowledge to control rather than passively accept the requisite symbols and concepts with which to illumine aesthetically the human condition in its cosmopolitan setting.

If the above approach to the "crisis" poems does justice to the inner conflict of Cavafy, then it is wasteful to look for corresponding events in his life which the "situations" in the poems literally describe. Whatever his private

---

[31]The Greek text in Cavafy 1983: 36. The plaintive note expressed here is recreated in the unpublished poem "Hidden Things" (1908).

experiences, it is their poetic transformation rather than the circumstances of their actual occurrence that counts. Nor does the compact meaning of these poems require endless debate and conjecture about intended persons masked behind mythical names and legendary places. There is nothing in the poems which is neither contemporary nor unrelated to the search for authenticity and completion. That the period of the "crisis" years was as prolonged as it was exhausting is clear indication of the complexity of his personal problem as well as witness to the enormous obstacles he had to overcome before he could find his authentic voice. However, the "crisis" poems alone, remarkable though they are in technique and thematic content, could hardly suffice to secure Cavafy a permanent place in world literature. In a way, they intimate what he resolved to hold back, as in the unpublished poem "Hidden Things," just as they document his explorations within the walls, the pensive cries and sullen thoughts, the consuming fears and inhibitions, which kept the mind and the passions in a state of ambivalence.

The writing of the *Ars Poetica* was a major step forward in the right direction, but whereas it sharpened the tools for mastery it still left the substantive issues of the crisis of his personality untouched. He could assign a high place to the idea of dignity among the "soft" virtues, but he had not yet found the wisdom to dignify his desires. Evidently, he could step back in horror once he had understood the implications of a life of futile effort and compromises. Then, when he tried to scale the walls from within, all he could find was another perimeter, another trench blocking the escape, and then at the sight of Achilles run back to hiding, as in the poem "Trojans." On the whole, throughout the "crisis" years he lived within his walls until the devotion to his art made him strong in spirit to conquer his fear and cope with the dead-ends of withdrawal, the lure of alcohol and the depleting anxiety over his demanding eroticism. Feeling his way to the exit, fumbling and groping in every step, he was getting gradually closer to the quality of mind the Greek genius had elevated to one of the supreme virtues: wisdom.[32]

It must have been in a moment of comparable intensive study when the poet felt the quality of mind that anticipated the sign of the exit. It must have been a high moment in poetry and self-illumination.

---

[32]The topic is discussed in chapter 10.

Chapter Seven

The Development of Cavafy's Poetics[1]

1. In The Year 1903: Ars Poetica. 2. The Persisting Problems. 3. Cavafy's Self-consciousness of His Poetic Inadequacy. 4. Disillusionment and the Possibility of Progress. 5. Progress and Poetry in the Ars Poetica. 6. The Editing of the Collections.

1. In The Year 1903: *Ars Poetica*

George Seferis once remarked "We can only learn the ideas and poetics of Cavafy by listening carefully to his poetry".[2] It is doubtful whether at that time Seferis knew of the existence of the 1903 manuscript Cavafy had written on the subject. The text was composed in English in a personal shorthand the poet had devised for his own use. It was found among the papers he had left to Alekos Sengopoulos and published for the first time in 1963 by M. Peridis, who also supplied the title *Ars Poetica*.

Seferis made a valid observation in recommending the method of listening to Cavafy's poems for the study of his poetic art. It is generally recognized that Cavafy was not born a poet but became one only through

---

[1] An earlier version of part of this chapter appeared in *Philosophy and Literature* 2, No. 1 (Spring, 1978): 85-109, also in Greek translation in *Nea Estia*, 114 (Nov. 15, 1983): 1393-1416.

[2] Seferis 1966: 124. He made this statement in 1946 in his lecture "Cavafy and Eliot—A Comparison." His interest in Cavafy's development is reflected in the notes he took on a number of early poems for a book he planned but never completed. His long essay with commentary on selected poems was published in his *Essays* (first ed. 1962: 287-360; second ed. 1974, v. 1: 364-457). Also Seferis 1974a; in the entry for October 9, 1946 he writes: "I read through Cavafy taking notes. I don't know at all, if it is possible now to finish the work I started in Pretoria—like so many others that have been put aside in the sort of life I lead" (44). Seferis' writings on Cavafy have been brought together in Seferis 1984, edited and with introduction and notes by G. Savidis, v. 1.

persistence and labor, reaching his "first step" sometime after the midpoint of his life. In his effort to assess the quality of his earlier poetic production and sharpen his sensitivity in facing self-criticism, he decided to put in writing his personal thoughts on his work sometime in 1903.

Taken as a whole, the text of the *Ars Poetica* has all the clarity and directness required of a testament designed to serve as a personal guide and handbook. The problems it discusses are limited to the particular needs of the poet. In this regard, the *Ars Poetica* has neither the range of topics nor the theoretical scope of, for instance, Aristotle's *Poetics*. It is quite certain that the ideas that preoccupy Cavafy in the *Ars Poetica* had been on his mind for a number of years. However, the *Ars Poetica* is his first prose piece in which he gives a systematic treatment to technical and critical issues directly related to the assessment of his work and his role as a poet. In order to project a clear image of Cavafy's struggle to reach his technical maturity which came after 1910, we need to discuss first the persistent problems he faced during this crucial decade, then examine the attitudes and values he embodied in certain representative early poems, and finally to relate them to the guiding principles he formulated in his self-addressed poetics of 1903.

2. The Persisting Problems

A number of interrelated problems confronted Cavafy in his late twenties and throughout his thirties. They emerged one by one to make more pressing the demand for a consistent solution and a complete recasting of his outlook. Coming to terms with these problems was extremely difficult. Aside from the emotional and sexual pressures he had to face alone, there was the absence of suitable ideas and conceptual tools to provide him with even the rudiments of a consistent intellectual framework. Whatever he borrowed from Europe and England, or resurrected from his own Hellenic heritage proved either beyond assimilation or insufficiently digested. The lingering issues fell roughly into four areas.

(i) Despite his determination to devote his life to the writing of poetry, the quality of his work was discouraging. He knew this and as a result he often expressed uncertainty about his ability to continue. Time and again he suffered from a feeling of inadequacy; nevertheless he sought to engage a reflective mood from which to draw encouragement and hope.

(ii) On the theoretical side, he identified with the long tradition which assigned a coveted cultural role to the savant-poet as discloser of truth and spokesman for humanity. It was a vain expectation for recognition, contrary to the prevailing climate of opinion in his immediate environment. Cavafy knew that his standing in the Greek community of Alexandria had gradually dwindled with the loss of family wealth and his lowly employment. His publications were hardly noticeable to make him an prominent name. This denial of personal recognition, in a society dominated by commerce and finance, contributed significantly to his mood of depression. The feeling of being an outsider, despite his successful associations in the upper social circles of Alexandria, became a constant irritant to his sense of pride.

(iii) The course of culture, the destiny of human institutions, the workings of history, became puzzles as he tried to view them through the opaque glass of disillusionment. These were grand themes actively discussed in the writings of leading European intellectuals, but to the young poet they had a different, personal urgency. His vital concern was not the understanding of science and its effects on social reconstructions, nor the adjustments it forced upon religious beliefs. His concern was how to assign meaning to the idea of progress and show whether this was possible at all, especially when his personal experiences led to the conclusion that all human effort, individual and collective, ended in futility. Following this trend of thought, he became convinced that the cosmopolis was cursed and that the very perfection of culture coincided with decadence.

(iv) The last and perhaps the most crucial problem Cavafy had to solve was that of finding his real place, his environment, something that would be tantamount to a *polis*, one to which he could belong physically and historically. Constantinople, Liverpool, Athens, Paris, even Alexandria, could not take the place of an Ithaka for this poet of the Greek *diaspora*. His attitude toward the modern cosmopolis was one of ambivalence; he viewed it alternately as a field of opportunities as well as a source of disappointment and loneliness. The place upon which one could fix an axis to give unity to significant events and experiences was lacking. Thus his search during the early years moved in random directions, anywhere and nowhere, roaming "in the same streets," ending behind the walls in a windowless dwelling; it brought the despairing poet to fear even the hope of finding an exit, and rendered him a prisoner clinging to the walls of the dark prison. It was a search without a clear concept of a *nostos* (homecoming), and with no other guide but a contrived sense of history and an empty myth. For all those years, Alexandria escaped him. So did the other cities which figure in some of his historical poems: Rome, Syracuse, Antioch—poetically evoked locales, backgrounds, too shadowy to blend with the spirit of man. We have to wait until 1911, with the writing of "The God Abandons Antony," to witness Cavafy's discovery of Alexandria. With it came the liberating resolution of the other deep-seated problems. It heralded his Ithaka.

3. Cavafy's Self-consciousness of His Poetic Inadequacy

It seems paradoxical that Cavafy, confident as in was in his sense of cultural mission, was also uncertain about his ability to articulate his thoughts and emotions with requisite perfection. Thematically, as well as technically, his early poems are thin and mediocre, and stand in sharp contrast with his compositions during the mature years, particularly in the treatment of the theme of poetic loyalty. A later poem, "Young Men of Sidon: (A.D. 400)" (1920/*1920*: B 16), offers a terse summary of Cavafy's unreserved dedication to poetry as the cause of his life:

> Give, I say, all your strength to your work,
> all your care, and again remember your work
> in times of hardship, or when your hour is nearing.
> This is what I expect and demand of you.

The words are those of a young man, spoken in the presence of five young Sidonians. The thought they express is an answer to the epitaph Aeschylus allegedly wrote for himself, to wit, that the significance of the tragedians's life stems from his having done his duty to his country rather than his poetry.

Another poem, "For Ammonis, Who Died Aged 29 in 610" (1915/*1917*: A 79), Cavafy reconstructs a scene in Alexandria:

> Raphael, they ask you to compose a few verses
> as an epitaph for the poet Ammonis;
> something elegant and polished.

Here, the poet Cavafy calls on an imaginary poet of the late Hellenistic period, to compose the epitaph for another poet:

> Of course, you will speak about his poems—
> but tell also about his beauty,
> about his delicate beauty we so loved.
>
> Your Greek is always fine and musical.
> But now we want all your mastery.
> Our grief and our love pass to a foreign tongue.
> Pour your Egyptian feeling into the foreign tongue.
>
> Raphael, your verses should be written, you know,
> to have something of our life within them,
> so that the rhythm and each phrase will declare
> that an Alexandrian writes about an Alexandrian.

The epitaph Raphael "wrote" does not matter, but the advice is clear. Cavafy dictates the content: reference must be made to the poet's work and his personal beauty; suitable rhythms and phrases are needed to gain perfection of expression; the character of the poem must embody the special circumstance of "an Alexandrian writing of an Alexandrian." The reader is drawn into the atmosphere of the poem, and the effect is consummate.

Let us now consider a poem written in 1895, and published in 1899: "The First Step" (A 101) one of the "approved" early poems. The scene is in Syracuse, where the poet Theocritus lived in the third century B.C. A young poet, Eumenes, visits Theocritus, and complains how after two years of persistent efforts he did not advance beyond the writing of one idyll. His plaintive tone continues:

> Alas, I see it, high,
> very high, is the ladder of poetry;
> and from this, the first step, where I stand here,
> I, unhappily, will never climb higher.

Theocritus, mature and experienced, retorts quite sharply:

> These words
> are unbecoming and blasphemous.
> Even if you are on the first rung, you should
> be proud and happy.
> To have come this far is no small thing;
> to do this much is a great glory.

> Even this one step, the first,
> is quite above the common world.
> To set your foot on this one rung
> you must in your own right be
> a citizen in the *polis* of ideas.

The meeting of the accomplished and the novice—the future and the present—are two voices that belong to the agonizing Cavafy. Both speak from the Hellenistic age. Theocritus is firm, secure and wise, reprimanding young Eumenes for belittling the achievement of his first step on the ladder of poetry. The moral is carefully drawn: completing the first step brings with it a notable distinction, one that makes Eumenes a person removed from the common world. It is precisely this special elevation that now constitutes "a great glory" and one which can belong only to the artist even if the work is but one idyll. Theocritus speaks with authority.[3] Eumenes is doubtful and uncertain. The problem is real, palpable, recognizable. Nothing appears out of place including the repetition of Theocritus' appraisal and command at the end of the poem. It was for good reason that Cavafy kept it on the list of his approved poems.

The same motif recurs in other poems written in the early and middle nineties. Here the uneasiness about his ability to ascend the ladder of poetry has none of the crispness of tone or the direct human cast of "The First Step." There are several poems, which were later disowned, that illustrate this distance. We see here a Cavafy who is withdrawn, engaged in artificial dialogue with himself, groping through the glimmering shadows of confused imagery, outworn romantic cliches. The poems are worthless, except to serve as indicators of the ground he had to cover to make "the first step." In all the

---

[3] In Idyll XI, Theocritus says: "No remedy is there for love . . . save the Muses." Hence the cure for love is the practice of poetry, an occupation at once painless and pleasant, but which all the same requires a certain genius and utter devotion. Cavafy had read Theocritus and accepted the dictum. Unlike Theocritus' themes, those of Cavafy are not enacted in idyllic settings. Alexandria was not the right environment for pastoral poetry. As in Theocritus there is also in Cavafy frequent reference to unrequited love, heightened sensuality and compassion. A celebrated Cavafian verse from "Tomb of Iasis" (1917/*1917*: A 75) goes: "If Alexandrian, traveller, you will not blame . . . ." Visitors to Alexandria were at least expected to feign understanding and suspend judgment on the ways of the city. The erotic frankness in Theocritus' poetry is less constrained than Cavafy's.

early poems which deal with the motif of the fate of the poet, we see moving in parallel lines the agony of personal inadequacy and the magic vision of poetic destiny. In one titled "Singer," (1891/*1892*: CP) we find Cavafy wallowing in fantasy, grateful for the power of imagination which has built for him "a strong house of the spirit that destiny cannot shake," and whose walls "are of magic emerald." Life is cold and futile, but the poet can be of good cheer for he is "a secret apostle."

The bitter consequences of his escape were felt shortly after Cavafy realized that there was no way of evading the realities of everyday life and the traffic of the cosmopolis. Faith in fantasy brought him nowhere near the first step of poetry; rather it hastened the transformation of the walls of magic emerald into the dark and dismal high walls in the poem "Walls." The desolate feeling is expressed in "The Windows" (1897/*1903*: A 105).

In the "Singer" there is no dramatic character like Theocritus, only the voice of fantasy, assuring the poet that "his nature is divine." All we see here is an artificial and shadowy world of Cavafy's own making, but it reveals a sad picture of a person on the verge of failure grasping passionately for survival. Yet, there is no mistake about the nobility of the effort. The concern runs so deeply and the search for adequacy persists so tenaciously that they push themselves to the center of his consciousness and reign there as powerful though vain themes. These early poems show no critical understanding of the motif of the poet *in the poem*. Even the sentimentality of the tone is borrowed from the last waves of romanticism. Yet, they serve one function: to offer some sort of assurance and self-confidence, to help the poet sustain his belief that he can bring light and truth to a world which denies him significance.

The earliest poem written in this vein goes back to 1886. It is entitled "The Poet and the Muse" (CP 18). The dialogue motif appears here for the first time, articulating the same agonizing question, but it is a far cry from the concreteness of the exchange between Theocritus and Eumenes. As a poem it fails lamentably to qualify Cavafy for the first step. The two sides of the immature Cavafy interlock in a mode of imaginative promise and protectiveness. Fantasy, Muse and Mother become fused. The "poet" speaks first, not so much to extract assurance as to receive an explanation of why he was chosen. The admission of inadequacy is striking:

> To what good, what gain did fortune seek,
> That in my frailty I was made a poet?
> Futile are my words, and the sounds of my lyre,
> Even the most musical ones, are not genuine.

After mentioning how cold and crafty this world is, how painful life has become, the poet still sings of love and joy; he finds his harp miserable and its sounds a parody. Then the comforting Muse assures him:

> Poet, you are not a liar. The world you envision
> Is the true one.

The consoling Muse confirms that he is "the priest of the world" and "a friend," one who is close to pleasures, flowers and valleys; what remains is to wait for the early dawn to dissolve the frightful mist. Nature is still eager to become his, promising garlands of roses and other rewards for his songs.

There is no special reason to elaborate further on Cavafy's early poetic failures. The main point in tracing in reverse the successive layers of the theme of inadequacy is to show the obduracy of this problem, how it was projected and finally understood as a significant topic for poetry and a personal obstacle in his development. By the time Cavafy accomplished the "first step," he had divested himself of all the foreign elements of Romanticism, Parnassianism, and Symbolism he had occasionally tried on in the process of transition. But the problem of poetic inadequacy was more than a question of native talent. It was closely connected to the broader issues that define the place of the poet in modern society. These issues did not stand by themselves, for the status of the poet, as Cavafy saw it, was not simply a matter of social prestige and rewards, or of personal passion. The words of the young man of Sidon addressed only one side of the poetic role. It was the public aspect that called for equal attention. No satisfactory answer could be given to this side of the issue without first coming to grips with the meaning of culture and the historical dimension of man. At the time that Cavafy felt the pressure of the issues, the debate had centered around the possibility of genuine progress in the course of civilization. His reflections on this basic theme exhibit three distinct phases: the skepticism of the early poems, his reconciliation with the possibility of progress as expressed in the *Ars Poetica*, and the final post-1911 mature period which allows for a tragic view of history within the conditions of the cosmopolis. It is the last phase that holds the secret to his enigmatic statement: "I too am Hellenic. Careful! not Hellene, nor Hellenizing, but Hellenic."[4]

4. Disillusionment and the Possibility of Progress

We rarely see Cavafy willfully divorcing his ideals from the political side of human nature and immersing himself in the exotic pleasures of sensuality to perfect the exquisite experiences of the aesthete. No doubt there are poems which lead the reader to draw such inferences. But unless they are treated as partial, though substantive, aspects of the total range of his poetry and personality, his full significance as a major twentieth century poet remains unilluminated. By way of heritage and social standing, to which we may add disposition and learning, Cavafy exhibited since his early manhood a detached, yet intense concern for political and cultural issues as well as a keen interest in historical developments.

The England he knew from his adolescent years was a country in the full sway of the Industrial Revolution, with all its benefits and social evils. It was an England reigning supreme as a world power, spreading its tentacles over all corners of the world, including Egypt. Alexandria, as he knew it as a child, had grown and prospered before the arrival of the British in 1882. His family played an active part in its social and economic progress long before the intervention. When he returned to his city, after spending his adolescent years studying in England, Alexandria was still a growing cosmopolis, but with a different future, one that affected adversely the fortune of his family. It still remained the cosmopolis of vast commercial opportunity, where the ingenuity for making fortunes rivaled the complexity of political intrigues, the power of colonialism, the display of wealth, and the deterioration of the natives. The mingling of diverse nationalities and languages continued to produce a colorful mosaic against the background of the local pattern of cults, superstition and massive illiteracy.

The Greek community to which Cavafy belonged fitted rather comfortably into this maze. It had its own caste system, its range of social strata, and on the whole had amassed collective wealth and resourcefulness

---

[4]Malanos 1957: 235; Seferis 1984, v. 1: 262 n8; Keeley 1976: 109-10, esp. 182, n3.

for survival and success. Intellectually, however, it was an extension of Athens, and to an appreciable extent, like Athens, the recipient of the overflow of ideas and movements originating in the cultural centers of Europe and England. Greece as a young state was a political product of the nationalist resurrections of the nineteenth century and was still in the process of carrying out the Great Idea: to free the unredeemed populations living under Turkish rule. The Greeks of the diaspora, freed or otherwise, no less than the mainlanders, shared passionately in this dream and gave generously to the cause.

The growing body of literature in the mainland was tuned to a dual role. Internally, there was the need to summon the experience of the past in serving the goals of the free nation to attain adequate education, moral regeneration, political enlightenment and social reform—all conjoined to the vision of regaining the ancestral land. Externally, there was the problem of establishing a spiritual continuity with the European nations whose cultural achievements had made spectacular gains, while Greece, left out of the Renaissance and the Enlightenment, had missed the benefits of progress by almost four centuries. The modern Greek poets had their role made to order. It grew naturally, so to speak, out of the facts of national life. The direction had been set by their national poet Dionysios Solomos. The tone was Greek but the style European. The problem was mainly one of consonance. The theme was public and the spirit optimistic. As the nineteenth century approached its close, the poet Costis Palamas was conspicuously in the lead.

Cavafy, a British educated Alexandrian Greek, found himself at the outer perimeter of this redemptive nationalism. In more ways than one, he was unable to identify fully with the cause. His historical consciousness and approach to his heritage could not generate the same patriotic enthusiasm which inspired the poets of the mainland. Nor could the problem of progress take its urgency for him from a cultural setting so different from that of his immediate environment, disposition and upbringing. At the very core of this issue was the need to relate his poetic mission to a broader conception of the nature of modern culture. However, he was aware that Alexandria was not London or Paris, where cultivation of the arts and letters bestowed a coveted assignment to the gifted. Not only was the cultural climate of Alexandria rather indifferent to such pursuits, but there was no comparable public interested enough to uphold the work of the poet. Cavafy found himself in an environment which, while not lacking in energy or even a mild concern for the arts, had no organized intellectual movement from which he could draw encouragement and sustenance. Particularly during the period of his early poetry, except for the small circle of friends and intellectual acquaintances, he was left to his own resources. There were his memories of England from his adolescent years, the Hellenic background of his parents' Constantinople, the social standing of his family, but none had the requisite depth and content to construct the self-image he needed to overcome the "degradation" of having accepted a position as a clerk in the Irrigation Service.

The task of defining his role as a poet proved difficult on two accounts. First, he had to grope for ways to raise the concept of poetry to a level of cultural seriousness and significance. The device of the Muse carried no real conviction since it belonged to Cavafy the dreamer talking to himself in the world of fantasy. Thus, the pronouncements on cultural mission lacked the persuasive power his situation demanded. Second, the search for a theoretical basis held no promise if only because there was nothing of the kind readily available, except for what he could borrow from the artistic philosophies and manifestoes of Europe. To an extent this is what he did, only to reject them later on. The fact remains that his own social and community circles could not and did not attribute to poetry or the arts, in general, the seriousness Cavafy's self-image expected. Having no wealth of his own, he could not become influential in the affairs of the Greek community. Progress and social affairs were in the hands of men of commerce and wealth and tied to the larger enterprises of government. Given these circumstances, Alexandria had no special relevance for his poetry, no significance and no appeal other than being a place, a cosmopolis, separate from the inner life of the poet. It was only a matter of time before his ties to the city deteriorated and lost whatever emotional and social color they had. They gradually took on the bleak, imprisoning and oppressive qualities we see in his poem "The City." It took him years to realize fully what miracles he expected Alexandria to perform, but until then he was unable to see what impossible gestures he demanded of a city which had no Goethe, Coleridge, Keats, Wordsworth, Hugo, Poe, Baudelaire, Mallarmé, Gibbon, Macaulay, Rousseau, Arnold, Tennyson, Hardy, Ibsen, Zola, France, Shaw—to mention some of the writers whose books were in his library. Because of what Alexandria had denied him he could not give it a prominent place in his poetry. It appeared timidly and for the first time in 1900, but not before he exhausted it in negation. However, the low point was not reached until after Cavafy's several attempts to project his poetic self on the city-community ended in aesthetic failure.

Cavafy discovered the meaning of Alexandria after he finally learned not to beg from the cosmopolis what it could not give. A close look at some of his early poems reveals how his cultural estrangement was intimately related to his uncritical conception of progress and even more naive idea of nature. Suffice it to state at this point that in 1891, Cavafy was under the sway of the anti-social views of Baudelaire and the firm belief in a mystical continuity between the inner human self and nature accessible only to the poet. The affairs of civilization, inescapable and binding, had a historical rhythm of their own but were destined to transmute progress into futility. His 1891 sonnet, "Builders" (CP 21), gives a vivid account of how the poet fits in this historical and cultural web.

> Progress is a great edifice—each person brings
> his own stone—one man reason and counsel, another
> his actions—and day by day it raises its top
> higher. But once a tempest, or sudden tumult
>
> comes, in mass the devoted workers
> rush on the scene to support their futile work.
> Futile, for each man's life is given to caring
> for the pains and woes of a future generation
>
> to make sure that generation will know happiness
> pure, longevity, and wealth, and wisdom,
> without demeaning sweat or slavish labor.
>
> But that fabled generation will never come to be;
> this work's own perfection will bring the edifice to ruins
> and their own entire futile toil will start it anew.[5]

As a whole, the poem is unsalvageable. The contours are fuzzy and the historical landscape uncertain. There is no hint from which to glean specific instances of progress. The treatment is speculative but several strong beliefs emerge rather clearly. Whatever this "progress" means, it results from the cooperation of men of ideas and men of action. The poet by being loyal to

---

[5] The Greek text in Tsirkas 1958: 205-6; reprinted in Cavafy 1983: 21.

the former, is an leading agent, a creative force, in determining the course of progress. However, in the end, even the poet's contribution is of no help in averting the dissolution. The cause is noble: happiness, not his own, but that of a future generation. There is an element of sacrifice and social mission in this way of casting the poet's cultural role, but hardly powerful enough to cope with the prospect of doom. Still, the cause of the demise of progress remains obscure. More precisely, Cavafy tells us enough about the agents of progress but nothing concrete about the negative forces, other than to mention the intervention of "a tempest, a sudden turmoil." One suspects that the poet wants to suggest that undetected human flaws operate mysteriously to rob the future beneficiaries of the fruits of progress. As a result, the hoped for "happiness, longevity, wealth and wisdom" and the elimination of "sweat and labor" remain forever beyond reach. Progress, except for the moral value it has for giving the toilers a sense of duty and direction, is ultimately a utopian pursuit. The theme is cast in the mould of Sisyphus' task: it is as futile as it is necessary. The boulder of progress will roll back to the base of the hill.

Cavafy, as this and many other poems indicate, was obsessed with the theme of culture as historical process in general, and the meaning of progress, the goal of civilization, in particular. It appears that these were issues that provided the context he needed to assign the poet a place in modern society. After stating that leadership and responsibility were in the hands of men of theory and action, he avoided mentioning the poet. This aspect was made explicit later on in the *Ars Poetica*. In "Builders," his intent appears to have been to underscore the role of ideas in erecting the edifice of progress. The tone is declarative and indirectly one of warning. The message asserts the importance of men of reason and wisdom but is silent on the extent of their participation and effectiveness. The reader begins to suspect at this point that Cavafy cannot or does not as yet know how to make his suggestion clear, namely that the sustenance of progress and the realization of its ends depend largely on men of wisdom to guide the men of action. The theme harkens back to Plato's political philosophy. But there is another obscure issue in the poem, stated as a paradox, one which Cavafy rephrased as artfully as he knew how in his much admired "Waiting for the Barbarians"—a poem of striking drama and originality but still heavily burdened with the opaqueness of the same paradox. The issue touches on the fear of cultural futility. Briefly stated, Cavafy's view suggests that the moment progress reaches the point of perfection it comes to exhibit fully how its own success causes thereby the collapse of the edifice: "Its own perfection will bring the work to ruins . . . ." The idea is intriguing yet remains unclear. Did Cavafy mean to say that the process is inherently defective precisely because the poet is either ignored or allowed a perfunctory role? Was the poem meant as a criticism of the pillars of the Greek community of Alexandria? Was Cavafy addressing himself to the inherent dangers of the progressive policies and philosophies of the European nations? At least this much seems to be certain: regardless of the nature of his warning there is no mistake about his passion to assign to himself the role of high leadership in the cause of progress and civilization. If the end is futile, the mission of the poet is not.

"Builders" expresses a position which, with minor variations, Cavafy held for almost an entire decade. The futile cycle of progress, always ending in ruins, occurs again in "The Intervention of the Gods" (1899: U 111). The cause has become more concrete but taken out of human hands. The poet uses "we" to exhibit a series of planned actions aiming for the better: yet,

> . . . The more we try, the more we will undo,
> we'll keep complicating things till we reach
> utter confusion. And then we will stop.
> That will be the hour for the gods to work.
> The gods always come.

The gods do their own work; some men are helped, others are removed from the scene. A new order prevails and the gods withdraw. In due course, men will embark on the same routine only to bring about another "intervention." Two years later, in 1902, the center of gravity shifted from mysterious, unknown, and impersonal forces to the specifically human factor. The reasoning deals not with futility but failure. Thus in the poem "Interruption" (1900/*1901*: A 102):

> We interrupt the work of the gods,
> we, the hurried and foolish creatures of the day.
> In the palaces of Eleusis and Phthia
> Demeter and Thetis commence good deeds,
> in huge flames and thick smoke. But
> always Metaneira rushes in from the royal
> chambers, disarrayed and terrified,
> and always Peleus is scared and intervenes.

Neither Metaneira, the queen of Eleusis, nor Peleus, the king of Thessaly, could understand how the gods were working to render the royal offspring immortal. Ignorance of the ways of the gods is a human limitation, and when the crucial moment comes to determine the future course of events, human failure to understand correctly causes irreparable damage. The collective "we" of 1899 has now been replaced by the more specific "we" of 1902 to stand for any human being who, like Metaneira and Peleus, acts through fear, impatience and ignorance. The poet's expression has become direct and mellow, tracing the delicate outlines of the tragic face of mankind. This explains why Cavafy approved for publication "Interruption,"[6] whereas "The Intervention of the Gods" was kept in his archives with a note scribbled in English on the paper: "This is a good poem."[7] The fact is that it was no better than the other poems of the *Ancient Days* group he had published in the meantime and intended to bring out as a separate collection. Eventually he condemned them, and for good reasons. They were manifestly Parnassian in influence and vintage, mirroring a contrived classicism and a superficial grasp of the ancient Greek epic and tragic themes.

The agonizing question of human progress had for Cavafy a deeply personal significance, and the final answer he gave to it decided his destiny as "the poet of the city." In this period between September 1893 and July 1896[8] he studied with considerable care the two volume *Selections from the Writings of John Ruskin*.[9] Cavafy's comments on Ruskin take the form of an intimate dialogue on such fundamental themes as the nature of art and poetry, the problem of the good and the beautiful, the controversy over realism and

---

[6]According to Seferis' reading of this poem Cavafy is saying that "humankind, which includes the poet, resembles a mouse running frantically between the claws of fate." 1974, v. 1: 386. Thematically, the poem belongs to the phase of Cavafy's quest for an answer to the problem of futility.

[7]First publication in Peridis 1948: 161; also Cavafy 1968: 231-32.

[8]During the same period Cavafy was reading Gibbon and wrote a number of extensive comments. See Liddell 1970: 116-21; esp., Haas 1982: 25-96.

[9]First series, 1843-1860: Vol I, p. 524; second series, 1860-1888. Vol. II, p. 488, (G. Allen and Unwin, London).

idealism, the dynamics and direction of civilization, the philosophies of individualism and human rights.[10] As other critics have noted, by the time Cavafy came to study Ruskin, he was ripe for a revision of his views and ready to become at least partly reconciled to the ideal of progress.[11] However, the tendency to come to terms with progress emerged more clearly, but not without some reservations, in the *Ars Poetica* of 1903.[12]

Of all his comments on Ruskin we can only refer to the ones that bear directly on our theme. Where Ruskin castigates the rampant spread of industrialization as the chief threat to civilization, Cavafy comments:

> The speed [Ruskin speaks of], the diverse and marvelous inventions are hardly useless. Ruskin makes the mistake of viewing them as ends whereas they are only means. They serve his own Utopia. "The pace of the clouds" which shortens distances, increases and strengthens human solidarity, hastens the coming of the "Kingdom of Peace"—which is what the poets of the past centuries prophesied; and the poets of today still hopeful expect it to come, with their eyes fixed on the horizon where one morning golden castles will appear (comment 202).[13]

Cavafy was now siding with Macaulay and the progressivists of the Victorian era, having modified the extreme position he took when he wrote the "Builders." Ruskin's moral and religious vision was not Cavafy's. Cavafy's predicament was rooted in a feeling of personal frustration. Ruskin's speculations were part of the romantic view that sought to ward off the onslaught of positivist science with its mechanical and materialistic conception of the universe. Cavafy had no special affinity for Ruskin's rhetoric extolling nature as the revelation of the divine unity of purpose. Neither did he share

---

[10] P. Anastassiadis, Cavafy's friend, preserved the manuscript of these comments. Portions of the manuscript were published by Peridis 1948, edited in its entirety and annotated by S. Tsirkas, it was printed in the commemorative issue of the journal *Epitheorisi Technis* (1963): 582-611.

[11] Tsirkas 1958: 609.

[12] Savidis 1966: 145.

[13] See also Liddell 1970: 118, for a slightly different translation of this passage.

with Ruskin the inclination to lament the moral loss incurred when mankind fails to grasp nature as the manifestation of God. This religious and moralistic outlook, together with the wedge it drew between art and science, did not suit Cavafy, especially at a time when what he wanted was to raise the poet to the level of a statesman of ideas. In response to a passage from *The Stones of Venice* (vol. III) where Ruskin discusses the difference between the scientist and the artist, Cavafy objects to Ruskin's "mania to legislate what is art and what is not," and concludes: "Of the few things one can state with certainty is the fact that no one is able to say where art begins and above all where it ends"(comment 79). To Ruskin's thesis that our ideas of the beautiful depend directly on our state of purity, Cavafy replied that "purity of heart is not indispensable for seeing Beauty . . . I have in mind the author's narrow conception of *purity* and *heart*, not the broader meaning of these words . . ." (comment 204).

These reactions reflect more than a difference in approach. They throw considerable light on Cavafy's persistent effort to overcome the depressive thought of cultural futility while preserving intact the political and aesthetic stature of the poet in the cosmopolis which denies him significance. One also suspects that they speak for his erotic sensibility against Ruskin's "narrow conception of purity and heart." The clash between internal demands and external conditions kept the search for a final answer to the problem of progress in continual suspense. While the theoretical ambivalence remained unresolved, the poetic mood struggled to find expression through the basic "crisis" themes of "The City," "Walls," "Trojans," "The Windows," "Waiting for the Barbarians" and "Thermopylae," poems which received their final form after the writing of his *Ars Poetica*.[14]

5. Progress and Poetry in the *Ars Poetica*

Cavafy's visit to Athens in August 1903, coincided with two major events in his development: a psychological one having to do with "a great crisis of liberation" related to the final clarification but partial acceptance of his

---

[14]The dates of composition of these poems fall between 1896 and 1901; during this period only one poem, "Walls" (1891), was revised in 1897.

homosexuality, and an aesthetic one leading to the formulation of the basic concepts of his poetics, "the procedures of Emendatory Work and Philosophical Scrutiny" of his poems. With the writing of his *Ars Poetica*, Cavafy crossed, at the age of forty, into his transitional period which ended in 1911. But, more significantly, it helped him sever most of his ties to the trends and movements of the nineteenth century in order to develop his own original style and become one of the major poets of the twentieth century.

What stands out with striking clarity in this document is how Cavafy was finally able to define and defend a conceptual framework to carry out a program of critical revision of his work and also present his role as a poet with forthrightness and confidence. Briefly put, with his *Ars Poetica* Cavafy, begins to put behind him the years of wavering sentimentality, dependence and imitative explorations. If the *Ars Poetica* is a statement of position, an account as well as a program for future revisionary work, the mood and climate which pervade it were clearly anticipated in the [unpublished] poem he wrote in June 1903, "Growing in Spirit" (U 133):

> He who desires to strengthen his spirit
> must go beyond respect and submission.
> He will retain some of the laws
> but for the most part he will break
> both laws and customs and will move away
> from the accepted and inadequate propriety.
> He will learn many things from life's pleasures.
> He will not fear the destructive act;
> half the house needs to be pulled down.
> It is thus he will grow virtuously in knowledge.

The text of the *Ars Poetica*, composed in English in a personal shorthand was meant exclusively for personal use and not as a general theory.[15]

---

[15] See Cavafy, *Unpublished Prose Texts*, 1963. English text on the even-numbered pages and Greek translation by Peridis on opposite pages; reprinted with an introduction and notes by A. Decavalles, *Charioteer*, 10 (1968): 69-80. The reading of Cavafy's English shorthand was done cooperatively by M. Peridis, Gwyn Williams and G. Savidis. The title *Ars Poetica*, was introduced by the editor M. Peridis. It is used here only as a convenience to identify the work. See Appendix.

It is certain that Cavafy never intended the *Ars Poetica* for the wider public, not even his close circle of friends. The style of the document indicates that its sole purpose was to provide a theoretical and laboratory guide for criticism. The position he elaborated in 1903 underwent further changes by 1911. In this respect, the significance of the *Ars Poetica* lies in being a key to his transitional period. As such, the *Ars Poetica* does not represent Cavafy's definitive views although its basic principles continued to find application. However, without it, the deeper layers of his poetic work during the years of crisis can be neither fully explored nor properly understood. If Cavafy had made this document available at some point during his lifetime, probably the bulk of the literature that grew around his "transitional" or "crisis" poems in particular would not have been so wrong-headed or innocuous. But that is another story.

In the opening statement of the *Ars Poetica* Cavafy mentions that the "Emendatory Work" is already settled and he should proceed with a "philosophical scrutiny" of his poems (36). What he means by "emendatory" will be explained shortly. It is a canon to proceed "by considering the poems attentively, reporting on them, making a batch of the reports, and afterward working at them on the basis and in the sequence of the batch" (48). Since this is part of his laboratory work, so to speak, it need not concern us here. Furthermore, the text includes no papers illustrating the emendatory procedure. On the whole, the *Ars Poetica* consists of two parts, both dealing with the procedure of philosophical scrutiny. The first part explains and defends the concepts he uses; the second applies one special aspect of this procedure to a single poem, or rather to two formulations of a key verse in the unpublished poem, "The Pawn" (1894: U 63).

On close inspection, this document reveals a reflective and critical side of Cavafy's personality one can hardly infer from a reading of his early poems. Another way of stating this issue is to say that Cavafy is a "studio" poet to whom the qualities of lyricism and inspiration are totally foreign. He wrote with deliberate slowness. Most of his verse had to be reworked and belabored for precision and compactness of meaning. In this respect, Cavafy became a poet; he was not born one. His awareness of the imperfections of each new poem and the pressing demand to formulate canons and principles to guide the emendatory work led him to the complementary procedure of "philosophical scrutiny." It is both a procedure and a doctrine, a method for attaining technical precision and a theory of thematic truthfulness. It involves commitment to a philosophy of life, a discriminating utilization of personal experience in poetic creation, and the employment of the formal rules for logical consistency.

We will try to follow the order in which Cavafy develops these topics. The first rule he vows to apply is one which can render the thought units in the poems logically coherent and believable.

> Flagrant inconsistencies, illogical possibilities, ridiculous exaggeration should certainly be corrected in the poems, and where the corrections cannot be made the poems should be sacrificed, retaining only any verses of such sacrificed poems as might prove useful later on in the making of new work. Still the spirit in which the Scrutiny is to be conducted should not be too fanatical (36).

Bringing meanings in line with artistic cogency calls for the removal of all those flaws which interfere with the poet's intent to render his message exact and communicable. Overstating some aspect, intensifying another via qualifiers beyond the requisite limits of measure, are as damaging as they are useless. Yet undue austerity, when pursued *fanatically* can cause the collapse of a suggestive verse and flatten it to the likeness of prose. Aside from the keen concern Cavafy shows here for the logic of verse, there is also that of preserving any verse, regardless of its initial ties to a given poem, for future use. Both concerns are related to Cavafy's practice of composition. As early as 1903, he recognized not only that canons of coherence and measure are required for the completion and perfection of any given poem, but also that any given poem, even when it should be sacrificed, is not a total failure if it contains usable units. Such units are like living cells of poetic thinking and can continue to live as functional parts of another body. This concept which recognizes wholeness in poetic units as individual verses with potential merits of their own, serves to indicate that by this time Cavafy had come to view his entire poetic program as an organic body growing and developing so that each new approved poem signaled a new stage of his work.

The model that emerges with the writing of the *Ars Poetica* brought to prominence the conception of poetry as a life-work in progress, a whole body to be realized in stages and cumulative phases as new poems are projected and completed, thus forming a chain of organic events like offshoots from the original seed. For this reason, there are no "representative" poems that summarize, as it were, the poet's work and views. This fact was ignored by certain of his critics who thought of Cavafy as a pessimist, a decadent, and hedonist, to mention only a few of their ill-fated characterizations. Evidently, Cavafy, throughout his life, grew increasingly tenacious in his adherence to the organic model of a work in progress. And it may well be that this is what he had in mind when he asked of his critics to judge him "aesthetically." If our interpretation is correct, it seems that he meant by this term a judgment that assumes and evaluates not just the wholeness of individual poems but ultimately one's entire *oeuvre*. In addition, the model helps us understand why Cavafy abandoned the "early" plan to publish *special* collections of poems in favor of a serially continuous set of editions, constituting at the end but one total collection: *Poems*.

The next large topic of the *Ars Poetica* concerns the limits and value of personal experience for the literary and philosophic activities, both seen as co-ordinate manifestations of the theoretical man. The problem he raises is whether it is necessary for the poet to restrict himself only to his own *personal experience*. The issue is frequently raised in theories of artistic creativity, but Cavafy feels it important enough to be answered anew. He defends the poet's right to explore emotional states and historical events which by necessity cannot and should not be directly experienced: e.g., a violent disease, old age, perturbed states of mind, events in the past—these are his own examples. The fact is that poets and philosophers do write about these things. It is just as well that they should for "the person who experienced them might not be the person talented to analyze and express them" (38). What is at issue is not so much the fact that poets go beyond "personal experience," but the rules and methods of doing it properly. Hence, the problem of "guesswork" and how to use it cautiously:

> Guesswork indeed—when intelligently directed—loses much of its riskiness, if the user transforms it into a sort of hypothetical experience. This is easier in the description of a battle, of a state of society, of a scenery. By the imagination (and by the help of incidents experienced and remotely or nearly connected) the user can transport himself into the midst of the circumstances and can thus create an experience. The same remark holds good— though it presents more difficulty—in matters of feeling (*sic*, 40).

The poet, with the aid of the knowledge he has of himself, can attain a high level of sympathetic understanding of the imagined conditions he seeks to reconstruct. Yet there is always a precarious element, especially when the objective is to penetrate into states of feeling, for such states can be "true and false, possible or impossible at the same time, or rather in turns" (40). The challenge here is one of proper identification and cognition; it is closely philosophical, but not in the sense of replacing or competing with philosophy. Somehow, the poet has the certainty that what he envisions, the aspect of the state he discloses, is the truest, or perhaps nearest the truth. The issue is not a matter of the duration, recurrence or transience of a situation, but how authentically the poetic guesswork is able to grasp its object. What Cavafy seems to be saying here is that the poetic goal in employing personal experience, which includes learning and erudition, is not to give a full description of the object or to work explicitly by way "of careful thought and weighing of causes and effects, and by inferences," in the manner of philosophers. Rather, it is to bring forth the tone and ambience of the object as condensed immediacy. What the poet achieves is a genuine insight into an actuality, a credible and convincing reconstruction of a situation as it should have occurred: logical possibilities which invite assent in truthful communication. That such insights may often have the character of a suggestion, "a vague meaning," is not a detriment. Their fuller realization may come at a later time, and in some cases it may even require the work of generations. What is essential is that the guesswork has proved fruitful. The contrast he draws with the philosophical type of guesswork is of minor importance. The real thrust of the argument is to underscore the interpretive power of the poet, the value of his mode of sympathetic recreation of human situations and the inherent fertility of his suggested meanings. The concept of guesswork leads directly to the defense of the major thesis of the *Ars Poetica*, which concerns the cultural role of the poet.

Interestingly enough, the concept of guesswork comes in for further elaboration again at the end of Part One and concludes it (48-55). As he points out, "the guesswork, or rather the intellectual insight into feeling of others may result in the delineating of more interesting intellectual facts or conditions, than the mere relation of the person experience of one individual" (*sic*, 48). This penetration into other persons and facts influences, in turn, the thinker and poet by creating new states of mind. The cumulative effect is an enrichment of personal experience. Cavafy is not claiming original psychological observations. Rather, he means to provide a basis for his poetic theory and practices. Once it is understood that guesswork is in principle capable of further correction and enrichment, personal experience can and must produce insight of wider validity. What is initially private and subjective becomes public in its reference and objective in its scope, provided that sympathetic understanding has been carefully utilized to increase the ability of the knower as a poet. Although Cavafy does not engage in refutation of alternative theories about the nature of the poetic self, he does mean to say that poetry is not to be reduced to the expression of a private self and its lyrical states. The poet's world is his personal experience but it is at once private and public. Without the delineation and assimilation of *other states of mind*, the objective reference of the poet's insights lacks direction and validity. The objective side of personal experience makes poetry publicly significant, capable of communicating shared feeling, universal truths, the essential nature of collective and private situations, whether unique or recurring. The special circumstances may be one's own or they may pertain to a group, but the needs and desires involved are common enough.

The poet has no particular preference for the general and unchanging ways of things. He seeks truthfulness anywhere and everywhere. He controls his guesswork by transforming it intelligently into "a sort of hypothetical experience."

> The poems one writes, though not true to one's actual life, are true to other lives—not generally of course, but specifically—and the reader to whose life the poem fits admits and feels the poem.... And when one lives, hears and searches intelligently and tries to write wisely his work is bound, one may say, to fit some life (50, 52).

Cavafy sees the problem of communicating the truthfulness of personal experience as having two crucial aspects: (a) How is it possible for a poet to write about an emotion which he has perhaps never himself felt, or about an action, for instance, murder, when he has never killed a person? (b) How can the poet convey to others his own experience, whether of private states or historical events, inaccessible to others, when they have never felt or known such things? Neither aspect is treated in depth in the *Ars Poetica*. The discussion shifts to the more practical concern of how to attain truthfulness when writing a poem. It is a matter of sincerity, which he defines as "necessary truthfulness in art" (52). The criterion is accordingly applied to some lines he had written in 1903 but upon reading them over found them "flat," "not good" yet "sincere." Cavafy develops the concept of sincerity in order to resolve a serious difficulty: How the element of time and the transitory quality of feeling are decisive factors in grasping correctly the special mood of truthfulness in a poem. Feelings, however fleeting, are true at the time of their occurrence, if sincere. A personal state may change with the passage of time but that event as it actually occurred remains what it was, if properly recalled and genuinely re-experienced as memory. However, Cavafy notes, it is only proper that all feeling situations should not last, otherwise we would be "all of a piece" and stagnate "in sentimental inactivity" (54). To illustrate the point he mentions two sincere poems, both expressing truthfully the erotic feeling he had at the time of their composition. They are the unpublished poems "September, 1903" and "December, 1903,"[16] and written, as he characteristically notes, after "the great crisis of liberation" (54). The lovers' indifference as it succeeds the period of passion does not make the poems false; "they remain true to the past," "they will be applicable to the feelings of other lives"; and he concludes by way of summary (56):

> The same, therefore, must apply to other works—really felt at the time. If even for one day, or one hour I felt like the man within "Walls," or like the man of "Windows," the poem is based on a truth, a short-lived truth, but which, for the very reason of its having once existed, may repeat itself in another life, perhaps with as short duration, perhaps with longer. If "Thermopylae" fits but one life, it is true; and it may, indeed the probabilities are that it must.

Before proceeding with the third thesis of the *Ars Poetica*, which seeks to establish the cultural significance of the poet, we must draw attention to the fact that by 1903 Cavafy had formulated clearly and firmly one of the cornerstones of his art: the aesthetic and thematic significance of memory, not only as the storehouse of private experiences but also as a condition for the further refinement and expansion of his intellectual insights. In the net of memory he will capture, preserve and distill the cherished moments of the personal past and the forsaken events of his historical heritage. When we read Cavafy's poems we are constantly aware of the presence of a poet who is writing through memory and recollection, and when the circumstance demands it, resorting to a re-creation of dramatic incidents of past history to

---

[16]Text in Cavafy, *Unpublished Poems*, 1968: 135, 137; translations by Keeley and Savidis in Cavafy, *Passions and Ancient Days*, 1971: 19, 21.

let them act as carriers of personal events recalled in reverie. The aesthetic value of memory is a controlling factor in the making and reshaping of his world. What he retrieves from the past is always an emotionally significant and sensuously charged situation. It is reborn through art, for art, and as art. It is recalled back to life, as it were, in all its dramatic freshness and compelling frankness. This wedding of aesthetics and memory is one of his chief characteristics.

The poet remains an artist even when he works philosophically. Cavafy makes a special point to stress the rational side of the poet's personality in order to settle two problems directly connected with his own crisis. First he had to brace himself through argument against his lingering skepticism about the futility of human culture, and second to defend the significance of the poet's mission. Without a positive answer to the former, the latter would have remained unsettled. Unlike the aesthetic theologians of Romanticism such as Coleridge and others, who subscribed to the divine reconciliation of matter and spirit in nature and in God's *Logos* as a literal fact, and then viewed the poetic imagination as an analogue of divine creation, Cavafy has no religious thesis on which to rest his case. Neither Nature nor God as the Great Artificer are appealed to as the ultimate grounds of value; for Cavafy, there is no realm for poetry and art other than man's social and cultural setting. His poetry is *a political and personal affair,* and even when the works of man, often perverse and misguided in the unwieldy complexity of the cosmopolis, fail to meet the demands of intelligence or satisfy human needs, the search must still continue inside the *polis*. Cavafy does not leave the city for Nature or the World or God any more than he considers the appeal to mysterious forces of inspiration a sufficient account for the poet's work. Cavafy does not take his disillusionments and feeling of despair to the doorstep of religion or the sanctuary of the absurd. The soundness of his argument is not the issue here, for what matters in the *Ars Poetica* is the manner in which he disposed of the case for extreme pessimism or, as he stated it, "the philosophy of the absolute worthlessness of effort and of the inherent contradiction of every human utterance" (42).

This "seemingly highest" philosophy the poet should by all means try to avoid, but he need not go to pains to deny it. By merely working, the poet denies it. Even if he accepts it, assuming he is still a poet, "he must work still, though with the consciousness of his work being but final toys—at best toys capable of being utilized for some worthier or better purpose, or the very handling of which prepares for some worthier and better work" (44). To the true artist, this "philosophy," is at once logically untenable and incapable of being put to practice. As a theorist, the poet can raise and debate the issue, but as artist he need not, for his main mission is the fulfillment of his work. The fact is, he observes, that few "natures" act on the belief in the vanity of human things, and even fewer can act accordingly, that is, "refrain from every action—except such as subsistence demands" (44). The acts of people may and often do produce vain things but it does not follow that the impulse to act and the activities are vain. Echoing the distant voice or Aristotle, Cavafy grounds the principle of acting in human nature; actions produce works which are valuable either for their immediate utility or their beauty. To produce the latter is the function of the poet. Hence, the artist responds to the natural desire for beauty in all its diverse forms: "love, order in one's surroundings, scenery" (46). Neither disdain for the shortness of human life, nor "separation" from one's work, justifies the view of "absolute worthlessness"; nor does the contestable belief in an after-life, presumably better than this one, make that view any sounder.

After repudiating this view of the worthlessness of effort, Cavafy proceeds next to explain its occurrence. It results, basically, from either of two errors: (a) the partial viewing of things and (b) an excessive emphasis on the individual. In a way, they involve each other, but the error of individualism appears to weigh the heavier since it persists by means of a partial view of the social and generic nature of the human person. Individualizing the person and the work of art leads to feeling of futility. But once we regain our full view of things and see the individual within the broad concept of mankind, a created work of art no longer appears futile. Within the reality denoted by the inclusive notion of mankind "there is not death." The species continues and endures. A body, *atomon*, has separate existence, but the concept of man does not. However, the individual, as it exemplifies the species, is a constituent of a society, a nation, all mankind, regardless of where or when it exists. On this premise then, absolute vanity disappears and only "a comparative vanity may remain for the individual." Yet, when the individual "separates himself from his work and considers only the pleasure or the profit it has given him for a few years and then its vast importance for centuries and centuries, even this comparative vanity disappears or vastly lessens" (46-48). The problems Cavafy is facing here have no direct relationship to those associated with Marxist views on alienation or the Existentialist diagnosis of estrangement and meaninglessness. Hence, an effort to press the comparison would be misleading. Cavafy's argument is clear: pessimism is ultimately an unsound view not only because it is incompatible with the common nature of human beings, their inherent drives to produce and act, their enduring historical and social continuity, but also because it is inconsistent with the facts of individual psychology of satisfactions, rewards and fulfillments. When all is told, the cure for such pessimism is more wisdom, more understanding of the generic conditions of humanity and the concrete contexts in which action occurs and pleasures are consummated.

Part Two of the *Ars Poetica* re-introduces the distinction between the theoretical and the practical person. The poet or philosopher is a man of ideas and insights, converts them into plans which he then pursues with determination and courage, and when the circumstances demand it, even self-sacrifice. Cavafy is quick to add that the life of ideas is not without its own demands and tolls, for quite often the work of the theoretical man is not appreciated in his life-time, and even after his death it may be ignored or underrated. Furthermore, one's discoveries, being imperfect, do not bring the recognition or profit they deserve. Of course, they are mankind's again. But often it is other persons, who later perfect such insights, that come to claim the honor. The basic thesis, one which belies Cavafy's own aspirations and hunger for renown, is that the poet, in his capacity as a theorist, occupies an indisputable place in the forces that shape and guide the destiny of cultural politics.[17] While Plato denied the poet a place among the philosopher-kings, Cavafy restored him by appealing to the richness and social usefulness of the poetic intelligence. And he does it by making the poet not a being of enthusiasm, inspiration and imagination, but a person of rational work and public relevance. He goes back to the Homeric tradition and the tragedians of the classical age to make the poet once again an educator of mankind. Thus as early as 1903, Cavafy had arrived at a clearer conception of the broad

---

[17]The distinction seems to relate to Oscar Wilde's statement: "There are two kinds of men in the world, two great creeds, two different forms of nature: men to whom the end of life is action, and men to whom the end of life is thought." Again: ". . . for art comes to one professing primarily to give nothing but the highest quality to one's moments, and for those moments' sake." *Essays and Lectures*, "The English Renaissance of Art," (New York and London, n.d.), pp. 151-2. Cavafy had read Wilde, but for Cavafy the political concerns of poetry were stronger than what Wilde's aestheticism would allow.

and politically significant function of poetry: the didactic—a function which is not to be confused with the species of didactic poetry which purports to inculcate moralistic precepts.[18]

The remainder of Part Two is given to the examination of a verse in a poem, "The Pawn" (U 63-4),[19] in accordance with the procedure of philosophical scrutiny. The connection with the preceding views is provided by the suggestion that the pawn in a game of chess is analogous to the man of action, since both may be called upon for an act of self-sacrifice. Cavafy compares it to the case where a theory is translated into successful action through the sacrifice of a heroic man of action. Yet, without the hero of theory, the admirable action of the practical man would never take place. Conversely, without action, the mere idea remains an idle insight. By comparison, works of theory precede those of action in order and value. It is this last point to which Cavafy appeals to decide whether the adjective "great" applies with equal force to ideas and acts. Exclusive attention to sacrifices of action is not sufficient, since "the theoretical life, the life of the artist and the philosopher, have also their sacrifice, bitter and unjust" (*sic.* 60).

The discussion in this portion of the *Ars Poetica* is somewhat strained; but the general thesis is clear: the theoretical man is a great benefactor, the equal of the practical man and comparably heroic, if not more so. Without great theories, for instance, the system which the Spartan legislators conceived and established, the sacrifice of men like Leonidas would lose much of its significance. Ultimately, it is great theories which are translated into action and bring such rewards as "the complete happiness and success to which a human being can aspire" (66). Here belong the contributions of "the leaders of the American and the Greek rebellions, Pasteur, Garibaldi, and a few other instances" (66, 68). Cavafy's examples are quite interesting in that they refer to wars of liberation and discoveries of great benefit. Curiously enough, he does not refer to wars of conquest as paradigms of cultural stratagems.

---

[18]Papanoutsos 1955: 121-2, has made an exhaustive analysis of the "didactic" aspect of Cavafy's poetry.

[19]The poem was written in 1894 and revised in 1911, but remained among the poet's papers. Though not a successful poem, it has interest mainly as an aid to trace Cavafy's development. The theme of the poem is stated in the *Ars Poetica* as "the domain of theory translated into action."

Napoleon, Caesar, even Alexander of Macedonia, are omitted. The theoretical work that such cases involve, if one can speak of it in these terms, perhaps would have been thought of by Cavafy as grandiose rather than great. One suspects he would call it the work of ambition, not involving a theory which aims at human happiness. In any event, the answer is not given in the *Ars Poetica*. The reader may retrieve it piece by piece from the "Hellenistic" poems, all of which take political wisdom to be a kind of theoretical work. It is proper background against which the poet can screen and judge the loud claims of emperors, kings and leaders to fame, honor and greatness. The drama of hubris in history generates its own pity and fear.

What stands out in the *Ars Poetica* are the ideas Cavafy used in producing an argument in favor of his own importance as a poet. There is nothing in the *Ars Poetica* that directly relates to the commercial climate of opinion in Alexandria or the familiar cries of despair due to his loss of social standing. Similarly, there is no reference to the inner voice of the Muse; neither do we find the reassurance he had once sought by calling the poet "divine." By 1903 Cavafy had written but a handful of good poems, all of which were in need of further work. Thus, he could not really appeal to this work in demanding recognition. The body of his accomplishment was still rather thin. The alternative was to resort to a defense of his role in theory. And we see him in the *Ars Poetica* doing precisely that: dreaming of progress, contributing to human happiness, being a cultural leader, aspiring to the heroism of the theoretical man. His effort to elevate poetry to a noble place, to give it a cultural mission within the context of political life, was genuine and had the backing of a powerful philosophical heritage, but his secret claim of belonging to this class when he wrote the *Ars Poetica* rested more on desire than on actual accomplishment. The passionate concern to become a cultural hero made him dependent on wishful thinking. While this dependence persisted, the attempts to change his life were more in the form of escapes. The end to his cultural fantasies came not with emotional readjustments, but with the slow and careful application of the most remarkable insight of the *Ars Poetica*: the procedure of the philosophical scrutiny of his poems.

The cumulative result was the final discovery of his own voice and the radical change of his poetry. Only later, when the crisis had passed, was he able to see the meaning of his own humanism embodied in a non-heroic hero, to put it somewhat paradoxically. This concept took final shape in 1910-1911 with the writing of "Ithaka" and "The God Abandons Antony," the former being his version of the modern odyssey of the non-hero. Suffice it to say there is no anti-hero in Cavafy' poetry. Still, if one must speak of heroic acts, as defined in the *Ars Poetica,* they are his poems, at once aesthetic and political, his acts of poetry.

6. The Editing of Collections

The writing of the *Ars Poetica* was accompanied and followed by the reworking of a number of poems and the further clarification of the rules for their edition. The study of Cavafy's editions has been the subject of a special undertaking by Professor G. P. Savidis. His book is a thorough and exhaustive discussion of all the pertinent facts and constitutes the best guide for the reader who wishes to trace the phases of this topic. One can do no better than present here in bare outline only what may be of assistance for a better understanding of Cavafy's work. We have already seen how the *Ars Poetica* reflects faithfully Cavafy's conception of the growing organic unity of his poems, "a work in progress," which forbids divisions into separate and autonomous collections. If the number and selection of poems differ from edition to edition, the explanation for such variations must take into account practical difficulties and technical reasons, not least among them the fact that Cavafy found it necessary to test his rules of editing before arriving at a definitive plan which would best project the interrelationships of the poems. The reader should also bear in mind that Cavafy did not publish "collections" in the usual manner of book printing. In fact, the printing and circulation of his poems, except in cases of particular printings in journals and other media, were intended for the eyes of the happy few, select friends and recommended persons. Cavafy kept careful lists of the names of those to whom he sent copies of each successive edition.[20]

Savidis divides the editions into three distinctive periods, each reflecting a special phase in Cavafy's creative life and consciousness of technique.

The first period of editions lasted for thirteen years and falls between 1891 and 1904, for a total of thirty-nine published poems. Cavafy used the

---

[20]The catalogues listing names, dates and number of copies are printed in Savidis 1966: 217-83.

term "*phylladia*" (leaflets) for the one-page printing of the poem "Builders," a term which Savidis suggests must be extended to all five separate editions of period A. At maximum the leaflets comprise only six of the thirty-nine poems: "Builders," "Walls," "Prayer," two under the group heading *Ancient Days* ("The Tears of the Sisters of Phaethon" and "The Death of Emperor Tacitus"), and "Waiting for the Barbarians." Savidis numbers them A 1-A 5.

The second period of five to six years falls between 1904-05 and 1910. Cavafy uses the term "*teuchos*" (booklet), for these editions, two in all, which Savidis numbers *Booklets* 1 and 2. They are the only ones that have the form of a book—the later collections are not strictly speaking books but pages bound together. *Booklet* 2 (1910) is a "second" edition of *Booklet* 1, corrected and augmented; both contain only two poems of period A: "Prayer" and "Waiting for the Barbarians." *Booklet* 1 is a thematic selection of fourteen poems. *Booklet* 2 continues the same arrangement and contains only the poems he published for the first time or rewrote between *Booklets* 1 and 2. Cavafy never announced either edition. He distributed copies only privately. Petridis based his 1909 lecture on *Booklet* 1; the caustic review R. Campos wrote was for *Booklet* 2.[21] *Booklet* 1 has special interest because it reflects the first fruits of Cavafy's "philosophical scrutiny" of his poems, the reworking of those that were salvageable, the rejection of others and the writing of new ones which were embodied in the *Booklet* 2. But the fact that *Booklet* 2 included all the poems of *Booklet* 1 and more, is a clear indication that by 1910 Cavafy had approved, though not definitively, only twenty-one poems.

The third period begins around 1912 and continues till the poet's death. It is the period of his "*sylloghés*" (collections), which Savidis numbers from *Collection* 1 to *Collection* 10, "the longest, richest, more systematic and mature." The period of *Collections* begins with the chronological arrangement of the poems selected for inclusion, but as the work increases in volume the method of arrangement is settled in favor of a thematic one. It is worth noting that Cavafy's third and mature period began when he was about fifty years old and only after the crisis was well behind him. By this time, he had reached full understanding of his eroticism and was able to cast off his temerity to publish "revealing" poems—neither *Booklet* 1 nor *Booklet* 2 contains poems of this sort. The "philosophical scrutiny" of the poems of the second

---

[21] Savidis 1966: 47.

period continued throughout the mature years. As the *Collections* 1-10 clearly indicate, Cavafy gave his *definitive* approval to only seven of his pre-1911 poems.[22] Notably absent are "Waiting for the Barbarians," "Voices," "Desires," "Thermopylae," "The Windows," "Candles." Yet these are among the poems which made Cavafy popular and established his reputation as a new voice. There is no evidence that he ever disowned them either. If anything, they are among the best poems of the "crisis" years.

---

[22]Definitively approved pre-1911 poems are the following: "The Footsteps," "That's the Man," "Monotony," "Dionysos and His Crew," "King Demetrius," "Trojans," and "The Funeral of Sarpedon."

Chapter Eight

The Barbarians and Other Things That Are Not

1. Insight into Decadence. 2. Cavafy Responds to Gibbon: the Background for a Fictional Drama. 3. "Waiting for the Barbarians": Thematic Elements. 4. The Gods Have Not Died. 5. Defenders of Thermopylae.

1. Insight Into Decadence

Several poems of Cavafy's middle period form a thematic sequence as an answer to the deeply disturbing question of the vanishing of the *builders*. The theme is part of the broader issue of the destruction of the Hellenic world and the gradual compromise of the life of the polis. I restrict my discussion in the early sections of this chapter to the symbols and historical experiences the poet invokes to project futility and decadence not as inevitabilities but as misplacements of values due to distortions of normal priorities or submission to violence. I return to Cavafy's understanding of the Hellenic conception of life later in the chapter.

The denial of leadership through the exclusion from the class of cultural builders was a blow to the pride of the poet. Refusing to accept responsibility for the fading social mission of the artist, he resolved to view the situation as a social malaise. As the predicament reached the point of intolerance, a painful dilemma began to shape, pointing to two possible solutions: either resignation and eventual death in passive acceptance of the condition of decadence, or effecting a decisive redefinition of the idea of the voyage with the help of a bold vista into a more promising future. The latter came to be thematically dominant but only after the feeling of resignation subsided, in reflection rather than in action. While the state of indecisiveness lasted, Cavafy went through a period of serious personal disturbance that brought him close to a state of chronic depression.

The poems he wrote during the period preceding and following the writing of the *Ars Poetica* form the background to two grand topics, the secret turns of the erotic voyage and the universal humanism of the Hellenic ideals.

Chapter 8: The Barbarians and Other Things That Are Not

This chapter deals with the suffering that accompanied the process of recovery, the poetic traveling, so to speak, through the meandering twists of contorted human acts and intentions that Cavafy sought to reveal by turning them into themes for poems, sometimes with consummate skill, at other times with only mild success. Many of the poems of this period were rightly condemned; they possess no worth save that of weak links in the long chain of "the work in progress." They help us appreciate the hard labor required of the poet to rise to the level of clarity of mind before he could dismiss the illusions and the false expectations he had been nourishing against his better judgment. As confessions, they intimate the painful preparation for the final act of boldness toward defining the new voyage that would bring him out of the closure.

The discussion concentrates on three major poems: "Waiting for the Barbarians," "Thermopylae" and "Ionic," together with a few satellite compositions that help illumine the main theme. Each poem exposes a different aspect of the problematic of the role of the builders once it became a distorted quest. As an epilogue to the section on "Thermopylae" we turn briefly to the poem "Poseidonians," a moving dirge song but hardly an epitaph, since it occupies a special place in the saga of the loss of the Hellenic polis, itself symbolic of the personal problem he felt so deeply in 1894. Still, the perception of the loss was under the sway of the emotional undercurrents of his reading history with a passion. Nevertheless, the stirred emotions proved beneficial; they deepened his concern not for force of destiny but for the mindful ways of political and phyletic survival.

In the late 1890's Cavafy made an attempt to clarify his cultural views. One of the powerful devices he used was the inversion of the classical mode. In March 1898, he published the poem "The Tarantinians Carouse" (CP 55):

> The theaters are packed and music everywhere;
> here debauchery and lewdness, and over there
> contests, athletic and sophistical.
> An unfading wreath crowns Dionysos' statue.
> No corner of the land is left unsprinkled
> with libations. The citizens of Tarans carouse.
>
> But the Senators withdraw from all these things,
> and sullen, they speak in angry tones.
> And then each barbaric toga as it flees

takes the shape of a storm-threatening cloud.[1]

In March 1898, Cavafy wrote "Like the Past," which he later revised and gave a new title, "Monotony." He stressed the haunting feeling of his *ennui*, the repetitiousness of non-events, the soul's barren landscape. The trimmings, jewels, togas, and other paraphernalia, he apparently saved for the "Barbarians." Convinced that monotony was there to stay, he summarized its essence by saying that "each tomorrow looks no longer like a morrow". In January 1898, when he wrote the poem "The Souls of Old Men," the theme was carried a step further.

Two other poems, written about the same time, "Death of the General" and "When the Watchman Saw the Light," are special extensions of the dominant theme of *ennui* and its suspected cause: the failure of leadership to trust the creative genius. Both poems were written after "Waiting for the Barbarians," and give the impression of being afterthoughts. They were kept in the file of unpublished poems; thematically, they belong to the set of compositions dealing with crisis in leadership.

In "Death of the General" (January 1899, U 109),[2] the people lament the impending death of their Great Leader, who is still in possession of his senses and knows he never possessed the virtues the people believe he always had. The people may be mistaken but their fear is real: "His death is our city's demise! / Alas, Virtue has died with him."

Cavafy wrote a number of poems on the theme of failure on the part

---

[1] It seems to be a prelude to "Waiting for the Barbarians" (December 1898/*1904* A 107-8). Savidis has suggested that Cavafy probably based this poem on his reading of a passage in K. Paparrigopoulos, *History of the Greek Nation*, II (1865), pp. 322-3. The passage refers to a diplomatic incident in 282 B.C that finally led to armed conflict between Tarentum and Rome. The defiance which the leaders of the former exhibited in an hour of exuberance precipitated the loss of its independence in 272 B.C. See Cavafy 1983: 117-9.

[2] Savidis gives January 1899 as the date of composition, i.e. one month after "Waiting for the Barbarians," but with certain reservations. The manuscript is in Cavafy's handwriting with the following note: "Not for publication. But it may remain here" (U 230-1). On the other side of the page he had copied the last 11 verses of "Waiting for the Barbarians." Savidis believes that the initial title of the poem was "*Proetoimasia*" (Preparation), in accord with a title found in the chronological list F5, immediately after the title "Waiting for the Barbarians."

of leaders to respond to the need for collective statesmanship. The defenders, the fighters, are blameless, as Cavafy will say in "Those Who Fought for the Achaean League" (1922/*1922*: B 31), and so is the poet. In their arrogance the leaders do not even suspect that he is wise, a *sophos*. As for the crowds, they are just followers, accepting their fate. The theme dwells on one of the causes of decadence, the creeping self-deception of the citizens, their dependence on the illusion of greatness their leaders had not attained.

"When the Watchman Saw the Light," written in January 1900 (U 127), underscores yet another side of the pretentious leader. Whereas the people know that every Agamemnon is in fact replaceable—the chorus always knows!—the leaders do not. Anyway, unlike the aged and dying general, Agamemnon is the great conqueror of Troy, soon to be murdered. The people sense his fate but can do nothing to change it. And though they fear the doom, they also know it is not their own; another king will be found just as good or just as bad. Once again the complex issue of leadership is brought to the foreground, this time for some caustic remarks about kings, generals, rulers, especially leaders who see themselves as indispensable and irreplaceable. The Watchman saw the light and announced the return of Agamemnon, King of Mycenae. A good omen, but just the same:

> Argos can do without the house
> of Atreus. Ancient houses are not eternal.
> Of course many people will have much to say.
> We should listen. But we won't be deceived
> by words such as Indispensable, Unique and Great.
> Someone else indispensable and unique and great
> can always be found at a moment's notice.
> (Tr. Keeley and Sherrard, p. 187 rev. ed.)

The rule of replaceability also holds in the case of intellectuals, sophists, and all the clever ones. In November 1900, Cavafy wrote another [unpublished] poem, "The Enemies" (U 127). The setting is in the mansion of the Roman Consul, who is conversing with three sophists, learned chroniclers of events, dedicated to preserving current events for posterity, who came to pay him their respects. But, they say, they have "enemies," other sophists, who are writing history from another point of view perhaps to minimize the achievements of the Consul; they inevitably do so by distorting the facts, since style and taste are bound to change. The Consul, aware of the whims of fortune and popular taste, makes fun of the sophists: "*You* have enemies," he warns them. The reversal of the caution takes them by surprise. He flatters the flatterers suggesting that their fame, rather than his, is at stake. Actually, it is their writing of history that has enemies, since it is their rivals who are also writing history. The visitors see the trap and try to soften the barb by suggesting that their real enemies are the future sophists who will undo their "elegant and correct accounts." Still, "the same things will be said," only differently. The substance remains. Where then is the danger? The real enemy is the change of style, and nothing can be done about it.

2. Cavafy Responds to Gibbon: The Background for a Fictional Drama

In November 1898, Cavafy wrote a poem that was destined to draw attention to his poetry as well as add to his fame. "Waiting for the Barbarians" was published by itself as a *Pamphlet* A5 in 1904, and was later included in the edition of the issue *Booklet* 1 (1904-1905) with thirteen other poems. On May 7, 1905, Cavafy sent a copy of "Waiting for the Barbarians" to Kimon Michaelidis, editor of the periodical *Panathenaia*, only to receive a rejection note.[3]

The writing of this poem comes at the end of a long period of studying great historical works. During the 1890s, Cavafy read Ruskin and took notes between September 1893 and July 1896. He also read the 1820 twelve-volume edition of Edward Gibbon's *The Decline and Fall of the Roman Empire*. His notes on this work were written between 1896 and 1899, while engaged in a parallel reading of K. Paparrigopoulos' multi-volume *History of the Greek Nation*.[4] Cavafy was a critical reader with a special point of view. In order to understand the revisions and the final form he gave to this poem, it should be mentioned that at the time he was reading Gibbon he found it necessary

---

[3]For Cavafy's letter to Michaelidis, see Savidis 1966: 41 and notes 24-25. The poem was reprinted in 1906 in the Skokos *Yearbook* (*Imerologion*) for 1907. The different versions of the text are printed in Savidis 1966: 146-47; Tsirkas 1958: 326-27. Cavafy revised this poem several times before deciding on its definitive form. For the textual differences between the versions of *Pamphlet* A5 and *Booklet* 1, see Savidis 1966: 147, notes 117 and 118.

[4]Savidis 1985: 91-9; Haas 1982: 21, 31.

Chapter 8: The Barbarians and Other Things That Are Not

to register his reservations and enlist, when convenient, the support of other authorities.

Throughout the 1890's and the middle of the next decade Cavafy was still clinging to his brand of understanding the historical role of Christianity as a companion to Hellenism in the making of Byzantium. Gibbon's sweeping condemnation of the Byzantine Empire struck Cavafy as being at once unjust and unjustifiable. Gibbon had given an elliptical historical account of the activities of the barbarians as these affected Greece toward the end of the fourth century. A perusal of the poem in its final form yields not a single clue to help the reader discern or even suspect hidden connections between those destructive invasions and Gibbon's historical account. The poet has intentionally obliterated all traces to identity of locale and chronology. "Waiting for the Barbarians" is printed here in the Keeley and Sherrard translation (revised edition 1992, pp. 18-19):

> What are we waiting for, assembled in the forum?
>
> The barbarians are due here today.
>
>
> Why isn't anything happening in the senate?
> Why do the senators sit there without legislating?
>
> Because the barbarians are coming today.
> What laws can the senators make now?
> Once the barbarians are here, they'll do the legislating.
>
>
> Why did our emperor get up so early,
> and why is he sitting at the city's main gate,
> on his throne, in state, wearing the crown?
>
> Because the barbarians are coming today
> and the emperor is waiting to receive their leader.
> He has even prepared a scroll to give him,
> replete with titles, with imposing names.
>
>
> Why have our two consuls and praetors come out today
> wearing their embroidered, their scarlet togas?

Why have they put on bracelets with so many amethysts,
and rings sparkling with magnificent emeralds?
Why are they carrying elegant canes
beautifully worked in silver and gold?

Because the barbarians are coming today
and things like that dazzle the barbarians.

Why don't our distinguished orators come forward as usual
to make their speeches, say what they have to say?

Because the barbarians are coming today
and they're bored by rhetoric and public speaking.

Why this sudden restlessness, this confusion?
(How serious people's faces have become.)
Why are the streets and squares emptying so rapidly,
everyone going home so lost in thought?

Because night has fallen and the barbarians have not come.
And some who have just returned from the border say
there are no barbarians any longer.

And now, what's going to happen to us without barbarians?
They were, those people, a kind of solution.[5]

---

[5] See Keeley 1976: 29-32 on the theme and technique of the poem. On the background of the theme Malanos 1957 reports the following: "One day when he talked to me about the barbarians I came to understand that he used the word to mean nothing more than barbarians, whereas in "The Satrapy" he used the word 'Susa' to mean a life of leisure, just as the word 'Alexandria' in "The God Abandons Antony" he meant more than life. In his interpretive analysis he expounded to me first Nietzsche's philosophical theory on the *eternal return*, to end later on the main problem that had preoccupied him once: Whether our civilization, going on for centuries, is stable or is it possible at some point in the future to be disrupted and a period of barbarism follow in its wake" (299). Noteworthy discussions of this poem in Ilinskaya 1983: 91-2; Liddell 1974: 84-86; Malanos 1957: 299-301; Melakopides 1983: 205-7; Melionis 1983: 197-204; Seferis: 1974, v. 2: 393-6; Tsirkas 1958: 321-46 and 1971: 48-54; Yourcenar: 1978, 26-7.

In the mythic time of the poem, the presence of the Barbarians, as a necessary element, stays silently in the background. In real history, however, barbarians did invade Greece and they brought upon the land of the gods shame and destruction. The imaginative setting in the poem says nothing about the invasion that took place in 396 A.D., and the sacking of the temples. The reader can only surmise Cavafy's preparation for the writing of this poem and his intention to establish a connection between poetic surface and historic fact. It is not an accident that Cavafy wrote his "Waiting for the Barbarians" in 1898, after completing his reading of Gibbon and other historians. The connection will become clear after the historical events and Cavafy's criticism of Gibbon's views on two central items are brought to the foreground. The latter concerns the prospective arrival of barbarians at an unnamed imperial city, while the theoretical issue addresses the idea of progress.

Commenting on Gibbon V, xxx, 179, Cavafy gives in Note 23 his own views on the Gothic invasion of the Greek mainland in 396 A.D:

> Eunapius accuses (Vit. Max.) the monks or Christian priests of having been privy to the treacherous surrender of Greece; and it is a matter for considerable surprise that Gibbon did not quote the curious passage:
>
> The impiety of the dark-robed [monks] that crept in unhinderedly pointed out to him (Alaric) these gates of Greece. [Τοιαύτας αὐτῷ (τῷ Ἀλαρίχῳ) τὰς πύλας ἀπέδειξε τῆς Ἑλλάδος ἡ τῶν τὰ φαιὰ ἱμάτια ἐχόντων ἀκωλύτως προσπαρεισελθοῦσα ἀσέβεια.]
>
> It is true that the words of Eunapius do not carry any extraordinary weight. Certain doubtful remarks of Zosimus about the respectable (pagan?) Antiochus, his two good (pagan?) sons Musonius [*verso*] & Antiochus, & his bad (Christian?) son Antiochus; and the fact that the great majority of the inhabitants of Greece proper were pagans, is all the extraneous evidence that comes to corroborate Eunapius' accusation. But it is insufficient, and the accusation can be disregarded.
>
> Still, we are not used to so much favour—or justice—to the Christian cause from the pen of Gibbon. —C.[6]

---

[6] First publication in Peridis 1948; repr. in Liddell 1974: 120; also Haas 1982, 56, with a passage from Paparrigopoulos v. II, Bk 8, 800, which Cavafy uses for his reply to Gibbon.

The main point is that Gibbon, in V, xxx, 179 [III, 242], where he discusses Alaric's march into Greece in 396 A.D., should not have put most of the blame on the Christians as does Eunapius when referring to the decision that left the Straits of Thermopylae unguarded, thus making the monks party to the treacherous surrender of Greece. Cavafy is convinced that Gibbon did not use this source and hence missed the evidence. Nevertheless, the accusation of treachery stands but not on the strength of Eunapius' saying.[7] Gibbon wrote:

> In this narrow pass of Thermopylae, where Leonidas and the three hundred Spartans had gloriously devoted their lives, the Goths might have been stopped, or destroyed, by a skillful general; and perhaps the view of that sacred spot might have kindled some sparks of military ardour in the breasts of the degenerate Greeks. The troops which had been posted to defend the Straits of Thermopylae, retired, as they were directed, without attempting to disturb the secure and rapid passage of Alaric (V, xxx, 179).

Cavafy meant to show that Eunapius' accusation is based on insufficient evidence. He does not deny Christian complicity in leaving the pass of Thermopylae unguarded and thus facilitating Alaric's march into Greece. He tries to be judicious and maintain that the accusation holds even if Eunapius is biased. As for Gibbon, Cavafy identifies two errors: missing Eunapius' testimony, even if a biased source, and calling the Greeks 'degenerate', that is, incapable of defending their land for lack of heroic qualities when facing the Christian treachery. Papoutsakis quotes Cavafy (*Prose* 1963, "Byzantine Poets" 47-48, note 18): "It is foolish to argue for the view [viz. Gibbon's thesis that Byzantium=Eastern Roman Empire] that it was a declining phase of the Roman Empire, since the historical reality proves the opposite." Cavafy could not forgive Gibbon's negative evaluation of the Greek character of the Eastern Empire. Gibbon failed to do justice to both Greeks and Christians. As for the treachery of the latter in 396 A.D., Cavafy puts the blame exclusively on the priests and not indiscriminately on all Christians.

The historic events of that period do not surface in "Waiting for the

---

[7]Comp. Haas 1982: 58, n100. According to Paparrigopoulos, "the Goths were followers of Arius but Christians nevertheless and eager to contribute to the triumph of their allies, particularly through the destruction of the holy shrines [of the pagans]" (II, Book 8, p. 700).

Barbarians," and should not be treated as constitutive elements of the mythic space of the poem. Cavafy's dispute with Gibbon is related to the making of this poem not as the evaluation of Eunapius' judgment but as the rejection of Gibbon's conception of progress and its place in history. In 1898, when Cavafy wrote "Waiting for the Barbarians," he was still clinging to the 1891 view he had stated in his "Builders."

The passage in Gibbon that seemed to have prompted Cavafy to respond with a special note on the idea of progress, was the following:

> The experience of four thousand years should enlarge our hopes, and diminish our apprehensions; we cannot determine to what height the human species may aspire in their advances toward perfection; but it may safely be presumed that no people, unless the face of nature is changed, will relapse into their original barbarism. (VI, xxxviii, 418 [IV, 167-8]).

Insofar as Cavafy is pitching his views on progress and perfection against Gibbon's, the poem is in part a satire on Gibbon's faith in the Enlightenment ideal and a rejection of his anti-Greek and anti-Christian views on the causes of the decline of the Roman Empire. The Romantic revolt against reason had openly precluded regression to barbarism. For Gibbon, "enlightened" Europe had already become secure from future irruptions of barbarism.[8] Cavafy was turning the tables on Gibbon's theory of perfection.

---

[8] Cavafy has in mind the concluding section of Chapter xxxiii, "General Observations on the Fall of the Roman Empire in the West," where Gibbon reflects on the improvement of mankind since the times of the *human savage*: "Cannon and fortifications now form an impregnable barrier against the Tartar horse; and Europe is secure from any future irruption of Barbarians; since before they can conquer, they must cease to be Barbarians. Their gradual advances in the science of war would always be accompanied . . . with a proportionable improvement in the arts of peace and civil policy; and they themselves must deserve a place among the polished nations whom they subdue . . . . His [the human savage] progress in the improvement and exercise of his mental and corporeal faculties has been irregular and various; infinitely slow in the beginning, and increasing by degrees with redoubled velocity: ages of laborious ascent have been followed by a moment of rapid downfall; and the several climates of the globe have felt the vicissitudes of light and darkness. Yet the experience of four thousand years should enlarge our hopes, and diminish our apprehensions: we cannot determine to what height the human species may aspire in their advances towards perfection; but it may safely be presumed, that no people, unless the face of nature is changed, will relapse into their original barbarism (371-72).

The *personae* in "Waiting for the Barbarians" suffer from an anachronism. One suspects that Cavafy shaped them to match the over-civilized and perfected Europeans of the Enlightenment. Should they happen to fall in a state of decline, they can be re-vitalized as a political and cultural group only by barbarians; hence the message of promise in the expected event whereby the decadent "Romans" will soon be gratefully dominated by the under-civilized or rather non-civilized barbarians. However, unless the barbarians are still barbarous, they cannot really consummately conquer. Ironically enough they can be "a kind of a solution," only if they relapse into their original barbarism, which, according to Gibbon, is impossible. In Cavafy's poem the *personae* do not address the issue. In their disarming innocence the poet has them totally oblivious to Gibbon's musings. They cannot even come to say that barbarians without barbarism are not essentially different from themselves, and hence no solution of any kind is to be expected. If so, the invasion is pointless.

If there are no barbarians, all human beings are either civilized or over-civilized. And the question now becomes: Can the over-civilized be revitalized without the barbarians? Perhaps it was a mistake to make Europe secure from any future irruption of barbarism. And now what is Europe to do without barbarians? Those people were a kind of a solution. Perhaps. But a solution to what problem? Is the choice between the persistence of *ennui*, the undesirability of perfection, and death due to over-civilization?

In 1898 Cavafy was still on the grandstand of his "Builders" trying to comprehend the magnitude of the human predicament. Not feeling like one of the *personae* in the first version of the poem, titled "Barbarian," he had no share in the predicament. Needing barbarians for a solution was not part of his outlook. His was a different problem, one that is rooted in the classical quest of how to integrate the lyrical self and the citizen. Herein lies the importance of the persisting message of his "Builders," i.e., not to compromise the role of the poet in civilization and the life of the polis. If there was a pressing problem staring at the poet, when he was writing "Waiting for the Barbarians," it had to do with understanding the adequacy of his answer rather than the quest for a new solution from without.

It seems that the last poem Cavafy wrote in response to his reading of Gibbon and to the tenets of the Symbolist movement was "Waiting for the Barbarians." Chronology allows this inference, given that the poem was composed in December 1898 and the "notes" on Gibbon's history stopped in

1899. However, the idea of loss of vigor in a highly cultured city came before his reading of Gibbon.

Cavafy, reading Gibbon more than a century after the publication of his history, saw how the turning of events in the nineteenth century threw cold water on the optimism of the Enlightenment view of history. Gibbon had underestimated the barbarous element lurking from within like a sleeping giant unable to secure its European self against its own dormant forces of destruction. Gibbon could violently oppose the American Revolution but sympathize with the French Revolution. When Cavafy wrote his "Waiting for the Barbarians," he composed a symbolic poem. It was as though he meant to tell us that either we all are barbarians and do not know it, or that there are no barbarians and we do not know it. There cannot be any barbarians after we enter the phase of culture that prepares us for death in perfection. Optimism must be ruled out from the course of history, so thought Cavafy at the time, and so demanded the paradoxical marriage of progress and perfection. Gibbon had predicated his optimism on the faith in progress. Cavafy, composing at the end of the nineteenth century, saw that this faith had become opaque. The idea of progress was deficient in design, flattering to the inflated cosmopolitanism of the times, and conspicuously contrived to assuage the deep-seated agony in the works of the Romantic cult of perfection. Cavafy's obsession with his own version of perfection, coloring as it did his view of history and poetic themes a number of years even after the turn of the century, reflects the persistence of his personal crisis. It ran so deeply that it prevented the confluence of his desire to coordinate the expressive needs of the lyrical self and the reflective powers of the citizen in search of a polis no longer within reach.

Gibbon's views on the idea of progress were directly opposite to what Cavafy held in "Builders" and reiterated in other poems of the middle period, namely that the attainment of perfection was tantamount to over-civilization, carrying with it cultural exhaustion, as pictured in "Waiting for the Barbarians" of 1898. Reading Gibbon was no mean challenge; it even irritated him. The change came later.[9] It seems then that Cavafy's initial reaction upon reading

---

[9]Savidis 1985: 93-97. In his discussion of this point he remarks that "Waiting for the Barbarians" was "written during the period he [Cavafy] was pondering over Gibbon's shrewd but overly optimistic guess that 'Europe is secure from any future irruption of Barbarians;

Gibbon was one of irritation, but the 1898 poem masterfully conceals it only to reveal it through the device of irony. If the poem is read as a response to a "conceivable" event in history, irony gives the poem the special quality of satire, made dominant in the 1904 version. By that time, Cavafy had written his *Ars Poetica* and formulated his principle of philosophical emendation for the scrutiny of his poems selected for revision with the help of rational criteria that ensured internal cohesion and thematic correctness.

Yet Cavafy's "pondering," to use Savidis' expression, went deep enough and surfaced as subtle satire, revolving around the idea of a complex paradox: expecting a practically undesirable event to happen and also wishing the barbarians, destructive, disruptive and "uncivilized" though they were, to come and breathe new life into the decaying institutions of the great capital of an empire, itself exhausted and unable to recapture its spirit of old and to sustain political creativity.

Cavafy recast the portrait of the barbarians and presented it obliquely by insinuating only what they dislike, what annoys them, etc. Seen through the eyes of the *personae* in the poem, the barbarians become transformed into barbarians who have ceased being "barbarous." Therefore, they cannot conquer any more than they can exist; they disappear from the scene of history as a revitalizing force. The other side of the paradox reflects the situation of the city: glorious yet no longer able to view itself as the agency of progress, and being a living dead, a remnant and a relic, grasping for significance, and not finding any, it grants its citizens license to decay. Their perfected over-refinement heralds the call to finality. But before reaching the edge of exhaustion the citizens will have contributed to the demise of the only outside source of rejuvenation; they will have made the savage invisible. When the city will need those people, they just will not be there.

One begins to wonder at this point whether Cavafy intended to talk about barbarians or about the exhaustion of the literary movement he was about to jettison, precisely because it was like the barbarians: non-vital. And here we sense the heightening of irony. Cavafy went to Symbolism and to the poets who held the secrets of the primitive and primordial world of emotions that the scientific culture had undervalued, only to find that their poetic visions could not provide a way to reunite the lyrical and the communal self,

---

since, before they can conquer, they must cease to be barbarous'" (96-7).

the poet and the citizen. Like the magistrates in the fictional city of the poem, he had reached the inner side of the walls from which there was no exit. Perhaps for a brief moment, he too expected the barbarians to come, aid from without, to offer a solution, any solution. The symbols had worked; the corresponding objects had been identified; the situation for the writing of a poem was ripe. Reading Gibbon provided him with the rudiments of a new theme. Yet nothing was to come from the outside.

When Cavafy revised this poem for publication in 1904, he applied the canon of "philosophical scrutiny" but only to the extent that he could rework the poem without destroying the connecting tissue of the initial symbolism on which the ironic element depended for effect. More specifically, the opaqueness, the element of "*suggestif*" that entices the imagination, had to be preserved along with the mode he used to weave the complex pattern of the insinuated paradoxes. Removing the opaqueness would have made the poem too literal to be relevant to recognizable situations and too concrete for the symbols to function as suggestive universals. As in the case of "The City," Cavafy did the best he could in bringing the 1898 composition in line with the principle of "Emendantory Work." Both poems belong to the Symbolist period, "Waiting for the Barbarians" less so than "The City," since the former contains strong elements of irony and an awareness of the haunting problem of the duality of lyrical self and communal identity. Both poems, once their initial impurities were removed, became landmarks in the transitional phase.

There is a sense in which "Waiting for the Barbarians" can be said to point to the case of barbarians and the Roman empire, where both are used as raw material for a symbolic analogue despite the difficulty of associating Rome with the mythic space of the poem. There is nothing that invites the reader to lament the loss of a higher quality of life implicit in the "Roman versus Barbarian" confrontation. Therefore, discussions that have sought to explore the symbolist elements in the poem in order to uncover Cavafy's interest in late Roman and perhaps European history have not brought noteworthy results.[10]

---

[10] Tsirkas 1963, for instance, has argued that the situation portrayed in the poem is meant to cover the condition of modern Egypt, one that turns the English into a barbarian agency. On the whole the predicament to which the poem refers has no relation to any events in modern Greek history.

The poem utilizes select elements from certain phases of Roman history mainly for the composing of a symbolic picture that alludes not to a historic period of decline but to an imaginative crucial moment of a collective impasse with no solution in sight. Close attention to the details in the poem shows that Cavafy made use of phrases from passages in Gibbon.[11] Gibbon's faith in science, the ideal of the Age of Enlightenment, the basis of his concept of Progress, is the real connection needed to explain Cavafy's interest in writing a satiric poem to expose the limits of that faith. "Waiting for the Barbarians" is a satire on Gibbon. If by suppressing superstition the Enlightened Mind has in fact made Europe "secure from any future irruption of Barbarism," then the people in the poem are over-civilized and consequently incapable of further progress. On that basis there can be no barbarians in the literal sense, and given the conversion to "culture," there is no chance that humanity may ever revert to its original barbaric state. Since the Barbarians are no longer "barbarians," whether they conquer is irrelevant. With revitalization no longer a possibility, the Barbarians are things that are not. But was Gibbon right?

3. "Waiting for the Barbarians": Thematic Elements

Sometime in 1903-4 Cavafy wrote in his own shorthand a note: "I was also smwt. doubtful ab. 'περιμ. τοὺς Βρ.' and there I found in rew. t. surmise that their recurrence is a possibility."[12] Since he intimates that he surmised the possibility of a recurrence, the question is whether he means the repetition of a past event. The note was written after the rewriting of the poem to give it its definitive form, and it suggests in effect that he realized at that time of the first writing he had surmised that the possibility of "their" [=the barbarians] recurrence. If the note is allowed to read "I was also somewhat doubtful about 'Waiting for the Barbarians', and there I found in rewriting the surmise

---

[11]Note 5 on Gibbon I, viii, 314, quoted by Haas 1982: 36, indicates moods and effects: "animating faith and vigour"; "industry of the people"; "loss" and "fled"; also expressions referring to inner conditions of the empire, and expressions to indicate the absence of barbarians due to acculturation.

[12]Quoted in Tsirkas 1958: 340.

that their occurrence is a possibility," Cavafy finally had realized that the issue of the existence or non-existence of the "barbarians" had to be resolved. The lingering of the ambiguity until the poem was brought "under the scrutiny of the Philosophical Principle" may well explain the postponement of publication.

Years later, Cavafy came to say: "It is futile to wait for them." One is tempted to add here the following: *even if their recurrence is a possibility*, but to do so would be to question the removal of the ambiguity. Down to 1917, Cavafy spelled the word 'barbarians' with a capital B. When the poem was reprinted in *Alexandrian Art* (1928, p. 125), he changed the capital letter to a lower case b. He was simply reiterating his position to remove any misunderstandings about the fictional status of what might otherwise be taken for a historical entity. The fact is that he did utilize materials from real events in history to construct a symbolic analogue suggestive of a weakness in the human condition *in extremis*. He needed certain ingredients to weave a pattern in which to place the psychology of *ennui* for the dramatization of cases illustrating loss of vitality, cultural exhaustion, and especially the closure of a personal impasse. He found what he needed in the accounts of the historians, especially in Gibbon, together with a challenging interpretation.[13]

The theme called for the specification of locale and time for a fictional city. The date had to accord with a *terminus ad quem* and in order to be fictionally correct such an "event" could not be allowed to be imagined as having taken place later that 541 A.D. The consulate was no longer practiced after that date. This is a detail Cavafy must have known.

Identifying the place has been subject to considerable speculation.[14]

---

[13] "Waiting for the Barbarians" was written twenty years before Spengler's *Decline of the West*. See Peridis 1948: 78-81 for Cavafy's response to Gibbon on this particular issue.

[14] Michaletos 1952 argues in favor of Rome. Malanos, with support from Peridis, favors an "ideal city." Tsirkas 1958 contends that the analysis of Cavafy's "learned sources" leads to the conclusion that the city is Byzantium, and only secondarily Rome. He states that Cavafy told A. Politis that he sought to find in Byzantium an environment for his *personae* and that in 1896 this interest was quite strong. Tsirkas concludes that "Waiting for the Barbarians" must be an early Byzantine poem. Liddell, who finds Tsirkas' contention excessive, draws attention to the personal element in the poem, which in his view is related to Cavafy's mood of realistic pessimism, also present in "Candles," "The City" and "Walls." The theme connecting these poems is the feeling of *impasse*, and "Waiting for the Barbarians" shows that it runs deeper than the mood of pessimism the poet shared with the Symbolist poets.

The problem of the topography of the scenery aside, it should be obvious that Cavafy constructed the "city" with elements traceable to Rome, Byzantium and Alexandria.

The thematic study of this poem invites interpretation at two levels: (a) the transformation of historical materials, and (b) the parameters of self-reference. The latter raises the difficult question of identifying the problems Cavafy was facing at the time he wrote this poem, and why he thought that their solution depended on the successful casting of the theme of the poem in accordance with the rules and technique of "correspondances." By 1898, Cavafy was steadily coming closer to realizing that he had exhausted the usefulness of the Symbolist technique to furthering his own artistic interests. He had reached the point where he had to search for alternatives to escape the lingering impasse dating back to the days of "The City." But before we continue with the analysis of the self-reference of "Waiting for the Barbarians," we must return once more to the transformation of the historical materials he assimilated from his readings.

In a lecture P. A. Petridis gave five years after the publication of "Waiting for the Barbarians," we have what seems to be an accurate account of thoughts on history and civilization Cavafy sought to express in the poem.

> Again another great social problem concerns Cavafy: the problem of Civilization. Cavafy thinks that Civilization did not bring us happiness. In an hour of dark pessimism and deep reflection Cavafy must have conceived the "Waiting for the Barbarians." It is a magnificent and fascinating vision of the poet, who is transported to an ideal city, in which its inhabitants developed a civilization of high quality, and now are taunted by a hedonic nostalgia for a life of past ages, the memory of which is lost in the night of the past. They imagine that returning to the life of a primitive civilization will bring them happiness. And their desire was almost fulfilled. The news arrived that the Barbarians are almost nearby . . . .. Night came and they were still waiting, but the Barbarians did not appear. And some who came from the frontier said that Barbarians no longer exist. The citizens return to their homes pondering the question: "And now what will become of us without barbarians? / Those people were a kind of solution."[15]

If this is a faithful summation of the central theme, a number of

---

[15] Greek text in Tsirkas 1958: 323.

questions come to mind: Why so much stock in the belief that the barbarians hold the key to "a solution"? What values do the barbarians possess that could be of real use to the decadent city? Why would a Greek poet think that the salvation of civilization, however decadent, could depend on the untested cultural potential of "barbarians"? Why does Cavafy select for his theme a case of civilized life with distinct late Roman features and hardly anything Hellenic? Why did he portray the *personae* as citizens lacking confidence in the power of their own institutions and traditions to effect a renaissance? Why the unrequited melancholy at the end of the poem as the citizens leave the meeting place after hearing that the barbarians are not coming? We begin to suspect that a literal reading of the poem will not provide answers to these questions. The alternative would be to turn to the doctrines of Symbolism.

Essentially, the rejection of literal references to the existence of barbarians together with the possibility of finding the noble savages to serve as forces to rejuvenate a tired civilization, makes the poem anti-romantic in character. The idea of pre-civilization barbarians, untouched by questionable political and ethical practices, contributes nothing to understanding the poem. There is no suggestion that the city, suffering as it does from *ennui* and exhaustion, can turn for therapy to an injection of barbarian purity. All solutions from without are illusory, temporary, cases of "a solution." The alternative would be to look for an agent from *within*. The news from the frontier allows this inference, even if the poet refrains from drawing it for whatever technical reasons. The effect remains the same: Cavafy delivered a severe blow to political and aesthetic romanticism. It signaled his disengagement from its literary faith.

Only the poet, impassioned spectator that he is, knows that the barbarians do not exist even before the first lines of the poem are put on paper. Non-existence conditions the fate of the city and its malaise. The mystique works, and the reader willingly suspends disbelief. For a moment we prefer to visualize the barbarians as the last and lost saviors. Given what the *personae* have done with themselves or what their culture has done to them, however one prefers to state the issue, futility reigns supreme. Nothing is forthcoming. The poet knows it; he is a *sophos* even about non-approaching things. The title of the poem contains an element of irony, not tragic, but pathetic. Only the poet knows that nothing is about to happen. Where, then, does the poem take the reader?

The fictional setting of the poem points to another problem, how to understand what the "real" problem is: the process of cultural reconstructing. Thus Cavafy suddenly distances himself from the crisis of the effete culture and the ineptitude of the citizens that let the distortion of their once robust institutions go undetected. Unable to cope with the severity of the crisis both leaders and people turn to fatalism. Drained of energy and still hoping, they hang their expectations on the coming of the barbarians. But, then, they seem to know next to nothing about them as a revitalizing force. The guesswork of the citizens only succeeds in deepening the sense of despair. At this level of fictive meaning, Cavafy becomes obliquely didactic: the reader may realize that the way to respond to the problem of cultural decadence lies in decisive action away from dependence on the outside by initiating reforms from within. This was also Plato's solution.

Thirty years later, in 1928, in his "In a Large Greek Colony, 200 B.C." (B 66-7), Cavafy returned to the theme of reforms from the outside, the barbarians long forgotten.

> That things in the Colony aren't what they should be
> no one can doubt any longer,
> and though in spite of everything we do move forward,
> maybe—as more than a few believe—the time has come
> to bring in a Political Reformer.
> (Tr. Keeley and Sherrard, p. 155 rev. ed.)

And the debate to decide whether this is the right solution begins. What takes place is believable; it occurs in what is almost a real city and a familiar agora, with citizens doing real thinking, whether sloppy or prudent, it does not matter, for what they say sounds convincing. At the end of the poem the proposal to bring in the Political Reformer is dropped in favor of using local talent to set straight the city's public affairs:

> Certainly, and unhappily, many things in the Colony are absurd.
> But is there anything human without some fault?
> And after all, you see, we do go forward.

It was a reasonable decision even if the solution did not work; the Colony did not last. Sooner rather than later, the Romans, the outsiders, came and took over. What counts is that the solution came from within. The citizens in the large Greek colony in 200 B.C. did not throw up their hands in despair asking: "Now what's going to happen to us without Barbarians?" But let us return to the poem. This verse continues to pose a haunting question. Suppose the barbarians existed and could have provided a solution, what would it be? This takes us to the mystery of the problem. The only information the poet has released amounts to a picture, a dramatic situation of people waiting but refusing to legislate, unwilling to govern and maintain control over the affairs of the republic. The opaque texture of the problem invites the reader to supply the rest and fill the gaps. The 1898 poem is *suggestif*, like "The City."

In "The City" we witness no exit, and hence no solution. In "Waiting for the Barbarians," in sharp contrast to the drabness of that other city, this one is replete with pomp and circumstance; nothing will affect the inertia of the "non-drama," except for the final dimming of natural light. There is no promise of redemption for the city. By refusing to legislate, the citizens have become the inhabitants of a "non-city" filled with artificial relations, empty hierarchies, hollow titles and worn-out etiquettes. The "we" in the last line of the poem bears close resemblance to the *persona* in "The City," comparably unable to master the formalism of resignation we see the celebrants in "Poseidonians" and "Alexandrian Kings" display with such consummate skill.

There is still another question to which Cavafy does not supply the answer. What happened to the fictional barbarians, assuming that they ever were?. Did they vanish for the same reason the inhabitants of the city are about to do? There is another twist to the question. The specter of cultural decline had waxed strongly toward the end of the nineteenth century and the beginning of the twentieth, and in many instances it was related to the search for means and sources to revitalize the arts. It is possible that Cavafy, when he wrote his "Waiting for the Barbarians," had thought it useless to invoke the power of the primitive to provide patterns of artistic vitality and new approaches to search for originality of style and content. Could it be that he was a spectator refusing to join the welcoming party waiting at the gate and burdened with tired beliefs, some as old as Byzantium itself, surviving in the mannerisms of neo-Alexandrian Europeans? The hypothesis may be difficult to entertain but it is still possible to consider the chance that Cavafy had viewed with suspicion the movement that recommended the summoning of a primordial force to put new life into the tired blood of Romanticism and its offspring, Symbolism. But if there are no "barbarians" it is futile to invoke their spirit to solve the aesthetic impasse. In the meantime Nietzsche, pressing in a different direction and turning the table on the Greeks, had worked out a powerful device, the inversion of the classical mode, to overcome what he thought was the tyranny of decadence. Cavafy was not sufficiently familiar with that radical solution and later, when he learned more about it, he did not find it of special interest. Cavafy had confidence in the efficacy of the cumulative record of Western wisdom, whereas Nietzsche did not.

On the surface of it, "Waiting for the Barbarians" may be read as a poem on the theme of total social and political exhaustion. There is also the personal belief hiding beneath the glimmering surface that dependence on outside help creates more problems than it can solve. The poem, one begins to suspect, has an autobiographical ring to it.

Cavafy's experimenting with the poetics of Symbolism was leading to an impasse since the technique could not address both needs of his personality, stemming from the lyrical self and the political being. One suspects what Cavafy was trying to make clear to himself in 1898 was a state of mind that was beginning to look more and more like the city whose people, magistrates and dignitaries were waiting for the barbarians. Given the Symbolist technique, the correspondence obtains.

Left out of the poem is the implicit belief concerning the full range of possible solutions, other than what the "barbarians" as a collective *persona* conceivably represent. Somewhere included in this range is the possibility that only a well-planned inner re-organization of creative energies can save the poet from the fate that awaits the inhabitants of the exhausted city, or if one prefers, the depleted soul. Admitting the non-existence of barbarians does not necessarily make prominent the reform from within. Neither the *personae* nor the reader see this aspect, for they are not ideal spectators. The pathetic irony thus is allowed to reach deeper. Cavafy was composing in the Symbolist mode a symbolic poem to grasp the essence of his impasse to which his own compliance to the Symbolist doctrines had brought him. He was not required to assign a special time to the "event" nor did he have to locate it in a recognizable geographical place. The city is fictional and with minimal historical dressing. Viewed in this context, the theme of impasse is comfortably cast in objectified imagery and social symbols. The reader is free to treat it, together with "The City," as expressive of the poet's disapproval of an imagined model of "total" political decadence and cultural exhaustion.

It would seem that Cavafy designed the poem in such a way as to conceal any premises from which one could deduce the existence of "barbarians." This well conceived move also blocks the possibility of an external solution. Only the false sense of expectation is allowed to linger on, but it can do no more than protract the agony of ambivalence and discord between the two basic concerns of the self. There is also another side to the personal problem: preserving one's dignity. Turning to the barbarians for help implies admission of spiritual poverty and loss of dignity, in sharp contrast with the color, wealth, pomposity, and pretentiousness the magistrates put on display.

The demise of the imaginative-symbolic city portrayed in "Waiting for the Barbarians" will not be witnessed; the city is only in the poem. It does not suffer physically, it is not besieged nor will it be ransacked. No external force is about to touch it one way or another. It is simply anticipated that the city will wither and vanish just as we find it in the poem: nameless. Anyway, Cavafy says nothing in the poem about how the city ended. However, he did make it clear that the city has no builders and no poets; its representatives are administrators, office-holders, bureaucrats, officials, and of course, an emperor. The spiritual forces, the edifices, are absent.

Perhaps the "city" is in the soul, serving as the image of the personal situation the poem was intended to convey. Yet, it is not a City of Ideas (πόλις τῶν ἰδεῶν). What was hinted in chapter 4 can now be restated. If "The Satrapy" is the twin poem of "The City," then neither the real city of Susa, nor the decadent city in "Waiting for the Barbarians" is the right environment where one can be a *polites*. And the same holds for the bleak city of "The City." What then is one to do? Where does Cavafy go next? One begins to suspect that he is readying himself for the voyage, as in "Ithaka," in search of harbors and perfumes, though not yet ready for the City of Ideas. The cosmopolitan hedonist connoisseur of perfumes and pleasures is a step higher than the self-exiled man of "The Satrapy." We have then two different voyages: the voyage of "The Satrapy" that makes the traveler become an *a-polis*, man without a city, and the voyage of "Ithaka" that opens to the cosmopolitan vista. How, then, does the poet arrive in the City of Ideas? Perhaps it exists only as the end of the ascent to the world of poetic wisdom, available primarily to authentic creators like Theocritus.

4. The Gods Have Not Died

Two years before the writing of "Waiting for the Barbarians," probably in May 1896, Cavafy composed a mildly interesting poem based on one of his notes on Gibbon. He titled it "Memory" (*Mneme*) and published it on October 13, 1896 in the journal *Asty*. Most likely he rewrote it nine years later, in 1905, i.e. a year after the publication of "Waiting for the Barbarians," and decided at that time to retitle it "Thessaly." Finally after another revision and a new title, "Ionic," the poem was published in 1911. These editorial changes would hardly be of any significance were it not for the fact that the poem was thematically related to his notes on Gibbon. The striking feature of the 1911 "Ionic" is that, unlike the views expressed in "Waiting for the Barbarians," it is closer to the new outlook Cavafy was developing to bring into harmony his belief in Christianity and his admiration for the Hellenic tradition. Gibbon had provided the challenge; Paparrigopoulos, the great nineteenth century Greek historian, had filled the poet with confidence in the continuity of the three phases of the Greek nation: ancient, byzantine and modern.

The controversy over the conflict between Paganism and Christianity in the late Hellenistic period was bound to become a problem for Cavafy. Gibbon was but one of the many historians who had addressed the confrontation between the two cultural forces and reviewed the role of Christianity in the shaping of Western civilization. Cavafy sensed the sharpening of his dilemma and opted for what he thought was the best of both worlds, except that in 1896, and even in 1905, his position was only "a solution." The problem of the antagonism would not disappear. The seed of doubt had thrown deep roots in the imagination of the poet. A rival religious hero, one who did not survive the battle of the cults, Apollonius of Tyana, had provided the poet with the theme for a 1897 composition, "Absence," which was later revised and published under a different title, "If Dead Indeed," in the journal *Asty*.[16] Evidently, reading Gibbon and the late Hellenistic historians

---

[16]Cavafy was familiar with the literature on Apollonius. He had read Philostratus' *Life of Apollonius* and had published in 1892. See Cavafy, *Prose,* 1963: 51-65) an essay titled "Lamia," dealing with John Keats' poem "Lamia," based on Philostratus (Bk. IV, ch 25). He translated for this essay a substantial portion of Keats' poem (CP 126-7, ed. Savidis). Referring to Apollonius, Cavafy wrote: "The figure of the great magus and philosopher of Tyana fascinates us as a magnificent, super-human personality" (51). Aside from "If Dead

of different religious persuasions, especially Zosimus, Eunapius, Sozomen and Socrates, had helped Cavafy realize what vast destruction religious fanaticism had perpetrated on the non-Christian cultural traditions and institutions. He began to see that the Greek heritage was caught in the snares of the tensions between Roman imperial authority and the Eastern spiritual cults. His notes and comments on Gibbon provided the background of the 1896 "Memory."

> The gods do not die. Only the faith
>   of the ungrateful crowd of the mortals does.
> The gods are beyond death. Silver clouds
>   hide them from our gaze.
> O holy Thessaly, they love you still,
>   their souls remember you.
> In the gods, just as in us, blossom memories
>   of the heartbeats of their first love.
> When in love, dawn kisses Thessaly
>   and ardor of the life of the gods
> passes through its atmosphere; and sometimes
>   an ethereal figure flies over its hills.[17]

The poem intimates another side of the problem of the Greek tradition as it relates to Cavafy's understanding of the rise and message of Christianity. There seems to be a deeper connection between "Memory," later changed to "Ionic," and Cavafy's increasing awareness of the vanishing of the classical world during the late Hellenistic period, with the spreading of the new religions and the persecution of the rites and religious practices of the Greeks. Cavafy's reading of Gibbon marked the beginning of a new phase in his

---

Indeed," Cavafy wrote two more poems about Apollonius: "But the Wise Perceive Things About to Happen" (1896/*1899*; rev. *1920*) and "Apollonius of Tyana in Rhodes" (1925/*1925*).

[17]Savidis 1966 offers a tentative view about the possible date of composition of the first version of the poem: "It follows from other documents in the archives of Cavafy that the initial title of the poem was "Thessaly" (comp. also the fifth line: "Ὦ Θεσσαλία ἱερά" [O holy Thessaly] etc. and also the ninth line: " Ὅτε ἐρῶν τὸ λυκαυγὲς φιλεῖ τὴν Θεσσαλίαν" [When in love, dawn kisses Thessaly]; this permits the conjecture that the poem perhaps was inspired by the climate of the Thessalian incidents in May 1886" (110, n18). The conjecture has been adopted by Haas 1982: 61 n109, and with certain reservations by Dallas 1986: 74 n30.

approach to the problem.[18] In 392 A.D., the Emperor Theodosius proclaimed the most unfavorable laws against the pagans. Other bad omens followed. The last celebration of the Olympic games took place in 393 A.D., and soon thereafter the famous statue of Zeus, the masterpiece of Phidias, was transferred from Olympia to Constantinople.

The theme of "Memory" reflects Cavafy's thoughts in Note 22, "Destruction of the temples in the provinces A.D. 381 &c," Note 23 V, xxx, 179 [III, 242] "Alaric marches into Greece, A.D. 396" [separate note], and more directly Note 24, "His [Adolphus] marriage with Placidia A.D. 414." The mention of Thessaly points to Note 23 and the events of 396 A.D. The Emperor Arcadius's minister, Rufinus, had secretly encouraged the Gothic chief Alaric whose army had already encamped in Thrace and was posing a real danger to the capital of the Eastern Roman Empire, Constantinople, to move instead against the pagans of Greece with license to invade and plunder Greece. The invasion brought paganism to its knees. Alaric's christianized Goths found no resistance at the pass of Thermopylae. With assistance from the Christian monks, the officials left the straits unguarded on secret orders from the Emperor. The barbarians swept through the land. They did not enter Athens, but they crossed the Isthmus, took Corinth, and after pillaging every major city they marched all the way to Olympia. Alaric's invasion of Greece, the passing through the land of Thessaly, where Mt. Olympus dominates the sacred landscape—a symbol for all of Greece—the plundering and destruction of the temples, was a sacrilege that defies description. In 398 A.D., Alaric was forced to withdraw from Greece under pressure from the Western Roman Armies only to find his way to northern Italy.

Cavafy was well informed about the historical accounts of these events. Nevertheless, in his Note 23 he shows no concern and displays no serious emotion, such as indignation, to protest the sufferings of the Greek pagans. The main thrust of the Note is to challenge Gibbon's judgment, his illicit generalization in which he blames the Christians *en masse* for letting the Goths pass through the straits of Thermopylae. The emphasis is on defending

---

[18]The comments on Gibbon have been discussed in detail by Haas 1982, and to some extent by Bowersock 1981. Cavafy found unacceptable Gibbon's thesis on Byzantium: "The empire of the East . . . from the reign of Arcadius to the taking of Constantinople by the Turks, subsisted one thousand and fifty-eight years, in a state of premature and perpetual decay" (ch. xxxii).

Christianity rather than condemning the barbaric destruction of Greece. How then are we to explain the plaintive tone in "Memory" that the gods do not die, only the faith of the ungrateful crowd of mortals does . . . ? Cavafy carefully avoids accusing the Christians for converting the Greeks or the barbarians for destroying the Greek temples. The decline of paganism is strictly attributed to the fickleness of the ungrateful crowd. This is easy diagnosis; it will be removed from the poem in 1911.

Note 24 refers to a deposed Emperor, Attalus, whose role Gibbon reconstructs in chapter xxxi by drawing information from diverse ancient authorities. It is recorded that he was a pagan prince later converted to the Christian faction of Arius (the same sect as the Goths): "a prince, who in his native country of Ionia had been educated in the Pagan superstition, and who had since received the sacrament of baptism from the hands of an Arian bishop." We find him later in Rome, praefect of the city. Due to a combination of strange circumstances he became Emperor in 409 with the support of the people of Rome, the senate and the suffrage of king Alaric, who had by that time summoned Rome to surrender. Attalus was but another willing usurper who took the purple seriously and believed his policies, always subject to Gothic approval, conducive to a new order. When it suited the designs of king Alaric, Attalus was dethroned and disgraced in 410 A.D., in the same year Alaric and his Goths sacked Rome.[19]

The change in the title from "Thessaly" to "Ionic" is indicative of Cavafy's design to be true to the facts. The degraded emperor was assigned in 414 A.D. to lead the chorus of the Hymeneal song at the wedding of Adolphus, Alaric's brother-in-law, now king of the Goths, and Placidia, daughter of Theodosius, sister of Honorius and Arcadius, Emperors of West and East. Gibbon writes (V. xxxi, 335):

> Attalus, so long the sport of fortune, and of the Goths, was appointed to lead the chorus of the Hymeneal song; and the degraded emperor might aspire to the praise of a skillful musician. The Barbarians enjoyed the insolence of their triumph; and the provincials rejoiced in this alliance, which tempered, by the mild influence of love and reason, the fierce spirit of their Gothic lord.

---

[19]Alaric died in 410 after a brief illness while leading an expedition against Africa.

Cavafy comments:

> The subject for a beautiful sonnet, a sonnet full of sadness such as Verlaine would write—"Je suis l'empire à la fin de la décadence."[20] Lost in the Gothic tumult and utterly bewildered, a melancholy emperor playing on the flute. An absurd emperor bustled in the crowd. Much applauded and much laughed at. And perhaps at times singing a touching song—some reminiscence of Ionia and of the days when the gods were not yet dead. —C[avafy].[21]

Years later, as deposed emperor, Attalus may be easily imagined reminiscing in 414 A.D. what he and others like him comprising the "we" in the "Ionic," as Greek converts, had done by being party to the policies that brought about the events of 396-398 A.D. Attalus, participant in the ceremonies of the Goth's wedding, the humiliated celebrant, is now a perfect candidate to serve as the *persona* in "Memory," although neither "Memory" nor its revised version "Ionic" of 1911 was written as a sonnet. By combining Notes 22, 23 and 24, Cavafy could easily transform the "Memory" to the "Thessaly" version of the poem.

> Because we broke their statues
> because we threw them out of their temples
> the gods did not die, on account of that, at all.
> O land of Ionia, it is you they still love,
> It is you their souls remember.

---

[20]The verses from Verlaine's "Langeur" (ed. Pleiade), p. 370.

[21]Peridis 1948 cites the comment on Gibbon—written in English—and adds: "Here, in recalling Ionia and the gods who did not die, is found the nucleus of the wonderful poem 'Ionic' which will be written later" (79-80). Haas 1982, 60 writes: "This reading note clearly falls into the category of Cavafy's artistic comments on the *Decline and Fall*. As did Gibbon's passage on Simeon the Stylite, the passage on the deposed emperor Attalus brought to the poet's mind an existing literary work and suggested to him another possible poetic development of the subject. As far as we know Cavafy never wrote 'a beautiful sonnet [. . .] full of sadness' about 'a melancholy emperor playing on the flute', 'lost in the Gothic tumult [etc]'. But the evocation of two historical themes, that of barbarism and decadence and that of the death of the pagan gods, had led Cavafy scholars to cite this reading note with reference to two of his poems, Περιμένοντας τοὺς Βαρβάρους ["Waiting for the Barbarians"] (1898/1904), and Ἰωνικόν ["Ionic"] (published in 1911)."

> When dawn comes upon you on an August morning,
> ardor from their life passes through your atmosphere;
> and sometimes the shape of an ethereal youth,
> indefinite, quick and transient,
> glides over your hills.

But why "Ionia" in 1911? He found, so it seems, further use for his Comments on Gibbon, particularly with reference to Attalus. Attalus, Alaric and the details of the invasion and destruction of Greece in 396 and 398 are kept off stage in the poem. Nevertheless, the 1911 "Ionic" presupposes Notes 23 and 24, with Attalus as a ghost figure deposed by the Christianized Goths, ordered to playing the flute in 414, and in his humiliation reminiscing the days prior to his conversion lost in his effort to understand why they broke the statues of the gods. He looks back only to find the events abhorrent. The *persona* now speaks in the plural, but the poet behind the *persona* is still unwilling to blame Christianity for the demise of paganism. One can only blame the faithless crowds.

The transition from "Memory" to the "Ionic" deserves a closer look. In neither poem do the gods die; they live in their own way and continue to love the Greek countryside, their Thessaly and Ionia. What is at issue is not their immortality but the mode of worship and ritual: religion. In "Memory," the demise of religion is attributed to conversion due to shallow faith, whereas in "Ionic" the cause is the acts of violence. Changing the location from Thessaly to Ionia brings the final version closer to Attalus' birthplace and also suggests the unalterable Hellenic character of the birthplace of science, philosophy, epic poetry and legends about gods and heroes.

The 1911 "Ionic" contains a major revision. It introduces considerations that specify time and action. The faceless crowd is narrowed to a concrete "we" that allows assigning responsibility. The reader can now recognize the actions of violence as persecutions, more precisely as actions by converted Greek pagans directed against the Greek gods and the Greeks who still worship them. What did not come through in "Memory" was the suggestion that the Greeks were participating in the destruction of their own heritage. The opaqueness of this theme in 1905, in view of the fact that Cavafy had formulated his Emendatory Principle, may mean that either he had not sufficiently clarified his attitude toward Byzantium or that he was unwilling to examine critically the impact of Christianity on the Hellenic cultural institutions. In 1905, at least he was keeping Christianity and Hellenism in two separate compartments, confident he could be equally loyal to both and use them as needed. At some point, the inherent contrariness emerged, but not with sufficient force to demand immediate response. What surfaced in 1905 was the problem, not the solution. The "Ionic" owes its importance, at least in part, to the removal of the opaqueness. The guilt due to self-destruction had now been exposed.

A closer look at the religious practices in late Hellenistic times in Greece proper shows that the mainland on the whole remained loyal to the practice of paganism in its traditional non-proselytizing form. On the other hand, Christian practices were waxing strong, and the proselytizing proved well programmed in the greater urban centers, foremost in Constantinople, Alexandria, Antioch, and other major cities of the Eastern Roman Empire. Yet persecutions in the fourth century were not necessarily motivated by purely religious concerns. Anti-pagan persecutions were initiated for political gains and military advantages, as in the case of Alaric's invasion of Greece ending with the destruction of the shrines in Olympia and most of Peloponnesus.

There is a difference between a Christian Goth, unrelated to Greece, and Attalus, the Ionian Greek pagan converted to Christianity. Only someone like Attalus could speak convincingly like the *persona*, implied in the "ὡς ἐν ἡμῖν" in the "Memory" of 1896, whether speaking is done in 390 or 414 A. D.[22] Why did Cavafy refrain from naming the pathetic figure of Attalus as the *persona* in the poem?

With the writing of the 1896 "Memory," he could comfortably and imaginatively internalize, in poetic acceptance, the collective guilt of the converted Greek Christians and articulate in a moment of pious soliloquy the hope of preserving the treasured past of his phyletic ancestors. Whether the *persona* is Attalus in 414 A. D., or a shepherd on the slopes of Parnassus after hearing of a sacrilege at Delphi in 398, makes little difference. The "Memory" of 1896 contains the incipient idea for the "Ionic" of 1911. The mood of ambivalence proved authentic, and nothing essential in it was canceled as the

---

[22]Haas 1982, makes an interesting comment regarding the situation of Attalus and the symbolic value it has for Cavafy in the "Ionic," suggesting that "the theme of the death of the gods is intimately tied here to that of the death of a civilization—ultimately Greek civilization—brought about by the arrival of the barbarians who put their destructive strength to the service of their adopted religion" (62).

poem went through its various phases of revision.

The hidden mood stems from Cavafy's own ambivalence about the role of Christianity as a benevolent spiritual force. The events of the last decade of the fourth century made it perfectly clear that the continuation of paganism was unacceptable to the official religion, yet the selective attitude of certain civic and religious leaders at the beginning of the next century, which allowed for the cultivation of useful features of the Hellenic mind was more than necessary. It came to be regarded as part of the substance of Christian pro-paideia. With certain modifications, the Greco-Roman basic virtues, with proper controls, could provide the programmatic prelude to assist in the inculcation of conduct suitable to the religious conception of virtue. The major problem was how to remove the barbarians from the court and deny them access to high public offices. Synesius had urged adoption of such a policy in his letter to the Emperor.[23]

Reading historical texts made Cavafy aware of the complexity of the problem of the two cultures, and while maintaining a strong affection for the Byzantine ancestors, he still had to discover for himself the subtle ties that had made aspects of Hellenism compatible with the Christian culture without compromising the humanistic foundations of the former.

At the time Cavafy was reading Gibbon, he was drawing a sharp line between the intellectual and humanistic outlook of Christianity of the liberal wing of the Cappadocian Church Fathers, who appreciated the deeper affinity of their Faith to the Hellenic mind with certain reservations, and the ultra-conservative monks who had become intolerant of anything Greek. The fanatics demanded the destruction of everything related to the culture of the pagans. According to Cavafy's Notes, Gibbon was wrong to treat Christianity the way he did. Whether Gibbon could be counted among the admirers of the classical mind of Greece is another issue.

Cavafy's view of Christianity during this period is closely related to his attitude toward the Emperor Julian.[24] Julian's policies were detrimental to

---

[23]Text in J.P. Migne, *PG* vol. 66; *The Letters of Synesius of Cyrene*, tr. A. Fitzgerald, Oxford, 1926; Bregman 1982: 41-59.

[24]The unpublished "Julian at the Mysteries" was written in November 1892, one month after the first version of "Memory." See Bowersock 1981 for a full discussion of the Julian poems.

the cause they sought to serve, precisely because the Emperor was unable to understand how dangerous it was to revive and restore the pagan religion. He was confident that by adopting the organizational model of the Christian Church he could effect the return to paganism. He employed the wrong means to ensure the preservation of classical Greece, especially at a time when Christianity was consolidating its dogma and power. Julian's tenacious beliefs prevented him from understanding that there was a liberal side to the Christian outlook, sympathetic to Hellenism, and willing to accept certain select intellectual and cultural features. Convinced that this deeper affinity between liberal Christianity and the Hellenic mind was still functional, Cavafy grew skeptical of extreme positions. He criticized Gibbon for not seeing what Byzantine Christianity had done to preserve what it found valuable in the Hellenic tradition, notwithstanding the Church's claim to superior truths. Although aware of the Emperor's interest in Greece, Cavafy found Julian's policy to revive paganism and his blindness to the positive role of Christianity deplorable.

Cavafy's views toward Christianity gradually changed a number of reasons. He came to realize that even the enlightened prelates were often too uncompromising in the domain of moral values to be trusted with the stewardship of the classical tradition. At any rate, in 1899, he was still confident that there were grounds for the co-existence of the two cultural traditions and the promotion of mutual respect in both camps.

When Cavafy brought up the death of the gods and the loss of faith, as in the opening lines of "Memory," it was mainly to blame the converts of moral weakness rather than accuse the new religion of using oppressive tactics to succeed in changing the ways of the "ungrateful." The collective *persona* re-affirms the belief in the immortality of the Grecian gods, but what the *persona* finds painfully disappointing, more than the mortal nature of human beings, is their fickleness, their weakened faith and their ingratitude. Although these mortals were blessed with such lovable and exquisite divinities, at the first sign of unfavorable *fortuna* they switched loyalties. Still, the gods did not die.

The broader problem of death Cavafy did not put in manageable perspective until 1911 and 1912. By that time he had crystallized his views and found a way to cope with his personal and cultural ambivalences. The latter demanded a re-evaluation of the historical role of Christianity and a compassionate appreciation of the emotional dislocations the changing loyalties had caused during the battle of the faiths in late Hellenistic times, especially in the predominantly Greek cities, where the erotic side of life and the system of worldly values were being deeply affected.

Common to both ambivalences, the personal and the cultural, was the agonizing problem of his own deep-seated fears. As his poetic themes show, fear figured largely as a powerful and persistent element in defining the situations Cavafy had selected for the actions of his poetic *personae*. Understanding the diverse tropes of fear Cavafy employs as part of the dramatic setting helps the reader see why and how Cavafy created a variety of portraits of Julian, the so-called Apostate Emperor. Although the Julian poems have been discussed by many critics, the changing technique Cavafy uses in this group of poems is basically a shift in the perspective from which fear is viewed. To be able to handle this technical task successfully, Cavafy had first to free himself from the ambivalence of his attitude toward two loyalties: pagan and Christian.[25] The difficulty was resolved with the aid of the classical virtue of *andreia*, courage, after he decided to become "a brave man of pleasure." He tipped the balance in favor of the classical, the guiltless and erotic side of life. The decision was "announced" in the unpublished poem of 1903, "Growing in Spirit."[26]

The puzzlement about Christianity versus Hellenism parallels the ambivalence he felt toward the symbolist and classical conceptions of the role of the artist. Having realized that he was toggling between two irreconcilable views while pretending he could use both with impunity, he revised the poem "Memory" and gave it a conspicuously Greek title. The poem reflects an episode resembling his own way of being "in part this . . . in part that" (ἐν μέρει . . . ἐν μέρει) as a poet. Savidis has noted that "the conflict between paganism and Christianity, like that between Hellenism and Rome, appears

---

[25] Note 37 shows clearly that by 1898 Cavafy did not and could not have come to terms with what Christianity really did to the Hellenic heritage. For instance in this Note he writes: "It is not certain that Justinian suppressed the schools of Athens," following in this Paparrigopoulos' pious account of the incident. Consider also Cavafy's Note 33. Haas 1982: 70-71 has identified a number of passages to show Cavafy's appreciation of the humanitarian side of Christianity.

[26] Text and translation In Cavafy, *Passions and Ancient Days* (1971), text and translation by E. Keeley and G. Savidis.

early at the center of Cavafy's feeling for history."[27] The point is well taken, and on that basis it would seem that Cavafy could at times empathize with representative *personae* on either side of the opposing parties, pagan and christian, riding as it were the fence of cultural loyalty by being "in part this . . . in part that." However, the same construction of *personae* is used very sparingly, if ever, in the case of *personae* trying to mix the Hellenic and the Roman. The rule included his reading of historians: Gibbon's preferential treatment is reserved only for things Roman.

It should not be too difficult to understand Cavafy's defense of Christianity in his pre-1911 outlook. The belief in its value is related to his conviction that Christianity had in fact entered the bloodstream of the Hellenic tradition, revitalized the culture, and as a result helped the nation survive the horrors and humiliations of two oppressive conquests of the fatherland, the Roman and the Ottoman.

About the same time he published the "Ionic" he also published "Dangerous Thoughts" (?/*1911*": A 46). This is the poem in which the phrase "in part this . . . in part that" occurs, where playing with danger refers primarily to one's flirting with hedonic habits while moving in and out of available religious and cultural traditions. The dramatic date for the action in the poem is set around 337-351 A.D. at a time when loyalties could still be shifted according to needs, admittedly a dangerous practice to be partly this and partly that, unless one is from Syria living in Alexandria, like Myrtias, a pagan passing for a Christian:[28]

> Said Myrtias (a Syrian student
> in Alexandria; during the reign
> of Augustus Constans and Augustus Constantius;
> partly pagan, and partly christianizing);
> "Strengthened with theory and study,
> I won't be fearing my passions like a coward.
> I will give my body to the pleasures
> to the dreamed of sensual enjoyments,

---

[27] See Savidis 1985: 147-54, reprint of his 1973 article "Was Cavafy a Christian?"

[28] Tsirkas 1958: 333-34 thinks that "Memory" and "Dangerous Thoughts" were the products of Cavafy's reading of Rangavis, Gibbon and Thomas Hardy. If Tsirkas is right, then "Dangerous Thoughts" may be dated as a pre-1900 composition.

to the most daring erotic desires,
to the lustful urges of my blood, without
a single fear, for when I want—
and I will have the will, strengthened
as I will be with theory and study—
at the critical moments I shall be finding again
my spirit, ascetic, as before."

5. Defenders of Thermopylae

"Waiting for the Barbarians" stands in sharp contrast to the events that are commemorated in poems where the *dramatis personae* refer to the invasions and conquests of Greece, events that changed the face of history: the Persian invasions of 490 and 480 B.C., the Roman conquest of 146 B.C., the Gothic invasion of 396-98 A.D., and the Ottoman conquest of Constantinople in 1453. In fact, the world of "Waiting of the Barbarians" bears no resemblance whatsoever to the events that form the background for "Thermopylae" (1903/*1904*), "Those Who Fought for the Achaean League" (1922/*1922*), and "Ionic" (1896/*1905*; *1911*). The poet found nothing heroic to underscore in the "Ionic"; the background events were kept below the surface.

The theme of the poem, as worked out in 1896, had set the tone, and no revision could alter the plaintive mood of the pathetic. The heroic element, recast as a dominant theme, presupposing as it does the choice of the honorable life of duty and sacrifice, figures largely in the 1901 composition, "Thermopylae." The poem, written in the symbolist style of the "*suggestif*," was published in Xenopoulos' journal, *Panathenaia*, in November 30, 1903:

Honor to those who in their lives
elect and guard Thermopylae.
Never wavering from duty,
just and righteous in all their actions,
and yet with pity and compassion;
generous when rich, and even when poor
generous still, in some small way,
still helpful as much as they can;
always speaking the truth,
yet never hating those who lie.

> And still greater honor becomes them
> when they foresee (and many do foresee)
> that Ephialtes will appear in the end
> and the Medes will finally pass through.

The poem projects a solemn image of duty-bound *personae*. The mention of the famous battle of antiquity brings to mind the Persian invasion, the destruction of the land of Greece, Xerxes' early victories, the sacrifice of the defenders of the straits of Thermopylae, and the beginning of the end of the invasion when the united Greek navy defeated the Persian fleet in the Bay of Salamis in 479 B.C. Centuries later the conquerors came from the West. The Roman armies defeated the Achaean League in 146 B.C., and virtually ended the independence of the city states of that confederation.

Cavafy wrote in his *Ars Poetica*: "If 'Thermopylae' fits but one life, it is true; and it may, indeed, the probabilities are that it must" (1963 UPT 60). The reader may want to ask what acts qualify one to be a defender of Thermopylae? The symbol is meant to encompass more than battles and soldiers. Two preliminary comments are in order. For one thing, the *Ars Poetica* ties "Thermopylae" to the poem "The Pawn," and if the *persona* in "Thermopylae" seems related to the *persona* of the "Pawn," the former exhibits the public side of self-respect whereas the latter displays the personal side of sacrifice. For another, the foreknowledge of such events, as will make a Thermopylae possible, is a perception from a distance that entitles a poet to be a wise man, a *sophos*, as in "Things to Come" (=*Epikeimena*, 1892). The poet is now one who is fortified with knowledge about forthcoming events and is prepared to face them.

There is no mistake about the ethical tone of the poem. R. Beaton 1983, writes: "Not the historical pass defended and lost in 480 B.C., but any crucial moral 'pass.' A Thermopylae is a historical metaphor for a contemporary and generalized dilemma, the purpose of the appeal to history is to illustrate a perennial and especially a present, moral truth" (24). Other critics have viewed it with mixed feelings. Bowra 1949, thinks that the poem is good but contains a number of defects due to a certain "abstract ring to it (35), and Michaletos 1952, following Bowra, finds it "defective even from a pure aesthetic point of view. Lines 3-10 consist of a burdensome pleonasm . . . . They are of the most prosaic sort Cavafy wrote . . . . Had he omitted the 'filler' of those eight in-between lines, we would be looking at one of the most distinguished masterpieces of world poetry" (57-8). Themelis 1970, agrees that the intermediate lines are fillings (96-107). Tsirkas calls it "the best poem of the first period," and goes so far as to recognize it as containing Cavafy's "condensed theory of life of that time."[29]

Essentially, the poem elaborates a theme treated in "Builders" and cast inversely in "Waiting for the Barbarians." It expresses Cavafy's deep concern for the integrity of the poet as builder and, in a broader sense, the proper standard for Hellenism in the modern cosmopolis. It is formulated with the aid of parallel images referring back to invasion and its impact on civilized life. The historical correlative is part of the strength of the poem. It alerts the reader to impending dangers. One hears in the background the approaching Medes with the intent to conquer, unlike the "non-existing barbarians," whose purposes are not disclosed. The Medes are real, dangerous, and determined to shatter the Hellenic way of life. In "Thermopylae" the invaders do in fact score a victory and for a short while take over the land of the gods. In "Waiting for the Barbarians" there is no will to fight, no resistance, only profound disappointment in hearing the news that "they" are no more. The situation opens differently in "Thermopylae." A disaster will be completed, and yet it cannot prevent the rise of a moral victory. The reader is prompted to think that the opening lines presuppose knowledge of a defeat and a victory.

Still, the historical incident of "Thermopylae" is only accidentally related to the heroic resistance of the ancient Spartans and to Leonidas' duty to die, as he must, for his country. Nevertheless, the symbols converge to create an ambience to envelop the new scope of the heroic. Cavafy pays tribute to defenders of worthy causes, be they art, country or cultural tradition, each having its own unsung heroes who are prepared to fight against all odds, thus deserving recognition and honor as much as the famous leaders, the wealthy

---

[29]Tsirkas 1958: 404-423 uses three keys to explain the poem: (1) Distant echoes of this theme in Herodotus and Simonides. (2) A modern comedy by B. Anninos, *The Victory of Leonidas*, performed in November 16, 1894 in Athens, which Cavafy must have seen in 1901 during his visit to that city. In the play, the hero Leonidas, a wealthy immigrant, may have been a portrait of Averoff. (3) A play by Pichat, *Leonidas at Thermopylae*, first performed in Paris in November 1825, translated by A. Vlachos into Greek and performed in Athens in November 29, 1870 (published in 1872). The play was performed in Alexandria on 10/23 August, 1901, by a group of actors from Athens; Cavafy apparently attended this performance.

and the powerful. The former no less than the latter know fully well that the Medes will pass at the end. The courage to do one's duty remains what it is: praiseworthy. "Thermopylae" is modest in what it claims. It projects the poet as moral hero, the poet's wisdom vis-a-vis the contributions of persons of wealth and valiance. The poets, too, defend cities, cultures, traditions and ways of life against the Medes. In "Waiting for the Barbarians" no mention is made of poets and wise men with the power to foresee the approaching enemy and the consequences of humiliation.[30]

The defensive war, with or without barbarians, has been widened to cover a new breed of Medes. The symbols of invasion and resistance include situations that can summon novel varieties of courage. The two poems, "Thermopylae" and "Waiting for the Barbarians," make a special diptych. First we have a contrast between the reality of invading Medes, and non-existing barbarians, who never arrive. There are cases in between, and hence we are asked to honor people determined to defend their cause as they see it, be it city or ideal, but not as duty to implore relief from *ennui*.

What needs to be explained in the case of "Thermopylae" is why Cavafy insists that greater honor should go the those who, in addition to being loyal to the assigned duty, foresee what is about to happen, and having understood the coming of the inevitable, decide to stay and defend a Thermopylae despite foreknowledge of the defeat. Of course the Medes will prevail and crunch the defenders, but the vanquished will gain in honor. Each side, in its own way, emerges victorious, one through force, the other through virtue. But only the latter deserve Honor. This brings us to "But The Wise Perceive Things About to Happen" (1896/*1899*, rev. *1915*). They are the *sophoi* who foresee the coming of dreadful things. They do not panic, nor do they implore; they understand, stand, defend and, one suspects, even die. They are the courageous still. Here we have a continuation of the theme of "Builders," with a twist.

The world in "Waiting for the Barbarians" is one of *unreality*. But so is that in "Ithaka." Hence, it would be a mistake to include "Ithaka" in the period of realism, especially since the voyage is carried out in imagination, and the stations where the traveler may stop or is told he should stop are but

---

[30]Melakopides 1983: 205, referring to "Thermopylae," calls it "an affirmative poem *par excellence*," and one that "pertains to personal and social morality."

constructs of the hedonic mind and symbolic instances of poetic accomplishments. Actually the whole sequence of stations in the poem is analogue of the poems that will make up the work in progress, if and when completed. "Ithaka" is a poem about the Cavafian conception of poetry, not about a hedonic sequence in real life; it comes at the end of Cavafy's apprenticeship in Symbolism.

Despite the unreality of the *personae* in "Waiting for the Barbarians," the poem still uses elements suggestive of symbolic correspondences: inner states of the soul and its analogue, a fallen city, as in Plato, rich in embellishments and poor in virtue. Cavafy constructed a city to mirror states of the human psyche, just as he did with "Monotony" and other poems of the same period. If the barbarians were "a kind of solution," the implication is that one could look for other solutions as well. However, in this case the barbarians are a solution coming from the *outside*. But their non-existence cancels the external solution as well. The alternative is to search for an internal solution. But so long as the situation of "The City" continues to prevail, the internal solution stays out of reach. It is not forthcoming because the *ennui* consumes the city-soul. Therefore, both the soul and the city it resembles need to be turned around, rehabilitated.

Cavafy's real problem was to learn how to be a poet in the city of ideas, which in essence is the problem of being both a poet and citizen. The poets of the Symbolist movement skirted around this issue. While working with that mode Cavafy could ignore the problem but eventually it would come back to haunt him. With the unreality of the barbarians out of the way, he was free to attempt the reconstitution of the self against the odds of finding a genuine city in contemporary life. There was only one thing to do, and he did it. He returned to Alexandria and accepted the city for what it had become. But he also accepted the responsibility to understand all the facets and features that made up his part in the loss of the city. Cavafy took the next step: he defined his Thermopylae as poet and judge. By so doing he also discovered the limits of irony.

Chapter Nine

Eros and Sensuality

1. The Transition. 2. Eros in Life and in Art. 3. The Fear of Eros. 4. The Path of Eros: **Ars Poetica** *and the Release of "The City". 5. Reconciliation and Adjustment. 6. Eros after the Return to the City. 7. Eros and the Limits of Irony.*

1. The Transition

Between 1902 and 1909 Cavafy wrote explicit erotic poems but did not find the courage to print them. It was during this period of transition that his agony over the uncertainties of his art started to subside, though he was still being torn between passion and timidity and was still unable to summon the boldness he needed to become a "brave man of pleasure." He was determined to assign to this venerable ancient Greek expression a meaning of his own. It was no easy task, for it called for bringing down "half the house," especially at a time when his personal crisis was reaching a climax around 1903 and lasted well into 1909. The first *daring* erotic poems were written during this period, yet his fear of eros, combined with the pangs of guilt, forced him to postpone their publication including the poems he composed upon his return from Athens and the writing of the *Arts Poetica*.

What sustained the poet's agony was a discrepancy between the intense craving for lyric expression and the need for existential nourishment of eros, on the one hand, and the paralyzing fear of public scandal were he to disclose what he left untold in the poem "Hidden Things." The force of eros and the demands of sensuality, hardly distinguishable at times, eventually emerged with his recasting of the meaning of the ancient virtue of courage to accommodate a different side of the faculty of desiring: the creative urge.

Cavafy understood what it meant to think and act as one of equal rank with the wise travelers on the highway of *hedonê*, "the brave men of pleasure." How far he practiced the principle in his personal conduct is a private matter. What counted, beyond the deepening of self-understanding, was the poetic use of the recast virtue. Evidently, the growing determination revealed to him a novel way to set limits to the use of irony in his compositions just as it helped him modulate the lyrical voice of his own persona in the self-referential poems once the last vestiges of self-deception were removed.[1]

In treating the theme of sensuality, my purpose is not to offer a survey of the erotic poems, including those in the form of epitaphs for fictional young aesthetes, and even less to comment on the vast body of literature that has grown around Cavafy's erotic poetry. Rather, the discussion concerns the formidable problem he had to solve, as I tried to underscore at the end of the preceding chapter: the redirecting of the role of eros, of the faculty of desiring in general, in determining the next phase of his development. Eros, as a motivating force, had fallen in a state of captivity and in the service of predicaments. Its liberation from a dysfunctional employment became the most crucial issue in his life. His creative goals as an artist would come to a dead end without a resolution. The cobwebs that had crowded the poet's perspective since his formative years had to be removed before he could define the authenticity of his identity.

His cultural convictions were seriously affecting his erotic thinking. His reading of the historians, Gibbon and Paparrigopoulos, for instance, helped him reflect on his loyalties as material for poetic themes. He also became conscious of the tenacity with which he held his belief in the phyletic continuity throughout the millennium of the Byzantine Empire just as he was confident in the positive role of Christianity toward the ethnic survival of the Greek nation. Gibbon's scathing criticism did not touch him but it did plant a seed of doubt, hidden though it stayed in the background of the "Ionic." What disturbed his confidence was not so much the peculiar historical ties between Christianity and Hellenism; rather, it was the austere demands that the moral code of religion as a system of values puts on the desires.

The morality that Christianity approved as principles of conduct posed existential and personal problems for Cavafy, who from his early youth and with cosmopolitan upbringing knew not how to cope with the confusion and guilt about his erotic urges. Eventually, his choices were clarified but not before considerable suffering: either submit in obedience to a principle of

---

[1]Horton 1989 has traced the element of self-deception as a device in poetry and as a feature of *personae* in Cavafy's poems. For a different view compare Vayenas 1979.

absolute continence accepting the monk's ideal of abstinence in return for peace of mind and freedom from guilt, or else act and bring down "half the house" moving with thoughtful defiance to avert the dangers of social disapproval and religious damnation.

For years he postponed the decision, and the result was a life of pretension moving in and out of the cesspool of sin and guilt, yet fully aware that his compromise was as painful as damnation itself. With eros at the crossroads, the poet continued to live at the fringes of symbolism, unable to release what a real "brave man of pleasure" would do: the erotic visions of his poetic being. The postponement proved costly. His poetry remained still *suggestif*, and the road to realism blocked. Eros was delegated to a hidden existence, masqueraded, guilty, a thief stealing by night. And so long as eros was held captive, the Hellenic pursuit did not advance beyond the level of phyletic conviction. The cultural principle needed to enter "The City of Ideas" was not forthcoming. Hence the liberation of eros was more than an emotional curiosity pointing to an artistic complex. Ultimately, the task that confronted Cavafy came within the purview of a long and venerable cultural tradition, rooted in Plato's *Symposium*: how the poet determines for himself the order of the rungs on the great Ladder of Love, the one that brings the poet to the heights of immortality.

If the confessional note embedded in the poem "Understanding" (1915/*1918*) is accepted for its relevance to the formation of his "intentions," the pertinence of the early poems waxes strongly as records of eros even if their quality as expressions of art does not. The "intentions" of his poetry, formed at a tender age and dormant for decades, waited for the call of eros to come to light and blossom. But eros as a cultural force can also serve divided loyalties when abused and allowed to fall into the class of the ambivalent things Cavafy called "partly this . . . and partly that." Eros, so long as it maintains its full integrity lies beyond the range of irony.

It was the recovery of this wholeness of eros, rather than the pursuit of gratifications of his own sexual preference, that gave Cavafy's erotic poetry a profundity rarely found in modern poetry.

2. Eros in Life and in Art

In order to delineate the main contours of Cavafy's response to Eros through internal, indirect or lyrical statements, we have only two paths open to us. The first is to collect the dates of composition of the erotic poems and read the latter in chronological sequence.[2] The second path is to identify the date of the incident mentioned in each erotic poem and order such dated incidents in sequence regardless of when they became the subject of a composition or mentioned in a personal note. No matter which path is followed, Cavafy's erotic poems on themes of pleasure and pain form a vast and complex topic.[3] The first erotic theme appears in 1899 in a poem titled "One of Their Gods," and is handled indirectly by means of the powerful device of vicarious identification. However, the earliest emphasis on eros emerged in the poems he wrote in 1903-1904.

Cavafy's attempts to free himself from the predicament of self-alienation and the bouts of suffering he experienced intermittently during the phases of the crisis period from 1894 to 1910, intertwine throughout with the erotic problem. Both found their way in his art and were given a prominent place in the thematics of his poetry. The predicament of self-alienation as a personal problem extended over a long period and climaxed in the entombing of the desires of the *persona*—Cavafy's poetic ego—in a mausoleum. The

---

[2]Keeley 1976 has made limited use of this device in his chronological tables to trace the parallels of the "metaphoric city/sensual city/mythical Alexandria/the world of Hellenism," and with considerable insights as a result.

[3]The sources, other than the poems, are Cavafy's own statements and confessional notes, his own comments on his poems, and related reports from intimate friends and acquaintances. The chronology is essential to any effort to review the phases of the poet's development before he finally understood and accepted his erotic side. Not only is the erotic verse of the period 1902-1909 better treated in correlation with the poet's attitude toward sensuality, but the major compositions of 1910, "Ithaka" and "The God Abandons Antony," are more fully appreciated once the reader has traced the meandering course of eros leading to the removal of the last vestiges of self-alienation thus allowing for adjustments and reconciliations with city and self. The new voyage, no longer a wish to escape or to withdraw, seems clearly to have been prepared through the exercise *(askesis)* in eros that gradually contributed to the amalgamated new perspective for the understanding of the precarious and lasting elements of human nature, whether as history or as poetry.

widest perimeter of the three distinct concentric circles, which stand for the three phases of his drama of self-alienation, coincide with the outer limits of the depersonalized city so vividly portrayed in "The City" (1894/*1910*).[4] The retreat to the inner perimeters followed with inexorable logic until the exterior environment contracted to form the inner wall of an utterly lonely existence inside a windowless structure.

Between the outer perimeter and the narrowest space, as in "The Windows," lies the blurred surface of the inner sides of "Walls." Not more than three years separate the first conceptualization of the outer circle of the city in "The City," and the strictest confinement in "The Windows." The repeated attempts to rationalize or tone down the predicament, as in the case of "Che fece ... il gran refiuto" (1899/*1901*), are closely related to the futile efforts to break through the walls of a self, besieged by its own fears, as in the poem "Trojans," and to the fumbles and compromises which provided the poet with a number of "escape" themes, among them that in "The Satrapy." Parallel to these developments run the meandering currents that lead to the gradual acceptance of his suppressed eroticism. The publication date of the three closure poems shows that they were published in the reverse order of the chronology of composition: "The City" (1894/*1910*); "Walls" (1896/*1897*) and "The Windows" (1897/*1903*). Whether the poet planned their publication in that order is open to speculation.

By 1897 the crumbling of the inner walls was under way allowing for a shaft of light to enter Cavafy's windowless poetic world. The two visits to Greece, in July 1901 and in August 1903, during which he composed his *Ars Poetica*, were the turning point. It was right before the second visit to Greece, when in June 1903 he wrote the poem "Growing in Spirit" (UP 133), stating there his determination to assert the erotic side of the *persona* in defiance of conventional mores. Paradoxically enough, he also published in 1903 the most "insular" of the crisis poems, "The Windows," juxtaposing despair and defiance, resignation and action, to coax the lyrical self out of the dark confinement of the mausoleum. The advice he gave himself in June 1903 was to learn from the pursuit of pleasure, whatever the form of the gratification, and to allow the erotic to flow into the stream of poetry. Thus in January 1904, he wrote three poems, "September, 1903," "December, 1903" and "January, 1904." They

---

[4] See the diagram of the three concentric circles in chapter 5, section 1.

signaled the finding of the windows, but he never published them. Instead, he wrote more erotic poems, some of which were eventually printed. However, the poems he released, as he was nearing the "mature" period, were deliberate, cautious and prudent, for instance, "As Much as You Can" (1905/*1913*: A 25), and "The Satrapy" (1905/*1910*: A 16); the latter dramatized the error of judgment, an unhappy choice of favors at the court of King Artaxerxes over civic honor.

Looking back, then, from the pivotal year 1903, the thematic development moves from the personal experiences and reveries covering the preceding decade to the post-1903 period, when the cracks in the walls became visible. The poet reshaped his attitude of adjustment to the demands of political existence and acceptance, at least mentally, of his erotic side, thus lessening the abhorred burden of guilt. He did not disclose poetically this move until years later. He fought the effects of self-alienation and managed to make some progress, but it was a slow recovery. It emerged at first as the protean *persona* of the many masks. Although the poems of 1905 "As much as You Can" and "The Satrapy" objectify the modes of overt and covert adjustments, neither was printed before 1910.

A major effect of the crisis years was that of prolonging the poet's attachment to the tenets of the symbolist movement and his dependence on the device of ambivalence. The experimental findings of this period were kept in secrecy; hidden poems laden with intriguing vacillation, punctuated by indecision, yet replete with artistic devotion. Nevertheless, the poems still exuded feelings of timidity, withdrawal, self-alienation, fear and despair, while in real life the poet would seek abandon in nocturnal debauchery, or withdraw to indulge imaginative pleasures, suffer the attacks of guilt, return to illicit eros, falling deeper in the pit of suffering. The erotic self had become the victim of incontinence. Yet at no time did the poet adopt or attempt to imitate Baudelaire's mode of sin and its salvational metaphysics.[5] The

---

[5] Beebe 1964 aptly states: "Among the monastic rules of dandyism is that of chastity. Applied to the artist, Baudelaire's strictures on the advisability of chastity are historically important, for he was one of the first writers to express himself on the subject. Whereas the Sacred Founts artists find their motivation in the pursuit of love and often confuse artistic inspiration with erotic stimulation, Baudelaire insisted that art and sex are irreconcilable. 'The more a man cultivates the arts the less he fornicates', he wrote in his journals, for 'to fornicate is to aspire to enter another; the artist never emerges from himself'" (134-5). The

difficulties he faced during this period were more fully understood only after his recovery from self-alienation, when the redesigning of the place of eros in art entered the thematics of the mature period. Consider, for instance, how the vision of the old man in the poem "Very Seldom" (1911/*1913*) differs from the image of the despondent old man in the 1894 poems, written when the poet was still in his thirties. The sensuality in "An Old Man" in 1894, and "The Souls of Old Men" also in 1894, is but a moving lament to opportunities lost. At the other end, and with the crisis years behind, Cavafy went back to that period, not to relive bleak sentiments, but to resurrect in reverie the exquisite creative moments he had stored in memory. Aesthetic recollecting in its new form gave every element of preserved sensuality a place in a luminous perspective. The dark rooms of the mansion are replaced with the rooms where erotic excitement was once enjoyed.[6]

There are two sides to Cavafy's sensuality: on the one, there is the suppression of desires, leading to the entombment of the unfulfilled longings. The result, poetically speaking, is the mausoleum as in the 1904 poem "Desires" [or "Longings"].[7] On the other side, there is the determination to break through and indulge the desires that strengthen and support the pursuit of eros to make him a "brave man of pleasure." Both views create memories to be recalled later and turned into thematic matter for poetry. In either case, poetry stands to profit whether it be denial or pursuit. This peculiar Cavafian conviction, which he entertained at that time, seems to be the reason why sublimation is not sufficient to explain all the erotic poems he wrote. Cavafy's erotic imagination was as powerful as his intellectual acumen was brilliant. But so long as he was unwilling, for whatever reasons, to unlock the erotic drive, he resorted more to introspection and fantasy than to practical reasoning. His poetry and prose pieces with autobiographical relevance show that he knew about this discrepancy, and the evidence shows that he tried to free himself from the beliefs that maintained control over his actions and

---

reference is to the *Intimate Journals* (Boston: Beacon Press, 1957), p. 49.

[6] References to the poetic function of memory in Themelis 1970: 81ff; Pieris 1983c has discussed this side of Cavafy in detail with the aid of the symbol of light.

[7] The theme is repeated in the context of recollection in "Body, Remember" (1916/*1918*: A 91); see also Jacobson and Colaclides 1966.

erotic expressions, but the liberation he longed for, as mentioned in the *Ars Poetica*, could not come soon enough. The confusion left him scarred. Meanwhile, the open wounds would often make the pain unbearable. One such wound had its beginning back in the tender years of his childhood, when his mother held him captive to her needs and insisted on dressing the child in girl's clothes beyond the time when memory was beginning to build its storehouse of early impressions. The ingredients for forming a model for future cases of "partly this . . . and partly that" lie buried in the remote past of memory.[8]

Cavafy became shy, inhibited, afraid of ridicule, withdrawn and serious, and hardly an aggressive person. As the self-image in his poems portrays, he was passionate and attentive to love affairs, at least in fantasy. The loves he seems to have actually experienced he cherished and savored only as fully as his fears permitted. Sareyannis has reported that the poet rarely, if ever, exhibited or discussed, even in closed circles, sexual preference. Being protective of his privacy, he exercised unusual prudence, probably due to upbringing and inclination, forbidding the flaunting of his personal desires. Self-control came naturally to him, as expected of a person with Phanariot background and a claim to "aristocracy" fashioned after an English model.[9] But his confusions and inhibitions eventually led to despair. However, while he was able to channel into poetic imagery more than what his overt erotic actions afforded, he was also becoming increasingly depressed and puzzled.

It would hardly be an exaggeration to say that his eroticism is the most misunderstood and most discussed aspect of his personality. He never was much of a "brave man of pleasure," certainly not one who compares favorably to a hedonic Cellini. The admiration in which he held the erotic heroes he perfected in imagination can easily be taken as a personal trait in action. The fact is that in real life he dissipated the fervor of the drive through the use of alcohol and self-indulgence.[10]

---

[8]Tsirkas 1958: 298-9.

[9]Tsirkas 1958: 292, referring to Sareyannis.

[10]On Cavafy's addiction to drinking, Malanos 1957: 55; Peridis 1948: 45-48; Savidis 1966: 182, esp. n106; psychosomatic disturbances and related poems, Sareyannis 1964: 37-38; Tsirkas 1958: 297. Many of the early critics sought to relate his poetry to the style of his life and

The question that deserves attention, but lurks in the background, is the role of fear and guilt as these emotions related to the poet's sensuality by being inhibitive factors, and whether the breaking of his emotional shackles was in a way responsible for inventing a mode of expression beyond that of the *suggestif* mode of symbolism. The road leading to maturity, beyond the level of expression intimated in the poem "Hidden Things" (1908), cuts through the domain of eros, not around it. What was a matter of feeling throughout the period of crisis, and even some years beyond, became the object of illumined cognition, *noesis*, in 1915.

In the poem "Understanding" ("Noesis" 1915/*1918*: A 64) the poet speaks in a self-confessional mode recounting the significance of events whose clarified meaning reveals now why freedom from suppression is vindicated:

> In the dissolute living of my youth
> intentions of my poetry were taking shape,
> the province of my art was being sketched.[11]

The sentiment and recognition are stressed in "Their Beginning" (1915/*1921*: B 22). But when we go back to the years of 1898 and 1899 we do not detect the admission of erotic force, at least not directly. However, in June 1899 Cavafy followed an indirect path of expression when he wrote "One of Their Gods," a poem that enabled him to enjoy obliquely the vision of a vicarious situation through the experiences of a *persona* situated in the Hellenistic city of Seleukeia. There, he talked about a young boy, tall and perfectly handsome, with the joy of incorruptibility pictured in his eyes . . . . It reads like a prelude to the poet's preparation for the day he will qualify for

---

condemn his erotic preference as deviant, using strong moral terms, while other sought to soften the judgment with an appeal to psychoanalysis. Melakopides 1983: 214ff, treats eros in relation to *eudaimonia* as fulfillment when discussing the poet's homosexuality and refers to the views of critics who analyzed with detachment this side of Cavafy: Friar, Bien, Keeley, Papanoutsos and Seferis. For "moral" judgment, see Malanos 1957: "no guilt, only prudence" (60); Panayotopoulos 1946 [1982]: "All his life he was tormented by his problem, his evil inclinations . . ." (160).

[11]The Greek text reads: Μέσα στὸν ἔκλυτο τῆς νεότητός μου βίο
μορφόνονταν βουλὲς τῆς ποιήσεώς μου,
σχεδιάζονταν τῆς τέχνης μου ἡ περιοχή.

a place in the company of "the brave men of pleasure."

These intimations reveal how incidents were transformed into disclosures with personal significance. Cavafy often felt compelled to confess the personal value and objectives of his art, to describe how his artistic mission took shape during his creative period and how the memory of erotic moments, when the feeling was especially strong and vital, intoned the urge for poetic expressiveness.[12]

The intentions were rooted in eros, but he could not relate the latter to the type of love the priestess Diotima had recommended to Socrates in the *Symposium*—the eros with the power to transport the soul to the transcendent realm of Beauty absolute. Rather, it was the eros that grants to the will the power to expand and fulfill, as Cavafy wished it, i.e. without suppression and guilt. By stressing the sensual side of eros, Cavafy raised the issue of the injustice our civilization has done to the affective side of the erotic drive in all its manifestations and modes that in one way or another determine our choices in political, social and cultural conduct. It is therefore not surprising that eros became a recurring and dominant theme in Cavafy's poetry. It was to the problematic side of eros that he turned to discover the fact that his early erotic experiences had provided the occasions and the motives for the formation of the intentions of his poetry. In January 1914, he wrote the poem "Passing Through" (1914/*1917*: A 86), which was published privately. Having cast off the last remnants of the gnawing guilt, he can disclose that

> The things he timidly fantasized as a student, are open,
> revealed before him. And he wanders around, stays out nights,
> and is carried away. And as is (for our art) right,
> his blood, new and warm,
> pleasure enjoys it. His body captivates
> illicit erotic elation; and his youthful limbs
> give in to it.

---

[12]The problem of the artist's intentions has been extensively debated in recent aesthetic theory but the theoretical issues have been formulated in way that are not germane to the subject of this book. There may be literary critics who can relate "the intentions," as Cavafy understood the meaning of this expression, to the recent controversy, and it would be interesting to read such accounts. For a discussion on the theory of intentions see M. Beardsley's *Aesthetics: Problems in the Philosophy of Criticism* (New York, 1958), ch. 1.

> And in this way a simple lad
> becomes worthy of watching him, he too for a moment
> passes through the High World of Poetry—
> the aesthetic boy with his blood being new and warm.

It was the haunting quality of select remembrances that helped keep the fires of desire burning. They defined the thematic perimeter of his erotic space. There is a kind of memory, a *mneme* that is primarily erotic and through which remembrances are revived though not without some difficulty. Over the years and with the passage of time, the contours of some became blurred and the details lost their focus. Yet the poet confidently believed that a particular film of memory could fully retain its initial vitality unaffected by time. Cavafy often refers to films of memory that recaptured intact the erotic quality of the first adolescent years, as he does in the poem "Long Ago" (1914/*1914*: A 57). The film of a remembrance is replayed with the aid of three elements; by invoking them the poet is able to retrieve the essentials of the original experience:

(a) The texture of the skin: "A skin as though of jasmine . . ."
(b) The time: " . . . that August evening"
(c) The color of the eyes: " . . . Blue, I think they were . . . Ah yes, blue: a sapphire blue."

To bring back this "faded memory," Cavafy must make effective use of a special device: invite an imaginary hearer—his own self—to join him to a quiet inspection of the dimly lit chambers of his memories. He says in the "Long Ago" (1914/*1914*: A 57):

> I should like to tell this remembrance. . .
> But how it has faded . . . as though nothing of it left—
> because it lies so long ago in my early adolescent years.
>
> Skin as though of jasmine made . . .
> That night of August . . . —Was it August;—the night . . .
> I barely remember the eyes; they were blue, I think . . .
> Ah yes, blue; a sapphire blue.

The last four verses achieve a double-effect. What was opaque suddenly becomes a clear, focused image, one that has brought back with it the related pleasure of the original perception. In itself, the pleasure is the reward for regaining the intensity of the highly valued moment of the past. Despite the slow movement from insinuation to revelation of erotic intimacy, the imagery transmits to the reader a sense of deep compassion. But aside from these two effects there is nothing there to touch, no sensuous reality to be felt. The idol in the imagination is but a shadow of the beloved. Of course Cavafy knows this; but his objective was not to record the disappointment. What is being conveyed is the lingering conviction that sometimes the poet's exquisite moments of erotic recollections are not mere substitutes for the actual. They belong to the substantive content of art.[13]

These remarks are meant primarily to alert the reader to the basic function of desires in Cavafy's poetry. Recollected desires, occasionally mixed with fears and guilt, often carefully stored despite the bitter feelings left in their wake, fill the screen of memory with vivid imagery powerful enough to stir the poet with more force than did the experiences themselves. They possess a special quality, perfected in imagination, that provide eros with a steady bond between the poet's past and whatever is left of the future. This may help to explain why, when he was writing "The Windows" (1897/*1903*) and other poems of that vintage, he depended on symbolic devices for the protection of desires. But the protection came at a high price, for the broader scope of the erotic perspective continued to escape him. Self-alienation was too deeply entrenched to be dislodged with borrowed tools.

3. The Fear of Eros

When eros finally entered in bolder ways in 1903, Cavafy had just turned forty, hardly the old man he portrayed in his earlier poems, yet not unlike one. It is very difficult to understand and envisage the drama and the agony of so

---

[13] In a similar vein Vagenas 1980 notes that Cavafy's "idolized hedonic images" stand "less for actual experiences the poet had and more for the experiences as he actually remembers them; they are, as it were, experiences idealized, like the artificial flowers the poet was so fond of, flowers that are perfected replica of the natural ones" (233).

sensitive a poet, especially in the relative absence of autobiographical records.[14] Whatever we have is tied mainly to his poetry, and even here the lyrical confession is often guarded.

In June 1918, he wrote a poem in which he refers to his early manhood and titled it "The Twenty-five Years of his Life." Publication was held back until June 1925 (B 45). The *persona* in the poem is in Alexandria sometime between 1886 and 1888, that is, when the poet himself was about twenty-three and twenty-five, also in Alexandria. As the biographical data show, this was one of the most unhappy and least creative years of his life. The poem ended on the following two verses:

---

[14]He wrote a number of notes to himself, 24 in all, over a period of nine years (1902-1911). Samples from October and November 1902 follow:

October 19, 1902: "Συχνὰ παρατηρῶ τί λίγη σπουδαιότητα ποὺ δίδουν οἱ ἄνθρωποι στὰ λόγια.... Γνωρίζω ποὺ εἶμαι δειλὸς καὶ δὲν μπορῶ νὰ πράξω. Γι' αὐτὸ λέγω μόνον. Ἀλλὰ δὲν νομίζω ποὺ τὰ λόγια μου εἶναι περιττά. Θὰ πράξει ἄλλος." Cavafy 1983, 26 (ed. G. Savidis). [I notice often how little significance people attach to words . . . I know that I am timid and cannot act. That is why I speak only. However, I do not believe that my words are thereby superfluous. Someone else will act.]

November 9, 1902: "Μ' ἐπέρασεν ἀπὸ τὸν νοῦ ἀπόψε νὰ γράψω διὰ τὸν ἔρωτά μου. Καὶ ὅμως δὲν θὰ τὸ κάμω. Τί δύναμι ποὺ ἔχει ἡ πρόληψις. Ἐγὼ ἐλευθερώθηκα ἀπὸ αὐτήν· ἀλλὰ σκέπτομαι τοὺς σκλαβωμένους ὑπὸ τὰ μάτια τῶν ὁποίων μπορεῖ νὰ πέσει αὐτὸ τὸ χαρτί. Καὶ σταματῶ. Τί μικροψυχία . . .". [It occurred to me tonight to speak of my love. Yet, I will not do it. How strong is the power of prejudice. I have freed myself from its clutches, but I think of those still under its yoke and whose eyes may by chance to read this paper. And I stop. What timidity . . .] Ibid., 27.

November 12, 1902: "Ποιὸς ξεύρει τί ἰδέαι λαγνείας προΐστανται εἰς τὴν σύνθεσιν φιλολογικῶν ἔργων! Ἰδέαι λαγνείας solitaires, ποὺ διαστρέφουν (ἢ μεταμορφώνουν) τὴν ἀντίληψιν." [Who knows what ideas of lasciviousness direct the composition of literary works! Ideas of lasciviousness *solitaires*, that pervert (or transform) the perception.] *Ibid.*, 28.

December 13, 1902: "Δὲν ξεύρω ἂν ἡ διαστροφὴ δίδει δύναμιν, κάποτε τὸ νομίζω. Ἀλλὰ εἶναι βέβαιον ὅτι εἶναι πηγὴ μεγαλείου." [I do not know whether perversion gives strength, sometimes I think so. However, it is certain that it is a source of splendor.] Ibid., 29.

See also E. M. Forster's letter to Cavafy dated July 1, 1917, in which he mentions the poet's urge to declare that the artist-poet feels the need to be deviant in order to create. The letter was occasioned by what Forster had heard from Valassopoulo, viz. that Cavafy is unhappy and perhaps he would not write more poetry. See *Times* Literary Supplement, No. 1356 (November 14, 1975); the letter is fully quoted in Pinchin 1977: 110-111.

> . . . It is not unlikely that this sort of life of his
> will lead to a ruinous scandal.

The strong desires are projected without the sense of guilt. One suspects and for good reasons an anachronism here, a deliberate interference with the moral quality of the recollected incident. The poet has purged the erotic emotion of the feeling of sin that was in fact dominant in 1886 and 1888. The center of gravity has shifted now from sin as a cause of fear to a different source: the consequences of social disapproval, loss of dignity once the *anomalous eros* become public knowledge; people will refer to it as eros "distorted" a "deviation," a διαστροφή.

The place of fear of eros in Cavafy's poetry went through two different stages and produced two different modes of recollection. During the crisis period, the element of fear in the recollection of erotic experiences was associated with two distinct causes: moral sin and social disapproval. After the mature period was well under way, the element of fear was purged of sin as a causal factor until it finally disappeared from the emotional ambience of the recollected image. However, the poet still found it necessary to preserve in his vocabulary whatever was fitting to the characterization of an erotic preference dear to the *persona* but objectionable to "others." Since the fear of loss of social standing was real at one time, its cause was recollected along with the incident, and unless the eros was distorted the associated fear would simply be illusory. The conclusion is that in the second phase, eros is called distorted but the fear involved is free of guilt. The sense of sin is gone. The transition to the second phase was completed when he wrote some of his strongest erotic poems. He wrote e.g. "In an Old Book" (1922/*1922*: B 33):

> The beauty of anomalous attraction . . .

and referring to a *persona*'s verse in "Theatre of Sidon (A.D. 400)" (1923/*1923*: B 37):

> . . . about a kind of eros
> the kind that leads to condemned and barren eros.

or where the modulated lyrical voice of the self-distanced *persona* speaks of the other lover, as "In Despair" (1923/*1923*: B 34):

> . . . he wanted to be saved
> from the tainted, the diseased pleasure,
> the tainted pleasure of shame.

or when recollecting sensuous events, as in "Days of 1896" (1927/*1927*: B 57):

> He became completely disgraced. An erotic proclivity of his
> excessively forbidden, held in contempt,
> yet innate just the same . . .

What was feared to be the cause of a personal disaster became the seeding ground for "the intentions of my poetry," as the verse in "Understanding" goes.[15] And, when alone, in the solitude of the late hour of the night, as in "To Call Up the Shades" (1920/*1920*: B 17), the poet waits:

> One candle is enough.   Its faint light
> fits more suitably,   will be more likable
> when the Shades of Love,   when the Shades will come.
> One candle is enough.   Tonight the room
> must not have much light.   Deep in reverie
> and in receiving mood,   and with the little light —
> thus in reverie   I will visualize
> to let the Shades of Love,   the Shades to come.

Alone in the late hour of the evening, he initiates a simple ritual of solitude to bring back from his psyche's erotic Hades the souls of loves long gone but not forgotten, with nothing of their former vigor except the illusion of pleasure. And the poet for a while lets the power of the brain do the resurrecting, until he drifts into sleep and the visions of beloved Shades return to the dark recesses of the soul waiting perchance for another visit at another night of reverie. None of this would have happened had the poet not become "a brave man of pleasure."

The acceptance of eros became the catalytic event that marked the

---

[15] Compare "Their Beginning" (1915/*1921*). It may well be that this poem was composed earlier than 1915, probably in December 1908, listed by Savidis as "lost." We should not exclude the chance that its original title was "Decadent Eros" (Ἐκφυλισμένος ἔρως), a title that later was changed to the more lyrical "illicit pleasure" (ἔκνομη ἡδονή), matching thus the opening verse of "Their Beginning."

beginning of a new poetic phase. It was an act of self-acceptance after which Cavafy felt free to transform his symbols, e.g. "windows," into powerful literary devices to function aesthetically far better than they did in the poem with the same title, or for instance, in the erotic poem, written in 1907, with the title "An Evening of Mine," latter changed to "One Night" and published in 1915.[16] By the time he wrote "The God Abandons Antony" (1910/*1911*: A 20), the windows were no longer burdened with symbolic messages. Comparably, with the passage of time, eros was no longer the tyrannical force dressed in suggestive yet ambivalent symbols. Particularly interesting is the transformation of the windows from a symbol feared for the unpleasant reality it may reveal to an object that opens new vistas of a world formerly forbidden and now desirable.

Eros gradually regained its full transformational power and the creative impetus needed to sustain the poet in his "work in progress." He did not have to read Baudelaire's *Intimate Journals* to understand the implications of Baudelaire's strictures for eros. Cavafy had created his own confinement from a different source of inhibiting factors. Nevertheless, his early acceptance of the symbolist movement, to the extent that he did, carried with it, and unknown to him, the demand for a certain code of conduct which was naturally unsuitable to a person of his temperament and cultural background. To go counter to anything erotic meant to make an impossible sacrifice as well as subscribe to a dangerous experiment in abstinence. However that may be, the contradiction that symbolism generated in Cavafy's outlook at that time, i.e. the conflict between the positive element that signaled the way beyond

---

[16] The poem "One Night" may well be the final version of a poem first drafted in March 1904, titled "Last Night" (Χθὲς Νύχτα) and revised three years later as "An Evening of Mine" (Ἕνα Βράδυ μου). Savidis lists this 1904 title as a "lost poem" in Cavafy UP 1968: 148, but takes no position on the issue whether the poem was preserved and revised under a different title. My own view—and it is only a guess—is that it is probable that Cavafy, when he revised the 1907 version for publication in 1915, found it necessary to change the title after the lapse of so many years, since what was once a "last night," happened twelve years ago. The draft of the poem was composed in 1904. What makes my view even more plausible is that the erotic theme of the 1907 poem could have just as easily been a similar theme for a 1904 poem, given the fact that a number of poems of this type were written after the end of 1903. The "Notes to himself" the poet wrote, dated October 19, 1902, November 9 and 12, and December 13, 1902, may be regarded as evidence that by this time Cavafy was ready to assert rather comfortably his acceptance of his homosexuality. See Cavafy 1983: 26-29.

romanticism, and the ascetic ideal of chastity imposing a non-erotic code of abstinence, simply added fuel to the flames that started with the sprouting of Cavafy's erotic ambivalence and the gnawing of the *ennui* associated with guilt and withdrawal. When the effect of the contradiction became unbearable, the tenets of symbolism had to be abandoned, which he found difficult to do while expecting to write poetry without distinguishing between technique and life style. The puritanism of the dandy was easier to reject since it did not suit Cavafy's temperament. Whether the reaction to symbolism after 1900 was instinctive and spontaneous or the result of careful reflection, is difficult to say; the evidence seems to favor the former. The fact is that Cavafy chose to affirm the positive side of eros. We may now try to retrace the steps that brought him to that choice.

4. The Path of Eros: From the *Ars Poetica* to the Release of "The City"

When Cavafy embarked on his special journey to retrieve and understand his eroticism, he first had to repudiate his pseudo-dionysianism, his artificial hedonism as well as the contrived self-image of the decaying self, especially his affected Christian pretensions due to sinfulness and to fear of loss of soul. He had borrowed from Baudelaire ideas to complement his definition of the role of the artist-poet and also how to gain insights into the role of eros in the poetic act. It is small wonder that in the early stage of his poetic career Cavafy became increasingly confused and finally locked in the gilded cage of inauthentic guilt. We thus see an Alexandrian Greco-Christian turned into a contrived Parisian symbolist poet. There was little that could be called classical in his background to be summoned for his needs, to surface as it were at that point and ease the tensions except for a distant feeling of cultural regret of past historical failures of late Hellenistic adventures which the poet could invoke as phyletic memories.

However confused Cavafy may have been at that time, he knew that the Gods had not died, just as he knew, to use a metaphor, that they would not speak to him so long as his mind was clinging to the vision and the language of French symbolism, to its conception of the role of the poet. As a result, he could not seek alternative ways to define his own sense of artistic mission except insofar as a certain strand of Platonism of the sort that we find present in the poem "Builders" would permit. The upshot is that Cavafy did not attain full authenticity until he was finally able to assert his own modalities, which in turn called for the recovery of his own erotic passion and cultural tradition. Bringing about the removal of guilt and the dismissal of artificial moods and pseudo-mystical escapes, could not longer be postponed.

By 1904, as the testimony of the poem "January, 1904" allows us to infer, Cavafy began to seek the erotic, but the fact of the situation is that he remained indecisive, giving the impression that his sensuality had been seriously, if not incurably, injured. But at least he had become aware that he had to accept the urge for the erotic and to understand it. With the first clarifications of his eroticism Cavafy entered a path that led to a hilltop from which to view the erotic force in light of a different perspective, one that takes eros out of the framework of the salvational metaphysic of symbolic poetry. He was about to become a different poet when he wrote in "September, 1903" (U 135):

> At least I should not fool myself now with illusions
> so as not to feel my empty life.
>
> And yet I came so close so many times;
> and yet how paralyzed I was, how timid I became.
> Why did my lips stay sealed
> when my empty life was weeping inside me
> and my desires were dressed in mourning.
>
> To have been so close so many times
> to the eyes and the erotic lips,
> to the body dreamed of, the beloved body;
> so close so many times.

And in the 1903 poem, "Growing in Spirit," the poet admitted that

> ... the pleasures will have many things to teach him.

What he was about to learn from the pleasures proved at once positive, concrete, constructive, liberating. But the lessons did not come about painlessly. There were disappointments and rejections, as it seems to have been the case with the encounter he had in Athens during his brief visit there. The time had come to let the "hidden things" surface and be faced without the dread of constant fear.

Between June 1903, when he wrote the unpublished poem "Growing in Spirit" (Δυνάμωσις UP 133), a poem in which he declares his intention to learn from pleasure as one who "will not be afraid of the destructive act," fully aware that "one half of the house must be pulled down"—and 1910, he wrote the following erotic poems:[17]

(1). January, 1904: "September, 1903" ('Ο Σεπτέμβρης τοῦ 1903) [UP 135].
(2). January, 1904: "December, 1903" ('Ο Δεκέμβρης τοῦ 1903) [UP 137].
(3). January, 1904: "January, 1904" ('Ο Γεννάρης τοῦ 1904) [UP 139].
(4). February, 1904: "On the Stairs" (Σταῖς Σκάλαις) [UP 141]
(5). March, 1904: "At the Theatre" (Στὸ Θέατρο) [UP 143]
(6). June 1904: "Memory of Pleasure," later revised in 1909 as "Come Back" ('Επέστρεφε) and included in *Collection 3, (1912)*.
(7). May, 1905: "Drunk" (Μεθυσμένος). The title was probably changed in July 1913 to "Tipsy" (Μισομεθυσμένος)=?" In the Street" ('Εν τῇ ὁδῷ), *1916*: A 84.[18]
(8). June 1905: "I Went" ('Επῆγα) *1913*: A 59, included in *Collection 3*.
(9). December, 1905: "Lust" (Λαγνεία)," later changed to "He Swears," and published in 1915 in *Collection 3*.
(10). September, 1907: "The Closed Coach" (Τὸ κλεισμένο 'Αμάξι) changed to "The Tobacco-Shop Window," ('Η Προθήκη τοῦ Καπνοπωλείου) *1917*: A 85 and included in *Collection 3*.
(11). March, 1909: "March, 1907," (Μάρτιος τοῦ 1907) later changed to "Days of 1903," (= Μέρες τοῦ 1903) *1917*: A 92, included in *Collection 3*.

---

[17] I think it useful to add to this list of eleven pre-1910 erotic poems a number of semi-erotic compositions, some of them listed as "lost," written between 1903 and 1910, for instance the January 1904 title "The Picture," listed by Savidis as lost (UP 140). There is a chance this is either the January 1923 "From the Drawer" ('Απ' τὸ Συρτάρι UP 187), or the April 1913 "Thus" ('Ετσι UP 157), both explicitly erotic. The word 'photographia' (picture) occurs in both.

[18] There is no hard evidence for including this poem in the list, which according to Savidis is "lost" [UP 144]. It is open to speculation whether this may be the first form of the "In the Street" (*1916*: A 82), recorded as "written" in July 1913 with the title "Half-Drunk" (Μισομεθυσμένος). The style is close to that of the 1904 compositions period. It would seem that Cavafy's expression in line 9 "as though hypnotized" (σὰν ὑπνωτισμένος) replaced the "half drunk" (μισομεθυσμένος)," maintaining the same number of syllables, and this replaced the original "drunk" (μεθυσμένος), obviously too strong a term for the condition of the *persona* to sustain awareness of the evoked erotic imagery in its details. Savidis, however, lists the poem as "lost" (UP 144).

The composition dates of the first five explicitly erotic poems indicate that the "liberated" desires enter as poetic themes shortly after the writing of the *Ars Poetica*, a turning point in Cavafy's development as a poet and *persona* in his poems. At the age of forty, he experiences a decisive change with two major developments: the direct and reflective surfacing of eros and the deepening of his understanding of his art, now with the aid of formulated criteria for revisions of old poems and the composition of new ones. Both developments took place after his visit to Athens.

All eleven erotic poems were written before 1910, the publication year of the "The City," and only six eventually included in one of the *Collections*. They were held "prisoners," so to speak, until such time as Cavafy was certain he was well past the gateway. In 1911, Cavafy writes the poem "Very Seldom" (Πολὺ Σπανίως) *1913*: A 49. Here the theme is about an old man, a poet, exhausted and stooping; if the *persona* represents Cavafy, he is not more than forty-eight years old, now returned to his "city" and walking in its streets, accepting the house in which he lives, and reflecting on the pain of aging. In the second stanza his mind goes to those young men who now quote from his poetry and are stirred by his own vision of beauty. The role of the builder-poet has now changed to serve as a fount of poetic visions to excite the creative sensuality of the young.

Both the city and the poet have been transformed, and both roles have been prepared since the time of the first envisioning of the *persona* in the "That's the Man" in 1898 and its timely publication in 1909 (Οὗτος Ἐκεῖνος), A 45. The fictional *persona*, a young man from Edessa, placed as a visitor in Antioch as a mythical-historical setting, projects his expectations to attain fame as a poet, for "he writes and writes" and with the last canto done he has "eighty-three poems in all." By co-incidence, about the same time that the poem was published, Cavafy appears to have written the same number of good poems.[19]

---

[19] Actually, Cavafy had "written" about 143 poems by August 1898. See Savidis' Preface to the edition of the condemned poems and the Tables in his edition of the unpublished poems (UP 253ff.).

5. Reconciliation and Adjustment

There is an important difference between Cavafy's experiential rediscovery of his city and his viewing Alexandria as a historical-mythical setting for certain poetic episodes that form his thematic material. The latter environment does not precisely correspond to the former. At any rate, from the experiential point of view after 1911, the city was no longer that of "The City." The transformation was complete by March 1916, when he wrote the poem "Alexandrian," revised and published in 1917 under a new title, "In the Evening" (A 87):

> Anyway things wouldn't have lasted for long. The experience
> of years makes that clear to me. Somehow Fate
> hurriedly came and ended all.
> The beautiful life was brief.
> But how powerful were the scents,
> and on what splendid a bed we laid ourselves,
> and to what pleasure we gave our bodies.
>
> A reminiscence of the days of pleasure,
> a reminiscence of the days came near me,
> something of the heat of the youth of both;
> I took again a letter in my hands,
> read it over and over till the light was gone.
>
> I went out to the balcony in melancholy mood—
> went out to change thoughts at least by watching
> something of the beloved city,
> something of the movement in the street and the shops.

Also related to this period is the poem "Outside the House," (1917/*1919*: A 89):

> Yesterday walking in a neighborhood
> out-of-the-way, I passed by the house
> I used to go when I was very young.
> Eros had seized my body there
> with his splendid power.
>
>   And yesterday
> as I walked along the old street,

> immediately the spell of eros made everything beautiful
> the shops, the sidewalks, the stones,
> and walls and balconies and windows;
> nothing there remained ugly.

Love has completely transformed the cityscape of 1894; these are not the same streets, not the same windows, nor the same walls. The ugliness is gone. What brought Cavafy back to the actual city, its tangible things—houses, streets, the lights, the shops, the taverns, after the disillusionment in the ideal of the "builder-poet" wore out, was the acceptance of the erotic element as it gradually surfaced and led him to undertake two tasks: (a) to put some order in his inner world so that he could view it with detachment and care by referring to it more openly and more concretely in relationship to his actual desires; and (b) to come to terms with his environment to make the necessary emotional adjustment to the real setting of the city of Alexandria and the possibilities it occasioned, and with whatever demands and opportunities it presented.

The process of conciliation and adjustment lasted for years, and the initial attitude of rejection and hostility receded only with effort and considerable pain. Gradually the feeling of deep resentment was replaced with an attitude of thoughtful resignation, which later changed to emerge as discriminating appreciation. Yet, the identification of the poet and the city never went beyond a certain degree of intimacy and enchantment. The imaginary exits, as heralded in "Ithaka," found their poetic fulfillment in the historic-mythical poems of hedonic cities, Alexandria and the other Hellenistic cosmopolitan epicenters. The actual exit Cavafy experienced was neither sudden nor as carefree as "Ithaka" suggests. Yet it seems to have been free from the subterfuge of symbolism. The conciliation with the city was a matter of expediency as well as survival.

That is why in revising the "The City" for publication in 1910 he could no longer leave in the expression "hatred" toward the city in the poem. The feeling was no longer true to his situation. He knew this to be the case even when he first wrote the poem.

The first poem which ties the tangible objects of the city to his erotic day-dreaming and recollection of cherished experience comes around 1904, and is titled "January, 1904" (UP 139). Preludes to it are the twins "September, 1903" and "December, 1903." Years later, in 1909, he will write

"Days of 1903," but will print it in 1917.

In February, 1904 he wrote "On the Stairs" (Σταὶς Σκάλαις, UP 141) which was found in the file of poems titled *Passions*. This is another indication that the *passions* brought him back to the city, although this poem deals with "illicit" love-seeking at a brothel where the *persona* narrating in the first person sees a man going up the stairs, when he was descending, both hiding their faces not to be detected by each other; neither found there the pleasure they sought since what they secretly desired was each other. Thematically comparable is a poem written in March 1904, "At the Theatre" (Στὸ Θέατρο). It relates a visit to the local theater. The play itself was boring, but when he cast his eyes around and saw a depraved young man about whom he had heard "things", he fantasized and compared images of fantasy and recollection. It, too, remained an "unpublished poem" (UP 143).

In June 1904 he wrote another hedonic poem, "Memory of Pleasure" (Μνήμη Ἡδονῆς), which he revised in 1909 and published in 1912 in *Nea Zoe* under a new title, "Come Back" (Ἐπέστρεφε, A 56). The theme is very close to that of "One Night."[20] However, the latter offers a detailed description of locale: a room, poor and cheap, above an ill-reputed tavern. The window looked out to a dirty and narrow side-street, and one could hear the voices of workers playing cards and indulging in song and drinking in the tavern below. The inexpensive and cheap bed where love-making took place; hedonic lips, rosy and drunk with passion—all these things the poet recalls years later in his lonely home one night and relives the hedonic intoxication. "Come Back" asks for the return of a cherished sensation to possess the poet again:

> Come back often and keep taking me,
> beloved sensation come back and keep taking me—
> when the memory of the body awakens,
> and an old desire runs through the blood again;

---

[20] In March 1904, he wrote a poem titled "Χθὲς Νύχτα" ("Last Night"), listed in Savidis (UP 142) as lost. It may be that Cavafy changed the title and published with a new on, "Μία Νύχτα" ("One Night") in *Nea Zoe* 1915 (A 55), incorporated in the canon as an approved poem: again, an erotic poem, reminiscing illicit love, much in the style of poems of 1904. However, according to Savidis, the poem "Last Night" is not the finished form of "Χθὲς Νύχτα" ("Last Night") but that of "Ἕνα βράδυ μου" ("One of My Nights"), composed in 1907 (UP 148). It is quite likely that three years later the former became latter, recast by the poet while in a mood of reminiscence.

> when the lips and the skin remember,
> and the hands sense as though they touch again.
>
> Come back often and keep taking me in the night,
> when the lips and the skin remember . . .

Another erotic poem, written in July 1904: "From the Hands of Eros" (Ἀπ' τὰ Χέρια τοῦ Ἔρωτος), published in 1915 with a new title, "At the Café Door":[21]

> Something they said those at my side turned
> my attention towards the café door.
> And I saw the handsome body that looked
> as if Eros had made it with his supreme skill—
> molding with joy its symmetrical limbs;
> raising its height like a statue;
> molding with emotion the face
> and leaving on it with the touch of his hands
> a feeling on the forehead, on the eyes and the lips.

In September 1904, Cavafy wrote "Desires" (Ἐπιθυμίες) and published it in 1904-05 (February 1905), for the first time in the edition *Booklet* 1. It is a dirge song, but not tied to anything concrete of his environment; there is no mention of locale.[22]

In June 1905, Cavafy composed an openly erotic poem, "I Went"

---

[21]Savidis lists the title without the date of publication, pointing out that this composition was be considered a lost poem (UP, Introduction, p. xii). He may be right, but there is still a chance that the poem is the first form of the [Greek] which Cavafy printed in December, 1915 "At the Café Door" (Στοῦ Καφενείου τὴν Εἴσοδο, A 54). Every word in the original title occurs in this poem (lines 4, 5, 7 and 8). It seems possible that Cavafy thought the original title unsuitable on the ground that it was either too sentimental or too vague to convey a personal experience which was tied to some familiar locale: the coffee house he frequented. The poem refers to an erotic response to a handsome young man who upon entering the coffee house aroused Cavafy's admiration to think that the beautiful body could have been shaped by Eros' own hands. Malanos 1957: 130 and Dalmati 1964: 79 suspect influence of Meleager in this use of Eros.

[22]I have discussed this poem at some length in chapter 6. I may add here that the rather opaque image view of the erotic in this poem made it sufficiently safe for publication.

(1905/*1913*: A 59) where he openly admits that he gave in and went all the way to drink the strong wine of the erotic pleasures, which up to that time were only "half-real" and "half-turning round" in his mind. He went into the brilliant night

> and drank the strong wines,
> the brave men of pleasure drink.

    The once erotically timid and hesitant *persona* who had come close to the point of self-destruction, driven by feelings of guilt and lost in self-alienation, has now moved in the other direction, to the pursuit of pleasures as a case of virtue. Cavafy had read his Plato. He was intentionally twisting the Platonic definition of the virtue of courage, *andreia*, of knowledge of what to fear and what not to fear; it was a clever move on his part to extend the meaning of that virtue to cover the conquest of the fears of the apolaustic love and sensual indulgence. However, the poem contains a note of special exhortation; the poet must still struggle to convince himself of his ability to summon defiance, until he can say with self-assurance: "I was no longer subject to bondage!" A lingering question remains: Was Cavafy telling the truth in 1905? Perhaps in some peculiar way he was. The relativism of his *Ars Poetica* would allow him to do so. Since the poem refers to one defiant act, not a permanently secured freedom from bondage, disillusionment would be waiting in ambush. The feeling of elation, at that moment, must have been overwhelming. Somehow, the poet must have suspected that he had not completely conquered his fears. In the late hour of the brilliant night of his sensuous city the temptation grows strong and willing to test the power of the burning passion. But the city, in full light of day, wears a different face, and comes to his poetry in symbolic and historical bits. In July 1905, he wrote one of his most revealing poems on the effect of compromised integrity: "The Satrapy." This and another poem, "I Went," stand at the extremes of an ambiguity tucked under the use of the expression "giving in."

    In December 1905, he wrote the last poem of the year, "He Swears" (*1915*: A 58), an erotic poem, mild in tone, expressive of remorse, unsure about ability to control the temptations of the evening hours. Unlike the "I Went," which opens with a personal admission, "He Swears" narrates the erotic event through the third person singular. The locale here is left unnamed and unspecified, and the *persona* is lost. The decision to yield comes not from knowledge but springs forth from the mystique of the night.

> He swears so often to start a better life.
> But when night comes with its own advice,
> with its compromises, and its promises;
> but when night comes with its own power
> of the body that wills and seeks, to the same
> fatal joy, lost, he goes again.

This is not exactly what is to be expected of a "brave" *persona* of pleasure. The persistent recurrence of doubt, remorse, the nagging anxiety over the divided self, keep pushing the poet back to a state of uncertainty. It may be recalled at this point that the "Trojans" (1900/*1915*: A 26) was published only one month before the publication of the poem "He Swears." "Trojans" had already underscored the futility of all efforts to defend one's world, be it city or self. But "He Swears" exposes the weakness of will, now projected in the form of excuse. The appeal to understanding indulgence becomes a motif later masterfully perfected and used in the poem "For Ammonis, who died at 29, in 610" (1915/*1917*: A 79) and "Tomb of Iasis" (1917/*1917*: A 75).

The sensual urge grows strong after dark. What the poet comes to rediscover in his Alexandria is restricted to what the pursuit of sensual pleasure can do to make life excitable at night and tolerable during the day. Actually the persistence of guilt, gnawing as it does at both sides of the poet's divided self, diverts him from thinking about the fullness of life to which cities and individuals should aspire. Instead, he moves defiantly to taste the forbidden fruits while turning his eyes away from the misshaped details of everyday life, the people and their problems, the hustling and bustling of workers and masters, the sweat and toil of sheer living. The pieces are there but their arrangement is left to chance. The poetic hand is not ready to put together the principles that give form to a total social and cultural environment. What takes precedence is the sensual opportunities rather than just the conciliation with the realities of the city that has become the paramount concern of the *persona* during the crisis period. In fact, even indulgence remained a problem until such time as he was able to accept his self and his erotic passions with full understanding of their peculiar demands and implications for civilized life. The mission of the "builder" was a haunting one.

In the poem "As Much as You Can"—the initial title was "Life" (1905) before it was revised and published in 1913—Cavafy is heard giving advice to himself on how to preserve his dignity. Having seen what sort of life goes on in the city, he is willing to distance himself from the "others." The vague symbol "city" covers little more than the humbug of the world, the traffic and the chatting, the mingling with acquaintances in social circles, in a word, the diurnal trivialities. The shift from the desolate sort of city of 1894 to the pedestrian concerns of "people" in 1905, is remarkable. He had come to realize that leaving the city was wrong. The new solution advocated a willful separation from the multitude.

The year 1906, shows that Cavafy did not compose explicit erotic poems. He turned his attention to writing poems mostly about historical-mythical themes. They give the impression that he was delegating the task of tracing the contours of his immediate environment to the mythical and historical *personae* in his poems. They are remarkable *personae* as surrogates in acting out assignments involving special predicaments, as in the case of the unpublished "Poseidonians" (1906 UP) and to some extent, and in reverse, the "Philhellene" (1906/*1912*: A 37).

In 1907 Cavafy returned to his erotic themes. According to Savidis, Cavafy wrote on July 1907 "One of My Nights," ("Ένα βράδυ μου"). The title of which was changed to "One Night," when the poem was published in 1915. Another composition, "The Window of the Tobacco Shop" (1907/*1917*: A 85) (original title "The Closed Carriage"), registers an important change: it specifies the locale of the meeting of the poet, portrayed as a *persona,* and another person; the sex is left vague but the reference to the window of a tobacco shop leaves no doubt that the encounter was between males. The final title is a marked improvement over the original one, for it names an ordinary "place" where meetings are accidental, not a closed room *where* illicit consummations take place after casual encounters. Moreover, the poet takes the reader right in the middle of busy places within the city, during day hours: there is the street, the side walk, and the scene of taking off in the closed carriage providing the needed privacy for the initial acquaintance to become

> the sensitive approaching of the bodies,
> hands that joined, the lips that met.

We are now inside the city of opportunities witnessing the cravings of those who dare and have the courage to indulge sensual pleasures. It is the real city with its stores and cafes, streets and lights, hidden lures, where human beings live and breathe, love and hate, meet and move, explore and seek, buy and sell cheap and precious things, including their souls. The poet has become one of the people, staying in their midst and yet so distant, removing himself at will yet longing to touch and relate to someone, fully aware of the human reality, with or without illicit desires. A way has been found to seek abandonment in the fleeting fragments of its sensual reality.

On April 1907, Cavafy wrote the poem "Hidden Things" (UP 151).[23] Whether he did it intentionally or not, the poem provides a clue to the *persona*'s identity, to "hidden" thoughts and acts, things he wanted to tell but could not, at least not at that time.[24] In view of the publications of sensuous poems after 1912, Cavafy kept no significant secrets from his readers. If "Hidden Things" contains a special message, it can only pertain to experiences and poems that precede 1908.[25] If a comparable poem was written in 1933 the situation would be different. Seen in retrospect, Cavafy was right to withhold its publication.

After the 1908-1911 period, he started on a new path, publishing far more revealing poems than ever before. Just the same, what he left unpublished or decided to make public before 1911 yields ample evidence to judge the quality of his compositions and the scope of his objectives.

We have only one erotic poem from 1908. According to Savidis, only

---

[23] First publication in *Nea Estia*, 74/872: 1531; reprinted in UP; translation in Cavafy 1971, Keeley and Sherrard. See chapter 3, section 1 for discussion of the personal relevance of this unpublished poem.

[24] Ever since its first publication by Savidis in 1963, a number of commentators have assigned special importance to the content of "Hidden Things," usually appealing to the poet's intention to keep the real secret of his poetry to himself by issuing only vague hints but never fully revealing the total message of his passion. The poem remained among the unpublished poems, and this fact rather prohibits making heavy biographical use of what it does not say. For this reason alone it should not be favorably compared to the published poems for relevant disclosures.

[25] However, it is interesting to note that Hadginis 1962: 27 makes a convincing case concerning the way in which "Hidden Things" complements the "Aimilianos Monai, Alexandrian, A.D. 628-655" (date of composition unknown) published in 1918.

the original title has been preserved: "Decadent Eros" ("Ἐκφυλισμένος Ἔρως").²⁶ Savidis may be correct since there is no supporting evidence to the contrary. It is still probable that fragments or the basic theme of this poem were utilized later in the writing of a 1915 composition, titled "Their Beginning" ("Η 'Αρχή των" B 22), and published in 1921 with the same title.²⁷ Although the "Their Beginning" uses the expression "illicit pleasure," the effect is softened in the last three verses:

> The fulfillment of their illicit pleasure
> was done. They got up from the mattress
> and hurriedly are dressing without speaking.
> They come out separately, furtively, from the house, and as
> they walk somewhat uneasily on the street, it looks as though
> they suspect something about them gives away
> the kind of bed they had been lying just a while ago.
>
> But how much the artist's life has gained.
> Tomorrow, the next day or years later will be written
> the powerful verses that had their beginning here.²⁸

In March 1909, he returned to erotic reminiscing in a poem originally

---

²⁶UP 152, dated December 1908.

²⁷If Cavafy revised a 1908 composition in June 1915 but refrained from publishing it, the explanation may be that he thought it exceedingly daring. The expression "beginning" in the 1915 composition may well refer to the "powerful verses" of 1908.

²⁸The word 'powerful' [plural of the Greek 'δυνατός'] would be closer to the original. The word occurs eight times in the canon; in a mythical setting Patroclos is called "courageous, and strong, and young"; e.g. in historical settings, Syria will be "powerful again," and Cratesicleia is said to be "strong." The remaining five instances occur in explicitly erotic settings, either directly or obliquely: "strong wines," "the chandelier's powerful fire," "how strong were the scents," "the strong verses had their beginning here," and "the work of a powerful artist." In the poem cited, Cavafy discloses an important personal detail: powerful verses had their beginning in memorable moments of illicit love that took place "years ago," and probably after the act praised as "growing in spirit" (June 1903) was accomplished. All uses of *dynatos* in erotic compositions are found in poems printed after 1913. In "On Hearing of Love," (1911 UP 153) the "hearing" spoken of is a sensing the presence of powerful love, δυνατὸς ἔρως.

titled "March, 1907" and later changed to "Days of 1903" (A 92). The reference to March in the original title makes no sense at all unless it was meant to record the date of composition. Perhaps due to a slip of the pen he wrote [190]7 instead of [190]9. The scene is that of a darkening street. The erotic nostalgia harkens back to an affair of 1903, admittedly short-lived. Evidently, the poem was not considered "safe" at the time it was composed, although it contains no hint to an illicit liaison, but in 1917 he thought it quite safe to be printed. The last poetic rehearsal of erotic memories, prior to the publication of "The City" in 1910, was done in September 1909, with the revision of the 1904 "Memory of Pleasure," later changed to "Come Back," deliberately perhaps omitting reference to place.

6. Eros After the Return to the City

The chronology of Cavafy's erotic poems supports the conclusion that prior to April 1910, when Cavafy made public his renouncement of the unnamed "city" from which there was to be no exit, as he wrote in 1894, he was constructing a symbolic analogue of his inner state of mind, by no means fixed and unalterable. The poem was descriptively correct to a felt situation. The same suggestive technique was used for the other compositions of the crisis period. A change, therefore, in the quality of the emotional states was bound to require some modification in the poetics. The turning point that signaled the qualitative change in perception, requiring thereby a corresponding review of principles, came after Cavafy's return from his visit to Athens in 1903 where he made the acquaintance of Mavroudis. Once back in Alexandria, he did two things: he wrote his *poetics*, and found the courage to understand the origins of his fears. Officially he closed this period with the publication of "The City," a poem that provided the right preface to lead his "editions" by having that poem indicate the crucial predicament of his life, the Hades to which he had descended and where the long journey of the return had started. If he wanted to use an erotic poem instead of "The City" to mark the beginning, in fact he had such a one which was composed in 1895, "Chandelier" (1895/*1914*: A 60), in which he recorded with unusual descriptive power the erotic space of an incident. As early as 1895 the poet proved that he had the power to understand the need to visualize erotic concreteness, especially when the experience warrants the preservation of the particulars.

> In a room bare and small, only four walls,
> covered with cloth deep green,
> burns a beautiful chandelier and glows;
> and in each flame a sensuous affection,
> a sensuous urge is kindled.
>
> In this small room, lit brightly,
> from the chandelier's strong fire
> the light that flows is hardly usual.
> The pleasure of this warmth
> was never meant for timid bodies.
> covered with green cloth—
> a beautiful chandelier burns, all fire;
> and each of its flames kindles
> a sensual fever, a lascivious urge.

The first poem (unpublished) on the same thematic matter to be written after 1910 was "On Hearing of Love" (June 1911), in which he acknowledged not the drabness and ruins of a life in a desolate city but gratitude for exquisite moments of loves had.[29]

> On hearing of powerful love, tremble and be moved
> like an aesthete. Yet, being fortunate,
> remember how many such things your imagination made for you;
> these first, and then the others—the lesser ones—in your life
> you had and enjoyed, truer and tangible.—
> You were not deprived of such loves.

The erotic poems that came after 1911 are further elaborations on the acceptance of sensuality and the value of eros in art and life. The richness and originality of his erotic poetry has deservedly drawn the attention of scholars and literary critics adding impressive novel insights on a theme that

---

[29]The poem elaborates a theme announced in "Timolaos the Syracusan" (1892/*1894*: CP 30), viz. the unexpressed music being superior to the expressed. The concept has been stated and defended in Plotinus' theory of art and beauty. But Cavafy's interest centers on a special aspect: "on hearing of powerful love." The responses to an erotic stimulus, be it imaginative or real, are sources of pleasure, and the authentic aesthete should welcome the occasion to be moved deeply by such "fantasized" loves; while the latter are not valued above the real ones they still deserve a high place in the poet's emotional world.

has deservedly become a *locus classicus* in contemporary erotic poetry.[30] These poems, arranged according to the date of composition as far as it can be determined in each case, yield an interesting sequence with "Dangerous Thoughts," published in July 1911, at the head of the list.[31] No attempt is made here to accompany the listing of the titles with brief descriptions of the themes, especially in view of the availability of the text and many excellent translations.

> October 1911: "I've Looked so Much," (*1917*: A 83).[32]
> April 1913: "Thus" (U 157).
> July 1913: "In the Street" (*1916*: A 84).[33] Also in July 1913: "Priceless Things,"

---

[30] Alexiou 1983 has offered a useful survey of recent writings on the subject and devoted the major part of her essay "not to recover the poet's symbolic or biographical journey, but to examine the work's poetic function and significance" (47). Her essay is one of the best treatments of the subject, even if one finds it difficult to accept without reservations the part of the thesis that claims that "none of the first-person erotic poems can be taken as autobiographical" (64). Others who have contributed significantly to this complex topic are: Bien 1964, Bowersock 1983, Caires 1980, Capri-Karka 1982, Keeley 1976, Liddell 1948, Nehamas 1983, Pieris 1982, Savidis 1983, Sherrard 1978, Vayenas 1980, Yourcenar 1978.

[31] This is the first "daring poem" expressing the intention to announce the erotic thoughts to appear in print (*Nea Zoe* 7/1: 28). Cavafy had just joined the liberal periodical under the editorship of progressive literati. It had just published a poem by a known leftist, Varnalis, "Θυσία" (Sacrifice). See ch. IV, section 2.

[32] The phrase "γιὰ τὰ ὡραῖα" is not in the 1917 version, where he speaks of "persons of my love." Keeley and Sherrard translate "figures of love." The reference is clearly to an imaginative grouping of select hedonic *personae,* seen and encountered secretly "in the nights when I was young."

[33] Original title "Half-Drunk" (Μισομεθυσμένος). It may well be that this poem is the May 1905 "Μεθυσμένος" (UP 144), shorter title but the same word, and revised as in July 1913. Both words were stricken out from the title as well as the text. Line 7 appears to contain a suitable substitution: ὑπνωτισμένος. This may be ground for not including this 1905 composition in the list of "lost" poems, as recommended by Savidis in his edition of Cavafy's unpublished poems (Preface). On the theme of the widening of space, see the keen remarks by Diskin Clay 1977 with reference to the conceptualization of movement in "The Four Walls of my Room" (1893: U 43) and "Walls" (1897), which in retrospect anticipate the theme developed further in 1913. See also note 18 of this chapter.

changed later to "When they Come Alive" (*1916*: A 81).[34]
September 1913: "To Sensual Pleasure" (*1917*: A 82):

> Joy and incense of my life: the memory of the hours
> I found, and saved, the pleasure as I wanted it.
> Joy and incense of my life: for me, as one who avoided
> every sensual pleasure of routine love affairs.

January 1914: "Passing Through" ("Πέρασμα" *1917*: A 86).
February 1915: "Understanding" ("Νόησις" *1918*: A 64):

> What needless repentances, how futile...
> But I could not see the meaning then.

June 1915: "Their Beginning." (*1921*).
September 1915: "And I Lounged and Lay on Their Beds" (UP 167).
May 1916: "Body, Remember" (*1918*: A 80).
January 1917: "Half Hour" (U 169).
February 1917: "Grey" (*1917*).
July 1917: "Outside the House" (*1919*).
November 1917: "Half Past Twelve" = "Since Nine o' Clock" (*1918*).
January 1918: In the "Next Table" (*1919*: A 90).
March 1918: "Comes to Rest" (*1919*: B 8).
June 1918: "The 25th Year of His Life" (*1925*).
November 1918: "The Afternoon Sun" (*1919*).
May 1919: "The Bandaged Shoulder" (U 179).

Between October 1919 and 1932, Cavafy composed about twenty, depending on the count, more self-referential erotic poems.[35]

---

[34] When Cavafy revised the poem for publication in 1916, the title was phrased more realistically to state the inner arousal rather than physical details. The poet, giving advice to himself, must preserve "in his half-hidden phrases" what the perfecting imagination has made tangible. By so doing, Cavafy still hesitated in 1913 to suspend the symbolist rules of poetic "suggestiveness," although he has advanced his style beyond the demands of the symbolist technique. Probably what explains the discrepancy is the perseverance of irrational elements blocking the free and open articulation of the aestheticized erotic experience.

[35] Editions of Cavafy's erotic poems almost invariably include most or all compositions in which the erotic impulse is treated in various situations, historical and fictional, not having necessarily traces of self-referential significance, and for this reason I have not discussed them

In 1925(?), late in his life, Cavafy wrote a poem, "Days of 1896" (*1927*: B 57). He seems to be recalling events that led to the days of 1896, to what happened to him when he was nearing thirty.³⁶ It must have been a time of pain and inner turmoil. Personal circumstances brought about a traumatic experience that left its indelible mark on the poet's mind. The poem alludes to days and events that wounded his sense of pride; the poem ends on a plaintive note that the poet "became totally disgraced" (. . . ἐξευτελίσθη πλήρως)." He confirmed in 1927 what had come to prevail three decades before and the emotions associated with that period. The poems composed in 1896 continued thematically the general mood of "The City," with only minor differences, depending on what the poet saw worthy of recording on the other side of the penumbra.³⁷ As I have already mentioned, Cavafy saved a peculiar self-addressed note dated November 1902. He jotted down that on that night he got the idea to write "about his eros" but for some reason, which he did not disclose, he decided not to follow through. Then he added: "What power prejudice has. But now I am no longer under its sway . . ."³⁸

---

in this section. The list of his self-referential erotic poems after October 1919 consists of 19 titles, published and unpublished: October 1919: "On Board Ship" (*1919*); July 1921: "Summer of 1895" (lost?); September 1921: "I've Brought to Art" (*1921*); December 1922-?-: "In an Old Book" (*1922*); January 1923: "From the Drawer" (UP 187); May 1923: "In Despair" (*1923*); January 1924: "Before Time Altered Them" (*1924*); July 1924: "He Had Planned to Read" (*1924*); January 1925: "In the Boring Village" (*1925*); 1926: "In the Tavernas" (*1926*); 1927: "Days of 1896" (*1927*), "Two Young Men, 23 to 24 Years Old" (*1927*), "Days of 1901" (*1927*), and "A Young Poet in His Twenty-Fourth Year" (*1928*); 1928: "Picture of a 23-year-old Painted by His Friend of the Same Age, an Amateur" (*1928*), and "Days of 1909, '10 and '11" (*1928*); 1929: "Lovely White Flowers" (*1929*); 1930: "The Mirror in the Front Hall" (*1930*) and "He Asked About the Quality" (*1930*); 1932 [1921?]: "Days of 1908" (*1932*).

³⁶In 1896 Cavafy was thirty-three, in the "crisis" period of "the loss of the polis." Although precise chronology is not germane to the mood of the poem, the expression, "he was nearing thirty," if taken literally may be explained as week recollection or, even better, as due to effective use of poetic distance.

³⁷This was discussed in chapter 5, section 5.

³⁸Entry for year 1902. As it happened, he may have felt free from prejudice though not free from fear. Writing explicitly erotic poems confirms the poet's insistence concerning the issue of prejudice, but the fact that he refrained from publishing them is strong evidence that

It seems that by 1902, Cavafy was fully aware of the need to cope with the problem of self-denial and self-alienation. The "crumbling of the inner walls" that was to put an end to his self-imprisonment, had become imperative by June 1903. It could be that the act demanded of the poet in "Growing in Spirit" was done about a month before his second visit to Greece in August 1903. Right after that visit or perhaps during, he set to writing the *Ars Poetica* between August and November 1903. It is not a coincidence that the *Ars Poetica* was written about the same time he composed the first *explicit* erotic poem. It would therefore seem that the crystallization of his principles regarding poetic composition could not occur without concurrently arriving at a level of self-understanding. Self acceptance meant nothing less than admitting the directional force of his erotic desires. Most likely the encounter he had during his visit to Athens proved catalytic.

"In the Evening," (1916/*1917*: A 87), though not an erotic poem, offers an excellent example of how cherished memories, "an echo from the days of pleasure," reconciled the poet to his city, Alexandria. In the mellow hour of the evening the poet can pause in serenity and see

> Something of the beloved city,
> something of the movement in the streets and the shops.

The attitude toward the city has undergone profound changes since 1896, even 1910 when "The City" was published. Another important detail has its place here: the original title of "In the Evening" was "Alexandrian" (1916). The title was probably changed deliberately so that readers of his poems would not be misled, when reading "The City" together with "Alexandrian," and be tempted to confuse the bleak city of 1894 or 1910 with the "beloved" city of "In the Evening." Actually the new title directs attention away from *the name* of the city to *the hour of the day,* the time element that gives the locale its lovely countenance. This poetic device makes sense especially if we remember that Cavafy considered the titles as parts of the meaning of the poems.

By 1918, with the "crisis years" behind him, wise as he had become after conquering his phobias, "the Laistrygonians, Cyclopes, fierce Poseidon," he had also come to terms with the demands of his erotic imagination and

---

he was still in the grip of fear. See Tsirkas 1963: 689.

recognized the fitful claims of his longings and desires that had tormented him in earlier decades. His approval of his erotic outlook is clearly reflected in the innuendoes and remarks which he interspersed in the text of the lecture he "dictated" to Sengopoulos, who presented it in Alexandria on February 23, 1918.[39]

7. Eros and the Limits of Irony

The poem "I Went" (1905/*1913*) contains no element of irony. Nevertheless, it invites further inspection of the special role that inversion of the classic plays as the alternative on which to base a defensible approach to the cardinal virtue of *courage*. What is in question is whether it makes sense to speak of the courage to be hedonic in response to the urgency of Eros without falling into the trappings of a self-defeating, self-contradicting ethical stance, as Plato would say.

Cavafy's reply, if we were to construct one with the aid of speculation, would be that, given the conditions of the modern, the classical conception of "brave" (*andreios*) is no longer a live option for a virtuous life. With the *polis* gone, the entire range of features that formed the conditions for political virtue and determined its meaning vanished. If one is to assign acceptable meaning to *andreia* in authentic conduct, given the absence of the conditions of the *polis*, one must first face the problem of identifying ways to uncover fearful objects and only then formulate directives to shape conduct in response to the dangers such objects pose. These objects would correctly then be called "the enemy." If we accept Cavafy's approach as a promise to find the answer to this quest, the enemy he came to see bears little, if any, resemblance to the Persian army the Athenians fought at Marathon and the Spartans faced at Thermopylae. With this clarification, the clue to the inversion of the classical virtue can now be better understood.

The *polis* of the ancients has changed character, structure and mission, after the emergence of the cosmopolis. The transformations that took place

---

[39] The full text of the Sengopoulos lecture is reprinted in *Review of Art* (Dec. 1963): 614-621. A manuscript variant was preserved by Timos Malanos and published in *Nea Estia* 96, No. 1129 (July 15, 1974): 1135-1149.

opened up new possibilities for the signification of the cardinal virtues that Plato and Aristotle sought to delineate with theoretical care and argument. There is little, if anything, in Cavafy's cosmopolis that resembles the city of Athens, that Citadel of Wisdom, and even less that would give it the right to claim the honor of being a city of ideas, and hence nothing that makes it imperative to summon a doctrine of virtues as the requisite means for the pursuit of the good life under the guidance of the common good. The new enemy turns out to be the pretentious institutions and the falsification of hard-won traditional values on which the fulfillment of public and personal aspirations once depended. It is the unexamined values of the modern cosmopolis at which Cavafy points the accusing finger when he uses such symbols as the Laistrygonians, Cyclopes and fierce Poseidon, in his "Ithaka." They have become burdens lodged within the soul, nourished and sustained by decadent and hypocritical attitudes, threatening the individual and persistently preventing one from reaching fulfillment. They are the enemies of longings. They delay the journey to Ithaka, and even worse, confuse the planning of the only promising journey left, the hedonic, for the preservation of what is left to the individual to do for the soul. The fearful objects, initially external, eventually become internal, and they threaten to destroy the last elements of the dismembered primordial Eros, the power to beget in beauty. Something of the ladder of love in Plato's *Symposium*, lingers imperceptibly in the back of Cavafy's mind as he tries in so many of his poems to make clear the misplaced mission of the erotic in the complex realities of the modern city. Whether the fearful objects are allowed to distort or frustrate the nature of Eros is not a matter of choice and hence there is no difference between them, for the result is the same: they open in their wake the abyss of self-alienation by crippling and blinding the remnants of the creative force.

With the *polis* no longer in place, only Eros can keep us going, issuing on occasion a glimmer of hope. Cavafy is confident that the stage is set for a new version of *andreia*, since life without at least a semblance of virtue cannot be worth living, and though valued biologically, the creative person finds it difficult not to retreat into the absurd and the meaningless. But latching on to Eros as a kind of savior, for Cavafy the only promising savior, requires the pursuit of the hedonic experience. To secure the latter, in order to nourish Eros and keep the daimon alive, if not alive and undistorted, acts of courage become acts of duty. They must be acts performed not through mimesis, but as the result of deliberate choice if they are to ensure the type of conduct that ends as excellence of habit, to speak with Aristotle. Cavafy no doubt understood the requirement. It is at this point that sensuality acquires a novel and radical moral twist for our poet: one becomes a courageous pursuer of pleasure (ἀνδρεῖος τῆς ἡδονῆς).[40] The poet has a duty to do so, in the name of Eros, and an indispensable virtue in the mission to save Eros, where *eros* stands for the creative force in the human individual who is confronted with the dehumanizing conditions of the impersonal cosmopolis and the crushing anonymity in the massive state. The first objective of the redefined virtue of courage is to "tear down half the house," and by means of courageous hedonic acts denounce the idols that forbid the rightful fulfillment of eros. The stance of courage is one of defiance, and hence dangerous, open to the possibility of generating a new sort of *hubris*, as the people on the other side of the wall will say. Once again, courage cannot be separated from knowledge of what to fear and what not to fear as enemies of Eros. The situation of indecisiveness can become permanent, as it were, or temporarily paralyzing when the choice is made by longings emotionally charged and at cross purposes with themselves.[41]

There are risks involved in undertaking to redefine the virtue of

---

[40] The expression is found in Plato's *Laches* at 191e 4-7: "Now all these are courageous, but some have courage in pleasures and some in pains, some in desires and some in fears. And some are cowards under the same condition, as I should imagine." Οὐκοῦν ἀνδρεῖοι μὲν πάντες οὗτοι εἰσιν, ἀλλ' οἱ μὲν ἐν ἡδοναῖς, οἱ δ' ἐν λύπαις, οἱ δ' ἐν ἐπιθυμίαις, οἱ δ' ἐν φόβοις τὴν ἀνδρείαν κέκτηνται· οἱ δέ γ' οἶμαι δειλίαν ἐν τοῖς αὐτοῖς τούτοις.

[41] A case in point is the difference between the emotional stance in "I Went" and "December, 1903." In the former the *persona* surrenders to the strong passion, "gives in," later to say with confidence that the pleasures were fully enjoyed, giving him the right to call himself a brave man of pleasure; in the latter poem timidity carried the day, and in order to derive something resembling the experience of pleasure, the *persona* had to turn to the power of the mind to recall the what was not said or done, yet completing in imagination what the circumstances denied him. Nehamas 1983 offers a perceptive although different explanation of the difference when he writes: "One difference is certainly constituted by the active presence of memory in "December, 1903" though this is not enough." But another difference is that in addition to remembering there is "the realization that what is remembered is to be written about, that it must be the source and content of poetry. "December, 1903" is the first of Cavafy's poems to relate erotic experience to writing" (310). One might object by saying that the occasion is erotic but the experience is not; what is said in the poem is clear: the *persona* did not "give in" to the demands the passion had made.

knowledge for the post-classical climate of cultural life, for no one can fully anticipate the developments that will give society its moral structure and its code of approval and disapproval, especially in view of so many unpredictable cross-cultural mixtures of values and attitudes. Living in societies that fail to provide integrated and coherent value systems, in addition to courting constant change in the name of progress, it becomes difficult, if not impossible, to know with precision what to fear and what not to fear, beyond the types of action prohibited by law and where the punishment for transgression is spelled out in depressing detail. The thickening network of legalities limit severely the hedonic range of deliberate choice. Clearly then, the individual is taking his/her chances, and society, whatever this means, and usually it means the code of ethics approved by the most powerful of institutions, is always ready to condemn. The issue of courage as virtue in relation to fear revolves around the concept of society and social approval while the meaning of the term "society" continues to remain opaque. Is society a community or is it a heap of human beings controlled by the changing whims of jurisprudence in an otherwise unstable cosmopolis without stable cultural boundaries? Questions of this type must have puzzled Cavafy when he set out to rediscover Eros in his own Alexandrian cosmopolis of modern society. What struck him as odd was the web of its pretensions.

While the modern modality refuses to acknowledge openly natural rights of sensuality, the responsibility of the poet as "the brave man of pleasure" remains unaltered. Sensuality, for Cavafy, calls for recasting the virtue of courage, albeit not exactly in the way Plato meant it. Yet, by being regarded as a requisite virtue to the modern, its relation to knowledge must be clarified. Thus, the new poet has become the spokesman for sensuality. The answer he gives will decide whether he is a wise man or not. It is part of the wise man's mission to know and to share his experience and knowledge even when he perfects them in imagination, as is in the case of poetry and art in general. And if poetic wisdom is of the latter kind, the flight to creative imagination and the visions it offers when the work is completed, are not lies. They are conscious yet privately staged illusions, not instances of self-deception intended to substitute escape for action.

The poet masters irony. But more than being cognizant of its artistic value as an instrument of intimations, the poet knows how to handle irony fully aware of its limited use for the articulation of the human condition. *Only episodes of misleading uses of self-deception call for the employment of irony.*

The poet as a wise person is never self-deceiving, especially when he intentionally resorts to constructing illusory experiences in privacy. Obviously they are but second-best replacements for what reality cannot afford or even refuses to grant.

The wise and courageous poet values the illusions of artistic fantasy for their vividness. And he is an even more courageous pursuer of select hedonic experiences, when he openly acknowledges what he makes of the world in remembrance, reverie and illusion. What perfecting acts complete "prudence" sternly admonishes against and tries to prevent. It is against this background that we can explain how and why Cavafy in the name of eros undertook in his poetry to recast the virtue of courage. He appears to have done so not because he thought he could reshape the classical view in a manner that would bring him beyond good and evil in the way Nietzsche did, but because he needed an alternative to face the invidious intrusions of the cosmopolis into the sacred domain of the erotic spirit of humanity. He had to find an answer to the challenge without compromising the perennial pertinence of the traditional virtues. Redefining the virtue of courage to conquer the fear of pleasure, and then transmute it into poetic expression, seemed like a good place to start. He followed through with decision he had reached, which in itself a courageous act. Once again, eros had become an authentic poet.

Chapter Ten

The New Voyage: Ithaka

> "Now I have gotten used to Alexandria."
> C. P. Cavafy. (Note of 1907)

1. "Ithaka" and the Return to the City. 2. "Second Odyssey": Background and Contrasts. 3. The Ambiguity of the Voyage. 4. The Reconstructive Assimilation of Symbolism. 5. "The God Abandons Antony": Postscript to "Ithaka." 6. The Poetic Side of Hedonism.

1. "Ithaka" and the Return to the City

The voyage the poet craved in 1894 had in every respect the features of an intended escape from the city. As such, it was nothing more than a cry of despair; he had thought of himself as a prisoner of the city, however "situational" may have been the feeling that pervaded the intent of "The City." While rehearsing in his imagination the voyage of escape, he stayed in his Alexandria not only at the practical level of the diurnal affairs, as his prose writings and engagements show, but also at the lyrical level of the imaginative reconstructions of historical events and the personal projections of emotional states that pervade his poetic themes.[1] The poet actually never left

---

[1] For the occurrences of "Alexandria" in Cavafy's poems, see Delopoulos-Kairis 1983: 33-35, 129-30; of special importance are the following: (i) "Sham el Nessim" (1892 CP), a poem, first of the kind, set in the native environment of modern Alexandria; (ii) "Alexandrian Merchant" (April 1893 UP), in which the city appears only as a merchant's birthplace, to which he is about to return after a successful trip to Rome where he sold a shipment of rotten grain; (iii) in "Lagidou Hospitality" (April 1893 U), the gullible king Ptolemy Philopator bestows favors on the pretentious sophist Medon, reader of the powers of the soul and the infinite, who had left a wealthy and uncouth Roman patron for richer gifts at the royal court of Ptolemy; (iv) "The City" (1894), although left unnamed, is understood to be the poet's Alexandria; (v) in "The Glory of the Ptolemies" (1896/*1911*) the king declares Alexandria "the teacher, the apex of all learning, and the wisest in all the arts"; (vi) in

Alexandria. Sixteen years later, in October 1910, Cavafy wrote his "Ithaka," his finest crystallization of the voyage theme and the bridge that signaled the final step toward the unfettered and full range of his own voice. With it became visible the measure of a unique poet.

> As you set out on the journey to Ithaka,
> wish that the road will be long,
> full of adventures, full of learning.
> The Laistrygonians and the Cyclopes,
> 5 angered Poseidon, do not fear,
> you will never meet with such things on your way,
> if your thought can stay high, if an exquisite
> emotion touches your spirit and your body.
> The Laistrygonians, the Cyclopes,
> 10 the fierce Poseidon, you will not encounter,
> unless you carry them inside your soul,
> if your soul doesn't raise them up before you.
>
> Wish that the road may be long.
> Many may be the summer mornings
> 15 when with what joy, what delight
> you will be entering harbors never seen before;
> to stop at Phoenician trading posts
> and purchase the attractive merchandise,
> mother of pearl and coral, amber and ebony,
> 20 and sensual perfumes of every kind,
> as many as you can of sensual perfumes;
> to go to many Egyptian cities
> to learn and learn from the scholars.
>
> Always have Ithaka in your mind.
> 25 Arrival there is your predestination.
> Yet do not hurry the journey at all.

"Herodis Attikos" (1900/*1912*) Alexandria is included in the list of illustrious cities, e.g. Antioch and Beirut, as the ones that educate the orators of the future; (vii) "The End of Antony" (1907 U) deals with the last scene of the Roman general's life in Alexandria; (vii) in "The Displeasure of Selefkidis," written two months before the publication of "The City," in 1910, the theme involves Alexandria only because although it centers on the infighting of the royal hostages from the courts of the Ptolemies and the Seleucids in Rome soliciting her support; (viii) the scene for "The God Abandons Antony" (1910/*1911*) is set in Alexandria.

> Better that it last for many years;
> and be quite old when you drop anchor at the island,
> rich with all you gained during the voyage,
> 30   not expecting Ithaka to give you riches.
>
> Ithaka gave you the beautiful journey.
> Without her you wouldn't have set out to go.
> Ithaka has nothing else to give you now.
>
> And if you find her poor, Ithaka did not deceive you.
> 35   Wise as you have become, with so much experience,
> you will by now have understood what Ithakas mean.[2]

Twenty years later Cavafy dictated to a trusted friend the following brief comment on the meaning of the poem:

> [12 (40)] The meaning of the poem is simple and clear: a person in his life while pursuing a purpose (Ithaka), acquires experience, knowledge and sometimes "goods," higher than the purpose itself. Sometimes, when he arrives at the end of his efforts, finds "Ithaka" poor and not up to his expectations; nevertheless, Ithaka has not deceived him because
>
> > Wise as you have become, with so much experience,
> > you will by now have understood what Ithakas mean.
>
> Although this poem is quite lucid, it would not be pointless to draw attention to the verses 18-26. The reader will notice an emphatic mention of perfumes, which here doubtlessly symbolize the hedonic enjoyments. Experts on Cavafy's style know well that the poet rarely makes use of emphasis, and when we encounter such an emphasis, it surely signifies something. It did not happen accidentally or by the sweeping force of lyricism. Indeed the aforementioned verses contain a double emphasis that refers to the phrase at the beginning of the poem "if an exquisite emotion touches your spirit and your body."[3]

---

[2] In translating this poem, rather than strive for literary merit, my concern was to render faithfully Cavafy's text by staying as close as possible to his own syntax and imagery.

[3] Translation mine. *Self-comments* (1930): 26-7. Here as elsewhere in his comments on his poems and in other brief prose pieces, Cavafy uses the third person pronoun when referring to himself.

To speak of Cavafy's return to Alexandria is but to use suggestive imagery to underscore his conciliation with his city, a return as a work of his imagination to acknowledge the qualities that were once only half-perceived. One suspects at this point that the "return" was not to the "City of Ideas." The civic reality in Cavafy's personal thematics was intentionally cast as a curse in the verse of 1894: "the city will always follow you." The reverse was also true. With the passing of time, the poet identified with the city and traced all of its sensual contours. As for the idea of the ideal polis it simply never was a real political entity except in the poet's own historical imagination and youthful vision of utopian perfection.

The city he learned to love was not different from the city he had condemned and cursed in 1894. The city in which he was born and had lived most of his life, the contemporary Alexandria, had all the trappings of misery and promises of sensuality of any teaming cosmopolis; it was not a City of Ideas, not even a modest *polis*, not more and not less than any other contemporary center of mixed populations. As for being a place for eros as a philosophical principle and guide for the soul to push forth with its imperatives, and to inspire all builders touched by the vision of Platonism, only a wilful liar could project such a picture. The city had no *agora* for citizens to gather, deliberate and agree to work together and to secure the future of their *polis* in accordance with the lofty principles Plato had articulated in his *Republic*.

Learning to accept Alexandria was no easy task. The meandering of Cavafy's fumbles and compromises eventually taught him to take what was available in his Alexandria without dreaming of political stature, or rather, without allowing his sense of personal importance to depend on glorious assignments for its fulfillment. He came to terms with Alexandria by way of understanding his own limitations, no longer thinking that his mission as poet and citizen was to effect the return to a life of sensual freedom in the hellenistic cosmopolis. Still, he was right to envision the potential of eros as the natural force that makes it possible for the spirit to climb the ladder of beauty. Cavafy was bright enough not to limit the span of the erotic to a particular form of gratification and demand that the whole be forced to suit the whims of the part. He came to understand why freedom fulfilled in the condition of the cosmopolis is only an illusion, for neither the total gamut of desires, nor the expression and pursuit of every erotic idiosyncrasy are granted license for capricious exercise.

2. "Second Odyssey": Background and Contrasts

In tracing the theme of eros in Cavafy's poetry, especially as it relates to the concept of the voyage, the oppression of sensuality takes on special significance, more so than the direction of his own sexual preference. Eros, being a pervasive element in his poetry, also defined the terms for overcoming the problem of his self-alienation. Finally, Eros became the main force in the transformation of the idea of the voyage from the way it was expressed in the "Second Odyssey" to its refined form in "Ithaka."

  The journey intimated and hoped for, when Cavafy wrote "The City" in August 1894, had already taken imaginative shape eight months earlier, in January 1894, in a poem titled "Second Odyssey" until recently thought to have been lost. The escape was conceived in light of the motif of a different "odyssey," one designed to continue the homeric hero's travel after the return to his island. The Odysseus of Cavafy and Homer's Odysseus part company at this point. The new theme was sustained with the aid of symbolic elements and dealt with a voyage to the interminable unknown.

  In 1894, Ithaka and Alexandria, having lost the magnetic feature of a fatherland as the end the *nostos*, parallel each other for a while as symbols of depressing habitats. Eventually, and not too surprising, Alexandria came to be invested with the meaning of an inverted Ithaka. The voyage that was heralded happened only in the soul of the poet. In 1910 Cavafy revised and published "The City" and also wrote a brand new poem which he titled "Ithaka." Whereas the revised version of "The City" served as a reminder of the predicament of enclosure, the new poem, "Ithaka," announced a radical conception of a voyage no longer designed to convey the compulsion to escape. By that time, the poet had made the transition to a reconstructed self in search of fulfillment. Fourteen years earlier, in contrast, "The City" had stated directly and in dramatic anguish what the "Second Odyssey" had comparably expressed in mythical imagery:

> Second Odyssey and greater
> than the first. But alas
> without Homer, without hexameter.
>
> My paternal house was small
> 5 and so was my paternal city
> and all of its Ithaka was small.

	Telemachus' affection, the faithful
	Penelope, the aging father,
	his old friends, the devoted
10	love of the people,
	the blissful quiet of the house
	entered as rays of joy
	in the navigator's heart.

And they vanished like rays.

15	The thirst
	for the sea awakes inside him.
	He hated the wind of the land.
	At night the ghosts of the West
	disturbed his sleep.
20	Nostalgia overran him
	for voyages
	and morning
	arrivals in harbors, where
	with what joy one enters for the first time.

25	Telemachus' affection, the faithful
	Penelope, the aging father,
	his old friends, the people's
	devoted love
	and the peace and the comfort
30	of the house tired him.

	When the shores of Ithaka
	gradually fainted from his sight
	and he sailed west full speed
	toward Iberias, on to the Herculean Gates
35	away from all that was the Aegean Sea,
	he felt he lived again, that
	he cast off the hateful bonds
	of things known and familiar.
	And his adventurous heart
40	rejoiced frozenly, emptied of love.[4]

---

[4] First publication in Savidis 1987: 196-7. Certain observations may be helpful to trace the poem's thematic connections to its sources. The second stanza places Odysseus in a setting similar to Tennyson's Ulysses. In the third stanza the poet's praise of the household

The distance that separates the two 1894 poems, "Second Odyssey" and "The City", from the 1910 "Ithaka," is both thematically and stylistically remarkable. Not only are the corresponding concepts of a voyage radically different, but the changing landscape and the tone of the lyrical expression in "Ithaka" are features nowhere to be found in the two early poems. The *ennui* and the drabness have disappeared in the latter poem along with the feeling of hopeless confinement. Why, then, did Cavafy suppress the "Second Odyssey" yet decided to publish "The City" after making only a few minor changes, which were done about the same time as he wrote "Ithaka"?

A comparison of the texts of the two voyage poems reveals some startling differences about the role of Ithaka in each poem. In the opening lines of the 1894 poem Odysseus states that he finds *now* his Ithaka small. In the 1910 poem the speaking *persona* insinuates to the reader, the novice traveler, what Ithaka may mean only *at the end of the voyage*. The affection of Telemachus, Penelope's faith, the aging father and the old friends, all mentioned in "Second Odyssey," third stanza, lines 7-13, and repeated in the sixth, lines 23-28, have been replaced in "Ithaka" with "Laistrygonians, Cyclopes and fierce Poseidon," who are certain to be encountered "if one carries them in his soul." They haunt us like lingering ghosts of the inner landscape. Only a few words and phrases of the vocabulary used in the 1894 poem found their way in the 1910 poem: the noun 'Ithaka' and certain words and images, occurring in lines 20-22:

and the morning arrivals in harbors, where with what joy one enters for the first time.	. . . mornings when with what joy, what delight you will be entering harbors never seen before.

---

is close to Dante's, but the associated feeling of attachment and its endurance are not. Whereas Cavafy sees Odysseus' motive to leave Ithaka originating in boredom combined with the passion for travel, Dante identifies the motive as the desire to acquire experience of the world, and Tennyson finds it in Ulysses' determination to follow knowledge "like a sinking star." Cavafy has Odysseus leave Ithaka alone, unlike Dante and Tennyson, who allow for comrades to accompany the hero. In style and vocabulary Cavafy stays surprisingly close to Dante's Canto but finds Tennyson's Ulysses "a more human and recognizable hero," probably because the latter resembles his own Odysseus in feeling depressed and bored on account of the *ennui* of the daily routine while the desire swells to "cast off the hateful bonds / of things known and familiar" (lines 38-8).

The theme of the post-*nostos* or post-Ithaka journey is not original. Mythical accounts abounded in antiquity about Odysseus who leaves his island soon after the return from Troy. The literature on the variations of the post-Ithaka voyage has reaped since late antiquity a rich harvest.[5]

There has been much discussion among critics about the literary background of "Ithaka" on whether the hitherto labelled "lost" poem, "Second Odyssey," may have been the first version of "Ithaka."[6] A close affinity between the two poems is no longer defensible, and for two reasons: (a) The recently recovered text of the "lost" poem, offers no support to the view that it was an early version of "Ithaka." (b) Cavafy's remarks in "The End of Odysseus," an essay he wrote in April 1894, only months after the writing of "Second Odyssey," afford no clue that this parnassian poem anticipates the symbolist elements in "Ithaka." In a letter to his friend Anastassiadis in 1895, he refers to this prose piece as a "curiosity of literature."[7] The essay does not mention the poem, yet the omission allows the supposition that Cavafy had already collected the requisite source materials for the writing of the "Second Odyssey." In addition to the presence of borrowed elements from Dante and Tennyson, there is the brief interval of time separating the "Second Odyssey"

---

[5] See Stanford 1968; this scholarly treatment of the Ulysses theme makes in passing only one brief reference to Cavafy in an "additional note" to chapter xv: "I regret that linguistic difficulties have prevented me from following the Ulysses theme further in modern Greek literature. For Seferis's *On a foreign line*, see chapter fourteen of this work. Another poem on a similar theme is *Ithaka*, by C. P. Kavafy, translated by John Mavrogordato in *The Poems of C. P. Kavafy* (London, 1951), pp. 47-48 (278)."

[6] Savidis, for instance, wrote in 1975, "The first version was probably written in January 1894. The final version, written in October 1910, was published November 1911" (210).

[7] The English text in Peridis 1948: "Dear Pericles, These lines are a general introductory notice to the 3 articles and 3 poems herewith enclosed. My article on 'The End of Odysseus' is simply a 'curiosity of literature' and I only hope it isn't tedious and that the translations are not too bad" (311). The other two articles were "A Night on the Calinder" and "The Mountain"; the three poems were "Candles," "In the same City," and "Artificial Flowers." There is no mention in the letter that Cavafy enclosed a copy of the "Second Odyssey." The translations of the verses from Dante's *Inferno*, Canto 26, and Tennyson's *Ulysses* he has used in the article were his own. See Cavafy, *The End of Odysseus*, (1974): 17f; repr. in Savidis 1987.

and "Ithaka." It would seem, then, that Cavafy was working on "The End of Odysseus" when decided he to write a poem of his own on a related topic.

The 1894 voyage theme does not follow faithfully the motif of Dante nor that of Tennyson, where the traveler leaves Ithaka forever. Cavafy's intent seems to have been that of introducing a novel element for a conception of a voyage rooted in motives other than those in Dante's or Tennyson's versions of Odysseus. Since the early experiment, "Second Odyssey," did not bring the desired results, the manuscript was filed away. The sentiments and convictions that defined the predicament in "The City" had ruled out the possibility of an escape, and by the same token stressed the futility of preparations for a voyage. The dramatic settings of the two "voyage" poems do not dovetail beyond the "starting point." One critic has claimed that the voyage motif in "Ithaka" goes back to another early prose piece, "The Mountain."[8] Since the top of the mountain, symbolizing the absolute, is forever beyond our reach, the voyage that leads to perfection can never come to an end. Without doubt, Cavafy was familiar with this poetic commonplace.

Be that as it may, the poem was never printed. Though it was safely filed away, the idea of writing a post-*nostos* poem was not abandoned. The concluding paragraph of "The End of Odysseus" shows that he was fully aware of the complexity of the task:

> At the point where Homer decided to stop and put a period, it is difficult and dangerous for anyone to want to continue the discourse. However, it is in such difficult and the dangerous undertakings where the great artists succeed; I also believe that on the basis of the excerpts and the summaries [of Dante and Tennyson] I gave, no matter how badly my translation and narrative rendered them—the reader will agree that Dante's imagination created an image in no wise unworthy of the "reigning poet" (16).
> [signed] K.F.K.

Heroic action aside, Cavafy's Odysseus in "Second Odyssey" is not a variation of Tennyson's modern Ulysses. We must, therefore, try to identify the radical changes the concept of the voyager underwent between 1894 and

---

[8]Ilinskaya 1983: 64-5, who suggests that "Ithaka" is related to the prose pieces "The End of Odysseus" and "The Mountain." She notes: "The open end of Tennyson, which Cavafy regards as a positive feature and the vagueness of the concluding verses, the unknown that awaits the hero 'has a fascinating effect on the mind'." The phrase in Cavafy 1974: 17.

1910, to understand why Ithaka was cast as a symbol and Odysseus was transformed into an available variable, an impersonal *persona* that could be replaced by anyone whose lifelong pursuit is the voyage itself.

"The City" and "Ithaka" contrast so sharply in style and theme as to create the impression that these two poems were written by different hands. The difficulty is resolved by asking whether we are dealing with two different *personae* inhabiting the same poetic space. The surface resemblance between the two journeys remains an immovable feature of both poems, just as is the use of the second person singular to indicate the speaker. The poet is the same; only the perspective changed over the years.

Actually, "Second Odyssey" is close to the perspective of "The City," and hence it may well be viewed as the imaginative voyage of the *persona* in "The City," on the assumption that the escape was not impossible. However, so long as the confinement persists, it also holds for Cavafy's *ennui*. Hence, the *persona* in "The City" can easily identify with Tennyson's romantic Odysseus as well Cavafy's own. Somewhere in the background of the post-*nostos* modern motif one suspects the presence of intense feelings of alienation. In 1894, the boredom Cavafy felt in Alexandria was projected on an alienated Odysseus in his inescapable Ithaka after the return from Troy. Having written the "Second Odyssey," Cavafy was ready to write, as he did, "The City."

The time separating the two voyage poems of 1894 and 1910 had left little in common between them, other than the fact that Ithaka in the "Second Odyssey" is abandoned in favor of pursuing a vacated *nostos*. Given the discontinuity of imagery, "Ithaka" uses very little from the 1894 composition. The name of the island becomes a title in 1910 and serves mainly as a symbol. By way of content, "Ithaka" announces boldly a new theme that lies mid-way between two compositional periods, the first one marking the end of Cavafy's attachment to symbolism, and the second announcing the swelling waves of realism. The poet needed a platform and a signpost to herald the coming of the new. The last poem of the middle period, ending in 1910, was written.[9]

---

[9]For "Ithaka" as the turning point in Cavafy's development, see Keeley 1976: 77. Nehamas 1983: 308, n21, agrees with this assessment. Other critics, while agreeing with the view that 1911 marks the turning point in Cavafy's development, see a discontinuity between pre-1911 and post-1911 poems, e.g. Seferis, Sareyannis, Tsirkas, Bien, and Yalourakis. However, see Malanos and Pinchin, who stress continuity. Liddell has argued that the two

For Cavafy, to be able to write a poem like "Ithaka," he first had to recapture Alexandria, accept the city as his aesthetic habitat and not merely as ordinary environment, and attain a level of personal maturity to keep eros steadily within his poetic sight. Confident that he had met these conditions, he wrote "Ithaka." Nothing in the poem indicates that he saw it as an escape poem expressive of the wish to leave the city, or making pretentious claims that the road that leads directly to the City of Ideas was discovered, nor is the poem to be read as a counter-statement to the "Second Odyssey." What is new in "Ithaka" is the theme of a post-romantic radical journey forged with the tools of symbolism. The voyage, however, is not so much about the ports of arrival as it is about the process itself. It moves away from contrived myth to stating the psychodrama of internal growth and personal development, not yet as reality but somewhere in the realm of imaginative planning. The poetic mind was ready to be touched by a high thought and an exquisite emotion.

Writing a poem with an original twist made doctrinal demands on the poet. The post-*nostos* motif had to be taken out of the environment of pure symbolism and reworked with the finest art of the inversion of the classical mode. Thus, Cavafy went beyond the traditions of both Dante and Tennyson to purge Odysseus of the heroic element in order to make the *persona* pertinent to contemporary perspectives. What Cavafy finally kept from Tennyson and Dante was indeed nothing substantive or even formal.[10] He even turned to Homer for thematic intimations before transforming Ithaka into a symbol of the inner landscape. Painted with attractive colors to suggest a three-dimensional dream-like reality, Ithaka was groomed to comply with the demands of the inversion principle. By 1910, he was ready to eliminate the

---

views are reconcilable. Tsirkas 1958 has aptly noted that Cavafy had become a reputed poet by 1911 and about this time "the orientation of his life from that point on changed. Poetry becomes an end in itself. Poetry of pleasure and the pleasure of poetry mean the same thing" (433).

[10] Maronitis 1983 has aptly noted that "Ithaka does not correspond to the traditional expectations of the post-Homeric types of Odysseus. Yet this departure, being a theme in Cavafy's poem, turns a negative element into a positive thesis as pleasure and experience are transferred from the final focal point of *nostos*, as tradition has it, to the intermediary long voyage, which in fact, as staged in Cavafy's poem, has silenced and has left out of its field of attention the event of the war. The reader of Cavafy's poem has no idea that the poem has any connection with a voyage that came at the end of a war" (67).

idea of a second voyage in favor of a first and only significant voyage. It meant recasting the ancient motif to suit a non-mythical context no longer to be found in the tradition of the modern. The experience which the inverted motif helped convey was suddenly endowed with the credentials of a novel universality.

"Ithaka" came to seal the concluding chapter of Cavafy's relation to the Symbolist movement. The latter had served him well by assisting him in finding the freedom of the inner landscape he needed to test the poetic worth of the experiences stored from years of suffering in pursuit of eros. The inversion of the classical mode has the external face of the Hellenistic outlook and the internal texture of the modern problem of self-alienation agonizing to re-integrate the powers of the soul.

The speaker in "Ithaka," it must be assumed, has knowledge and wisdom. The *persona* knows and reveals. If a *sophos*, about what is he wise if not about the *thymos* (spirited will) and the *epithymetikon* (appetitive), the parts of the soul that had puzzled Plato all his life? It must also be assumed that the wise *persona* is not one burdened with fears of the Laistrygonians, Cyclopes, or fierce Poseidon. On the other hand, the *persona* of "The City" is so bitter and despondent that his imagination, deadened and paralyzed, cannot but remain in this state so long as despair prevails and his heart, "like the dead, lies buried." Since neither poem points to a concrete *nostos*, the movement is away from the birthplace or the *patria*. Therefore, no departure actually occurs, only planning. Motion takes the form of flights of the imagination performed in stationary positions. *Nostos*, for all practical purposes has been literally suspended. "Ithaka" stated the problem with elegance and charm but offered no hint toward its solution. The only way to meet it was to re-invent *nostos*. Either eros must become a poet or the poet must save eros. Plato had seen things correctly: a psyche divided cannot rise to the heights of truth and beauty.

What was said in chapter 9 about Cavafy's erotic poems and the diversity of the erotic imagery in his pre-1910 compositions, renders support to the thesis that he had to explore the tortuous and meandering path of eros before he could turn the *daimon* into a real source of creative energy. His own erotic dichotomy parallels the adversities of rigid control and yielding to the passions. It took decades before his erotic side gained enough buoyancy to overcome the contravening defenses of private fears and cultural ambivalence and was able to steady his course with a modicum of wisdom.

It should be of little surprise that Cavafy finally decided to print erotic poems considerably past their date of composition. His own erotic memories and actions were kept in strict privacy. His reluctance to refer to them in explicit memoirs or in conversations with close friends is well known. What was left untold in 1894, namely the causes that account for the ruination of the *persona* in "The City", emerged in 1903 with the vagueness of guarded caution when he decided to record certain "liberating" experiences in his reflections on his art. The phases of his erotic disclosures followed a winding path leading the desires out of the Mausoleum and into the light of day for the poet to view them without the burden of guilt. Such was the personal Ithaka of the early phase of his own emotional unfolding: an expanding of eros from vicarious sensuality in private reverie to acts of intense pleasure, however infrequent. The quality of both was eventually transmuted into poems of rare sensibility. Equally important is the fact that he brought together the shards of political eros.

"The City" is the appropriate prefatory poem to the collections of his mature period.[11] It presents the subjective side of his *political* consciousness *in extremis*, but it also states vividly the bifurcation of commitment and the impasse to which it leads. The publication of "The City" also served as the unofficial announcement that the crisis periods had ended. As the preface to the *Collections* it throws into sharp relief the most crucial moment of the poet's self-estrangement. A line was drawn between the end of the "crisis" and the dawn of a new phase in the poet's development. The crumbling of the subjective walls allowed Cavafy's poetic imagination to objectify his personal agony and thus alleviate the burden of the pain over mixing the private experience with the peripheral values of the cosmopolis. As the poet acquired sharper tools to work on themes of social consciousness, he became increasingly able to deepen his interest in historical events. After 1910, the historical themes were handled in more subtle and profound ways than when he was still under the sway of the powerful waves of Romanticism, still in the grip of the Symbolist movement.

For the rest of his life Cavafy would frequently turn to the past and

---

[11] See Bien 1983: 119-20, for a different view on why Cavafy used this poem to preface the 1905-1915 *Collection*; he refers to sentiments expressed in Cavafy's unpublished note of April 28, 1907.

make it a living part of his Ithaka, but with a passion different in quality and scope from that of the historian, be he Thucydides, Polybius, or Gibbon. He approached his subject sensibly, yet not without a comparable protest against the losses and failures associated with ethical failures and arbitrary shifts of power. As a result, his poetry gained by his sharpened ability to conceal the didactic element under the carefully constructed surface of irony and occasional sense of gloom. The political message is always there, and can be more fully understood when voiced through a dramatic recasting of the events of history.

The poems of the post-1910 mature period in general are carefully designed studies of the private and public side of the cosmopolitan personality resorting to adjustments, compromises, intricate involvements, subterfuges and, on the whole, covert and overt attempts to salvage the fragments of humanity the *dramatis personae* consider worthwhile. They all speak, move and act without definite assurance for lasting success, playthings, as it were, at the mercy of their opaque destiny. They move in whatever cultural milieu the new goddess, the cosmopolitan Fortuna, afforded, seeking the blessings of the new divinities that had replaced the rule of cosmic order. By trusting his *personae* in the hands of Fate and Fortuna, Cavafy proved to be one of the wise contemporary poets who understood the role of the passions in the interplay of vicissitudes, the successes and failures in the lives of those whose atrophied sense of political mission had blunted the will to believe in perfectible communities. Cavafy's fascination with political failure proved to be of lasting interest, whether expressed with reference to groups, as in "Poseidonians" (U) and "Waiting for the Barbarians," or to individuals and royal houses, as in "From the School of the Renowned Philosopher" and "Alexandrian Kings." His early obsession with the role of the *political* poet as builder and citizen in the "City of Ideas" dissipated as he went through a prolonged phase of withdrawal ending in the mausoleum of the "The Windows."[12] Once he came to understand the practical limitations of the

---

[12] The political mission of the poet goes back to the venerable tradition of law-givers/poets of ancient Greece. Cavafy sees himself as a poet-statesman and projects this image with the aid of a powerful symbol, viz. the "builder" (*ktistes*). Comp. Plato's *Politicus* at 259, where he states that a man who understands politics, the art of ruling, even if he holds no office should be called a statesman. Vrissimitzakis 1975 (34-42), was the first to draw attention to Cavafy as a *politikos* poet in an article he published in 1926.

poetic consciousness as a creative contributor to the quality of life in the cosmopolis, Cavafy broke through the prison of his self-alienation at the same time that he felt ready to jettison the remaining vestiges of his dependence on Symbolism. The poem "Ithaka" can well be seen as the last stop in this phase.[13] It steadied the course of the "work in progress."

3. The Ambiguity of the Voyage

Commentators and critics of Cavafy have expressed sharp disagreements over the poetic merits of "Ithaka." Melakopides sees it as "the least understood work" yet "the poet's final synthesis of virtues and values".[14] Others, without necessarily using the same criteria, register serious reservations, even view it as a poetic failure. Savidis, in close agreement with Sarakinos, has concluded that the "failure of Ithaka" is due to the burdening role of the sources, viz. Homer, Dante and Tennyson. Commenting on Cavafy's indebtedness to Homer, he notes that whereas the *Iliad* provided the poet with a number of themes, the largess from the *Odyssey* amounted to nothing more than "the

---

[13]Tsirkas 1958: 434-5, follows Malanos, who in 1943 published his views on the connection between Cavafy's "Ithaka" and [Pseudo?] Petronius' "*Exhortatio ad Ulyssem*," a translation of which appeared in the Alexandrian journal *Nea Zoe* (January 1910, 156). Cavafy's alleged dependence on Pseudo-Petronius is still in doubt. Evidently, both Malanos and Tsirkas took it for granted that the "Second Odyssey" was the real precursor of "Ithaka," although neither critic had ever seen a copy of the 1894 composition and hence could not have known of the serious dissimilarities between "Ithaka" and "Second Odyssey, on the one hand, and certain similarities between the latter and the Pseudo-Petronius poem, on the other. Comp. Malanos 1957: 304-5. It would be of philological interest to trace all the literature on the Ulysses theme with which Cavafy was familiar when he wrote "The End of Odysseus." Baudelaire's "Le Voyage" is a possible influence in formulating the idea of "Ithaka," especially the verses, "Mais les vrais voyageurs sont ceux-là seuls qui partent / Pour partir . . ." (But the true travelers are only those who depart for the sake of departing) *The Penguin Book of French Verse* (Hartley), p. 341.

[14]Melakopides 1983: 208-9, notes ". . . one of his [Cavafy's] best-known and perhaps least understood works. Its importance lies, I suggest, in the expansion and enrichment of his first set of values, such as aesthetic creativity, wisdom, knowledge, courage, dignity, pity, compassion; for it introduces, in 1911, the beginning of what I see as the poet's final synthesis of virtues and values."

eccentric or exotic crystallization of "Ithaka."[15] That "Ithaka" suffers from flaws, despite its evocative power and appealing message, has been admitted even by ardent admirers of Cavafy's poetry. The explanations offered to account for the flaws, especially in view of the recovery of the copy of the "Second Odyssey," need to be revisited. While the latter poem has little aesthetic merit, particularly when compared with Tennyson's "Ulysses,"[16] "Ithaka" is too far from the 1894 climate to be held to the same negative judgment solely on the grounds of surmised thematic continuity. The presence of the ambiguity which frames the flaws in the poem is better explained as originating with the *suggestif* conception of composition. The fact is that the lingering principles of Symbolism in Cavafy's technique found in "Ithaka" their most subtle application. The denial of *nostos* worked well for Dante and Tennyson, but when Cavafy used *nostos* with the inversion of the classical mode as a symbol, an incurable ambiguity crept into the poem. The inflated symbol of Ithaka simply overpowered the intended meaning. Cavafy's "comment" of 1930 on the poem offers no hint about the presence of a flaw.

The problem of clarifying the meaning of Ithaka continues to haunt the reader. The poet assures us—or is it himself?—that "Ithaka gave you the beautiful journey." Assuredly so, but what else can it give, aside from what an inclusive vision of life may suggest? We know that we are about to start on a journey. And we hear of things to expect, cities and harbors in between, in

---

[15]Savidis 1974, in a comment he appended to his edition of Cavafy's "The End of Odysseus," states that he viewed the crystallization as "the result of the triple pressure of Homer, Dante and Tennyson on the sensitivity and ambition of Cavafy" (21). When Savidis expressed this view he did not have the text of the "Second Odyssey" before him; he had listed the poem among the "lost" compositions. It is not known to me whether he would be willing to hold the 1974 view today.

[16]Willey 1956: 71, referring to Tennyson, states in his *More Nineteenth Century Studies*: "In *Ulysses* the sense that he must press on and not smoulder in idleness is expressed objectively, through the classical story, and not subjectively as his own experience. He [Tennyson] comes here as near perfection in the grand manner as he ever did; the poem is flawless in tone from beginning to end: spare, grave, free from excessive decoration, and full of firmly controlled feeling." No comparable praise can be heaped on "Second Odyssey," but it cannot be denied that Cavafy made a genuine effort to cut loose from both Dante and Tennyson, although he stayed closer to the former in the selection of imagery and nearer to Tennyson for the model of dramatic dialogue.

short the total gamut of pleasures. None of the harbors and cities can equal Ithaka itself. The reader is forewarned that he may find Ithaka poor at the end of the journey. Poor in what sense? As a barren land, void of further pleasures? The vagueness of the symbol thickens as the effort to identify the terminus, the last harbor, is met with disappointment. One can no longer be sure whether the symbol stands for the course of a full life or whether it points to the cumulative experience the journey has granted, the affective wisdom. If the latter, the end comes with, though not as, "wisdom and experience." The defining element is missing, for the end was unknown when the journey began. To call 'Ithaka' the balanced life, as Melakopides insists (ibid. 210), adds more to a presumed message than the text allows.[17]

It could be that the poet purposely left his symbols vague while exploring the means to come closer to the realism of his post-1910 poetry. If so, the plan fell short of success. The concepts of pleasure and *sophia* (wisdom), like the idea of the voyage, could not be relieved of their opaqueness once they were projected through the technique of *suggestif*. Furthermore, there is a certain hidden *circularity* in the poem, a poetic *petitio principii*: the theme presupposes that the *persona* possesses that which it aims at acquiring: *sophia*. More concretely, the poem assumes that the *sophia* of pleasure is a property of an accomplished "brave man of *hedone*," the speaker. The reader cannot help but wonder whether one can ever choose to embark on this sort of voyage unless already wise enough to know how to remove from the psyche the fear of the Laistrygonians and the Cyclopes before taking off. One must be somewhat *sophos* at the start, and at the end one is again *sophos*, perchance more *sophos*. An expected conclusion must be drawn at the end of the voyage: there should be no disappointment if Ithaka is found to be poor. Still, the sentiment is left vague, for Ithaka is not a kingdom, nor a life of civic duty, *politikon chreos*, at least no hint is made to that effect.

---

[17]Melakopides' statement "Cavafy elaborates on and qualifies pleasure as a crucial value of *Eudaimonia*" (*supra* 214f), seems intended to bring Cavafy close to an Aristotelian view in ethical theory about the *summum bonum*. It is an interesting point, but given the breadth of the symbol no such claim can be substantiated. The lyrical imagery of the poem is no substitute for an argument on which to rest so demanding an ethical principle. The claim made defies substantiation. Not enough information can be extracted from the poem to show that such a position dominates Cavafy's message in "Ithaka." The requisite elements needed to say that the poem adheres to the classical conception of *eudaimonia* are missing.

The voyage cannot be that of a *polites*. If so, the wisdom gained is not political. Somehow, Homer and Aristotle are not represented in "Ithaka," only a highly modified Epicurus, smiling enigmatically from a serene nook in his invisible garden. Ithaka, being a place without a definite identity, cannot have the beloved shores of the familiar island, nor the boundaries of the *polis* and its heritage. There are no prescribed or unwritten civic expectations here to respond and to find one's assigned place in the body politic. Hence the poem bears no resemblance to the city in "The Satrapy," nor to the island of "Second Odyssey." The real setting is in the projected landscape of imaginative pleasures. Wisdom demands of the traveler in "Ithaka" not to prolong the visits, nor stay permanently at any particular harbor. No traveler can afford the abandon of the lotus-eater, for it would signal the death of experience. Homer had correctly rhapsodized this last point.

The reader is looking at an Ithaka without the promise of a *terminus*, other than natural death. Upon closer inspection, once the magic is gone, the prospect of the voyage gives the impression of the open road away from the *ennui* of the cosmopolis. But what if the voyage is illusory and every exit is succeeded by another exit, all fixed on concentric circular walls? What if Ithaka is but a brilliantly painted curtain hiding the stage on which the real drama of life is acted? Raising the curtain may reveal a chain of endless links alternating between depressions and elations, unavoidable episodes in the traffic of the vast cosmopolis. This episodic drama of adventures is not an extension of the Homeric world, and no symbolic conversion can transform the latter to cover the Cavafian modern voyage. The difference between the Homeric and the modern voyages is so vast that it renders comparison almost meaningless. What characterizes the distinct phases of the modern voyage is not just the occurrence of concatenated pauses with the attendant hope of arriving at the last exit, but the mode of agonizing over the prospect of an abrupt encounter with a fixed "no exit" sign.

Once the grounds for the exchange of modes to portray the on-going alteration between crises and exits were understood, Cavafy could finally succeed in making superior use of the inversion device in his poetry. In the case of "Ithaka," however, the inversion of the classical mode was forced to suit and serve the poetics of Symbolism. The result was a failure, but it had the charm of an original experiment. If a counter-Ithaka situation is needed to illustrate the non-hedonic journey, the ill-fated voyage, so to speak, the reader can do no better than to turn to "Things Ended" (1910/*1911*: A 19), written about the same time:

> In fear and in suspicions
> with mind disturbed and frightened eyes,
> we waste ourselves designing ways
> how to escape the certain danger
> that threatens us so horribly.
> And yet we are mistaken, that is not what's coming;
> the messages were false
> (either we did not hear them, or didn't understand them).
> Another disaster, one we didn't quite imagine,
> a sudden and swift one descends upon us,
> finding us unprepared—with no time left—and sweeps us away.

A number of Cavafy's poems illustrate the idea of the ill-fated journey. They are about persons, real and imaginary, who fall prey to their own vices and their thoughtlessness. As such, they are negative versions of the *persona* in "Ithaka."[18] The rich harvest of this variety of possible deviations includes a number of masterworks, among them "The God Abandons Antony." The Roman Antony, as Cavafy reconstructed his last day, stood a fighting chance to prove that he could attain the rank of a "brave man of pleasure" when he was presented with the opportunity to end his Ithakian voyage in Alexandria. The poem does not rewrite history; it enriches a select event with an improbable possibility. Whether Antony heeded the exhortation is not as important as is the wisdom that was made available to Antony the *persona*, an unusual gift from poetry to prevent a pedestrian type of death from stealing the last word in the decisive hour of defeat.

When Cavafy's poems are read not as isolated entities but as distinct acts comprising a life's "work in progress" and as a continuous thematic dialogue between despair and pleasure, surrender and hope, false starts and grand illusions, dead-ends and fearful exits, failures and renewed efforts, they gradually reveal the promised meaning of wisdom which an Ithaka is expected to grant. What Cavafy had intimated in "Ithaka" became incarnate in the total

---

[18]Vrissimitzakis 1975 was perhaps the first to show that there is a correlation between the general idea of Ithaka and the life stories of individual *personae* in the poems. He writes: "Cavafy likes to narrate private odysseys, e.g. "From the School of a Renown Philosopher," and certain "tomb" poems, such as "Tomb of Ignatios" and "Tomb of Iasis" (26, n1).

output of his art. But, to return to the poem itself, a significant change is announced in the last verse, where the plural *Ithakas* has replaced the singular form of the name. Evidently, the Symbolist technique was still in operation, and it succeeded in shattering into bits the very symbol on which the poet had relied to convey his message.

Inadvertently, the poem missed its mark and ended in a spectacular failure. The hedonic journey in "Ithaka" promises *sophia*. As the imaginative journey progresses, the reader comes to the realization that he is listening to the speaker—to the poet's own voice—who is already wise, and shares the secret of his method but not the contents. Whatever else that wisdom may be, it is not philosophical knowledge; yet it has the makings of profundity as it insinuates the importance of understanding the affective soul, the desires and the passions of the spirited will, what Plato called *thymos*. It is a *thymosophia*, a sort of wisdom about the passionate soul that intuits how the desires work, how the experienced gratifications anticipate the consequences of pains and pleasures. It is a wisdom not limited to issuing the commands of prudence but geared more to perfecting the art of hedonic pursuits, to doing justice to the affective side of human nature. If to be wise is also to be just, the next move must aim at revitalizing yet another cardinal virtue: courage or *andreia*. Without it, the appeal of the exhortation weakens for lack of completeness. Cavafy's "Ithaka" anticipates rather than initiates the poet's search for the model of wisdom that would enable him to put new life into the classical mission of the poet-theorist.

Cavafy never seems to have doubted the belief that the man of wisdom is a better judge of actions than the common man. By opting for a wisdom that includes rational judgment as a guide and test of values, while illumining the demands of the desires, he moved out of the shadow of Romanticism as well as that of Symbolism. In a note, written in September 16, 1902, he asked what is truth and what is falsehood.[19] "Do truth and falsehood really exist, or is it that only the New and the old exist,—and Falsehood is simply Truth in old age?" He was pondering whether falsehood is nothing but a truth grown old and no longer useful. Even on such an urbane and pragmatic criterion, action and reflection on action work together to decide whether a certain truth is still workable and relevant to pressing problems. He went a step further to

---

[19] Cavafy 1983: 24.

conclude that there is nothing to prevent an accepted truth, now seen as "false," to return and re-install itself, if found to have more useful applications. No truth therefore becomes totally false, if there is a chance that it may become pertinent to future circumstances. The obsolescence of a truth cannot and should not be decided independently of the changes that attend the human condition. One just never knows when an old truth will be called upon to serve a *persona* in trouble, or a nation in danger. Ignorance of this simple rule aids and abets *hubris*; it breeds catastrophes. This is as close as he came to the outlook of the Greek tragedians.

It was for good reasons that wisdom was made part of the central theme in "Ithaka," although the determination of the meaning of the concept was left up to the reader's intuitive powers. Most of his poems, at least the ones he would label "philosophical," may be read as notes on the grand theme of wisdom. At the practical level, the *personae*, as agents of wisdom, help humanity rise above the level of helplessness and confusion. They offer dramatic proof that knowledge is attainable even if not in the form of perfectly complete eternal truths. The real difficulties in conduct arise not because of the limitations of human intelligence, but because of our reluctance to base action on wisdom. Errors are frequently made, some with irreversible consequences. Aside from those due to the abuse of reason, there are others that result from distorting the role of the desires in civilized conduct. Sometimes in the same place some persons are wise but powerless, others are powerless and foolish. Rarely are the destinies of people trusted in the hands of leaders who are at once wise and powerful. Nero knows not how to listen, and Oedipus rules himself innocent before deciphering Tiresias' utterances. As two verses insist in "But the Wise Perceive Things About to Happen" (1896/*1899*/*1915* revised with new title: A 17), "only the gods know what the future holds / for they alone possess all the lights." Following the ancient tradition, the poet assigned to human wisdom a place between omniscience and ignorance.[20]

The infrequent attainment of wisdom implies the predominance of conduct filled with half-truths and pretensions of conceit. Cavafy's themes abound with cases of the pathetic and a deeply felt sadness for the victims of

---

[20]For the wise man, as intermediate between the wholly wise gods and the ignorant mortals, see Plato: *Lysis* 218B; *Symp.* 204A; *Phaedrus* 278D.

unintended paucity of information. There is the case of the *persona*, in the poem "Interruption," who could not act on time to avoid the "inevitable." Mortals hear only what they can. Acting in fear and ignorance, not knowing that what seemed to be a threat was a blessing in disguise, interfere and disrupt the work of the gods. A great number of *personae* in his poems act, think, wish, and dream, while in a state of deficient reflection, *a-sophia*. They are forced throughout their lives to play without a full deck of cards. But play they must, not suspecting that the purpose of the marvelous journey is to deliver them, including the poet-speaker, from the confusion of *a-sophia*. Prudence to anticipate and avoid pain aside, the wisdom "Ithaka" recommends is not what belongs to the gods; it refers to what is indispensable knowledge in pursuing the *hedonic* possibilities of life. Cavafy remained a *hedonic* poet not out of preference for the unhindered pursuit, but mainly because he was convinced that there can be no short-cuts to wisdom and courage. Only wisdom protects what life offers and *andreia* obtains. Together they prevent the hedonic side of life from collapsing into vulgarity.

We may now ask our poet: To whom is the journey recommended and who in fact qualifies? In principle, the answer to the first part is: "to all, by nature." The difficulty lies in identifying suitable candidates who can in fact continue the journey and, while in transit, acquire the needed wisdom to finish as brave men of pleasure. By reading "Ithaka" in isolation from the other poems, the intended answer does not surface with sufficient clarity. A related difficulty in grasping the poem's message lies in the elliptical projection of its dominant imagery, when at the critical moment the poet cajoles the reader: "You will by now have understood what the Ithakas mean." As a promise it is but a poor substitute for direct disclosure. Perhaps the poet was left with no alternative once the inverted symbol of Ithaka was attached to the process and not to the concrete *nostos* that ties the subject's wisdom to *politikos eros* and civic duty. The inflated symbol forced the poet to suspend the concept of the *polis*. *Nostos* was displaced in favor of the open-ended quest, so central to modern consciousness. The concept of the *polis*, not being false, was forgotten on the shelf of old truths. The situation in "Ithaka" was not stated as a problem that demands the return of the *polis*. Cavafy had more ground to cover before he could travel between the two worlds, the classical and the contemporary, with the surety and security that wisdom affords. The excitement of the modern journey carried the day.

4. The Reconstructive Assimilation of Symbolism

Around 1910, Cavafy had redesigned the useful elements he borrowed from the Symbolist movement during the transitional phase before arriving at the definitive position of his poetics. This section supplements what was said in chapter 4, "The Long Shadow of Symbolism," where the discussion was focused on Cavafy's response to Baudelaire. The writing of "Ithaka" presented the opportunity he needed to bring into sharp focus the useful features of Symbolism he was employing selectively.

Cavafy gives the impression that he simply accepted the poetics of Symbolism as a free gift from the outside with which one could experiment and use to meet the demand for adequate poetic expression. He was not really touched by the Symbolists' poetic mysticism, and there is no indication that he ever explored that type of experience. Cavafy was simply looking for a means to advance beyond the fading romantic clichés. As for the loss of belief in traditional religion,[21] he expressed no interest in the *metaphysical agony* that many intellectuals, artists, poets, and philosophers considered central to their experience. The confrontations between science and religion that mark almost every movement and phase of modern European culture, were not among his primary concerns. As for his attitude toward Christianity, it resembled closely that of Myrtias, the *dramatis persona*, in "Dangerous Thoughts" (?/*1911*: A 46): "in part this . . . in part that."

In certain respects Cavafy was a kind of poetic experimentalist in search of artistic tools. First he went to Romanticism, as did so many of his contemporaries, and finally to Symbolism without intending to adopt the "truths" of its artistic dogma. His tempered acceptance of the world picture of Orthodox Christianity had none of the theologian's academic profundity.[22]

---

[21] Comp. Maronitis and Pieris whose articles in the commemorative issue, *Cavafy Circle* 1983, touch on this issue.

[22] However, see Savidis 1985a: 147-54, also Haas 1983a on Cavafy's views on Christianity. This is a complex topic and difficult to unravel in its details, especially in light of Cavafy's response to Christianity as related to eros and views on Hellenism. The feeling of guilt and his liberation from its stronghold are the keys to the study of the phases through which his ideas on religion went and how they found their way, and in what form, into his early and later poems.

Notwithstanding his attraction to Symbolism as aesthetic technique, he was by way of temperament closer to the Realists.[23]

The ideal of the beautiful that Cavafy counterposed must be sought within the context of his notion of "the City of Ideas," to be sure a Platonizing model with strong political overtones. Cavafy did not go to Symbolism as a protestor. He more or less drifted toward that fashionable direction and found it increasingly useful as a tool of expression as his expectations turned sour. So long as his native proclivity towards a naive acceptance of a realistic outlook was not fully trusted to assume command over his creative life, the dependence on the borrowed tools was merely habitual. Yet, for Cavafy, *real things,* whenever they would become distasteful, were judged on a direct personal level and not in connection to inscrutable transcendent causes. Nevertheless, his disillusionments were related to *real* difficulties as he perceived them from his particular station in life. Cavafy, as a young man, simply resisted coming to grips with the practical exigencies to adjust and make certain concessions to the demands of earning a living. He feared it would lead to loss of status. But his determination to become a poet and to be recognized as such reflects an unshakable loyalty to a cultural ideal of life, not one rooted in religious devotion or derived from communion with entities of a metaphysical nature.

His flirtation with Baudelaire's "Correspondances" was strong but not overpowering in its effects. Where Cavafy differs from the Romantic and Symbolist poets is mainly in his conception of the function and ideal of poetry. He viewed his art primarily in the tradition of his own heritage as well as in response to his own special circumstances, and only secondarily as part of a

---

[23] See Bowra 1943 (reference to the 1961 ppb. edition, chapter 1), for a discussion of these movements: "In this art of [like of Zola and Heredia] mysticism had no place. The Realists had no use for that belief in a superior world above the senses which had been familiar in Europe since Augustine absorbed the doctrines of Neo-Platonism; they had a stern conviction that what mattered was truth and that truth could be found empirically in this world . . . . In the third quarter of the nineteenth century the Realists and the Parnassians held the field in France, and even in England something of the same spirit may be seen in . . . Browning and . . . Tennyson . . . (2). Against this Scientific Realism the Symbolists protested, and their protest was mystical in that it was made on behalf of an ideal world which was, in their judgment, more real than that of the senses. It was not in any strict sense Christian . . . .. It was a religion of Ideal Beauty, of 'le Beau' and 'l' Idéal.' . . . For Baudelaire the Ideal of the Beautiful gave force and purpose to his tortured and tormented soul" (3).

"reaction" either to the Romantic or the Symbolist movement in the search for truth. Other related areas of controversy, where science, politics and religious institutions sought to deny poetry and art a significant place in the domain of action and values, fell outside his immediate interests. The value of poetry was not debatable.

It is important at this point to identify what it was that Cavafy was not looking for and what he found in Baudelaire's sonnet. It was noted in chapter 4 that Cavafy inserted verses of his own with which he introduced special elements adumbrating his eventual parting with Symbolism and return to the familiar things of everyday life, though at a different and more direct level than Zola, for instance, did. Whatever he gleaned from Baudelaire's conception of ideal beauty, he filtered through the pleasures of fulfilled desires and the vision of a *polis* where eros functions to make a person complete, without guilt, waste, corruption and subterfuges. Unlike Baudelaire, whose quest for ideal beauty required the God-Satan duality, Cavafy simply strove to expunge the soul of both guilt and agony. His erotic preference had taken the form of a true conviction in the value of liberated desire, although he had on occasion used expressions insinuating deviation from normalcy. There is no preoccupation with a descent to Hell in his poetry and no deliberate exercise in self-abasement, except for those periods of crisis when confusion and fear would unleash a heavy surge of guilt. But since the disturbances of soul had no convincing "metaphysical" framework to brand them condemnable acts of original depravity, and lacking covert complexes to explain these disturbances as symptoms of illness, the "crises" left no permanent scars.

At the end, Cavafy suffered no personal defeat. The alienation he experienced was nothing out of the ordinary or different from the sharp and painful perception any sensitive person feels when loneliness and rejection persist beyond the normal threshold of tolerance. In Cavafy's case, the intensity and range of his feeling of alienation would at times show signs of paranoia and confusion. Unable to perceive correctly the changes around him, he was temporarily weakened to prevent the loss of self-esteem and the encroaching sense of self-imprisonment. While a prisoner of his own making, he neither condemned the sensible world in hope of a better one, nor did he share the hope of transporting his spirit to the heavens of the Symbolist's world of ideal beauty and eternal meanings.

Neither by temperament nor by way of predicament was Cavafy a follower of the Symbolist movement. His was only a temporary liaison, one that provided a needed palliative and an opportunity for apprenticeship. Yet the association was not without certain risks; and it could have been destructive had he not the insight to turn it into a profitable exchange. Had the movement reached him in the form in which it was felt in France, or had its impact on him lasted longer, it could have defeated his genius by turning him into a disciple, drawing his themes from the confused feelings that would inundate his imagination during the "crisis" period. Fundamentally, Cavafy was a political poet of affective wisdom. He was confident that it was the poet's responsibility to address the world of individuals, their reason and desires, their values and aspirations, lest the affective domain of experience remain dark and misdirected, and as a result throw into disarray the ideals of the political community.

When Cavafy went to Symbolism to enrich his art, he had to posit and clarify his own symbols. But as his private objectives deepened in meaning, he had to reach beyond the limits of personal concerns. He may have taken his clue from Baudelaire in learning how to develop the technique of inverting groups of old and new symbols. Whatever the case may be, he inverted the relationships of things and their names as he explored their setting in classical and post-classical Greece. He inverted the classical mode to express his understanding of how poetry can cope with the modern and counter the sense of alienation that emerged after the loss of the *polis*.

Where the Symbolists sought to loosen the ties to political concerns by stressing the withdrawal of the individual to the recesses of the soul, Cavafy, in contrast, found it necessary to move in a different direction. He came from a different tradition. The history of Greece, its politics, successes and failures aside, the meaning of cultural glory, famous men and cities, were all major components of his phyletic memory. He was steeped in a culture that had formulated, defended and expressed the idea of beauty in sculpture, poetry, and architecture, city architecture in particular, as well as the art of the civic life, rhetoric and philosophy. Making ideal beauty exclusively a subjective value was not Cavafy's way of art. Delving into the realm of the mysterious self, to discover there the abode of perfect truth, would in his case only force a contrived effort before he could lay claim to having experienced it. At any rate, the effort would have been induced through the importation of foreign doctrines, rather than originating in his native tradition.

Cavafy's devotion to an ideal reflects an affinity to one of the more appealing features of Symbolism, but the texture was hardly the same. It was the influence in technique that left a deeper mark. It surfaced assuredly in poems where the power of suggestiveness tends to dominate the themes. It also proved to be one of the lasting effects of Symbolism, no matter how modified it was, to serve the idiosyncrasy of Cavafy's outlook. In effect, Symbolism became a technique adapted to the presentation of his world.

The evocative and suggestive devices of poetic compositions in the pre-1903 period, remained in force even after the writing of his *Ars Poetica* in 1903, when he formulated the Principle of the Emendatory Work. "Waiting for the Barbarians" and other poems of that vintage testify to the influence of Symbolism. After 1910-1911, the technique was largely modified to maintain suggestiveness. It was employed for the elimination of items where vagueness was a problem. The expanding use of situations from history made Cavafy increasingly responsive to the demand for precision and correctness. Suggestiveness was employed mainly through the subtle use of poetic *synecdoche*, the mechanism of bringing into the text the secondary detail, the forgotten anecdote, the becoming gestures and phrases in character with each *persona*, the marginalia of major events, all of which in turn could call to the foreground an expanse of experience to illustrate critical moments in what was to be an unsuspected turning point in history.

Awareness of certain limits, which Cavafy was extremely careful not to ignore, alerted him to the dangers of the temptation to become a faithful disciple of Symbolism. He had found in its tenets a way to reinforce his already formed conviction about the importance of the poetic self. His own tradition had always demanded this self-affirmation. But Cavafy's notion of self was Hellenic in character, not French. However, neither the metaphysics of Symbolism nor the model of pure music in poetry were congenial elements to his conception of self. His themes and language inevitably took him in a direction away from the one that brought fame to Baudelaire and Mallarmé. By 1907, he was tired of Baudelaire; in fact so tired that he admitted there was nothing left for him to learn from *Les Fleurs du mal*. Baudelaire "is locked in a small circle of pleasure."

Aesthetic withdrawal in the case of the Symbolist poets was willed; Cavafy found it useful only after he realized that there was no other way he could exercise the right to claim the public role of the poet. He did not cherish the exile of "Walls." Because of the fact that eros and withdrawal are countervailing forces, Cavafy had to resolve their antinomy. The knowledge that eros cannot be found in a state of withdrawal saved him from misanthropy, including milder forms of anti-social conduct. He never rejected the *polis* as such, only the conditions of the modern cosmopolis and its unprecedented mixture of indifference, vulgarity, puritanism, self deception and political callousness. That he learned to come to terms with the unsavory realities of the modern city does not lead to the conclusion that he therefore accepted them as something other than an aberration or an anomaly legitimated through convention, power and greed. He loved his Alexandria and its opportunities, and came to view them as occasions for enjoyment. The life of "thoughtful adaptations"[24] is never without lures, traps and dangers, but there can be no other play, except a life of self-denial or some form of monasticism. But Cavafy was confident that the legitimated anomalies were not laws of nature, and hence they did not have a permanent hold on human destiny. He was no orthodox Stoic to declare that whatever is, is good and inevitably so. He learned to accept existence primarily for whatever promise it held for a life becoming to "the brave men of pleasure," what a good Epicurean, minus the speculative atomism, would accept.

He studied history, and history made him wiser; he explored and identified the range of human desires. He was confident that a better *politeia* can be effected, one more humane and compassionate than what the prevailing realities allowed. Human ingenuity assured him of the possibility of a future *politeia*, where human understanding and desires can find free expression in the light of day, and where guilt and condemnation would not function to distort eros through vile and sordid abuse. Cavafy reached back to the past centuries of his tradition to telescope the leaders who had failed through negligence, ignorance or refusal, just as he sought in the understanding of his own desires the answer he needed to illumine the predicament of his generation with the suggestive force of poetry. His message, ever since the writing of the first symbolic poem "Builders," was essentially and broadly political. And it remained as such, except that with the passage of time it expanded into a poetic vision of statesmanship of culture. The ideal that lurks in the background of his poems as a "work in progress," and emerges with the power of suggestiveness, is a *politikos eros*, the eros that alone can transform the *cosmopolis* into a viable *polis* where ideas are given

---

[24]The expression occurs in one of the last poems he published, "In the Year 200 B.C." (1916/*1931*: B 88-89).

a proper home and desires are allowed to blossom in reasoned measure.

That Cavafy borrowed from the technical practices of Symbolism certain ways to cultivate and express his own range of sensibility cannot be denied. However, the substance of the tenets of Symbolism remained foreign to his outlook and needs. We have no way of knowing whether he studied its metaphysical doctrines with the care of the devoted disciple. One suspects that he had no such curiosity or inclination. Learning what he could take from the movement to advance his own development carried with it a price to be paid, particularly since the borrowed elements he employed were used as palliatives to assuage the pains of his disturbed soul. Some of his better known popular poems were written during this period. The best fruits of his association with the Symbolist movement were destined to come after the critical recasting of the features he thought best suited to throw into sharp relief the failures of the modern cosmopolis. Cavafy, a poet of the *polis* by choice and tradition, returned to realities of the city with a deepened understanding that graced his poetry with the glow of the wisdom he gained after he steadied his course on the way to Ithaka.

5. "The God Abandons Antony": Postscript to "Ithaka"

One month after the writing of "Ithaka," Cavafy composed, in November 1910, the first major non-symbolist poem, "The God Abandons Antony." It illustrated a journey and its end surprisingly different from what the concluding lines of "Ithaka" predict.

> When suddenly at midnight, you hear
> an invisible procession going by
> with exquisite music, voices,
> don't mourn your luck that's failing now,
> work gone wrong, your plans
> all proving deceptive—don't mourn them uselessly.
> As one long prepared, and graced with courage
> say goodbye to her, to Alexandria that is leaving.
> Above all, don't fool yourself, don't say
> it was a dream, your ears deceived you:
> don't degrade yourself with empty hopes like these.
> As one long prepared, and graced with courage
> as is right for you who were given this kind of city,

> go firmly to the window
> and listen with deep emotion, but not
> with the whining, the pleas of a coward;
> listen—your final delectation—to the voices,
> to the exquisite music of that strange procession
> and say goodbye to her, to the Alexandria you are losing.[25]
>
> (Tr. Keeley and Sherrard, p. 33, rev. ed.)

The *persona* is about to face death away from the glory of the battlefield. The dramatic moment in the poem is not Antony's confrontation with death but the hour that has come for him to make his last decision, the one that will confirm the way of life he had claimed to be his. The poem ends without an answer to the question put before Antony. And we are left to ponder whether the Roman did in fact rise to the occasion and thus prove that he understood what an Ithaka means. His journey, one of the stormiest, is described in Plutarch's account. Cavafy drew heavily for this and other poems related to that period: "Alexandrian Kings" (1912/*1912*: A 35), "Kaisarion" (1914/*1918*: A 69), "In Alexandria, 31 B.C." (1917/*1924*: B 41). It was indeed full of adventures, risks, excitements, conquests, victories, hatreds, intrigues, battles and defeats. What happened on the night before the journey of Antony's life was about to end, leaves much doubt as to whether or not he met the high standard of hedonic courage intimated in "Ithaka." The poet treated the Roman more generously than the reported events allow. When the end was nearing, Antony was presented with the finest of opportunities to demonstrate his claim to hedonic wisdom. Twenty years after the date of this composition, Cavafy dictated a "comment" in which the grandeur of the acute dilemma took second place to the didactic intent of the theme:

---

[25]Plutarch, *Life of Antony*: "That night, it is related, about the middle of it, when the whole city was in deep silence and general sadness, expecting the event of the next day, all of a sudden was heard the sound of all sorts of instruments, and voices singing in tune, and the cry of a crowd of people shouting and dancing, like a troop of bacchanals on its way. This tumultuous procession seemed to take its course right through the middle of the city to the gate nearest the enemy; here it became the loudest, and suddenly passed out. People who reflected considered this to signify that Bacchus, the god to whom Antony had always made it his study to copy and imitate, had now forsaken him" (The Dryden translation, 476-7). For interpretations of the poem: Ilinskaya 1983: 142ff; Malanos 1957: 126f, 303f; Michaeletos 1952: 52ff; Seferis 1974b, v. 1: 335-40.

> The poem refers to the times when the defeated Antony was besieged by Octavian in Alexandria (See Plutarch, *Life of Antony*), and at the moment when even his protector god, Dionysos, abandoned him (invisible procession). The poem teaches us that we must face disaster with dignity.[26]

The center of gravity has shifted to the suspense built into the high drama as we wait to hear Antony's last decision. The historical details of the end do not matter. We have them from Plutarch. Facing final defeat after his army deserted him and the navy crossed over to the side of Octavian, and when the (false) message that Cleopatra had died reached him, Antony went to his chamber and decided to end his life. There is a twist of irony here. Plutarch reports:

> He had a faithful servant, whose name was Eros; he had engaged him formerly to kill him when he should think it necessary, and now he put him to the promise. Eros drew his sword, as designing to kill him, but, suddenly turning round, he slew himself. And as he fell dead at his feet, 'It is well done, Eros,' said Antony; 'you show your master how to do what you had not the heart to do yourself;' and so he ran himself into the belly, and laid himself upon the couch. The wound, however, was not immediately mortal.[27]

He died later, after he was brought to the monument where Cleopatra had sought refuge.

Cavafy, assuming the reader's familiarity with Plutarch, made a masterful move in the poem: he withheld judgment. Indirectly, however, he placed high value on the crucial moment at which the *persona* shows whether he masters the flow of events or succumbs in obedience. The stage was set to perfection. Everything, now that Ithaka is not a symbol but the glorious city of Alexandria, hangs on the prospect of the last act. Antony, the *persona* entrusted with the role of the exemplar, is about to furnish the evidence that can confirm the attainment of an Ithaka. It is his to prove, while savoring the final *hedone*, whether his life can have as great an end as befits Alexandria

---

[26]*Self-comments* (1942): 24.

[27]The Dryden translation, 487.

herself. The suspense is there. The reader is waiting to see whether Antony will conduct himself at the most crucial moment as required of a man who had enjoyed the appellation Bacchus and proclaimed himself the descendant of Dionysos,[28] and thus be counted among the brave men of pleasure. The time for Antony to have said farewell to Alexandria, and by so doing prove his wisdom, was at the hour of the final pleasure, while listening "to the voices / to the exquisite music of that strange procession." Antony took no secrets with him to his grave. Cavafy had studied Plutarch's text and saw that Antony, with all his passions and extravagant action, never quite became an Alexandrian.[29] In fact, Cavafy had composed in 1907 a poem, "The End of Antony," stating exactly this very point.

> When he heard the women weeping
> and lamenting him for his plight,
> the leading lady with her oriental gestures
> and the slaves women with their barbaric Greek,
> the pride in his soul
> arose, his Italian blood disgusted,
> and all these things became foreign and indifferent,
> things till then he'd worshipped blindly—
> his whole fiery Alexandrian life—
> and said: "Weep not for him. It's unbecoming.
> Rather they should give him praise,

---

[28] Plutarch reports that Antony traced his ancestry back to Hercules and Dionysos. He expected festivities in his honor to reflect his divine lineage. "When he made his entry into Ephesus, the women met him dressed up like Bacchantes, and the men and boys like satyrs and fauns, and throughout the town nothing was to be seen but spears wreathed about with ivy, harps, flutes, and psalteries, while Antony in their songs was Bacchus, the giver of joy, and the Gentle. And so indeed he was to some, but to far more the Devourer and the Savage" (*op. cit.*, 437). Comparable scenes took place in Athens in anticipation of victory against Octavian.

[29] "Antony, stopping her lamentations as well as he could, called for wine to drink, either that he was thirsty, or that he imagined that it might put him the sooner out of pain. When he had drunk, he advised her [Cleopatra] to bring her own affairs, so far as might be honorably done, to a safe conclusion, and that, among all the friends of Caesar, she should rely on Proculeius; that she should not pity him in this last turn of fate, but rather rejoice for him in remembrance of his past happiness, who had been of all men the most illustrious and powerful, and in the end had fallen not ignobly, a Roman by a Roman overcome" (Ibid., 478).

> that he had been so great a ruler,
> and had acquired many good things.
> And if he'd fallen now, he doesn't fall humbly.
> Still Roman he's vanquished by a Roman."

The poem remained among the unpublished papers with a note "Too sti[lted?] however." It was a wise decision. The mature "The God Abandons Antony" shows clearly the weakness of the older poem and what it is: it was derivative and contributed nothing to the "work in progress." It simply dealt with the dramatization of a *persona* that had exploited eros and finished on the side of the pathetic, leaving behind no moral substance except for the last flurry of pride. He belittled Cleopatra and denounced everything, as Plutarch informs us, except his lust of power. His last act was to admit proudly that he suffered defeat as a Roman overcome by a Roman.

In 1910, with the scattering of the last clouds of Symbolism, the weight shifted from historical reportage and suggestiveness to the concreteness of affections.[30] Cavafy was now free to recast the *persona* of Antony and bring him before the tribunal of eros to face the test of wisdom. What matters now is not whether the Roman Bacchus failed, for that he did, but whether he was denied the opportunity to choose the fitting end.

Antony as a *dramatis persona* in "The God Abandons Antony," though not so much in "The End of Antony," presents a serious difficulty to interpretation: the *persona* in each of these two poems is not identically related to *personae* in other poems on comparable themes, and hence disturbs

---

[30]Ilinskaya 1983, refers to Cavafy's method of expressing his views on life through incidents from history, rather than abstract symbols or aphorisms, and points out that the technique is creatively used in poems written in the first decade of the century: "Orophernes" (1904/*1916*), "Demaratos" (1904/*1911; 1921*), "Manouel Komninos" (1905/*1916*), "Philhellene" (1906/*1912*), and "The Displeasure of Selefkidis" (1910/*1916*). These poems viewed as evidence that Cavafy started working with realist motifs prior to 1911, and that he began leaving behind the symbolist camp earlier than 1910. She concludes that "His [Cavafy's] theory of life is shown here ["Ithaka"] more developed" than in "The God Abandons Antony." The attendant thesis that the latter poem reflects a kind of *finale* that emerges from "Ithaka," is too strong to elicit conviction. The view I have tried to defend is that "Ithaka" contains dominant symbolist features hindering the emergence of its special message.

the continuity of Cavafy's "work in progress."³¹ To begin with, "The God Abandons Antony" stands in sharp contrast to the theme of "The Satrapy." Unlike the affinity between the "inseparable diptych" of "The City" and "The Satrapy," as Savidis calls the thematic continuity of the two poems, there is something of a chasm, or perhaps a carefully designed distance, between "The City" and "Ithaka." In the case of the former two, the affinity is clear: the exit, were it to become available and the wished for escape successful, the road would take the fugitive to Susa, not to Ithaka. The disillusioned poets-citizens, as self-exiles, end in someone's court, say that of Artaxerxes, as gilded prisoners. The intertwining of the two motifs could still cover the case "The End of Antony," so close to the date of composition of "The Satrapy" (July 1905), but its theme was too narrow to address the full spectrum of hedonic action that "Ithaka" announced in 1910. As such the motif was foreign to "The God Abandons Antony," which requires "Ithaka" as its prelude.

"The Satrapy," outlining as it does a remarkable a case of a wrong-headed journey gone sour, should not be read as a bitter counter-statement to "Ithaka."³² It is a "failure" poem, not an *exit* poem, in which the *persona*, here as a citizen, embarks on a solution that ends on a note of moral demise. The city to which the *persona* goes is not an Alexandria. Hence this voyage is not about an Ithaka but about a place that provides refuge to an unfulfilled self, one that has divested itself of its political identity. If so, "The Satrapy" and "Ithaka" stand for radically dissimilar voyages.

In his own way, Antony never left his Rome, even after the Actium debacle, when he found himself a refugee in Alexandria. He never became an Alexandrian. Instead, he stood his ground as a leader in the hope of initiating action to regain the empire. Nor did he intend to live securely in the

---

³¹Yourcenar 1958: 100, has argued that there is a contradiction in the two Cavafian poems: "The End of Antony" (1907 U) and "The God Abandons Antony" (1910), since in the former poem Antony, led by the ideal of Roman virtue, feels pangs of conscience for having yielded to the temptations and fascination of Alexandria, whereas the same traits are not present, or rather not conspicuous, in the latter poem. I fail to see why Yourcenar must insist that an inconsistency obtains between the two poems. The inconsistency arises only when the message of "Ithaka" is forced to pertain to both "Antony" poems.

³²Written in 1905 and published in *Nea Zoe* (May-June 1910 issue), it was included in the thematic *Collection*, and printed next to "The City."

city that gave him exquisite hedonic experiences. He continued to view Alexandria as a foothold from which to recapture Rome herself. He miscalculated the potency of the role of Alexandria in the scheme of his ambitions. The *persona* in "The Satrapy" had no imperium of his own, only a bruised *thymos*. The difference between Athens and Susa, on the one hand, and Rome and Alexandria, on the other, lies less in the origin than in the terminus of the two voyages, one Greek and the other Roman. Alexandria, the poet tells us, is worth the price, Susa is not.

"The God Abandons Antony" was Cavafy's first dramatic application of the spirit of "Ithaka," the new canon for adventure, but with a difference brought out by the ultimate decision of the *persona*. The end of the journey was prepared through the twists of *Fortuna*, leaving open to suspicion that the last word belongs to *pathos*. Antony was urged to be brave in a novel way, quite foreign to the Roman nobleman and soldier. He was asked to produce credentials he did not have but had boastfully claimed all along. The New Bacchus lacked the requisite wisdom to hear the message of the exquisite music of the passing troupe of his ancestor. If we believe Plutarch, Antony was not, nor did he become, one of the brave men of pleasure. He died captive of the ethos of power. "The End of Antony" underscored the obvious and the pedestrian: the return of Antony's soul to Rome. The poet knows when he fails. The poem was not published.

6. The Poetic Side of Hedonism

Cavafy delineated an attractive motif for poetry: the voyage without a *nostos*. It owes its appeal to its power to symbolize whatever idea the poet selected to introduce as a theme through the device of the inversion of the classical mode of limit and destination. Yet, it would seem that sailing on a course that defies finiteness can only mean, to someone who is attached to the classical tradition, that the unintelligible is suddenly raised to the level of an ultimate principle. Cavafy understood the implications of such a thesis and found it useful, if not compelling, to follow them. He thought so, at least for a while and with reservations, particularly when the emotional stress during his own crisis kept him close to the Symbolists. However, none of his poems shows signs that he ever succumbed to the lure of the alleged artistic mission to capture and express the infinite. To say that his "Ithaka" prescribes invisible boundaries around the concept of the open-ended voyage has the ring of a paradox. But closer inspection of the poetic mixture of determinate limit and continuous process may lead us to think otherwise. Actually there is no flaw to be found in the projected constructs of his poetic technique. The voyage may be continuous, but it need not be interminable; and its purposiveness, while appearing opaque under the layers of strong emotional urges at the start, gains in clarity and definiteness as it gets closer to the end. Thus, what was initially restrictive, yet attractive enough to serve as a motive, the unfolding of the voyage was gradually replaced with a broader and higher objective. In due course, and after a wider span of hedonic encounters, along with deeper insights of our human potential, the storehouse of experience eventually turns itself into a kind of wisdom. The inversion of the classical mode as a poetic device was not a source of substance but of style, a means to serve poetry by addressing the conditions of the cultural mood of the contemporary and without losing sight of the valuable record of the past. Therefore, critics who appeal to Cavafy's use of irony and inversion to conclude that a pervasive skepticism prevails in his poetry overextend the limited application of the device.

After the formulation of the new Ithaka, Cavafy went on with his creative explorations of the psyche and the imaginative excursions into the Hellenistic and modern cosmopolis. He did not accept the death verdict others had pronounced on the classical mode and the Hellenic spirit, any more than he ever questioned the truth of the hedonic vision of life. He made the most of a confused situation. And while he salvaged what he could from the classical heritage by treating it thematically, either in the direct or the inverted mode, he also sought to expose the contemporary distortions of eros and the subterfuges they forced upon the unprepared voyager. Something of Cavafy's greatness is contained in the symbolic surface of his "Ithaka," whether it is viewed as an index to a program, style, viewpoint, or cultural messages. Its theme still touches the reader's curiosity when one's way of life no longer inspires confidence in its pretensions to stability and enduring pleasures.

"Ithaka," despite its ambiguities and flaws, remains a poem that holds one of the keys to understanding the restless *persona* of our times. Its appeal will continue so long as the conditions that breed disbelief in the resurrection of the *polis* persist. Whether the *polis* can return or a civic arrangement comparable to it can be effected in the future, does not detract from the value of the poet's disclosure. Cavafy courageously addressed a period of human history that found itself wallowing in the vortex of its own restlessness and opting for a voyage of unending gratifications. He deserves special recognition for seeing how non-hedonic these utopian odysseys become at the end, mainly because the voyagers fail to see that the snares of self-alienation make every departure a false beginning.

Cavafy's "Ithaka" speaks for a journey radically different from the type that Nietzsche and Kazantzakis recommended. It is also totally unlike the journey of the poet in the world of Baudelaire, where we witness a descent into vileness, from the vanishing point of spiritual ambition to the litany to Satan and away from all illumination. Furthermore, it is unlike the radiance that comes with the quest of St. John's of the Cross that calls for going into the Dark Night of the Soul.[33] Cavafy's "everyman's "Odysseus needs to acquire a different set of virtues to be able to attend to tasks so unlike the undertakings of the amoral athletes who move beyond good and evil, or others who try to negate every relation to either good or evil, though not both.

Somewhere in the distant background of the speaking *persona* in "Ithaka" one can hear the echo of Epicurus' ancient wisdom, advising what to fear, what not to fear, and how to select intelligently from the vast array of possible pleasures. Nothing in the poem is said about the gods, though one suspects they are still there, still loving the land of Ionia. The expected wisdom confirms no preset teleology, discernible at the starting point, other than the unrequited desire to embark on a homespun idea of a voyage. When the poem ends, the reader comes to realize that the idea of the imperturbable and venerable life in an Epicurean Garden is but a state of painless innocence. It would be vain to expect it to be found in the shops of any of the trading posts and the sunlit harbors. A subtly modified epicurean message had imperceptibly defined Cavafy's mature outlook.

Neither nature nor community can assign to Ithaka a perennial meaning. What nature and the cosmopolis do not make available, we, the voyagers, must discover by trusting the yearning for the journey. The only choice we have is to ignore the suspicion that the world is but the playground where we enact the *nostos* we must invent, with or without the prospect of reunion with the faithful Penelope we imagine weaving patiently at the loom of duty. As the poem ends, we are not surprised at her absence.

---

[33] See also Zweig 1968: 229, with reference to Baudelaire.

The magic of the "work in progress" has done its part. The voyager is confident, clear-headed, if not already somewhat wise, and ready to proceed with the testing of the enduring quality of a new form of courage, still a cardinal *excellence*. He may be called a contemporary Epicurean disinclined to slaughter the helpless phantoms that wiggle in the cobwebs of salvational missions and romantic infinities, or cavort in the game of power seeking. To be sure, Cavafy was not the only one with a deep sense of disillusionment over the political pretensions of his time. Many a poet and philosopher throughout the centuries had withdrawn from the messy affairs of the *vita activa*. Being an ardent student of history, he knew well how the abuse of political power, once it gets out of hand, shatters the remains of virtue in both leaders and followers. Sometimes Ithaka can do no more than preserve one's sanity by encouraging the indulgence of the interminable as an antidote to the dark passage of hopelessness.

Cavafy founded no Garden. He withdrew to his flat on Lepsius Street, near the buzzing port of Alexandria. And though he had friends and followers, also a growing circle of admirers as he advanced in age, he lived the rest of his life stationed at a slight angle to the universe, as Forster said.

The Epicureans of ancient times, the philosophical spokesmen for the hedonic side of life in the Hellenistic cosmopolis, had found their way to the pleasure of imperturbability. Some twenty-three centuries later, Cavafy sought to restate their hedonism for his own age, perchance for all ages, as a poet, refining the pursuit of pleasure not as aesthetic withdrawal but as reflective acceptance of the desires. He saw the poetic side of hedonism as a reasonable, if not the only, alternative to the despairing lust with which the *alienated* individual snatches crumbs of pleasure from stale loaves of ideals. Where Epicurus could claim that the nature of things provided a solid foundation for hedonism, Cavafy, the modern western gentleman of Alexandria, had found nothing comparable to which he could turn for support. Science had already so dehumanized nature that it could no longer be viewed as the ground for what is good, and beautiful, and pleasant, in the political and aesthetic visions. Scientific explanations and ethical aspirations had parted company. Once nature, and all things in it, had become neutral facts, the inscrutable ways of culture, bent on working furiously with a sense of vengeance, never fail to transform transparent values into mysterious subjective entities.

Science, once dehumanized, and politics, once debased, combine to make Ithaka unavailable to humanity. Working alone against this trend, our modern Alexandrian poet, talking in strange ways, re-introduced Ithaka with a calmness only the wisdom of affective experience knows how to articulate through the power of art. The arrow of the exquisite thought and emotion points to a road away from the enclosures of the cosmopolis and towards the openness of the teaming harbor by the sea. Should the voyager be ready, intelligence may steer a course towards a life in a *polis* where the pleasure of ideas and the ideas of pleasure converge. This, one suspects, was the hedonism Cavafy sought to champion within the brief span of his "work in progress," the one-hundred-fifty-four poems of the canon.

Appendix

Constantine P. Cavafy: Ars Poetica[1]

First Part

After the already settled Emendatory Work, a philosophical scrutiny of my poems should be made.

Flagrant inconsistencies, illogical possibilities, ridiculous exaggeration should certainly be corrected in the poems, and where the corrections cannot be made the poems should be sacrificed, retaining only any verses of such sacrificed poems as might prove useful later on in the making of new work.

Still the spirit in which the Scrutiny is to be conducted should not be too fanatical.

The profit of personal experience is undoubtedly a sound one; but were it strictly observed it would limit tremendously literary production and even philosophical production. If one ought to wait for old age to risk a word about it, if one ought to wait for the experience of a violent disease in order to mention it, if one ought to experience every sorrow or perturbed state of mind in order to speak of it—one would find that what is left to write of is very little, and indeed many things might not be written at all obviously, as the person who experienced them might not be the person talented to analyse and express them.

Guess work, therefore, is not to be avoided by any means in a wholesale manner; but of course it must be used cautiously. Guess work indeed—when intelligently directed—loses much of its riskiness, if the user transforms it into a sort of hypothetical experience. This is easier in [the] description of a battle, of a state of society, of a scenery. By the imagination

---

[1] First publication C. P. Cavafy, [*Unpublished Prose Texts*, M. Peridis ed.] 1963; the title was supplied by the editor. See also Decavalles 1968: 69-80, for the English text, introduction and notes. Decavalles notes that this title was quite justified, and that "the few pages we are in possession of give us a most revealing insight into the theoretical background, the poetics that stood behind and shaped Cavafy's poetry as we know it" (69).

(and by the help of incidents experienced and remotely or nearly connected) the user can transport himself into the midst of the circumstances and can thus create an experience. The same remark holds good—though it presents more difficulty—in matters of feeling.

I should remark that all philosophers necessarily work largely on guess work—guess work illustrated and elaborated by careful thought and weighing of causes and effects, and by inference. I mean knowledge of other reliable experience.

Moreover, the poet in writing of states of mind can also have the sort of experience furnished by his knowledge of himself and has, therefore, very reliable gauging of what he would feel were he placed in the imagined conditions.

Also care should be taken not to lose from sight that a state of feeling is true and false, possible and impossible at the same time or rather by turns. And the poet—who, even when he works the most philosophically, remains an artist—gives one side: which does not mean that he denies the obverse, or even—though perhaps this is stretching the point—that he wishes to imply that the side he treats is the truest, or the one oftener true. He merely describes a possible and occurring state of feeling—sometimes very transient, sometimes of some duration.

Very often the poet's work has but a vague meaning; it is a suggestion: the thoughts are to be enlarged by future generations or by his immediate readers: Plato said the poets utter great meanings without realising them themselves.

I have said above that the poet always remains an artist. As an artist he should avoid—without denying—the seemingly highest—seemingly, for it is not quite proved that it is the highest—philosophy of the absolute worthlessness of effort and of the inherent contradiction in every human utterance. If he deny it: he must work. If he accept it: he must work still, though with the consciousness of his work being but finally toys—at best, toys capable of being utilised for some worthier or better purpose, or the very handling of which prepares for some worthier or better work.

Moreover, let us consider the vanity of human things, for this is a clearer way of expressing what I have called "the worthlessness of effort and the inherent contradiction in every human utterance." For few natures, for very few, is it possible-after accepting it—to act accordingly, that is refrain from every action except such as subsistence demands. The majority must act; and though producing vain things, their impulse to act and their obedience to it are not vain, because it is a following of nature, or of *their* nature. Their actions produce works, which can be divided into two categories, works of immediate utility and works of beauty. The poet does the latter. As human nature has got a craving of beauty manifested in different forms—love, order in his surroundings, scenery—he purveys to a need. Some work done in vain and the shortness of human life may declare all this vain; but seeing that we do not know the connection between the after-life and this life, perhaps even this may be contested. But the mistake lies chiefly in this individualization. The work is not vain when we leave the individual and we consider the man. Here there is no death, at least no sure death: the result may perhaps be immense; there is no shortness of life, but an immense duration of it. So the absolute vanity disappears: at best only a comparative vanity may remain for the individual, but when the individual separates himself from his work and considers only the pleasure or the profit it has given him for a few years and then its vast importance for centuries and centuries even this comparative vanity disappears or vastly lessens.

My method of procedure for this Philosophical Scrutiny may be either by taking up the poems one by one and settling them at once—following the lists and ticking each on the list as it is finished, or effacing it if vowed to destruction; or be considering them first attentively, reporting on them, making a batch of the reports, and afterwards working at them on the basis and in the sequence of the batch: that is the method of procedure of the Emendatory Work.

It may also very well happen that the guess work or rather the intellectual insight into the feelings of others may result in the delineating of more interesting intellectual facts or conditions, than the mere relation of the personal experience of one individual. Moreover—though this is a delicate matter—is not such study of others and penetration of others part of what I call "personal experience"? Does not this penetration—successful or not—influence the individual thought and create states of mind?

Besides, one lives, one hears, and one understands; and the poems one writes, though not true to one's actual life, are true to other lives. ("Τὸ πρῶτο φῶς των" ["Their First Light"], "Τείχη" ["Walls"], "Παράθυρα" ["Windows"], "Θερμοπύλαι" ["Thermopylae"])—not generally of course, but specially—and the reader to whose life the poem fits admits and feels the poem: which is proved by Xenopoulos' liking ("Τείχη" ["Walls"], "Κεριά" ["Candles"]) and

Pap[antoniou]'s ("Κεριά" ["Candles"]) and Tsocopoulos' ("Φωναὶ Γλυκεῖαι") ["Sweet Voices"]. And when one lives, hears and searches intelligently and tries to write wisely, his work is bound, one may say, to fit some life.

Perhaps Shakespeare had never been jealous in his life, so he ought not to have written *Othello*; perhaps he was never seriously melancholy, so he ought not to have written *Hamlet*; he never murdered, so he ought not have written *Macbeth*!!!

On Sunday, (16 August 1903) I wrote some lines beginning "Σὰν ἔρχεται καμμιὰ ἡμέρα ἢ μιὰ ὥρα" [When a certain day comes or a certain hour]. I was absolutely sincere at the time. In fact the lines as they now stand are not good, because they have not been worked: it was throwing on paper an impression. In the evening of the very same day I was ill, and the lines seemed to me flat. Yet they *were* sincere: they had the necessary truthfulness for art. So is every sincerity to be laid aside, on account of the short duration of the feeling which prompts its expression. But then art is at a standstill; and speech is condemned—because what is always lasting? And things cannot and should not be lasting, for man would then be "all of a piece" and stagnate in sentimental activity, in want of change.

If a thought has been really true for a day, its becoming false the next day does not deprive it of its claim to verity. It may have been only a passing or a short-lived truth, but if intense and serious it is worthy to be received, both artistically and philosophically.

25 November 1903

Here is another example. No poems were sincerer than the "2Ms," written during and immediately after the great crisis of liberation[2] succeeding on my departure from Athens.[3] Now, say that in time Ale. Mav. comes to

---

[2] The Peridis rendition of the shorthand version "gr. cr. of lib" is "great crapulence of libations." I have adopted the Savidis reading "great crisis of liberation," which I believe reflects more faithfully the intent of the expression. See Savidis 1966: 144, n.110.

[3] The meaning of the shorthand expression "2Ms" has been variously interpreted. According to Peridis ("Introduction" 21-22) it stands for two poems written in 1901, whereas Savidis 1966: 144, n104, commenting on this passage, offers the reading "two M[onth]s." Decavalles 1968: 79, n7, supports the view that "2M"s means "two Μέρες" (Days), in which case the reference must be to poems where "Days" is part of the title.

be indifferent to me, like Sul. (I was very much in love with h[im]. before my departure for Athens), or Bra.; will the poems—so true when they were made—become false? Certainly, certainly not. They will remain true in the past, and, though not applicable any more in my life, seeing that they may remind of a day and perhaps different impression, they will be applicable to feelings of other lives.

The same, therefore, must apply to other works—really felt at the time. If even for one day, or one hour I felt like the man within "Walls," or like the man of "Windows" the poem is based on a truth, a short-lived truth, but which, for the very reason of its having once existed, may repeat itself in another life, perhaps with as short duration, perhaps with longer. If "Thermopylae" fits but one life, it is true; and it may, indeed the probabilities are that it must.

Second Part

Verses reported on:[4]

Ἔτσι τελειώνει ἡ ὑψηλὴ προσπάθεια [Thus the high endeavor ends].[5]

Ἔτσι πληρώνεται ἡ μεγάλη προσπάθεια [Thus the great endeavor is rewarded]

My only doubt is whether I have not qualified too much; and yet one might say the statement "ἔτσι τελειώνει ἡ ὑψηλὴ προσπάθεια" [Thus the high endeavor ends] is not exaggerated. The poem deals mainly with the domain *of theory translated into action*. If a great artist or philosopher is not brought to quite the same sacrifice, it may be said, however, that he also undergoes sacrifice in another way by his never being appreciated as is his eed during his lifetime, by even after his death a great part of his struggles and his toil being underrated or ignored, and by his making discoveries and

---

[4]The verses refer to the July 1894 unpublished poem, "The Pawn," clearly a "penumbra" poem; see chapter 5, section 5. A translation of this poem is given at the end of the Appendix.

[5]A close expression was presumably used in a line of the older version of the poem "The Pawn"; see Cavafy (UP) 1968: 221-222.

laying foundations which, necessarily imperfect in his case, do not and cannot perhaps bring him honour or profit, but being perfected and brought to fruition by others bring those others—whose "προσπάθεια" [endeavor] has been but small—honour and profit. But, again the poem deals *with theory translated into action*. It deals with the pioneer, with the act, with the man—like in "Thermopylae"—of abnegation. An objection might be the way in which the word "ὑψηλὴ" [high] seems to specify the superiority of this "προσπάθεια" [endeavor] which deals, as I have stated, with practical effort; but is not this being too minute? And am I not contradicting myself now? Seeing that I have stated that the theoretical life, the life of the artist and the philosopher, have also their sacrifice, bitter and unjust.

And also what if the translation into action is to be paid for in this way? Its results are good. And the glory and the merit remain to the theorist, that is he who mastered out and who planned and thought out the salutary system, the ideal demeanour, which works for good even though in its carrying it out it demands sacrifices (fruitful in final consequence and happy) in the actor; it demands to be applied by a hero.

Without the teaching, the sacrifice (from which so much good will result, so much happiness) would never take place; the hero, brave but unable to think, would be useless, no asset of profit to the world.

And is not the pawn's fate, and the sense of the two last verses, merely symbolical of the *pain exacted from every great effort for its lofty aims—sometimes in one form, sometimes in another*: sometimes greater, sometimes less: but always to be paid: in sufferings, in humiliations, in surrender.

"Πάει καὶ θυσιάζεται" [goes to its sacrifice] I say "Θυσίαις" ["Sacrifices"] are of different varieties.[6]

And then the "pawn" applies the thought and does the player's action, because he can. He *is* the "pawn." He is fit. The theorist is fit for other

---

[6]The expression was crossed out and replaced with another at a later date. Peridis believes that Second Part is older than Part One (17). An exact date of the writing of Part Two cannot be fixed. The last sentence of the Second Part makes it clear that Cavafy intended to revise the poem "when The Scrutiny is taken up." Since the First Part clearly refers to "a philosophical scrutiny of my poems," the revision of "The Pawn" presumably took place after the formulation of the procedure. If so, the writing of the two parts of the *Ars Poetica* may not have been so far apart in time. Probably the revision of "The Pawn" took place sometime around 1903 and definitely before 1911.

work. He pays his pain in other fashions. He is no "pawn"; he acts as he can and as he must.

The theorist is of course the great benefactor. The millions that will be saved by the retreat of the "queen" owe their happiness to them. To the hero thanks are due too; he by his sacrifice realises or rather hastens the good planned. But even without him the good planned would have been realised. Only it would take a longer time, it would have to traverse paths toilsome and troublesome. His sacrifice is honourable to him in the first degree; it is profitable to the community; but the theorist is a great and honourable benefactor still.

In fact, the theorist is rather not considered in this poem. We are praising the heroic action which carries theory into effect. Great or different, the theorist is to be considered apart.

Great were the legislators of Sparta who made out the System out of which Leonidas's sacrifice came.

/O/ But what about great theory translated into action and bringing regard, that is, the complete happiness and success to which a human being can aspire. The leaders of the American and the Greek rebellions, Pasteur, Garibaldi, and a few other instances.[7]

All the objections former to that /O/ marked are I find groundless.

/O/ is the only logical one.

It may not be unsurmountable but as I had to pass to other work, and had already spent almost a month on considering the poem, I decided to leave out the puzzling two lines and to insert in their place the line

ἔτσι ἡ ὡραία προσπάθεια τὸ ἀπαιτοῦσε
[The beautiful endeavor demanded it thus]

and to "renvoyer" the whole thing for consideration when the "The Scrutiny" is taken up.

---

[7]The next two repetitions of the mark /O/ refer are used as shorthand notation to refer to the same idea.

THE PAWN[8]

Often watching players at a game of chess
my eye follows a pawn
as it moves slowly finding its way
and arrives on the last line.
It goes to the end with such eagerness
that makes you think that surely here is where
its enjoyments and rewards begin.
It encounter many hardships on the way.
Pedestrians throwing spears aslant;
castles attacking it with their broad
lines; in the squares the swift knights
seeking with trickery to make it immobile;
and here and there using angular threat
a pawn sent from the enemy's camp
blocks its advance.

Yet it is saved from all the dangers
and reaches the last line.

How triumphantly it arrives here,
on the terrible line, the last one;
how readily it touches it own death!

For it is here the Pawn will die,
and all its travails were only for this,
for the Queen, who will our savior be;
to resurrect her from the grave
it descended to the Hades of the chess.

---

[8]Text in Cavafy UP 1968: 63-64; on the extant MS the poet wrote: "It may stay here."

BIBLIOGRAPHY

I. *TEXTS AND TRANSLATIONS*

For the most frequently cited works one or two capital letters are used to indicate abbreviations inside brackets at the end of each bibliographical item, followed by the page number.

1. Poetry

Cavafy, C. P. 1963. *Ποιήματα* [Poems]. Ed. George Savidis. 2 vols. Athens: Ikaros. [A], [B].

———. 1968. *'Ανέκδοτα Ποιήματα 1882-1923* [Unpublished Poems]. Ed. George Savidis. Athens: Ikaros. [U]

———. 1983. *Τὰ 'Αποκηρυγμένα ποιήματα καὶ μεταφράσεις* [The Condemned: Poems and Translations]. Ed. with notes, G. P. Savidis. Athens: Ikaros. [C]

2. Prose

———. 1942. *Καβαφικὰ αὐτοσχόλια* [Cavafian Self-comments]. Ed. G. Lechonitis with introduction by T. Malanos. Alexandria. 2nd ed., Athens: D. Harvey and Co. (Probably composed around 1930).

———. 1948. *Ἡ Γενεαλογία μου.* [My Genealogy]. *Nea Estia* 43, no. 501 (May 15, 1948), 622-28. (First publication of the 1909 document). [G]

———. 1963. *'Ανέκδοτα πεζὰ κείμενα* [Unpublished Prose Texts]. Ed. M. Peridis. Athens: Fexis. [UPT]

———. 1963. *Πεζά* [Prose]. Ed. with notes, G. Papoutsakis. Athens:

Fexis.

———. 1963. Ἀνέκδοτος χρονολογικὸς πίνακας σύνθεσης ποιημάτων 1891-1925 [Unpublished Chronological Table of Composition of Poems 1891-1925]. Ed. with notes, by G. Savidis. *Epitheorisi Technis* 18, no. 108 (December 1963), 567-81. (Last date in the listing is 1926); reprinted in Savidis 1987, *Mikra Kavafika*, vol. 2, 49-85 (with additions). [UT]

———. [1918] 1963. Περὶ Ἐκκλησίας καὶ Θεάτρου [Church and Theater]. Ed. with introduction by G. Savidis. Athens. First publication in *Grammata* 4, no. 39 (Alexandria, January-July, 1918), 686-90.

———. 1963. Σχόλια στὸν Ράσκιν [Comments on Ruskin]. Ed. with notes, by Stratis Tsirkas. *Epitheorisi Technis* 18, no. 108 (December 1963), 582-611. (Written between September 23, 1893 and July 1896). [CR]

———. 1972. "Αἱ σκέψεις ἑνὸς γέροντος καλλιτέχνου" [The Thoughts of an Old Artist]. Presented by G. Savidis. *Tram--A Carrier*, no. 5 (Thessaloniki), 101-4. (Probably written sometime after 1894 and before 1906).

———. 1973. Τιγρανόκερτα [Tigranokerta]. Presented with notes, by G. Savidis. *Theatron* 6, no. 32 (March-April 1973), 10-12. (Unpublished blueprint for a poem, probably prepared in 1929).

———. 1974. Τὸ τέλος τοῦ Ὀδυσσέως [The End of Odysseus]. Ed., commentary and notes by G. Savidis. Ioannina: Dokimasia. Reprinted in G. Savidis, *Mikra Kavafika*, vol. 2, Athens: 1987, 169-81. (First publication of a prose piece written between 1894 and 1895).

———. 1977/8. "Ἡ συνάντησις τῶν φωνηέντων ἐν τῇ προσῳδίᾳ" ["The Meeting of Vowels in Prosody"]. Ed. with notes, by G. Kehaghioglou. *Hellenika* 30 (1977-1978), 353-82. (Written circa February-August 1902).

_____. 1979. *Ἐπιστολὲς στὸν Μάριο Βαϊάνο* [Letters to Marios Vayanos]. Ed., introduction, comments and notes, by E. N. Moschos. Athens: Estia. (Forty-three letters written between March 3, 1924 and March 17, 1931).

_____. 1979. "Ἀνέκδοτη εἰσήγηση γιὰ τὸν Βαλαωρίτη" [Unpublished essay on Valaoritis]. Ed., introduction and commentary by G. Savidis. *Nea Estia*, Special Valaoritis Issue, 106 no. 1259 (Christmas 1979), 215-6. (Probably written in 1924 or 1925).

_____. 1982. *Reading Notes on Gibbon's 'Decline and Fall'*. Ed. with notes, by Diana Haas. *Folia Neohellenika, Zietschrift fur Neograezistik*, Amsterdam 1982, 25-96. (The text of fifty-eight Cavafian "comments" written in English). [GB]

_____. 1980. *Τρεῖς ἐπιστολὲς τοῦ Καβάφη* [Three Letters of Cavafy]. Ed. P. Modinos. Athens: Greek Literary and Historical Archive. (Letters dated September 1, 15, 1920, and January 23, 1921).

_____. 1983. *Ἀνέκδοτα σημειώματα ποιητικῆς καὶ ἠθικῆς* [Unpublished Notes on Poetry and Ethics]. Ed. with notes, by G. P. Savidis. Athens: Ermis. [UN]

Kavafis, Costantino. 1979. Εἰς τὸ φῶς τῆς ἡμέρας [In the Light of Day]. Un racconto inedito a cura di Renata Lavagnini. Palermo: Universita di Palermo, Istituto di Filologia Greca (Quaderni-8). Pp. 59. A short story, written between 1895-1896.

3. English Translations of Poems

Cavafy, C. P. 1924. "Ithaca." Valassopoulo, G. trans. *The Criterion*, 2, No. 8 (1924), 431-32.

_____. 1952. *The Poems of C. P. Cavafy*. Mavrogordato, John, trans. Introd. Rex Warner. London: Chatto and Windus; New York: Grove Press, n.e. 1964.

_____. 1961. *The Complete Poems of Cavafy*. Ray Dalven, trans.; introd. W. H. Auden. New York: Harcourt, Brace and World, 1961; London: The Hogarth Press. Expanded edition: Harcourt, Brace and Jovanovich, 1976.

_____. 1967. *Fourteen Poems*. Chosen and Illustrated with twelve etchings by David Hockney. Stangos, N. and Stephen Spender, trans. London: Alecto Ltd.

_____. 1971. *Passions and Ancient Days*. Keeley, Edmund and Savidis, George, trans. New York: The Dial Press.

_____. 1992 [1975]. *Selected Poems*. Keeley, Edmund and Sherrard, Phillip, trans. Princeton: Princeton University Press. Revised edition.

_____. 1975. *Collected Poems*. Keeley, Edmund and Sherrard Phillip, trans. Savidis, George, ed. Princeton: Princeton University Press. Bilungual edition; pb. translation only.

Keeley Edward and Sherrard Phillip, trans. 1961. *Six Poets of Modern Greece*. London: Thames and Hudson, 1960; New York: A. A. Knopf.

Friar, Kimon. 1973. *Modern Greek Poetry: From Cavafis to Elytis*. New York: Simon and Schuster.

4. Literature on Translations

Friar, Kimon. 1978. "Cavafis and His Translators into English." *Journal of the Hellenic Diaspora*, V/1 (Spring 1978), 17-40.

Ioannidi, Helene. 1972. "Le travail du poète et le probléme de la traduction." *Critique* [Paris] 229 (Avril 1972), 354-68.

Keeley, Edmund. 1975. "Problems in Rendering Modern Greek." *Essays in Memory of Basil Laourdas*. Thessaloniki. Pp. 628-36.

Peri, Massimo. 1982. "Κριτικὴ ἐπισκόπηση τῶν καβαφικῶν μεταφράσεων" ["Critical Review of the Translations of Cavafy's Poems"]. *Mantatoforos* (in Greek), 18 (November 1981) and 19 (April 1982).

Raizis, M. Byron. 1977. "Cavafy and His English Translators." *Balkan Studies*, 18/1, 91-97.

II. GENERAL

1. Bibliographical Works

The names of Greek authors and titles of journals are transliterated, and same of authors and the titles of books and articles are listed in the original with the translation inside brackets [ ] in each case. Titles of books and journals in Greek are in italics; quotation marks are used to indicate titles of articles.

Daskalopoulos, D. 1983. "῾Η βιβλιογραφία Κ. Π. Καβάφη" ["Cavafian Bibliography"], Part I: Problems; Part II: Select Bibliographical List]. *Diabazo* [I Read], no. 78 (October 5), 141-64; esp. 149-64.

Haas, Diana and Michalis Pieris. 1984. *Βιβλιογραφικὸς ὁδηγὸς στὰ 154 ποιήματα τοῦ Καβάφη* [Bibliographical Guide to the 154 Poems of Cavafy]. Athens: Ermis. Pp. 305-46.

Katsimbalis, George. [1932] [1983]. "Σχεδίασμα καβαφικῆς βιβλιογραφίας" ["Draft for a Cavafian Bibliography"]. *Kyklos* 2/3-4 (November 1932), 134-39; repr. the Society for the Greek Literary and Historical Archives, Athens, 1983.

Journal of the Hellenic Diaspora, 10/1-2 (1983), 167-71.

2. Anthologies and Commemorative Issues of Journals.

Pieris, Michael, ed. 1985. *Εἰσαγωγὴ στὴν ποίηση τοῦ Καβάφη. Ἐκλογὴ ἄρθρων καὶ μελετημάτων* [*Introduction to the Poetry of Cavafy:*

Collection of Articles and Essays]. Rethymno: School of Philosophy, University of Crete.

ΕΠΙΘΕΩΡΗΣΗ ΤΕΧΝΗΣ [*Review of Art*] 18, No. 108 (December 1963).

ΕΥΘΥΝΗ [*Responsibility*]: Μέρες τοῦ ποιητῆ Κ. Π. Καβάφη. Πενήντα χρόνια ἀπὸ τὸν θάνατό του. [Days of the Poet C. P. Cavafy. Fifty Years After His Death]. *Tetradia Efthynis*, No. 19 (May 1983).

Journal of the Hellenic Diaspora, 10/1-2 (Spring-Summer 1983).

Η ΛΕΞΗ [*The Word*] No. 23 (March-April 1983).

ΚΡΙΤΙΚΑ ΦΥΛΛΑ [*Critical Pages*] 5 (1978).

ΚΥΚΛΟΣ ΚΑΒΑΦΗ [*Cavafy Circle*]. Issued by the Society for the Study of Modern Greek Culture and General Education. Foundation of the Moraitis School. Athens, 1983.

La semaine égyptienne. Numero special consacre au poète Alexadrin C. P. Cavafy. Avril, 1929.

Mind and Art: The Mind and Art of C. P. Cavafy. Essays on His Life and Work. Athens: Denise Harvey & Co., 1983.

ΝΕΑ ΕΣΤΙΑ [*Nea Estia*] 74, No 872 (November 1, 1963).

Ο ΚΥΚΛΟΣ [*The Circle*] 2/3-4 (1932).

ΟΡΙΖΟΝΤΕΣ [*Horizons*] 1/2 (April, May, June 1970).

ΠΑΝΑΙΓΥΠΤΙΑ [*Panegyptian*] 5, No. 223 (July 8, 1933).

ΠΡΑΚΤΙΚΑ ΤΡΙΤΟΥ ΣΥΜΠΟΣΙΟΥ ΠΟΙΗΣΗΣ: ΑΦΙΕΡΩΜΑ ΣΤΟΝ ΚΑΒΑΦΗ. [*Proceedings of the Third Symposium on Poetry: Dedicated to C. P. Cavafy*]. University of Patras, July 1-3, 1983. Athens: Gnosi Publications, 1984.

ΧΑΡΤΗΣ [Chart] Nos. 5-6 (April 1983).

3. Books and Articles.

Agras, Tellos. 1980. *Κριτικά* [Critical Essays]. Vol. 1: Cavafy-Palamas. Athens: Ermis. Repr. of the following articles previously printed in various journals: "'Η Ειρωνία τοῦ Καβάφη" ["The Irony of Cavafy", *Alexandrini Techni* (September-October 1930), 281-88, also in *Nea Estia* (November 1, 1933), 1397-1402]; "Καλοὶ κι' Ἀγαπητοί" ["Good and Beloved", *Kyklos* 2/3-4 (November 1932), 127-33]; "Καβάφης" ["Cavafy"], *Megali Elliniki Enkyklopaideia*, v. 13, p. 435].

Alexiou. Margaret. 1983. "Eroticism and Poetry." *Journal of the Hellenic Diaspora*, X/1-2, 45-65.

Alissandratos, G. G. 1982. "Οἱ 'Θερμοπύλες' τοῦ Καβάφη" ["Cavafy's 'Thermopylae'"]. *Parnassos*, 28, 509-36.

Anagnostakis, M. 1963. "Συζητῶντας γιὰ τὸν Καβάφη" ["Discussing Cavafy"]. *Epitheorisi Technis* (December), 670-71.

Anton, John P. 1973. "Γύρω ἀπὸ τὴ συνάντηση Καβάφη Καζαντζάκη" ["The Meeting of Cavafy and Kazantzakis"]. *Neo-Hellenic Logos*, 5-15.

_____. 1977a. "'Ο Βάρναλης καὶ ὁ ἱστορισμὸς τοῦ Καβάφη" ["Varnalis and Cavafy's Historicism"]. *Neo-Hellenic Logos*, 25, 13-25.

_____. 1977b. "Alexandria: The History and Legend of a City." *Conspectus of History*, Annual Publication of the Department of History, Ball State University, IV, No. 1, pp. 13-33.

_____. 1978. "C. P. Cavafy's *Ars Poetica*." *Philosophy and Literature*, 2/1, 85-109.

_____. 1987. "'Ο αἰσθητικὸς-κριτικὸς Παπανοῦτσος καὶ ἡ ποίηση τοῦ Κ. Π. Καβάφη" ["The Aesthetician-Critic Papanoutsos and the Poetry of

C. P. Cavafy"]. *Proceedings of the Symposium on E. P. Papanoutsos, Educator and Philosopher.* University of Ioannina, pp. 141-49; reprinted in *Nea Estia*, 121 (March 15, 1987), 366-72.

_____. 1993. "Γλώσσα καὶ Ἑλληνικὸς πολιτισμὸς στὴν ποίηση τοῦ Καβάφη" ["Language and Hellenic Culture in Cavafy's Poetry"], *Nea Estia*, 134 (July 15, 1993), 905-914.

Barnstone, Willis. 1977. "Real and Imaginary History in Borges and Cavafy." *Comparative Literature*, 19, 54-73.

Baudelaire, Ch. [n.d]. *Les Fleurs du mal.* Texte présenté par René-Louis Doyon. Paris: R. Rasmussen.

Beaton, Roderick. 1981. "C. P. Cavafy: Irony and Hellenism." *The Slavonic and Eastern European Review*, 59/4, 516-28.

_____. 1983. "The Historic Man." *Journal of the Hellenic Diaspora*, X/1-2, 23-44.

Beebe, Maurice. 1964. *Ivory Towers and Sacred Founts: The Artist as Hero from Goethe to Joyce.* New York: New York University Press.

Bertocci, Angelo Philip. 1964. *From Symbolism to Baudelaire.* Carbondale: Soutern Illinois University Press.

Bevan, Edwyn R. 1966. *The House of Seleucus.* New York: Barnes and Noble.

_____. 1968. *The House of Ptolemy: A History of Egypt under the Ptolemaic Dynasty.* Chicago: Argonaut.

Bien, Peter. 1964. *Constantine Cavafy.* New York: Columbia University Press.

_____. 1983. "Cavafy's Three-Phase Development into Detachment." *Journal of the Hellenic Diaspora*, X/1-2, 117-36.

Bowersock, G. W. 1977. "Gibbon and Julian." *Gibbon et Rome à la lumière de l' historiographie moderne*, Université de Lausanne, Publications de la Faculté des Lettres, XXII (Geneva).

_____. 1978. *Julian the Apostate*. Cambridge: Harvard University Press.

_____. 1981. "The Julian Poems of C. P. Cavafy." *Byzantine and Modern Greek Studies*, 7, 89-104.

_____. 1983. "Cavafy and Apollonius." *Grand Street*, 2/3 (Spring 1983), 180-89.

Bowra, C. M. [1943] 1961. *The Heritage of Symbolism*. [Reprinted from the 1943 edition.] New York: Schocken Books. (References to this paperback edition).

_____. 1949. *The Creative Experiment*. London: Macmillan. Ch. II: "Constantine Cavafy and the Greek Past," pp. 29-60.

Bradbury M. and D. Palmer, eds. 1979. *Decadence and the 1890s*. London.

Bregman, Jay. 1982. *Synesius of Cyrene: Bishop-Philosopher*. Berkeley and Los Angeles: University of California Press.

Brodsky, Joseph. 1977. "On Cavafy's Side," *New York Review of Books*, (February 17), 32-34.

Browning, Robert. 1976. *The Emperor Julian*. Berkeley: University of California Press.

Caires, Valerie C. 1980. "Originality and Eroticism: Constantine Cavafy and the Alexandrian Epigram." *Byzantine and Modern Greek Studies*, 6, 131-55.

Capri-Karka, Carmen. 1982. *Love and the Symbolic Journey in the Poetry of Cavafy, Eliot and Seferis*. New York: Pella Publishing Co.

Carter, A. E. 1958. *The Idea of Decadence in French Literature 1830-1900.* Toronto.

Castillo, D. Miguel. 1970. "Algunos Aspectos de la Poesia de Constantino Kavafis. *Byzantion-Nea Hellas*, (Santiago, University of Chile), 52-107.

Catraro, Atanazio. 1970. *Ὁ φίλος μου ὁ Καβάφης* [My Friend Cavafy]. Trans. into Greek by Aristea Rallis. Athens: Ikaros.

Catsaouni, Helen. 1983. "Cavafy and the Theatrical Representation of History." *Journal of the Hellenic Diaspora*, X/1-2, 105-116.

Christidis, B. Ph. 1958. *Ὁ Καβάφης καὶ τὸ Βυζάντιο* [Cavafy and Byzantium]. Athens: Biochart.

Clay, Diskin. 1977. "The Silence of Hermippos: Greece in the Poetry of Cavafy." *Byzantine and Modern Greek Studies*, 3, 95-116, reprinted 1983, *The Mind and Art of C. P. Cavafy*, pp. 157-81.

———. 1987. "The Poet in the Reader." *Journal of Modern Greek Studies* 5/1, 65-83.

Colaclidis, Petros. 1984. "Ἡ γλῶσσα τοῦ Καβάφη" ["Cavafy's Language"]. *Proceedings of the Third Poetry Symposium 1983*, 119-46.

Dallas, John. 1974. *Καβάφης καὶ ἱστορία* [Cavafy and History]. Athens: Ermis.

———. 1983. "Οἱ δύο ὄψεις τοῦ νομίσματος τοῦ Ὀροφέρνη" ["The Two Sides of the Orophernis Coin"]. *I Read*, No. 78, 104-13.

———. 1984. *Ὁ Καβάφης καὶ ἡ δεύτερη σοφιστική* [Cavafy and the Second Sophistic]. Athens: Stigmi.

———. 1986. *Ὁ Ἑλληνισμὸς καὶ ἡ θεολογία στὸν Καβάφη* [Hellenism and Theology in Cavafy]. Athens: Stigmi.

Daskalopoulos, D. 1988. *Κ. Π. Καβάφης: Σχέδια στὸ περιθώριο* [C. P. Cavafy: Drawings in the Margins]. Athens: Diatton.

Dalmati, Margarita. 1964. *Κ. Π. Καβάφης* [C. P. Cavafy]. Athens: Society of Hellenic Editions.

Decavalles, A. 1968. "The *Poetics* of Cavafy." *The Charioteer*, 10, 69-80. (Introduction to the reprint of the English text of Cavafy's *Ars Poetica*, pp. 72-79, and notes 79-80).

Delopoulos, K. 1972. *'Ιστορικὰ καὶ ἄλλα πρόσωπα στὴ ποίηση τοῦ Καβάφη* [Historical and Other Persons in Cavafy's Poetry]. A Bibliographical Guide. Athens.

Delopoulos, K. and Maria M. Kairis. 1983. *Καβάφη γεωγραφικά* [Geographical Names in Cavafy]. Athens: Greek Literary and Historical Archive.

Dimakis, Minas. 1963. "Γενικὸς καὶ ὁ ἀτομικὸς ἄνθρωπος στὴν ποίηση τοῦ Καβάφη" ["The Universal and the Individual Man in Cavafy's Poetry"]. *Nea Estia*, 74, No. 872, 1602-6.

Dimaras, K. Th. 1932. "Μερικὲς πηγὲς τῆς καβαφικῆς τέχνης" ["Certain Sources of Cavafy's Poetry"]. *The Circle*, 2/3-4, 69-86.

―――――. 1956. "'Η Τεχνικὴ τῆς ἔμπνευσης στὰ ποιήματα τοῦ Καβάφη" ["The Technique of Inspiration in the Poems of Cavafy"]. *Philologhiki Protochronia* 13, 97-102.

Dimiroulis, Dimitris. 1983. "Cavafy's Imminent Threat: Still 'Waiting for the Barbarians'." *Journal of the Hellenic Diaspora*, X/1-2, 89-103.

Dragona-Monachou, Myrto. 1964. "'Ο Σενέκας—Ἕνας φιλόσοφος κοσμοπολίτης γιὰ τὸ ταξίδι κ' ἡ 'Πόλη' τοῦ Καβάφη" ["Seneca—A Cosmopolitan Philosopher Speaks of the Voyage, and 'The City' of Cavafy]. *New Times*, (Spring-Summer), 138-43.

Durrell, Lawrence. 1956. "A Cavafy Find." *London Magazine*, 3/7, 11-14.
      1973. Review of *C. P. Cavafy: Selected Poems*. *The New York Times Book Review* (January 21), 2-3.

Eliot, T. S. 1923. "Ulysses, Order and Myth." *The Dial*, 75 (November 1923).

Fiedler, Theodore. 1973. "Brecht and Cavafy." *Comparative Literature*, 25, 240-46.

Flores, Angel. 1958. *An Anthology of French Poetry, from Nerval to Valery in English translation*. Ed. A. Flores. New York: Doubleday, Anchor.

Forster, E. M.[1] 1958. "C. P. Cavafy: 1863-1933." *Umbrella*, 1 (October), 5-7.

———. 1961. *Alexandria: A History and a Guide*. New York: Doubleday.

———. [1923] 1962. *Pharos and Pharillon*. New York: A. A. Knopf; the essay, "The Poetry of C. P. Cavafy," reprinted in *The Mind and Art of C. P. Cavafy* (1983), pp. 13-18.

———. 1965. *Two Cheers for Democracy*. London: Penguin Books. The essay, "The Complete Poems of C. P. Cavafy," repr. in 1983, *The Mind and Art of C. P. Cavafy*, pp. 40-45.

Fotiadis, Th. 1983. "'Αχαιοὶ καὶ Τρῶες στὸν Καβάφη" ["Achaeans and Trojans in Cavafy]. *Contemporary Times*, 3, 109-112.

Frangopoulos, Th. D. 1983. "Τὸ κεραμεοῦν" ["Of Common Clay"]. *Efthyni: Days of the Poet C. P.Cavafy*, No. 19, 253-63.

Fraser, M. P. 1963. "Cavafy and the Elgin Marbles." *Modern Language Review*, 58 (January), 66-68.

---

[1]Forster's letters to Cavafy, 1917, 1923, 1924, are quoted in Pinchin 1977.

Friar, Kimon. 1953. "One of the Great." *New Republic*, 128 (January 26), 19-20.

_____. 1973. *Modern Greek Poetry: From Cavafis to Elytis*. New York: Simon and Schuster.

Ganoulis, Elias 1975. *Κριτικὰ σημειώματα* [Critical Notes]. Athens.

Georgiou, M. 1963. "'Ο Καβάφης καὶ ἡ ἄρνηση: σταθμοὶ τῆς ἀντικαβαφικῆς κριτικῆς" ["Cavafy and Rejection: Stages of Anti-Cavafian Criticism"]. *Epitheorisi Technis* (December), 652-69.

Ghivalou-Katsini, Anastasia 1979. "Τὸ ἐπίθετο στὴν ποίηση τοῦ Κ. Π. Καβάφη" ["The Use of Adjectives in Cavafy's Poetry"]. *Nea Estia*, 106 (no. 1253), 1284-87, and (no. 1254), 1373-78.

Gibbon. Edward. 1925. *The History of the Decline and Fall of the Roman Empire*. 2 vols. London: J. M. Dent. Reprint.

Golffing, Francis. 1955. "The Alexandrian Mind: Notes Toward a Definition." *Partisan Review*, 22, 73-82; repr. in *The Mind and Art of C. P. Cavafy* (1983), pp. 115-26 (reference to this edition).

Gregory, Horace. 1953. "A Twentieth Century Alexandrian." *Poetry*, 81 (March), 383-88.

Haas, Diana. 1982. "Cavafy's Reading Notes on Gibbon's *Decline and Fall*." *Folia Neohellenika: Zeitschrift für Neogräzistik*, 4, 25-96.

_____. 1983a. "'Αἱ ἀρχαὶ τοῦ Χριστιανισμοῦ': ἕνα θεματικὸ κεφάλαιο στὸν Καβάφη" ["'The Beginnings of Christianity': A Thematic Chapter in Cavafy"]. ΧΑΡΤΗΣ, Nos 5-6, 589-608.

_____. 1983b. "Στὸν ἔνδοξό μας Βυζαντινισμό: σημειώσεις γιὰ ἕνα στίχο τοῦ Καβάφη" ["To our Glorious Byzantinism: Notes on a Cavafian Verse"]. *Proceedings of the Third Poetry Symposium*, pp. 183-95; repr. *I Read*, 78, 76-81.

———. 1984. "Early Cavafy and the European 'Esoteric' Movement." *Journal of Modern Greek Studies*, 2/2, 209-24.

Hadgifotis, I. M. 1973. *Ἡ Ἀλεξάνδρεια κι' ὁ Καβάφης* [Alexandria and Cavafy]. Athens: Editions Alkaios.

Hadginis, I. 1962. *Ἡ Ἀλεξάνδρεια τοῦ Καβάφη* [Cavafy's Alexandria]. 2nd ed. Athens: Estia.

Halvatzakis, M. 1967. *Ὁ Καβάφης στὴν ὑπαλληλικὴ ζωή* [Cavafy in Public Service]. Athens.

Haris, Petros. 1983. Ὁ ποιητὴς Κ. Π. Καβάφης [The Poet C. P. Cavafy]. *Proceedings of the Academy of Athens*, 58: 294-309.

Hitti, P. K. 1937. *A History of the Arabs*. London.

Holton, David. 1989. "Cavafy and the Art of Self-Deception." *Modern Greek Studies Yearbook*. Minneapolis: University of Minnesota, 5, 143-62.

Ilinskaya, Sonia. 1983. *Κ. Π. Καβάφης: οἱ δρόμοι πρὸς τὸ ρεαλισμὸ στὴν ποίηση τοῦ 20 αἰώνα* [C. P. Cavafy: The Road to Realism in Twentieth Century Poetry]. Athens: Kedros.

Jacobson, Roman and Peter Colaclides. 1966. "Grammatical Imagery in Cavafy's Poem *Thimisou soma . . .*". *Linguistics*, 20, 51-59.

Jusdanis, Gregory. 1987. *The Poetics of Cavafy*. Princeton: Princeton University Press.

Kapsalis, S. D. 1983. "'Privileged Moments': Cavafy's Autobiographical Inventions." *Journal of the Hellenic Diaspora*, X/1-2 (1983), 67-88.

Karakassis, Stavros. 1963. *Ο Καβάφης* [Cavafy]. Athens: Diphros.

Karavias, Panos. 1963. "Ὁ Καβάφης καὶ ὁ κρυφὸς σπαραγμός" ["Cavafy and the Hidden Despair"]. *Nea Estia* 74 (November), 1553-65.

Karayannis, V. 1983. *Σημειώσεις ἀπὸ τὴν γενεαλογία τοῦ Καβάφη* [Notes from the Genealogy of Cavafy]. Athens.

Katope, Christopher G. 1969. "Cavafy and Durrell's *The Alexandria Quartet*." *Comparative Literature*, XXI/2, 125-37.

Kazantzakis, N. 1965. *Ταξιδεύοντας Β* [Traveling B: Egypt]. 2nd edition. Athens, pp. 78-83.

Kazazis, J. N. 1976. "Studies in Kavafis: A Commentary on T. Malanos' Theory of Hellenistic Influences in the Poetry of Kavafis." *Hellenika*, 29/1, 132-54.

Keeley, Edmund. 1952. *Constantine Cavafy and George Seferis: and their Relation to English and American Poetry*. Unpublished doctoral dissertation. Oxford University.

_____. 1971. "'Latest Poems' Increase Cavafy's Appeal to Students." *University*, A Princeton Quarterly, (Spring).

_____. 1972. "The 'New' Poems of Cavafy." *Modern Greek Writers*. Eds. Edmund Keeley and Peter Bien. Princeton: Princeton University Press, pp. 123-43; repr. 1983 *The Mind and Art of C. P. Cavafy*, pp. 46-59.

_____. 1976. *Cavafy's Alexandria: A Study of a Myth in Progress*. Cambridge: Harvard University Press.

_____. 1983. "Cavafy's Voice and Context." *Grand Street*, 2/3, 157-77; repr. in Keeley, *Modern Greek Poetry: Voice and Myth*. Princeton: Princeton University Press. 1983, pp. 3-30.

Kitroeff, Alexander. 1983. "The Alexandria We Lost." *Journal of the Hellenic Diaspora*, X/1-2, 11-21.

Klingopoulos, G. D. 1983. "E. M. Forster's Sense of History: and Cavafy." *Essays in Criticism*, 8/2, 156-65.

Kokolis, X. A. 1976. *Πίνακας λέξεων των 154 ποιημάτων του Κ. Π. Καβάφη* [Table of Vocabulary in the 154 Poems of C. P. Cavafy]. Athens: Ekdotiki Ermis.

———. 1983. "Γλωσσική άσυμβατότητα, ποιητική τεχνική καὶ πολιτική έγρήγορση στὸ 'Πάρθεν'" ["Language Unconventionality, Poetic Technique and Political Awareness in the Poem 'Parthen'"]. *I Read*, Commemorative Issue, 61-73.

Komis, Andonis. 1935. *Κ. Π. Καβάφης* [C. P. Cavafy]. Corfu.

Korfis, Tasos. 1983. "Τρία σχόλια στὸν Καβάφη" ["Three Comments on Cavafy"]. *Contemporary Times*, 1/3 (January-February), 106-8.

Korsos, D. 1978. "Τὸ έλληνικὸ πρόσωπο τοῦ Καβάφη" ["The Hellenic Face of Cavafy"]. *Critical Pages*, Commemorative Issue, 67-93.

Lambropoulos, Vassilis. 1983. "The Violent Power of Knowledge: The Struggle of Critical Discourses for Domination Over Cavafy's 'Young Men of Sidon, A. D. 400'." *Journal of the Hellenic Diaspora*, X/1-2, 149-66.

Lardas, K. 1968. "Our Soul is Shaken, Paralyzed." *Ararat*, No. 34 (Summer), 24-33.

Lavagnini, Bruno. 1954. *Trittico Neogreco. Porfiras-Kavafis-Sikelianos*. Edizioni dello Istituto Italiano di Atene.

———. 1955. *Storia della letteratura neoellenica*. Milano.

Lavagnini, Renata. 1974. "Kavafis e Rodenbach." *Siculorum Gymnasium*, 27/2, 536-45.

———. 1975. "La poesia 'Nous n'osons plus chanter les roses' di K. Kavafis." *Folia Neohellenica*. Amsterdam, Band 1, 85-94.

———. 1981. "The Unpublished Drafts of Five Poems on Julian the

Apostate by C. P. Cavafy." *Byzantine and Modern Greek Studies*, 7, 55-88.

_____. 1983. "῎Ενα Διήγημα τοῦ Καβάφη: Εἰς τὸ φῶς." [A short-story by Cavafy: "In the Light"]. *To Dentro*, Nos 35-36 (May issue), 618-28.

Leontaris, Byron. 1983. *Καβάφης ὁ ἔγκλειστος· Δοκίμιο* [Cavafy the Imprisoned: Essay]. Athens: Erasmos Editions.

Liddell, Robert. 1945. "Cavafy." *Personal Landscape, An Anthology of Exile*. London: Editions Poetry London, pp. 100-10.

_____. 1948. "Studies in Genius: VII--Cavafy." *Horizon*, 18, No. 105, 187-202; reprinted 1983 *The Mind and Art of C. P. Cavafy*, pp. 19-32.

_____. 1974. *Cavafy: A Critical Biography*. London: Duckworth.

Lorentzatos, Z. 1977. *Μικρὰ ἀναλυτικὰ στὸν Καβάφη* [Minor Analytical Scholia on Cavafy]. Athens: Ikaros.

Magnes, Petros. 1963. "Τὸ ποιητικὸ ἔργο τοῦ Κ. Π. Καβάφη" ["The Poetry of C. P. Cavafy"]. *Epitheorisi Technis*, No. 108, 640-44; repr. from the 1912 edition, Cairo.

Malanos, Timos. 1943. *Ἡ μυθολογία τῆς καβαφικῆς πολιτείας* [The Mythology of the Cavafian City]. Alexandria.

_____. 1953. *Καβάφης-῎Ελιοτ: Εἶναι πράγματι παράλληλοι;* [Cavafy-Eliot: Are They Really Parallel?]. Alexandria.

_____. 1954. "῾Ο Καβάφης γιὰ τὸν Παλαμᾶ" ["Cavafy on Palamas"]. *Nea Estia* 55, 338.

_____. 1963. *Καβάφης 2—Φύλλα τετραδίου καὶ ἄλλα* [Cavafy 2: Pages from a Notebook and Other Notes]. Athens: Fexis.

_____. 1971. *Ἀναμνήσεις ἑνὸς Ἀλεξανδρινοῦ* [Recollections of an

Alexandrian]. Athens: Boukoumanis Editions.

———. 1978. *Καβάφης 3—Κριτικὰ διάφορα* [Cavafy 3: Sundry Critical Notes]. Athens: Editions Argo.

———. 1981. *Ὁ Καβάφης ἀπαραμόρφωτος* [The Undistorted Cavafy]. Athens: Prosperos.

———. 1986. *Ὁ Καβάφης ἔλεγε* [Cavafy Was Saying]. Athens: Prosperos.

Malevitsis, Ch. 1983. "'Η τραγικὴ σοφία τοῦ Καβάφη" ["The Tragic Wisdom of Cavafy"]. *Efthyni* Commemorative Issue, 19, 105-117.

Malkoff, K. 1987. "Varieties of Illusion in the Poetry of C. P. Cavafy." *Journal of Modern Greek Studies*, 5/2, 191-205.

Maronitis, D. N. 1972. "Arrogance and Intoxication: The Poet and History in Cavafy." *Eighteen Texts: Writings by Contemporary Greek Authors*. Ed. Willis Barnstone. Cambridge: Harvard University Press, pp. 117-34.

———. 1980. *Ὅροι τοῦ λυρισμοῦ στὸν Ὀδυσσέα Ἐλύτη* [Lyrical Boundaries in the Poetry of Odysseas Elytis]. Athens: Kedros; esp. "Poet and History: Cavafy's Realism and Elytis' Surrealism," pp. 155-60.

———. 1983a. "'Ο μεταφορικὸς Καβάφης" ["Cavafy and the Use of Metaphors"]. The Sunday *Vima* (October 2), 4.

———. 1983b. "Κ. Π. Καβάφης, ἕνας ποιητὴς ἀναγνώστης" ["Cavafy the Reader"]. *Cavafy Circle*, 55-79.

Melakopides, Constantine. 1983. "Cavafy: The Philosophical Poetry." *The Mind and Art of C. P. Cavafy*. Athens: Denise Harvey and Co., pp. 195-223.

Menas, K. 1985. *Ἡ γλῶσσα τοῦ Καβάφη* [The Language of Cavafy]. Ioannina: The University, School of Philosophy.

Merrill, James. 1975. "Marvellous Poet." *New York Review of Books*, (July 17), 12-17.

Michaletos, John. 1952. *Ἡ ποίηση τοῦ Καβάφη* [The Poetry of Cavafy]. Athens.

_____. 1955. *Καβαφικὰ θέματα: Ἀντίλογος* [Cavafian Themes: Disputative Reply]. Athens.

Michals, Duane. 1978. *Homage to Cavafy*. Danbury, N. H.: Addison House.

Milne, J. Grafton. 1898. *A History of Egypt*. 6 vols. London: Methuen.

Minucci, Paola M. 1979. *Costantino Kavafis*. Firenze: La Nuova Italia.

Modinos, P. 1980. *Τρεῖς ἐπιστολὲς τοῦ Καβάφη* [Three Letters of Cavafy]. Athens.

_____. 1983. "'Ο Καβάφης ὅπως τὸν γνώρισα" ["Cavafy as I knew Him"]. *Nea Estia*, 113, No. 1341 (May 15), 634-42.

Moutsopoulos, E. 1961. "Le Temps dans l'univers cavafien." *Annales de la Faculté des Lettres et Sciences Humaines d' Aix*, 35, 5-9.

Nehamas, Alexander. 1983. "Memory, Pleasure and Poetry: The Grammar of the Self in the Writing of Cavafy." *Journal of Modern Greek Studies*, 1/2, 295-319.

Nikolareizis, D. 1931. "'Ηδονισμὸς καὶ ἡ ποίηση τοῦ Καβάφη" ["Hedonism and Cavafy's Poetry"]. *Nea Estia* (November 1), 1148-53.

_____. 1963. "'Η διαμόρφωση τοῦ Καβαφικοῦ λυρισμοῦ" ["The Shaping of Cavafy's Lyricism"]. *Nea Estia* (July 15); repr. in special 1963 issue, 1462-67.

Ouranis, K. n. d. *Δικοί μας καὶ ξένοι* [Our Own and the Others]. Vol. 2. Athens: Estia, esp. ch. 2: "Cavafy," pp. 125-48.

Palamas, C. v. d. *Άπαντα* [Collected Works]. Vols. 12, 14. Athens, Biris, n. d.; esp. v. 12, pp. 1, 66-89, and v. 14, p. 217.

―――. 1981. *Αλληλογραφία* [Correspondence]. Vol. 3: 1929-1941 (ed. K. G. Kasinis). Athens: The Palamas Institute.

Panayotopoulos, I. M. 1982. *Τὰ πρόσωπα καὶ τὰ κείμενα* [Persons and Texts]. Vol. 4: *C. P. Cavafy*. 2d ed. Athens: Editions of Friends.

Pantelodemos, D. 1983. "'Ο Καβάφης μεταφράζει καὶ ἑρμηνεύει Baudelaire" ["Cavafy Translates and Interprets Baudelaire"]. *New Estia* 114, No. 1354 (December 1), 1499-1505.

Papadakis, N. A. 1969. "Ἡρώδης Ἀττικὸς ὁ Μαραθώνιος" ["Herodis Atticus the Marathonian"]. *Nea Estia* 86, No. 1015 (October 15), 1414-26.

Papanghelis, Th. D. 1986. "Spiritus in toto corpore surgit: Μία λειτουργία τοῦ ἐρωτικοῦ σώματος στὸν Προπέρτιο, στὸν Μπωντλαὶρ καὶ στὸν Καβάφη" ["*Spiritus in toto corpore surgit*: A Function of the Erotic Body in Propertius, Baudelaire and in Cavafy"]. *Hellenika*, 37/2, 280-305.

Papanoutsos, E. P. 1955. *Παλαμᾶς, Καβάφης, Σικελιανός* [Palamas, Cavafy, Sikelianos]. Second Edition. Athens: Ikaros.

―――. 1963. "'Ο διδακτικὸς Καβάφης" ["The Didactic Cavafy"]. *Nea Estia* 74 (November 1), 1505-7.

Papatzonis, T. K. 1932. "Συμβολὴ στὴ κριτικὴ τοῦ ἔργου τοῦ Κ. Καβάφη" ["Contribution to the Criticism of Cavafy's Work"]. *The Circle* 2, 87-93.

―――. 1948. "'Ο ἔνδοξός μας Βυζαντινισμός" ["Our Glorious Byzantinism"]. *Nea Estia* 43 (May 15), 659-65.

Papoutsakis, G. 1933. "'Ομιλία" ["A Lecture"]. *Panegyptia* 5, No. 233 (July 8), 11-13.

Peri, Massimo. 1978. "Κ. Π. Καβάφη ''Ο Καθρέφτης στὴν εἴσοδο' (Καβαφικὲς δομές)" ["Cavafy's 'The Mirror in the Front Hall' (Cavafian Structures)"]. *Speira* 7 (November), 290-302; trans. into Greek by J. Kephaloglou.

_____. 1976. *Strutture in Kavafis*. Padova: Universita di Padova, Studi Bizantini e Neogreci (Quaderni, 11).

_____. 1978. *Quatro saggi su Kavafis*. Milano: Universita Cattolica.

Peridis, M. 1948. *Ὁ βίος καὶ τὸ ἔργο τοῦ Κωνστ. Καβάφη* [The Life and Work of Const. Cavafy]. Athens: Ikaros.

Pernot, Hubert. 1921. *La Grèce actuelle dans ses poètes*. Paris.

Petridis, K. 1961. *Ἀπὸ τὸν Παλαμᾶ ὡς τὸν Καβάφη* [From Palamas to Cavafy]. Athens.

_____. 1966. *Ὁ Καβάφης καὶ ἡ διαλεχτική* [Cavafy and Dialectics]. Athens: Diptycho.

Petridis, Paul. 1909. "Ἕνας Ἀλεξανδρινὸς ποιητής: Κ. Π. Καβάφης" [An Alexandrian Poet: C. P. Cavafy.]. *Nea Zoe*, 5, No. 54 (April), 201-206.

Pieridis, Yiangos. 1965. *Ὁ Καβάφης: χαρακτηρισμοί, ἀνέκδοτα* [Cavafy: Characterizations and Anecdotes]. Second Edition. Athens: Orion.

Pieris, M. 1982. *Κ. Π. Καβάφης: Ἔφοδος στὸ σκοτάδι (Ἡ ἐξελικτικὴ πορεία)* [C. P. Cavafy: Sortie in the Night (The Develpmental Process)]. Edition *To Mikro Dentro*. No. 6.

_____. 1983a. "Σιωπὴ καὶ λόγος στὴν ποίηση τοῦ Καβάφη" ["Silence and Speech in Cavafy's Poetry"]. *I Read*, No. 78 (October 5), 82-96.

_____. 1983b. "Καβάφης καὶ ἱστορία: θέματα ὀρολογίας" ["Cavafy and History: Themes in Terminology"]. *Proceedings of the Third Poetry Symposium*. Athens: pp. 373-85.

_____. 1983c. "Τὸ φῶς καὶ τὸ σκοτάδι στὴν ποίηση του Καβάφη" ["Light and Darkness in the Poetry of Cavafy"]. *Cavafy Circle*, 113-49.

_____. 1985. Ed. *Εἰσαγωγὴ στὴν ποίηση τοῦ Καβάφη* [An Introduction to the Poetry of Cavafy]: A Collection of Articles and Essays]. Rethymno: The School of Philosophy, University of Crete.

Pierrot, J. 1981. *The Decadent Imagination 1800-1900*. (Tr. D. Coleman). Chicago and London.

Pikros, Petros. 1970. "Γνώμη γιὰ τὸν Καβάφη" ["An Opinion about Cavafy"]. *Horizons*, 1/2, 9-10.

Pinchin, Lagoudis, Jane. 1977. *Alexandria Still: Forster, Durrell and Cavafy*. Princeton: Princeton University Press.

Plutarch. 1950. *Twelve Lives*. Translated by John Dryden and with Introduction by Carl Van Doren. Cleveland: Fine Editions Press.

Poggioli, Renato. 1959. "*Qualis Artifax Pereo!* or Barbarism and Decadence." *Harvard Library Bulletin*, 13/1, 135-59; reprinted 1983 *The Mind and Art of C. P. Cavafy*, pp. 127-56.

_____. 1962. "L' Automne des ideés." *Diogene*, 38 (Paris 1962), 78-90.

Politis, Athanasios. 1930. *Ὁ Ἑλληνισμὸς καὶ ἡ νεωτέρα Αἴγυπτος* [Hellenism and Modern Egypt]. 2 vols. Alexandria: Editions Grammata, 1930; extract repr. in *Epitheorisi Technis*, "Cavafy" (December 1963), 645-48.

Pontani, Filippo Maria. 1940. "Saggio sulla poesia di Costantino Cavafis." *Epitheoresie, Rivista di cultura greco-italiana*, IV/8-9, 521-40, 590-604.

_____. 1940a. "Fonti della poesia di Cavafis." *Epitheoresie, Rivista di cultura greco-italiana*, IV/10, 657-69.

_____. 1946. "Metrica di Cavafis." Extract from *Atti della Reale Academia di Scienze, Lettere ed Arti di Palermo*. Ser. 4, vol. 5, pt. 2 (1944-1945). Palermo, pp. 163-219.

_____. 1970. "Motivi Classici e Bizantini Negli inediti di Kavafis." *Atti dell'Istituto Veneto di Scienze, Lettere ed Arti*, vol. 128 (1969-1970). Venezia, pp. 291-319.

_____. 1972. "Kavafis e Keats." *Studi classici in onore di Quintino Cataudella*. Universita di Catania, Facoltà di Lettere e Filosofia, pp. 141-74; repr. *Siculorum Gymnasium*, N. S. XXXI (1978), 383-416.

_____. 1983. "Νεκρολογία" ["Obituary"]. *Nea Estia* 114, No. 1350 (October 1), 1234-36.

Porfyris, K. 1963. "Ἡ πολιτικὴ στάση τοῦ Κ. Π. Καβάφη" ["The Political Stance of Cavafy"]. *Epitheorisi Technis* (December), 672-75.

Sareyannis, I. A. 1964. *Σχόλια στὸν Καβάφη* [Comments on Cavafy], (ed. Z. Lorentzatos; Preface. G. Seferis). Athens: Ikaros.

Savidis, George. 1963. *Οἱ πέντε πρῶτες ἐκδόσεις ποιημάτων τοῦ Κ. Π. Καβάφη. Βιβλιογραφικὸ δοκίμιο* [The First Five Editions of the C. P. Cavafy's Poems. A Bibliographical Essay]. Athens; reprinted with corrections and additions in *Epitheorisi Technis*, 104 (August), 132-45.

_____. 1964. *Γιὰ μιὰ πρώτη ἀνάγνωση τοῦ Καβάφη σὲ δίσκους. Φιλολογικὸ δοκίμιο*. [For a First Reading of Cavafy on Records. Philological Essay]. Athens; repr. *Epoches* 18 (1964), 56-65.

_____. 1966. *Οἱ Καβαφικὲς ἐκδόσεις* [The Cavafian Editions]. Athens: Tachydromos.

_____. 1973. *Πάνω νερά* [Upper Waters]. Athens: Ermis.

_____. 1975. "Cavafy and Forster." *The Times Literary Supplement*. (14 November).

_____. 1978. *Ἐφήμερον σπέρμα* (1973-1978) [Transient Seed (1973-1978)]. Athens: Ermis.

_____. 1982. "῎Ενα ἄγνωστο συγκριτικὸ κείμενο τοῦ Karl Shapiro γιὰ τὸν Καβάφη" ["An Unknown Comparative Text by Karl Shapiro on Cavafy"]. *Nea Estia* 111 No. 1317 (May 15), 635-6.

_____. 1983. "Τί ἐκόμισε στὴν τέχνη ὁ Καβάφης" ["What Cavafy Brought to Art]. *I Read*, No. 78, 35-36.

_____. 1985a. *Μικρὰ καβαφικά* [Minor Cavafian Essays]. Vol. I. Athens: Ermis.

_____. 1985b. "The Burden of the Past and the Greek Poet." *Grand Street*, 5/1, 186.

_____. 1987. *Μικρὰ καβαφικά* [Minor Cavafian Essays]. Vol. II. Athens: Ermis.

Savvas, Minas. 1972. Review of [1971] C. P. Cavafy, *Passions and Ancient Days*, (trans. E. Keeley and G. Savidis). *The Yale Review* (Winter), 308-12.

Seferis, George. 1966. *On the Greek Style*. Trans. Rex Warner and Th. Frangopoulos). Boston: Little Brown & Co., pp. 119-63; esp. ch. VII "Cavafy and Eliot—A Comparison," 119-62; reprinted 1983, *The Mind and Art of C. P. Cavafy*, pp. 60-88.

_____. 1974a. *A Poet's Journal: Days of 1945-1951*. Trans. Athan Anagnostopoulos. Cambridge: Harvard University Press.

_____. 1974b. *Δοκιμές* [Essays]. 3d ed. 2 vols. Athens: Ikaros.

_____. 1984. *Ὁ Καβάφης τοῦ Σεφέρη* [Seferis' Cavafy]. Ed. G. Savidis. Athens: Ermis.

Sengopoulos, A. 1963. "Διάλεξις περὶ τοῦ ποιητικοῦ ἔργου τοῦ Κ. Π. Καβάφη" ["A Lecture on the Poetry of Cavafy"]. Alexandria, 1918; repr. *Epitheorisi Technis*, 108 (December), 614-21.

_____. 1983. "'Ανέκδοτα σχόλια σὲ ποιήματα τοῦ Καβάφη (1918)" ["Unpublished Comments on Poems by Cavafy (1918)"]. Presented and with Notes by G. Savidis. *Chart*, Commemorative Issue 5/6, 549-61.

Sengopoulou-Karayanni, Rika. 1970. "Ὁ Καβάφης" ["Cavafy"]. *Horizons*, n.s. A/2, 1-9.

Sephers, Pierre. 1948. "Un Poète Grec Moderne, Constantine Cavafy." *Le Nef* (October-December).

Sherrard, P. 1956. *The Marble Threshing Floor*. London: Vallentine, Mitchell, 1956; esp. ch. 3: "Constantine Cavafis," pp. 83-123.

_____. 1978. "Cavafy's Sensual City: A Question." *Byzantine and Modern Greek Studies*, 4, 133-37; reprinted 1983, *The Mind and Art of C. P. Cavafy*, pp. 94-99.

_____. 1983. "Ξανακοιτάζοντας τὸν Καβάφη" ["Taking Another Look at Cavafy"]. *I Read*, No. 78 (October 5), 136-40.

Sikelianos, A. 1983. *Πεζὸς λόγος* [Prose Works]. Ed. G. Savidis. 4 Vols. Athens: Ikaros.

Souloyannis, Thymios. 1983. "Κωστῆς Παλαμᾶς καὶ Κωνσταντῖνος Καβάφης, διαμάχη καὶ ὀπαδοί. Ἕνα χρονικό" ["K. Palamas and C. Cavafy Conflict and Fellows. A Chronicle"]. *I Read*, No. 78 (October 5), 50-55.

Spender, Stephen. 1972. "Cavafy: The Historic and the Erotic." *The New York Review of Books* (January 15); reprinted 1983, *The Mind and Art of C. P. Cavafy*, pp. 89-93.

Sphaellou, C. 1977. *Καβάφης ὁ ἑλληνικός* [The Hellenic Cavafy]. Athens.

Spieros, M. 1983. "Παρατηρήσεις ἐπάνω στὸ Καβαφικὸ ἔργο" ["Observations on the Cavafy's Work"]. *The Circle*, 2/3-4 (November), 98-126; reissued 1983.

Stanford, W. B. 1968 [1963]. *The Ulysses Theme: A Study in the Adaptability of a Traditional Hero*. Ann Arbor: The University of Michigan Press.

Stasinopoulou, Maria. 1983. "Χρονολογία Κ. Π. Καβάφη" ["Chronology of Cavafy"]. *I Read*, No. 78 (October 5), 18-34.

Tennyson, Lord Alfred. 1987. *The Poems of Tennyson*. 3 vols., second edition, ed. Christopher Ricks. Berkeley and Los Angeles: University of California Press.

Themelis, G. 1970. *Ἡ ποίηση τοῦ Καβάφη: διαστάσεις καὶ ὅρια* [The Poetry of Cavafy: Dimensions and Limits]. Thessaloniki: Editions Constandinidis.

Theotokas, George. 1961. *Πνευματικὴ πορεία* [Spiritual Journey]. Athens: Fexis.

Tsafaras, K. P. 1975. "Μία ποιητικὴ διαμαρτυρία" ["A Protest for Poetry"]. *Platon*, 25/53-54, 238-42.

Tsirkas, Stratis. 1958. *Ὁ Καβάφης καὶ ἡ ἐποχή του* [Cavafy and His Times]. Athens: Kedros.

_____. 1963. "Κ. Π. Καβάφης: σχεδίασμα χρονογραφίας τοῦ βίου του" ["C. P. Cavafy: An Outline for the Chronography of His Life"]. *Epitheorisi Technis*, 18 No 108 (December), 676-706.

_____. 1971. *Ὁ πολιτικὸς Καβάφης* [The Political Cavafy]. Athens: Kedros.

Trypanis, C. A. 1951. *Medieval and Modern Greek Poetry*. Oxford: The Clarendon Press.

_____. 1981. *Greek Poetry: From Homer to Seferis*. Chicago: The University of Chicago Press.

Valaoritis, Nanos 1983. "Κ. Π. Καβάφης καὶ 'Ε. 'Α. Πόου μεταξὺ ἄλλων" ["C. P. Cavafy and E. A. Poe, Among Others"]. *Chart*, Commemorative Issue 5-6 (April), 650-57.

Valassopoulo, G. 1931. "An Alexandrian Poet." *Echanges*, Paris (December), 10-13.

Valetas, G. 1976. *Τῆς ρωμιοσύνης· δοκίμια* [For Romiosini: Essays]. Athens: Editions Pigis, esp. pp. 47-62.

Valieri, Harikleia. 1963. "'Ο θεῖος μου ὁ Κώστας" ["My Uncle Costas" (Cavafy)]. *Tachydromos*, (April 27), 20-1.

Varnalis, K. 1958. *Αἰσθητικὰ-κριτικά* [Aesthetic and Critical Essays]. Vol. 2. Athens: Kedros; esp. "The Historicism of Cavafy," pp. 191-94.

Vasiliev, A. 1968. *History of the Byzantine Empire*. 2 vols. Madison: University of Wisconsin Press.

Vayenas, Nasos. 1979. "The Language of Irony. (Towards a Definition of the Poetry of Cavafy)." *Byzantine and Modern Greek Studies*, 5, 43-56; reprinted 1983, *The Mind and Art of C. P. Cavafy*, pp. 100-14.

_____. 1980. *'Ο ποιητὴς καὶ ὁ χορευτής* [The Poet and the Dancer]. 2d ed. Athens: Kedros; esp. ch. III: "Seferis, Sikelianos, Cavafy," pp. 185-245.

Veloudis, G. 1972. "K. Kavafis und die Ironie." *Hellenika* II/III, 48-55.

_____. 1983. *'Αναφορές· Ἕξη νεοελληνικὲς μελέτες* [Reports. Six Neohellenic Essays]. Athens: Philoppotis; ch. 4: "Cavafy's Irony," pp. 44-57.

Vrissimitzakis, George. 1975. *Τὸ ἔργο τοῦ Κ. Π. Καβάφη* [The Work of C. P. Cavafy], augmented edition. Athens: Ikaros.

_____. 1921. *Ἀλεξανδρινοὶ γέροι* [Old Men of Alexandria]. *Pharos* 32.

Welch, Cyril and Lilian. 1973. *Emergence*. State College, Pennsylvania: Bald Eagle Press.

Willey, Basil. 1956. *More Nineteenth Century Studies*. New York: Columbia University Press.

Xenopoulos, Gregory. 1963. "Ἕνας ποιητής" ["A Poet"]. *Panathenaia*, (November 30, 1903); repr. *Nea Estia*, **74** (November 1), 1443-9.

Xydis, Th. 1963. "Καβάφης καὶ Σικελιανός: δύο ποιητικὰ ὁρόσημα" ["Cavafy and Sikelianos: Two Poetic Landmarks"]. *Nea Estia*, 74, No. 872 (November), 1591-1601.

Yalourakis, M. 1963. "Καβάφης καὶ Παλαμᾶς" ["Cavafy and Palamas"]. *Nea Estia* 74 (November), 1584-89.

_____. 1974. *Στὴν Ἀλεξάνδρεια τοῦ Καβάφη* [Cavafy's Alexandria]. Athens: Olkos.

_____. 1975. *Καβάφης—ἀπὸ τὸν Πρίαπο στὸν Κὰρλ Μάρξ* [Cavafy: From Priapus to Karl Marx]; reprint of the 1959 booklet *Cavafy of the Capital T*, pp. 17-138. Athens: Olkos.

Yiakos, D. 1963. "Ἕνας νέος ἀπ' τὴ Σιδώνα" ["A Young Man from Sidon"]. *Nea Estia*, 74, 1630-2.

Young, Kenneth. 1948. "Introduction to Modern Greek Poetry." *Life and Letters*, 56 No. 126, 107-26.

Yourcenar, Marguerite. 1978. *Présentation critique de Constantin Cavafy, 1863-1933, suivie d'une traduction des Poèmes par Marguerite Yourcenar et Constantin Dimaras*. 2nd ed. Paris: Gallimard.

Zweig, D. 1968. *The Heresy of Self-Love: A Study of Subversive Individualism*. New York: Basic Books.

INDEX A: TITLES

Editions, Poems, Translations, Prose Works

EDITIONS

Booklet 1 127, 129, 133, 147, 152, 155, 158, 220, 226, 283
Booklet 1909-1911 121n5
Booklet 2 48, 127, 128, 129, 133, 147, 152, 155-158, 220-221

Collections 70n36, 129, 133, 138, 156-157, 163, 172, 181, 279, 312, 312n11, 333n32

POEMS

"A Poet" 40n21
"A Young Poet in His Twenty-Fourth Year" 292n35
"Absence" 156, 244
"Addition" 126n9, 163, 172
"Again in the Same City", see also "The City" 118, 123n6
"Aimilianos Monai, Alexandrian, A. D. 628-655" 12, 142n21, 287n25
"Alexandrian Kings" 4, 8, 58, 241, 313, 329
"Alexandrian Merchant" 300n1
"Amphora" 156, see "Artisan of Craters"
"An Evening of Mine" see "One Night"
"An Old Man' 133, 147, 165, 266
"And I Lounged and Lay on Their Beds" 292
"Apollonius of Tyana in Rhodes" 244n16
"Artificial Flowers" (formerly "The Secrets of Flowers") 101, 307n7
"Artisan of Craters" 156
"As if in the Past" 156, see "Monotony"
"As Much as You Can" (original title "Bios" [Life]), 45, 46n29, 157, 181, 187, 265, 285
    quoted 45-46, 182
"At the Café Door" (formerly "From the Hands of Eros") 283
    quoted 283
"At the Theater" 51n1, 129, 278, 282

"Bacchic Song" 34, 34n15, 78, 126n9, 160

"Baudelaire" 84
"Before Time Altered Them" 292n35
"Body, Remember" 266n7, 292
"Builders" 31, 80, 93, 98, 103, 135, 138-139, 166, 177, 184, 186, 201-204, 220, 231-233, 257-258, 276, 327
    quoted 201
"But the Wise Perceive Things About to Happen" 156, 244n16, 258, 320

"Candles" 123, 221, 237n14, 342
"Chandelier" 289
    quoted 290
"Che fece . . . il gran rifiuto" 40, 176n22, 264
    quoted 176
"Come Back" (formerly, "Memory of Pleasure") 129, 156, 278, 282, 289
    quoted 282-283
"Comes to Rest" 99, 158n5, 292
    quoted 99
"Confusion" 133, 133n16, 150
    quoted 150
"Dangerous Thoughts" 42n23, 254, 254n28, 291, 322
    quoted 254-255
"Days of 1896" 274, 293, 292n35
"Days of 1901" 292n35
"Days of 1903" 129, 157, 278, 281, 288
"Days of 1908" 73, 292n35
"Days of 1909, '10 and '11" 292n35
"Death of the General" 224
"Decadent Eros" 274n15, 288 193, 284-285
    quoted 193-194
"December, 1903" 129, 159, 213, 264, 278, 297n41
"Degenerate Eros" 100n24
"Demaratos" 156, 332n30
"Demetrios Soter (162-150 B.C.)" 21n9
"Desires" 129, 130, 158-159, 162, 171, 221, 266, 283
    quoted 158
"Dionysos and His Crew" 155, 221n22
"Drunk", see also "Tipsy" 278
"Dünya Güzeli" ix, 163n8

"For Ammonis, Who Died at 29, in 610"
"For the Shadows to Come" 59
"From the Drawer" 278n17, 292n35
"From the School of the Renowned
    Philosopher" 313, 318n18
"Futile, Futile Love" 79

"Grey" 54, 292
"Growing in Spirit" 52, 129, 207, 253,
    264, 277-278, 294
    quoted 53, 207
"Half an Hour" 51n1, 292
"Half Past Twelve" ("Since Nine
    O'Clock") 292
"Half-Drunk" 278n18, 291n33
"He Asked About the Quality"
    292n35
"He Had Planned to Read" 292n35
"Herodis Attikos" 301n1
"He Swears" 157, 278, 285
    quoted 285
"Hidden Things" 43n25, 50, 51, 52,
    188n31, 189, 260, 268, 287, 287n25
    quoted 51
"Hours of Melancholy" 100

"I Went" 95, 157, 159, 278, 283, 295,
    297n41
    quoted 95
"I've Brought to Art" 292n35
"I've Looked so Much" 51, 54, 291
"If Actually Dead" 156, 172n19, 244,
    244n16
"Illicit Pleasure", 274n15
"Images" or "Icons", 79
"Impending Things" 156
"Impossible Things" 172
"In a Large Greek Colony 200 B.C." 21n9,
    240
    quoted 240
"In Alexandria, 31 B.C." 329
"In an Old Book" 273, 292n35
"In Church" 11n5, 156

"In Despair" 273, 292n35
    quoted 274
"In the Boring Village" 292n35
"In the Evening" (formerly "Alexandrian")
    280, 294
    quoted 280, 294
"In the House of the Soul" 36, 133n15, 161
    quoted 145-146
"In the Month of Athyr" 54, 56, 58
    quoted 56
"In the Same City" 123, 123n6, 133n15,
    137, 156, 161, 164, 307n7
"In the House of the Soul" 145
    quoted 145-146
"In the Street" 278, 291
"In the Tavernas" 292n35
"In the Year 200 B.C." 20, 21n9, 327n24
    quoted 20
"In Vain" 133n15, 144
"Injustice" 133n15, 144
"Interruption" 177, 203-204, 321
    quoted 203
"Ionic" (formerly "Memory" and
    "Thessaly") 39, 79, 163, 172n19, 223ff,
    254-255, 261
    "Memory" quoted 245
    "Ionic" quoted 248-249
"Ithaka" 48-49, 53-54, 69, 86, 90, 104, 115f,
    121, 127-129, 138, 156n3, 157, 160, 175,
    186-188, 218, 243, 258, 263n3, 281, 296,
    301, 307, 309, 310f, 314-319, 321f, 328f,
    332n30, 333ff
    as turning point in Cavafy's
        development 309n9
    comment on meaning of 302
    quoted 49, 175, 301
    relation to "The End of Odysseus"
        and "The Mountain" 308n8
    voyage motif in, 308
    wisdom as part of theme of 320

"January, 1904" 129, 265, 278, 281
"Julian at the Mysteries" 144n23, 251n24

"Kaisarion" 329
"King Demetrius" 155, 221n22
"Kleitos' Illness" 144n23

"Lagidou Hospitality" 300n1
"La Jeunesse Blanche" 149
    quoted 149
"Langeur" 248n20
"Last Night" 274n16, 282n20
"Life" see "As Much as You Can"
"Like a Generation of Flowers" 78
"Like Dead" 133
"Like the Past", see "Monotony"
"Like the Trojans", see "Trojans"
"Logos and Silence" 88, 89, 93
"Long Ago" 270
    quoted 270
"Lovely White Flowers" 292n35
"Lustfulness 157, see "He Swears"

"Manouel Komninos" 332n30
"March, 1904" 157, see "At the Theatre"
"March, 1907" 157, 288, see "Days of 1903"

"Memory of Pleasure" 156, see "Come Back"
"Memory" see "Ionic"
"Monotony" 172n19, 259
    quoted 49, 171
"Next Table" 292

"On Board Ship" 292n35
"On Hearing of Love" 48, 288n28
    quoted 48, 290
"On the Stairs" 278
"One Night" (formerly "One of My Nights") 275, 282, 286
"One of Their Gods" 156, 263, 268
"Orophernes" 332n30
"Our Art" 101
"Outside the House" 280, 292
    quoted 280-281
"Passing Through" 269, 292

quoted 269-270
"Philhellene" 157, 286, 332n30
"Picture of a 23-year old Painted by His Friend of the Same Age, an Amateur" 292n35
"Poseidonians" 223, 241, 286, 313
"Prayer" 220

"Rain" 133n15, 148
    quoted 148
"Return to Alexandria" 79n4

"Second Odyssey" 86, 122, 133, 156n3, 157, 163-165, 304, 307, 308-310, 314n13, 315, 317
    quoted 304-305, 306n4
"September, 1903" 42, 129, 159, 212, 263, 264, 277-278, 281
    quoted 42, 277
"Sham-el-Nessim" [Breath of the Breeze] 18, 300n1
    quoted 18-19
"Singer" 196
"Summer of 1895" 292n35

"Terror" 37 133n15, 139, 144, 146, 148
    quoted 145, 148
"That's the Man" 155, 172n19, 221n22, 279
"The 25th Year of His Life" 292
"The Afternoon Sun" 158n5, 292
"The Bandaged Shoulder" 51n1, 292
"The Batttle of Magnesia" 21, 21n9
"The City" 38, 48, 70, 81, 95, 103, 106, 108, 112, 114, 116, 118-121, 121n5, 122-24, 126-31, 131n12, 132n13, 132n14, 133-35, 137-138, 138n17, 139-140, 140n20, 141-42, 144-147, 150, 156-157, 162, 164, 167, 182, 188, 200, 206, 235, 237n14, 238, 241-243, 259, 264, 278-281, 289, 293-94, 300, 304, 309, 312, 333
    changes in, 129-130
    quoted 125, 141-142
"The Closed Coach" (see also "The

Tobacco Shop Window")
"The Death of Emperor Tacitus" 220
"The Displeasure of Selefkidis" 157, 301n1, 332n30
"The Elegy of Flowers" 78
"The End of Antony" 127, 301n1, 329, 331, 332, 334
  quoted 331
"The Enemies" 225
"The First Step", see "The Last Step" 120, 163, 193, 195
  quoted 120
"The Footsteps" 155, 221n22
"The Four Walls of My Room" 291n33
"The Funeral of Sarpedon" 172n19, 221n22
"The Glory of the Ptolemies" 3, 156, 172n19
"The God Abandons Antony" 48, 58, 65, 121, 127, 138, 157, 193, 218, 228n5, 263n3, 275, 301n1, 318, 328-334
  quoted 328-329
"The Ides of March", 157
"The Inkwell", 99n23, 133n15, 140
"The Intervention of the Gods" 203-204
  quoted 203
"The Last Step" 120
"The Mirror in the Front Hall" 292n35
"The Pawn" 115, 133n15, 143-144, 208, 217, 256, 343n4, 343n5, 344n6
  quoted, see Appendix 346
"The Picture" 278n17
"The Poet and the Muse" 78, 88-90, 196
  quoted 197
"The Satrapy" 47, 81, 121, 131, 138n17, 157, 182-184, 186-188, 228n5, 243, 264-265, 284, 333f
  quoted 182
"The Souls of Old Men" 133, 172n19, 224, 266
"The Tarantinians Carouse"
  quoted 223-224
"The Tears of the Sisters of Phaethon" 220

"The Twenty-five years of His Life" 272
  quoted 273
"The Tobacco Shop Window of" 129, 133, 157, 158, 278, 286
"The Windows" 38, 40, 40n21, 70, 81, 94, 103, 103n26, 108, 118-119, 130, 133, 162-164, 170, 172n19, 173n20, 179, 196, 206, 221, 264, 271, 313, 341, 343
  quoted 162
"Theatre of Sidon" 273
  quoted 273
"Their Beginning" 100, 268, 274n15, 288, 292
  quoted 288
"Their First Light" 341
"Theodotos" 69
"Thermopylae" 40n21, 126n9, 131, 177-178, 179, 180n27, 206, 221, 223, 255-258, 258n30, 341, 344
  quoted 178, 255-256
"Things Ended" 157, 318
"Things Impossible" 99
"Things to Come" 256
"Those Who Fought for the Achaean League" 66, 225, 255
"Thus" 278n17, 291
"Timolaos the Syracusan" (formerly Timolaos the Musician") 98, 141, 290n29
"To Call Up the Shades" 274
  quoted 274
"To Sensual Pleasure" 292
  quoted 292
"Tomb of Iases" 54, 195n3, 285, 318n18
"Tomb of Ignatios" 318n18
"Trojans" (formerly "Like the Trojans") 70, 122, 130-131, 131n12, 134, 154, 168n17, 173-175, 177-179, 189, 206, 221n22, 264, 285
  quoted 174
"Two Young Men, 23 to 24 Years Old" 292n35

"Understanding" 155, 262, 268, 274, 292
  quoted 155, 268
"Very Seldom", 177n23, 266, 279
"Voices" (formerly "Sweet Voices") 133, 133n15, 149, 152, 221, 342
  quoted 149

"Waiting for the Barbarians" 7, 40-41, 70, 130, 172n19, 173n20, 180n27, 187, 202, 206, 220-238, 241-244, 248n21, 255, 257-58, 313, 326
  quoted 227-228
"Walls" 38, 40, 48, 70, 103, 108, 118-19, 130, 133, 156, 164ff, 166n12, 167, 168n17, 172n19, 173n20, 175, 177-79, 185ff, 206n14, 220, 237n14, 264, 291n33, 341-343
  interpretations of 165-167, 168n17, 187n30
  quoted 165
"When the Watchman Saw the Light" 224-25
  quoted 225
"When They Awaken" 52
"When They Come Alive" (formerly "Priceless Things") 291
"Whoever Has Failed" 35, 133n15, 141-142
  quoted 35, 141

"Young Men of Sidon: A.D. 400", 193
  quoted xxii

TRANSLATIONS

Cavafy's translations of

Baudelaire 82, 105,   112-113
Keats 100
Lindsay-Barnard, Lady 79
Shakespeare 78
Tennyson 78

PROSE WORKS

Ars Poetica, xvii, 30n8, 32, 41, 45, 75, 103, 108, 127, 135, 152-155, 160, 169, 178, 189, 191, 197, 202, 205-219, 222, 234, 256, 260, 264, 267, 276, 279, 284, 294, 325, 344n6, see Appendix pp. 339-346

Prose 31n10, 31n11, 32n13, 36n16, 45n27, 64n25, 79n3, 80n6, 80n7, 81n8, 81n9, 109n32, 147n25, 229n6, 244n16
  "A Night on the Calinder" 122
  "Byzantine Poets" 80, 229n6
  "Give Back the Elgin Marbles" 31
  "Lamia" (essay), 244n16
  "Professor Blakie in Modern Greek Language" 31
  "Shakespeare on Life" 31
  "The Coral from a Mythological Point of View" 79
  "The Inhuman Friends of Animals" 79
  "The Mountain" 123, 307n7, 308

Self-comments 23n1, 139n19, 177n23, 302n3 330n26

"The End of Odysseus" 86, 307-308, 308n8, 314n13, 315n15

INDEX B: GENERAL

Achilles 173
Adolphus 247
Aeschylus xxii, 192
Agallianou, Rika 61n20, see Sengopoulos
Agras, Tellos 59n15, 69, 73
   lecture on Cavafy, 58-59
Alaric 10, 230, 247, 249
Alexander of Macedonia 218
Alexandria,
   accepted as Cavafy's aesthetic
     habitat 310
   occurrences of in Cavafy's poems 300n1
   scientific center 3
   setting for Cavafy's poems 11
   spritual ancestry of 1
   stormed by Napoleon's troops 12
Alexandrini Techni (*Alexandrian Art*) 23n1, 69, 237
Alexiou, M. 77n44, 290n30
Ali, Muhammad 13-17, 24-25
Alienation 111-115, 118, 121, 263, 271, 311, 325, 337
Alithersis, Glafkos 64
American Revolution 233
Amr 12
Anastassiadis, Pericles 23n1, 38, 39-40, 55, 70n36, 76, 120, 122, 123n6, 124, 132n14, 166, 205n10
   letter from Cavafy 307
Ancient Days, poems dealing with classical themes 37, 204, 220
Anninos, B. 257n29
Antioch, as setting for Cavafy's poems 11
Antiochos III (the Great) 21n9
Anton, J. P. 71n37
Apollonius of Tyana 244
Apostolopoulos, A. xxiv
Arcadius, Emperor 246-247
Aristotle 2, 109 136, 215, 296-297
   Poetics 191
   Politics 2

Arnold, M. 200
Artaxerxes, 187, 265, 333
Asty 79, 244
Atheneum 57, 69
Attalus, Emperor 247-249
Attikon Mouseion 31n12
Auden, W. C. xxv
Averoff, G. 17 257n29
Avgeris, M. 45n27
Barnard, Lady 30
   "Auld Robin Gray", tr. 79
Baud-Bovy, S. 106
Baudelaire, Charles xxv, 36, 82-84, 84n12, 85, 86-90, 90n18, 91-93, 93n20, 94-98, 100-102, 105-107, 109, 112, 115-116, 200-201, 265, 275-276, 322ff
   "Correspondances" 80, 82, 84-88, 90, 95, 97-98, 103, 105, 109
   quoted 82-83
   Intimate Journals 93n20, 265n5, 275
   Les Fleurs du mal, 85-87, 116, 113n34, 326
   "Le Crepuscule du Matin" 112-113
     quoted 113
   "Le Voyage" 314n13
Beardsley, M. C. 115, 269n12
Beaton, R. 179n25, 256
Beebe, M. 86n13, 91n19, 93n20, 265n5
Benaki Museum 23n1, 45n28, 123n6
Bertocci, A. P. 116
Bevan, E. D. 14
Bien, P. xxv, 267n10, 290n30, 309n9, 312n11
Blackie, J. 80
Bouche-Leclercq, 14
Bowersock, G. W. 11n4, 246n18, 251n24, 290n30
Bowra, C. xxv, 179n25, 256, 323n23
Bregman, J. 251n23
Browning, R. 106
Butler, Samuel 38

Byron, Lord 15
Byzantine Empire 12, 227, 241

C. P. Cavafy: Commemorative Issue, 75n43
Caesar 7, 218
Caesar-Cleopatra Affair 7-9
Caires, V. 290n30
Callimachus 106, 107
Campos, Robertos 53, 220
   pseudonym for P. Magnis 53n2
Capri-Karka, C. 290n30
Catraro, A. 58, 58n12, 65
Cavafy, Alexander 26, 40, 42
Cavafy, Aristeides 26, 40
Cavafy, C. P.
   biography 23-24, see genealogy
   brave man of pleasure 318ff
   Christianity, views of 322, (see also Gibbon)
   city of ideas 180, 243, 323
   conflict with Palamas 60-65
   correspondence with Forster 56n5
   crisis period 35-36, 94, 117-119, 121, 125, 152, 156, 163-164, 167, 173, 188-89, 293n36, 294; ch.6 passim;
   "crisis" poems 129-130, 137, 146, 150, 152- 155, 159, 178, 188, 263-264
   decadence xix, 9, 71, 222, 225, 240, 242
   Emendatory Principle 249, 326
   Emendatory Work 207-208, 235, see Appendix, 339-346
   erotic disclosures 312
   erotic poems 290, 312
   exposure to classical ideas and values 27
   genealogy of 23n1, 26, 45, 74
   "hedonic" and "historical" themes 70
   historical consciousness of 10n3
   homosexuality 42
   idea of progress 231ff
   indebtedness to Homer 314
   loneliness, theme of 160-161
   penumbra poems 140n20, 143, 147, 149f
   philosophical scrutiny 41, 48, 51, 110, 152, 163, 207-208, 217-220, 235, 237, see Appendix, 339-346
   political mission of 313n12
   postponed publication of 129
   predicament of enclosure 304
   return to Alexandria, 303
   symbol of the builder 313n12
   theory of truth 319
   view of truth 154
   voyage motif 86n14, 308, 311, 334ff
   will of 67
   work in progress xvii, xxii, 85, 186, 219, 223, 314, 327, 332-333, 336
Cavafy, George (Brother) 26, 27, 31, 40
Cavafy, George (Uncle) 26, 28, 31
Cavafy, Helene 26, 67
Cavafy, John 26, 36n16, 42, 67, 145n24, 147n25
Early Verses 29, 67
   translations 29, 40
Cavafy, Pandelis 28
Cavafy, Paul 26, 42, 44, 52, 58
Cavafy, Peter-John 26
Cavafy, Petros 26, 31
Chiari, J. 109n31
Christophidis, Lukas 61
Claudel, P. 109n31
Clay, Diskin 290n33
Cleopatra 5, 7-9, 13, 330f
Colaclides, P. 266n7
Coleridge 200
Constantine the Great 9
Constantinides, K. N. 75n43
Countess de Noailles 63
Courage 95, 168, 296ff, 321
Criterion 69
Cynoscephalae, battle of 21

Dallas, J. 122n5, 187n30, 245n17
Dalmati, M. 283n21
Dalven, R. xxv, 39n18, 117n2
Dante 176, 176n22, 306n4, 307-308, 310,

314, 315n15, 315n16
The Divine Comedy 176n22, 187n30
The Inferno 175, 307n7
version of Odysseus, 308
Daskalopoulos, D. xxiv, xxv
De Lesseps, Ferdinand 25
Decavalles, A. 207n15, 339n1, 342n3
Dederick, B. xxv
Delopoulos-Kairis 300n1
Demakis, M. 84n12
Democratia 70
Dieterich, K. 59
Dimaras, C. Th. 73
Dinocrates of Rhodes 2
Diotima 269
Durrell, L. 65
Dutton, D. xxiv

Egypt 26, 29, 162n7
Egyptian Gazette 58
Eleusis 204
Elgin Marbles 80, 81
Eliot, T. S. 39, 69, 106
Embros 60n17
Epicurus 7, 317, 327, 336ff
Epitheorisi Technis 53n2, 57n10, 205n10
Ethniki 31n11
Ethnos (Nation) 63
Eunapius 230, 245

Forsdyke, Sir John 55
Forster, E. M. xx, xxv, 39, 55, 57, 58n11, 65, 66n28, 69, 272n14
  letters 56n5
  Alexandria: A History and A Guide, 65
  Pharos and Pharillon 68
France, Anatole 14, 72, 200
French Revolution 233
Frere, Sir Bartoll 55
Friar, K. xxiii, xxv, 267n10
Furness, R. A. 55
Ganoulis, Elias 131n12
Garibaldi 217, 345

Gautier, Théophile 93
Gianos, Mary xxii
Gibbon, E. 103, 130, 200, 204n8, 226, 229-233, 235-237, 245-248, 251-252, 254n28, 261, 313
  Decline and Fall of the Roman Empire 248n21
Gide, André
  Palludes 166
Gissing, G. R. 168
Goethe 200
Grammata (Letters) 53-54, 59, 76
Gritsanis, P. 80

Haas, D. xxiv, xxv, 94n21, 144n23, 164n9, 204n8, 226n4, 229n6, 230n7, 236n11, 245n17, 246n18, 248n21, 250n22, 253n25, 322n22
Hadginis, I. 14n7, 287n25
Halvatzakis, M. 14n7
Hardy, Thomas 166-168, 200
  Jude the Obscure 166
Haris, P. xxiv
Heraclius, Emperor 12
Herodotus 257n29
Herondas 111
Homer xxn4, 173, 188, 308, 314, 315n15, 317,
  Iliad 314
  Odyssey, xxn4, 2, 188, 314
Honorius, 247
Holton, D. 261n1
Hugo, Victor 88n17, 200

Ibsen 200
Illinskaya, S. 79n5, 90n18, 94n21, 121n5, 122n5, 132n14, 142n22, 145n23, 228n5, 308n8, 329n25, 332n30
Industrial Revolution 198
Inversion of the classical 95, 104, 135-140, 175, 188, 223, 242, 295, 310, 317, 325, 335
Irrigation Service of the Ministry of Public

Works 32, 65, 141, 200
Ismael 17, 27

Jacobson, R. 266n7
Joyce, James 55

Julian, Emperor 251-253
Justinian, Emperor 253n25

Kahl, E. xxiv
Karavias, P. 84n12
Karydis, N. xxiii
Katsimbalis, G. xxiii, 62-63
   bibliography of Cavafy 73
Kazantzakis, N. xx, 70-71, 336
Keats, John 99, 100n23, 200, 244n16
   "Lamia" tr. 100n23, 244n16
   "Sonnet to the Nile" 100n23
Keeley and Sherrard, tr. xxv, 225, 227,
   240, 287n23, 291n32
Keeley, E. xxiii, xxv, 14n7, 51n1, 81, 121n5,
   122n5, 127n11, 132n14, 138n17, 154n2,
   198n4, 213n16, 228n5, 253n26, 263n2,
   267n10, 290n30, 309n9
Keller, Katherine Z. xxiv
Kitroeff, A. 14n7
Klaras, H. 84n12
Koumoulides, J. xxiv
Krumbacher, K. 80
Kyklos 73
Kyklos Kavafi 164n9

L'art pour l'art 106
La Grèce actuelle dans ses poètes 59
La Semaine Égyptienne 62, 63
Lagoudakis, S. 68
Lambropoulos, V. xxiv
Lavagnini, R. xxvi, 58n12
Lawrence of Arabia 69
Lebésque, P. 58
Lechonitis, G. 73, 124, 177n23
LeDante, Y-G 112n33
Lekakis, M. xxii

Leonidas 177, 230, 257, 345
Leonidas at Thermopylae 257n29
Letters to Marios Vayanos 68n33
Libre 68
Liddell, R. xxvi, 14n7, 79, 105-107, 121n5,
   143n22, 166n15, 173n20, 204n8, 205n13,
   228n5, 229n6, 237n14, 290n30, 309n9
Life of Apollonius 244n16
Lorentzatos, Z. 14n7
Louÿs, P. 14

Macaulay 103, 200, 205
Maeterlinck, M. 110
Magnis, P. 53n2
Mahaffy, J. P. 14
Malanos, T. xxvi, 10n3, 14n7, 56, 57n9, 68,
   132n14, 173n21, 176n22, 198n4, 228n5,
   237n14, 267n10, 283n21, 295n39, 309n9,
   314n13, 329n25
Mallarmé, Stephan 110, 200, 326
   influence of, 103n26
Marc Antony, 8
Marinetti, F. T. 58, 58n12
Maronitis, D. N. 104, 310n10, 322n21
Marshall, J. 55
Mascaro, V. 58n12
Maskaleris, T. xxii, xxiv
Maurois, André 73
Mavrogordato, J. xxv, 55, 73, 307n5
   The Poems of C.P. Cavafy 307n5
Mavroudis, A. 289
Melakopides, C. 228n5, 258n30, 267n10,
   314, 316
Meleager 283n21
Menelaus 2
Mercure de France 58
Meredith. G. 63
Merrill, J. 168n17
Metaneira 204
Michaletos, G. 132n14, 165n11, 179n25,
   237n14, 256, 329n25
Michaelidis, K. 226, 226n3
Migne, J. P. 251n23

Minucci, R. M. 58n12
Mitropoulos, D. 73
Modern Greece 73
Modinos, P. 57, 66
   Three Letters 66n29
Montale, E. 58n12
Moréas, J. 110
Moschos, E. N. 68n33
Moskoff, C. xxiv

Napoleon 12, 218
Nea Estia 23n1, 42n23, 45n28, 63n23, 65n27, 73, 84n12, 131n12, 190n1, 287n23, 295n39
Nea Grammata 74n42
Nea Techni (New Art), 68
Nea Zoe (New Life) 44-45, 46, 47n31, 48, 53, 119, 124, 165n10, 282, 291n31, 314n13, 333n32
Nehamas, A. 168n17, 290n30, 297n41, 309n9
Neon Asti 41n22
Nietzsche, F. 228n5, 241, 299, 336
Nostos 6, 18, 81, 192, 308-310, 321, 336f
Noumas 47n31

Octavian, Emperor 8, 330
Odysseus 6, 307ff
Omar, Caliph 12
Orambi 29
Othóni 62n21

Palamas, Costis 53, 60-63, 63n23, 63n24, 64-65, 69, 71, 199
   conflict with Cavafy 60-65
Panathenaia 40n21, 226, 255
Panayotopoulos, I. M. xx, 69, 267n10
Panegyptia 73
Pangalos, T. 70
Papadiamandis, A. 45n27
Papanghelis, T. D. 106, 107
Papanoutsos, E. P. xxiii, 73, 166, 217n18, 267n10

Papantoniou, Z. 47
Paparrigopoulos, K. 224n1, 226, 229n6, 231n7, 244, 253n25, 261
   History of the Greek Nation, 224n1, 226
Papatsonis, T. K. 73
Papazis, Constantine A. 28-29, 82, 114
Papoutsakis, G. 80n7, 229n6
Pappas, C. N. 53n2
Paraschos, Kleon 62
Pargas, S. 53, 56, 59, 76-77
Parnassianism xx, 82n10, 83, 197
   poetics 86
   poetry 168
   poets 83, 94n21
   themes 86, 96, 143
Passions and Ancient Days 51n1, 213n16, 253n26
Pasteur, L. 217, 345
Pea, E. 58n12
Peri, M. 58n12
Peridis, M. 44n26, 46, 54-55, 56n5, 59-60, 60n18, 61n19, 64, 67n32, 72, 76-77, 80n7, 101n25, 108, 123n6, 126n10, 190, 204n7, 205n10, 207n15, 229n6, 248n21, 267n10, 339n1, 342n2, 342n3, 344n6, 307n7, 342n2, 342n3, 344n6
Pernot, H. 59
Pessimism 132n13
Petridis, P. A. 46, 58, 60n18, 67, 165n10, 220, 238
   "An Alexandrian Poet" 47
Petronius (Pseudo) 314n13
   "*Exhortatio ad Ulyssem*" 314n13
Philip V of Macedonia 21
Philostratus 244n16
Photiades, Charicleia 26-27, 29-30, 40, 63
Pieridis Y. 56n6, 63
Pieris, M. xix, xxiv, xxv, 86, 87n15, 122n5, 266n6, 290n30, 322n21
Pinchin, J. L. 39n18, 272n14, 309n9
Placidia 247
Plato 1, 7, 165n12, 202, 217, 240, 259, 262,

276, 284, 295-296, 298, 303, 311, 319, 320n20
Laches 297n40, 320n20
Phaedrus 320n20
Politicus 313n12
Republic 1, 166n12, 303
Symposium 262, 269, 296, 320n20
Plomer, W. 73
Plotinus 99, 290n29
Plutarch 329, 331, 334
   Life of Antony 329
   quoted 329n25, 330, 331n28, 331n29
Poe, E. A. 81, 86, 111, 115, 200
Polemis, I. 31, 31n12
polis 8, 144, 295, 324ff, 338
   life of 222-232
   loss of 137f
   return to 321
Politis, A. 237n14
Politis, P. 11n3, 68, 73
Polybius 5, 313
Pontani, F. M. xxvi, 58n12
Pre-Raphaelitism 106
Presocratics 109
Printezis, P. 38
Prisons 119, 133
Propertius 106
Ptolemy, King 300n1
Ptolemy II Philadelphus, coronation of 4
Ptolemy(ies) xxi, 1-9

R. J. Moss Company, 67
Raizis, M. B. xxiv
Rallis, M. 29, 31, 40 78, 126
Rallis, P. 80n7
Rangavis, A. 254n28
Realism 104, 111, 145n23, 258, 309
Renier, H. 63
Review of Art 295n39
Revista Quindicinale 31n11
Rimbaud, A. 97
Rodenbach, G. 146, 149
Rodokanakis, J. 29, 40

Rolland, R. 64
Romanticism xx, 83, 94n21, 96-97, 101, 114-115, 197, 214, 241, 312, 319, 322ff
   Romantic perfection 233
   Romantic movement 324f
   Romantic outlook of Cavafy 103
   Romantic poets 154
   Romantic themes 96
   Romantics 109
Rousseau, J. J. 200
Roussel, L. 68
Rufinus 246
Ruskin, J. 32, 204-205
   Selections from the Writings of John Ruskin 204, 204n9.

Said Pasha 24, 25
Said Pasha, son of Ali, Muhammad 24
Sarakinos, T. 314
Sareyannis, Y. 14n7, 73, 74n42, 103n26, 166n12, 267, 309n9
Savidis, G. P. xviii, xxiii, 29n5, 29n6, 30n7, 30n8, 32n13, 32n14, 34n15, 37n17, 40n20, 43n24, 43n25, 44n26, 46, 48n32, 51n1, 54n3, 55, 56n5, 57n8, 70n36, 76, 79, 82n10, 84-86, 87n16, 94n21, 99, 100n23, 101n25, 103-104, 115n35, 117, 121n3, 121n5, 122n5, 123n6, 127n11, 133n16, 138n17, 146n25, 156n3, 182, 190n2, 205n12, 207n15, 213n16, 219n20, 220, 224n1, 224n2, 226n3, 226n4, 233-234, 244n16, 245n17, 253, 254n27, 267n10, 272n14, 274n15, 275n16, 278n17, 278n18, 279n19, 282n20, 283n21, 286-87, 290n30, 305n4, 307n6, 307n7, 314, 315n15, 322n22, 333, 342n2
Seferis, George xviii, xx, xxvi, 10n3, 11n3, 19-20, 32n13, 55, 67n31, 94n21, 104f, 106f, 132n14, 161n6, 165n11, 173n21, 176n22, 190, 198n4, 204n6, 228n5, 267n10, 307n5, 309n9, 329n25
Sengopoulos, A. 57, 61n20, 67, 190,
   lecture on Cavafy, 295n39

Sengopoulos, Rika 23n1, 74
Shakespeare 28
Shaw, G. B. 200
Sherrard, P. xxvi, 132n14, 138n17, 290n30
Sikelianos, A. 102
Simonides 257n29
Sisyphus 202
Skokos, K. 68
Skokos' *Yearbook* 226n3
Skylitsis, S. 29
Smyrna, burning of 75n43
Socrates 136, 245, 269
Solomos, D. 60, 105, 199
Sophia (wisdom) 97, 319
Souloyannis, E. 60n18
Soutsos, A. 28
Sozomen 245
Spengler, E. 237n13
   Decline of the West 237n13
Stanford, W. B. 307n5
Stanlick, N. xxiv
Suez Canal 14, 25
Sylloghés 220, see *Collections*
Symbolism xxi, 79n5, 82, 82n10, 84, 86, 89, 92, 94n21, 95, 96, 100-101, 103-105, 107-12, 115-16, 145, 197, 234, 239, 241-42, 259, 265, 281, 310-311, 319f
   effects of 315
   influence of 82, 97, 107, 82
   symbolist framework 308
   symbolist poetry 276-277, 334
   symbolism, Baudelairian 34, 92, 116
   symbolism, psychology of 95
   symbolism to Realism, period of 104, 145n23
   symbolism Cavafy's withdrawal from 107
   symbolist movement 312, 322ff
   symbolist style 255, 319
   symbolist phase of Cavafy 104, 235
   symbolist poetics 86, 97, 238, 242, 291n34

Symbolist poets 98, 106, 109, 111
symbolist themes 86
Synesius 251
   The Letters of Synesius of Cyrene 251n23
Tachydromos 61n20, 63
Taedium Vitae, modern theme of 106
Tantalides, Elias 28
Tennyson, Alfred Lord 78, 156n3, 200, 305, 306n4, 307-308, 309-310, 314, 315n15, 315n16
   Ulysses 156n3, 307n7, 315n16
   versions of Odysseus 308
Tewfik 27
Thaniel, G. xxiv
The Apuans 57
The Great Hellenic Encyclopedia 73
The History of the Decline and Fall of the Roman Empire, see Gibbon 130, 226
The Nation 69
The Southern Review 127, 127n11
The Stones of Venice, see Ruskin 206
The Tempest, see Shakespeare 28
The Times Literary Supplement 56n5, 272n14
Themelis, G. xxiii, 178n25, 257, 266n6
Theocritus 111, 120, 194-196, 243
Theodosius, Emperor 246-247
Theotokas, G. 71
   Elefthero Pnevma, (Free Spirit) 71
   Pnevmatikí Poreía (Spiritual Journey), 71n40
Thomson, James 38, 167,
   "The City of the Dreadful Night" 139n19
Thrylos, Alkis 62
Thucydides 313
Toynbee, A. 39, 69
Travels: Spain, Italy, Egypt, Sina, 71n37 see Kazantzakis
Tsirkas, S. xxvi, 14n7, 23n1, 28n2, 28n4, 39n19, 57n9, 58, 59n13, 68n33, 123n6, 124n7, 126n9, 132n9, 132n14, 139n19, 142n22, 162n7, 165n10, 166, 169n18, 179n24, 201n5, 205n11, 226n3, 228n5,

235n10, 236n12, 237n14, 238n15, 257, 267n8, 267n9, 267n10, 293n38, 309n9, 314n13
Tsokopoulos, T. 39n19, 342
Two Gentlemen of Verona 28, see also Shakespeare

Ungaretti, G. 58n12

Valassopoulo, G. 55, 56n7, 58, 65, 69, 73, 272n14
  "An Alexandrian Poet" (essay) 73
  translations of Cavafy's poetry, 58
Valieri, Charicleia 67
Varnalis, Costis 53, 70, 169n18
  "Sacrifice" 291n31
Vayanos, M. xxiii, 68, 69, 75n43
Vayenas, N. 112n33, 145n23, 261n1, 271n13, 290n30
Vema 182n29
Verhaeren, Émile 110
Verlaine, P. 248n20
Vikelas, D. 80, 81
Vitti, M. 58n12
Vlachos, A. 257n29
Vrissimitzakis, G. 57, 59, 69, 71, 131n13, 313n12, 318n18

Welch, Cyril and Lilian 93n20
Wilde, Oscar 216n17
  Essays and Lectures 216n17
Willey, B. 315n16
Williams, Gwyn 207n15
Wordsworth 200
World War I 45, 53, 55, 66
World War II 18

Xenopoulos, G. 40, 166n12, 168n17, 255, 342
Xerxes 256

Yalourakis, I. 14n7, 57n9, 60n18, 62n21, 62n22, 63n23, 131n12, 309n9
Yannopoulos, P. 47
Yourcenar, M. xxvi, 228n5, 290n30, 333n31

Zachariadis, D. 53
Zacharopoulos, G. xxiv
Zelita, Eutychia N. 23n1
Zervos, C. 53
Zeus 246
Zola 200
Zosimus 245
Zweig, P. 115, 336n33